White Ethnic New York

White Ethnic New York

Jews, Catholics,
and the Shaping of
Postwar Politics

Joshua M. Zeitz

The University of North Carolina Press Chapel Hill

© 2007 The University of North Carolina Press
All rights reserved
Set in Quadraat and Bureau Grotesque
by Keystone Typesetting, Inc.
Manufactured in the United States of America
The paper in this book meets the guidelines for
permanence and durability of the Committee on
Production Guidelines for Book Longevity of the
Council on Library Resources.

Library of Congress
Cataloging-in-Publication Data
Zeitz, Joshua
White ethnic New York: Jews, Catholics,
and the shaping of postwar politics /
Joshua M. Zeitz

  p. cm.
Includes bibliographical references and index
ISBN 978-0-8078-3095-6 (cloth: alk. paper)
ISBN 978-0-8078-5798-4 (pbk.: alk. paper)
1. Jews—New York (State)—New York—History—
20th century. 2. Catholics—New York (State)—
New York—History—20th century. 3. New York
(N.Y.)—Politics and government—20th century.
4. New York (N.Y.)—Religion—20th century.
5. New York (N.Y.)—Ethnic relations. 6. United
States—Religion—1945–1960. I. Title.
F128.9.J5Z45   2007
305.892407471'09045—dc22
2006033636

cloth   11 10 09 08 07   5 4 3 2 1
paper   11 10 09 08 07   5 4 3 2 1

In memory of

Abraham and Ann Zeitz,

Jack Bagan, and

Elaine Bagan Zeitz

Contents

Tables

Acknowledgments

In the course of writing *White Ethnic New York*, I have incurred countless personal and intellectual debts. Whatever faults this book suffers are my responsibility alone, but whatever strengths it possesses are very much the collective achievement of many friends and colleagues.

First thanks go to Jim Patterson, who has been a great supporter of this project, and whose balance of intellectual rigor and steadfast encouragement helped me see the book to print. Over the past several years I have been lucky to count Jim as a friend and colleague, and I can only hope that the final product lives up to his high example.

I owe a deep debt of gratitude to members of the Brown University community. Howard Chudacoff and Maud Mandel were a steady source of sage advice and probing criticism. Mike Vorenberg read sections of the manuscript and offered important early feedback that helped shape my approach to the revision process. Mike has also been a generous colleague and friend over the years. Like countless other Brown alumni, I will always remain indebted to Jack Thomas, whose dedication to teaching—and to the life of the mind—was a source of inspiration to everyone who was lucky enough to sit in his classroom or spend an afternoon at his house discussing books, ideas, music, and other subjects. Jack passed away last year, but I am very pleased to acknowledge his role in seeing *White Ethnic New York* to fruition.

Since my graduate school days, and in these early years of my career, I have been lucky to be part of a close circle of friends. Jim Sparrow, Alan Petigny, Andrew Huebner, Liam Brockey, Nathaniel Frank, and Dave Hamlin continue to set a standard of academic excellence that I aspire to match as a writer and teacher, and their camaraderie—past and present—has made my life a lot richer. To that list also belongs Robert Fleegler, who has been one of my closest friends for fifteen years. We have studied together and grown up together, and I have scarcely written a word that he has not read or developed an idea that he has not challenged. This book would look much different—and be far weaker—without his influence and support.

Along the way, several scholars read and commented on this book. I am particularly indebted to Hasia Diner, Joshua Freeman, and Eli Lederhendler for their insights. I would also like to thank Bryant Simon, who painstakingly read through a full draft and provided extremely incisive, detailed comments for revision. At a joint Cambridge University–Boston University conference on political history, Bruce Schulman and Julian Zelizer offered probing questions based on a related paper. Julian also read and commented on the manuscript, which I greatly appreciate. Don Critchlow read the manuscript, too, and gave generously of his time and expertise on American conservatism. Above all, very special thanks go to Gerald Gamm and John McGreevy, who began their association with this project as University of North Carolina Press anonymous readers but soon broke anonymity to offer several pages of pointed criticism and advice. Since then, John has read subsequent drafts, helping me sharpen the chapters on urban Catholicism. I did not take all of his advice, but I tried to take most of it; much of what is strong about this book is the result of his input, as well as that of Gerald.

Several colleagues at Cambridge University—particularly Paul Warde, Jon Parry, and Mark Wormald—have been very supportive of my career, as I have labored to make the transition from the American to the British academy. Pembroke College generously allowed me a term's leave to finish the manuscript, for which I am most grateful. John Thompson, a teacher and writer of great accomplishment, has been a source of encouragement and has asked challenging questions that helped sharpen my work; while, together, Tony and Ruth Badger have made sure that my life in Cambridge has been both intellectually and socially rich. At Oxford University, Jay Sexton, Stephen Tuck, Gareth Davies, and Richard Carwardine gave me an early opportunity to present parts of the book. Their questions and comments were of the highest caliber and informed many of my revisions.

My students at Brown, Harvard, and Cambridge—some of whom remain good friends, even as they have gone off in the world to start their own lives and careers—have, in ways they probably do not always appreciate, contributed mightily to my intellectual development. They often helped me hash out some of the issues in this book, even if they did not know it. It has been a privilege to work with and know them all.

Grants from the Gilder Lehrman Institute of American History, American Jewish Archives, John Nicholas Brown Center for the Study of American Civilization, Woodrow Wilson Foundation, Brown University, and American Academy for Jewish Research helped support the work that went into this book. I am also grateful to the staffs of the Dorot Jewish Division of the New York Public Library, American Jewish Archives, American Jewish Historical Society, Fordham University Library, Archives of the Diocese of Brooklyn, Columbia University Library's Special Collections and Oral History departments, Jewish Theological Seminary of America, and New

York City Municipal Archives. Thanks also to Chris McNickle, who raided his private research collection and loaned me several remarkable, unpublished political polls dating from the early 1960s.

Elaine Maisner, my editor at UNC Press, has been a steady and invaluable champion of this project for several years now. Elaine helped shepherd the project through in-house and reader reviews and played an enormous part in helping me refine and reshape many of the ideas in the book. I am deeply grateful for her tremendous support. Ron Maner provided early assistance, which I deeply appreciate. Many thanks also go to Jay Mazzocchi, my project editor at UNC Press. Jay's careful and skilled work made this a far more polished book, and for that I am very grateful.

I am especially indebted to friends and family members who listened to me prattle on for eight years about New York Jews and Catholics. Troy and Kath Rondinone, good friends and fine scholars, cheerfully discussed the project in its many stages and incarnations, while Helene Sinnreich helped me stay connected to the Jewish history universe and hosted me in Youngstown, Ohio, where I was able to present parts of the book to an audience of scholars and interested community members. My aunt and uncle, Deede and Larry Snowhite, regaled me with stories of the 1968 Ocean Hill–Brownsville controversy, which saw Deede on strike with other members of the UFT and Larry working as a replacement teacher in central Brooklyn. My brother Nate has kept close tabs on my career, even as he has pursued a very different line of work; and my father, Carl Zeitz, has read most everything I have written—from the accessible to the overly academic—with equal enthusiasm.

In writing a book on Catholics and Jews, it was more than a little helpful to be part of an interethnic marriage. My wife, Juli-anne Whitney, has been my best friend, closest companion, fiercest intellectual critic, and favorite goofball for over ten years now. She has suffered through this project since its inception and has been its strongest and best-informed booster. Accordingly, this book is as much hers as mine. I would like to thank Jules for everything—especially her love and support.

Finally, I would like to acknowledge my grandmother, Bea Bagan, my great-aunts Fay and Mary, and my great-uncles Harry and Charles. The historian in me has long valued what they have to say about the generation that made the American Century, and the grandson and nephew in me loves them unconditionally.

This book is dedicated to my grandparents, Ann and Abe Zeitz and Jack Bagan, and to my mother, Elaine Bagan Zeitz. They did not live to see the book to print, but they are very much a part of the story it tells and of my life.

White Ethnic New York

Introduction

In the fall of 1954 Rabbi Ben Zion Bokser, the spiritual leader of the Forest Hills Jewish Center in Queens, used his Rosh Hashanah sermon to trumpet the harmony between traditional Judaism and social criticism. It was a theme he revisited often with his congregants on the High Holidays (Rosh Hashanah and Yom Kippur), when his synagogue was filled to peak capacity. "The refusal to be comforted has been the secret passion of our people's history," Bokser intoned. "We lived in exile for two thousand years. We created special institutions to keep us maladjusted, to remind us of our troubles, to perpetuate our grief."

According to Bokser, the Jewish people's sustained longing for independence taught them to reject the proposition that "man must learn to accept himself and his circumstances. We do not have to assume that the circumstances are final. . . . When they clash with deeply cherished ideals, it is important to resist circumstances. Religion, at least Judaism, does not only teach us to accept, but also to resist. When Abraham was told by God that He is about to destroy Sodom, he did not bow his head in humble submission. He protested. He challenged God to justify His actions." Bokser encouraged his congregants to interpret Abraham's insubordination in the matter of Sodom and Gomorrah as an imperative to "foster [a] sense of maladjustment," to resist "blind fatalism."[1]

Writing of his years as a student at St. Philip Neri Elementary School in the 1950s, novelist Michael Pearson recalled learning the same biblical story of Sodom and Gomorrah. A poor liar, Pearson failed to convince Mother Concepta, his first-grade teacher, that he was not the chief culprit in a pencil fight that had broken out while she was away from the room. Making an example of Pearson, Mother Concepta reminded the class that "Lot's wife turned around. She looked back. She disobeyed, boys and girls. And God turned her into a pillar of salt. Remember Lot's wife, children. Remember her." According to Pearson, "At least once a week for the rest of the year Mother Concepta told the story, working the drama exactly the same way each time."[2]

In New York City, Catholics and Jews encountered many of the same biblical passages in their religious schools and houses of worship, but they often extracted different lessons from them. It is the central argument of this book that from the mid-1940s through the early 1970s, millions of "white ethnic" New Yorkers—Jewish and Catholic—adhered to two sharply divergent worldviews that defined the way they approached a broad range of political and cultural questions.

In an important reinvention of their shared heritage, many Jewish New Yorkers in the postwar period identified political dissent and intellectual freedom as core elements of their secular and religious traditions and came to view the individual as the fundamental building block of society. These values stood in sharp contrast to the main themes pervading the religious, domestic, and political institutions of New York's large Catholic subculture, which promoted obedience to authority—rather than skepticism of it—as a Christian and American virtue. Unlike Jews, who tended to regard individual rights as paramount, millions of Irish and Italian New Yorkers in parochial schools and local parishes learned and reaffirmed that an individual's interests were subordinate to the community's and that legitimate ecclesiastical, political, and social authority derived from a common, divine source.

Underlying these conflicting views were two fundamentally different approaches to faith. Whereas New York Jews were an overwhelmingly secular group for whom religion was a malleable cultural and political tradition, Irish and Italian Catholics often viewed the world in spiritual terms, through the lens of their religion.

These divergent ideas about faith, community, and citizenship enjoyed a powerful, majoritarian influence within each community. Importantly, however, neither worldview went uncontested. Throughout the early Cold War era, the city was home to a vibrant liberal Catholic minority that would assert itself with greater force by the mid-1960s. Many Jews, in turn, often placed their status as homeowners, businesspeople, taxpayers, or union members ahead of their commitment to secular liberalism. *White Ethnic New York* addresses the diversity within—not just among—the city's Jewish, Irish, and Italian communities, while still treating ethnicity as a powerful engine that drove city politics in the years between 1945 and 1970.

This book makes three central contributions to scholarship on postwar America. First, most studies of the postwar period propose that ethnicity—defined here as the intersection between religion, national origins, and class—ceased to be a meaningful force at almost the very instant the first potato fields on Long Island gave way to suburban sprawl. Group histories of American Jews and Catholics frequently conclude with such telling chapter titles as "Assimilation," "From Ghetto to Suburbs: From Someplace to Noplace?," "The End of Catholic Culture," and "Conclusion: The End of Immigrant Memory—Who Can Replace It?" These works lend credence to the popular, if not entirely accurate, view of postwar American history as a swift trajectory from city to suburb, from working class to middle class, and, hence, from pluralism to white homogeneity.[3]

It is precisely this route that novelist Philip Roth's fictive Seymour "Swede" Lvov follows. Swede, a second-generation American Jew, "could have married any [Jewish] beauty he wanted," according to his curmudgeonly younger brother. "Instead he marries the bee-yoo-ti-full Miss Dwyer. You should have seen them. Knockout couple. The two of them all smiles on their outward trip into the USA. She's post-Catholic, he's post-Jewish, together they're going out there to Old Rimrock to raise little post-toasties."[4]

Many of the best-regarded general histories of the Cold War era either ignore the topic of ethnicity or echo Eric Goldman's more explicit conclusion that "by 1949, the nature of the population had changed so much that only a minority could feel genuinely old stock; the typical American . . . was a third-generation immigrant. Rising to the middle class left [him or her] only the more anxious to achieve the further respectability of unhyphenated Americanism."[5]

The notion that pluralism diminished after World War II—at least among white Americans—can be traced to the early 1950s. Many public intellectuals writing at that time were reluctant to acknowledge the survival of the immigrant generation's hybrid, hyphenated culture—none more so than Will Herberg, whose celebrated tract, *Protestant, Catholic, Jew* (1955), announced the death of ethnicity and its replacement by formal religious identification, devoid of meaningful spirituality. "However important the ethnic group may have been in the adjustment of the immigrant to American society," wrote Herberg, "and however influential it still remains in many aspects of American life, the perpetuation of ethnic differences in any serious way is altogether out of line with the logic of American reality." Herberg introduced the term "triple melting pot" to the lexicon of American pop sociology. The Irish, Poles, Italians, Jews, and other white ethnics, he argued, had melded into three distinct groups: Protestants, Catholics, and Jews. These groups stood as faint remnants of ethnic America, with their members committed to a vague "American way of life" and divided only nominally on significant social and cultural questions.[6]

Herberg's assertions were consistent with trends in contemporary scholarship and popular culture. *Protestant, Catholic, Jew* appeared just as many "consensus" historians were concluding that America had, from the start, been free of permanent social divisions so endemic to European nations.[7]

The theory of the triple melting pot was also a neat complement to films like *Gentleman's Agreement*, winner of the 1947 Academy Award for Best Motion Picture, in which Gregory Peck plays a non-Jewish reporter who probes the depths of American anti-Semitism by posing as a Jew for a few weeks. A telling scene depicts Peck, as Phil Green, explaining to his young son that religious differences are entirely superficial. Some people go to "church" on Sundays, he says, while others go on Saturdays. Otherwise, people and religions are pretty much the same.

It was not until many working-class, white Americans soured on racial and economic liberalism in the late 1960s that writers once again emphasized the enduring importance of "ethnicity"—always a slippery term, but now summoned up to represent a range of groups (Catholics of every stripe, working-class Jews, and even working-class Protestants) whose principal connection seemed to be their resentment of black radicalism and the welfare state.

Social scientists like Andrew Greeley, Jonathan Rieder, and Michael Novak viewed this cultural reaction—and the concurrent resurgence of white ethnic pride—with sympathy.[8] Others treated the "unmeltable ethnics" with measurable derision and argued, as have James Shenton and Kevin Kenny, that the ethnic revival of the 1970s was essentially a "reaction against the heightened race consciousness of African Americans and the social and political gains they have made since 1960."[9]

Two well-known scholars stand out for their early appreciation of the lasting importance of ethnicity in postwar American life. Writing in 1963, Nathan Glazer and Daniel Patrick Moynihan famously observed that "the point about the melting pot . . . is that it did not happen. At least not in New York. . . . On the contrary, the American ethos is nowhere better perceived than in the disinclination of the third and fourth generation of newcomers to blend into a standard, uniform national type." Focusing on five groups in New York—the Irish, Italians, Jews, African Americans, and Puerto Ricans—Glazer and Moynihan maintained that "one group is not as another and, notably where religious and cultural values are involved, these differences are matters of choice as well as of heritage."

Glazer and Moynihan earned critical acclaim for their incisive analysis of cultural pluralism in the postwar years, but their book failed to produce an extensive body of follow-up work to test and refine their principal conclusions. This study is deeply indebted to Glazer's and Moynihan's pioneering effort, and in many ways it picks up where they left off.[10]

This book's second contribution to postwar historiography relates to the burgeoning field of whiteness studies. Over the past two decades, scholars have produced a treasure trove of material on the historical development of whiteness as a category of social identity, economic privilege, and political classification. Though writings on the historical problem of whiteness have branched off in multiple directions, most scholars working on the larger question of racial formation have argued that the process by which European immigrants and their progeny asserted their status as white Americans—and with that status, their fitness for American citizenship, with all its attendant political privileges and material trappings—was complete by the years immediately following World War II.[11] This book does not challenge the central claim of whiteness scholars. To be sure, in achieving their standing as white Americans, immigrants came into possession of a host of political and economic entitlements. But whiteness did not equal sameness. Jewish, Italian, and Irish Americans continued to view the world through distinct prisms and to interpret a range of political, social, and cultural issues differently from each other. In grafting race so tightly onto ethnicity, historians have lost perspective on the diversity among and between different white urban dwellers in midcentury America.

White Ethnic New York makes a third contribution to scholarship on postwar America in its reconsideration of the decline of the storied New Deal coalition between African Americans and urban Jews and Catholics. In general, most scholars believe that race played a central role in this story and argue that the children and grandchildren of European immigrants replaced once-primary bonds of ethnicity with a new American identity predicated on both "whiteness" and either working-class or middle-class solidarity.

While historians disagree considerably on the timing and nature of such transformations, they see eye to eye on the fundamentals: the white middle class emerged from World War II as a transcendent category, united in its distance from blackness. Whiteness replaced Catholicism and Judaism—as well as Italian, Jewish, and Irish identity—as the primary political and social tie that bound second- and third-generation Americans to each other and to other "old-stock" Americans. Much of this new identity was implicitly rooted in the economic and political privileges that these postethnic Americans derived from their newly secure standing as white—chief among them, access to suburban housing, higher education, and better-paying industrial and white-collar jobs.[12]

If this interpretation has altered the chronology of "white backlash"—which now appears to have had roots in the 1930s rather than the late 1960s—it still views the collapse of the liberal coalition as intimately associated with the politics of race[13] and, more specifically, as stemming from the efforts of white Americans to defend the racially exclusive, middle-class privileges they began to enjoy in the 1930s.[14]

The example of New York City complicates this interpretation. In Gotham and its surrounding areas, the Roosevelt coalition began to rupture long before Black Power entered the American political vocabulary, and this political breakup had little to do with race. As early as the 1940s, highly salient cultural differences between Catholics and Jews drove a wedge between the Roosevelt coalition's two principal white ethnic constituencies. Though Jews and Catholics shared a fierce loyalty to the New Deal state throughout the 1930s, in 1944 Franklin Roosevelt polled less than half of New York's Irish vote and only 41 percent of the city's Italian vote, while garnering an overwhelming 87 percent of the Jewish vote. Roughly thirty years later, half of all Jews considered themselves "liberals" and another 27 percent "moderates," compared with just 13 percent of Catholics who identified themselves as "liberals." In effect, a process that began around the time of World War II came full circle by the close of the Vietnam War.[15]

Because they disagreed on fundamental questions about citizenship and community, authority and dissent, the nature of totalitarianism, and the relationship between citizens and the state, Jews and Catholics often clashed over such diverse political phenomena as domestic anticommunism, the civil rights movement, the youth counterculture, and the Vietnam War. Ultimately, these cultural divergences fractured the liberal coalition, as a slim majority of Catholics grew uncomfortable in a Democratic Party that increasingly prioritized individual liberties and entitlements, and as a vocal and disruptive minority of young Jews gradually came to regard liberalism as an unsatisfactory political option, turning instead to the decidedly antiliberal New Left. The liberal coalition thus suffered attrition from the left and the right, for reasons not owing to race politics.

Indeed, though Catholic voters were far more supportive than their Jewish neighbors of law-and-order backlash candidates in the late 1960s, surveys revealed that Jews were marginally *more* skeptical and fearful of racial integration than Catholics. Race explains a good deal about postwar politics, but not everything.

I n the late 1960s and early 1970s—ironically, just when Jews and Catholics were the most politically polarized—two important developments began to reconfigure the sharply bifurcated world of white ethnic New York. First, schisms emerged within the city's Irish and Italian communities over civil rights, student activism, and religious worship. Part of the general revolt against authority that wracked America in the late 1960s, and given extra force by the ecclesiastical reforms of Vatican II, the increased tendency of many Italian and Irish New Yorkers to question religious and civic authorities signaled an end to the insular and cohesive Catholic culture of the early Cold War period. This process was aided by the entry of many third-generation Catholics into postsecondary academic institutions and middle-class professions, bringing an end to the Italian and Irish communities' overwhelmingly homogenous working-class composition. Second, the postwar migration of a critical number of Jews from Eastern Europe changed the political demography of New York Jewry, delivering a sizable minority of ultratraditional, ideologically conservative Jews to the city's outer boroughs. At the same time, the 1970s saw a large exodus of city Jews to the suburbs and the Sunbelt. These changes aside, what stands out about the period between 1945 and 1970 is the surprising degree to which ethnicity retained a central place in the city's cultural, social, and political landscape.

Two notable exception to the prevailing tendency of scholars to downplay the lasting importance of pluralism among whites in the postwar period are John T. McGreevy and Gerald Gamm. In his monograph on Catholics and race in the twentieth century, McGreevy notes that "the role of religion in the literature on modern race relations is especially circumscribed. Otherwise shrewd analyses of 'white' racial formation scrutinize the trajectories of Irish, Polish, and Italian identity while barely acknowledging the role of religious belief." McGreevy's central argument—"that American Catholics frequently defined their surroundings in religious terms"—isolates religious conviction as instrumental in driving postwar politics. By implication, his book suggests that not all white ethnics held to the same ideas and beliefs.[16] Gamm's study of postwar Boston finds that the democratized character of Jewish religious culture eased the way for the relocation of urban synagogues to the suburbs and hence facilitated Jewish "white flight," while the economic and emotional dimensions of the Catholic parish system precluded any such easy abandonment of neighborhood institutions. Both studies tacitly agree that explanations of postwar history that hinge solely on race are overreductive, and that significant cultural, political, and social differences between white groups—in this case, between Jews and Catholics—persisted well into the 1960s.

This book takes a cue from McGreevy and Gamm. Rather than assume that white ethnics forged a comprehensive union predicated on race, the following pages examine the endurance of heterogeneity in the ways different white Americans understood politics, social change, and contemporary culture. If, in the years following World War II, race became a more important category of identity than ethnicity—as indeed it did—the process by which this transition occurred was gradual. In Cold War–era New York and elsewhere, the same intersection between religion, national origins, and class that had played a guiding role in nineteenth-century political culture continued to exert a profound influence on how Americans understood rights, responsibilities, and government.[17]

In its treatment of ethnic politics, this book assumes that ideas and ideology—both secular and religious—mattered a great deal to ordinary New Yorkers. At the same time, people's beliefs and actions were not always in perfect accord. Though many New York Jews embraced secular liberalism in the abstract, Jewish predominance in the city's manufacturing, real estate, and commercial sectors meant that, as individuals, many Jews were complicit in denying African Americans access to good jobs, fair prices, and decent housing. Conversely, though increasing numbers of Irish and Italian New Yorkers embraced a deeply conservative ethnic worldview, the heavy participation of Catholics in left-leaning unions—such as the Transport Workers Union, the International Brotherhood of Electrical Workers, and the American Federation of State, County, and Municipal Employees—meant that many of the city's Irish and Italian residents acted out of self-interest to promote liberal economic policies and a strong labor movement, even if they remained uncomfortable with the culture of postwar liberalism.

White Ethnic New York draws on a wide variety of sources, some of which are not typically regarded as explicitly political in nature. These sources include synagogue and church sermons, public and religious school documents, oral histories, neighborhood newspapers and organizational newsletters, literary works and films, political speeches and position papers, and opinion polls and surveys. When taken together, however, these sources point to a fundamental divide between Jews and Catholics on broad sociopolitical questions that often informed popular approaches to electoral politics.

Readers may wish to bear in mind that Chapters 1 through 3 rely primarily on quantitative evidence, whereas Chapters 4 through 8 also incorporate a good deal of qualitative data. It is impossible to draw broad conclusions about popular ideology just from synagogue sermons, oral histories and literature, or polls and surveys. But when such diverse sources point to a common collection of themes, it becomes possible to draw conclusions about the ideas that ordinary people shared about the world around them.

In some respects, the case of New York City offers an instructive glimpse at the lasting influence of ethnicity among white Americans.[18] In 1960 as many as 4.2 million Jews, Italians, and Irish still lived in Gotham, where they accounted for 63 percent of the white population and continued to exist in social, residential, and economic isolation from each other.[19]

In other respects, New York City stands out as unusual. Most New Yorkers, both white and black, whether Catholic, Protestant, or Jewish, proved unusually accepting of—or at least reconciled to—differences among their fellow city dwellers throughout the postwar period. Racial prejudices proved less explosive in New York than in many other urban centers. Much of this uniqueness owed to the city's cosmopolitan outlook—a collective sensibility rooted in its historic pluralism and vibrant system of public transportation, education, and culture. In this sense, political patterns in New York City may have been atypical: since the city's racial tensions were relatively tame, the divide between Catholics and Jews was perhaps artificially pronounced.

Yet New York is instructive precisely because it was uncommon. Although ethnicity was an important category of identity elsewhere—in Detroit, Philadelphia, and Chicago, for example, where race was always a more salient issue in the 1950s and 1960s—it was easier to discern in postwar New York. Examining ethnic trends in a city like New York helps reveal them in other places, where the primacy of race politics rendered them more invisible to the naked eye.

Though they grew up just across the Hudson River from Manhattan, Philip Roth's characters must have known these things to be true. Try as he might, Seymour Lvov could never really escape being Jewish. And his wife, Mary Dawn Dwyer, could never really escape being Irish Catholic.

1 Communities

Reflecting upon his childhood in the New York City suburb of Scarsdale in the 1950s, Joshua Koreznick recalled that "virtually everyone was Jewish." On Yom Kippur, Judaism's most sacred day, "the school was open, but it was a little ludicrous . . . almost like playing a game, [pretending] that it was not a Jewish community."

Koreznick's mother, Emily, had grown up in a comparable environment —"a gilded ghetto on West End Avenue in Manhattan . . . amongst so many Jews in a similar situation." Even after she left home to attend Vassar College, Emily found that "from a Jewish point of view, you were somewhat more segregated. I don't mean that we didn't make friends with non-Jews, but even living patterns tended to be that Jews bunked with roommates who were also Jews. Certainly the dating patterns were along those lines." The memories of both mother and son point to a high degree of continuity between generations.[1]

Brian McDonald also recalled his formative years in the 1950s and 1960s in Pearl River, a bedroom community of New York, as parochial and insular. The son and grandson of New York City police officers, McDonald characterized the department he knew as a child as "a paramilitary organization, with overwhelming[ly] homogenous ethnicity and culture (read: Irish, Catholic). . . . For city cops living in Rockland County at this time, the brotherhood was intensified even further." Officers and their wives "carpooled and socialized together. They joined fraternal organizations like the Knights of Columbus . . . [and] our families went on vacations together to the Police Camp in the Catskills."

McDonald's mother was a devout Catholic who remained intensely committed to her old neighborhood in the Bronx, the Grand Concourse, which was once a center of Irish American culture in New York City. She "tenaciously held on to her Bronxness" and, with her husband, worked to re-create for her son a childhood as ethnically and religiously seamless as her own. Mrs. McDonald's friendships "were with the wives of other city cops. Like their husbands, they kept to themselves. My mother belonged to the sister organization of the Knights of Columbus. . . . Most of these women had young, growing families, and accordingly, a great deal of time was spent in St. Margaret's School–related activities."[2]

As the stories of Joshua Koreznick and Brian McDonald suggest, the erosion of tight-knit ethnic communities was not an overnight phenomenon but instead occurred gradually after World War II. By several key standards—residential concentration, schooling, economic and social relationships, and organizational affiliation—ethnicity had considerable staying power in New York well into the late 1960s.[3] Even as they participated in the postwar housing and suburbanization booms, Italian, Irish, and Jewish New Yorkers continued to occupy separate spheres.

The story of this continuity is not uniform, however. Between the close of World War II and the early 1960s, Irish and Italian New Yorkers gradually constructed a more united cultural and social front, as historic divisions between these two predominantly Catholic groups lost their saliency. Despite the dual influences of suburbanization and economic prosperity, Catholic New York—often a world in which parish and neighborhood, church and society, were synonymous—continued to thrive.

New York Jews never constructed parallel institutions on the same order as their Catholic neighbors. But they continued to segregate themselves residentially and socially, and they erected an enormous philanthropic network that set much of the tenor of Jewish identity in the postwar period.

The story of white ethnic New York in the 1940s and 1950s is thus one of gradual change and relative continuity, not sudden disruption. Even as commentators marveled at the swift erosion of white ethnicity, the powerful combination of religion, national origins, and class continued to provide New Yorkers with a way of ordering and understanding their world.

Calculating the number of white ethnics (Jews, Italians, and Irish) living in New York at any given time is an extraordinarily complicated task. Because the U.S. Census Bureau has traditionally excluded questions regarding religion from its decennial surveys, no government statistics exist detailing the number of Jews living in the city or the proportion of Catholics among those counted as Irish or Italian. Moreover, until 1980 the census kept records only on the foreign born and "persons of foreign stock," whom it defined as children with one or two immigrant parents. This policy effectively excluded the third generation, and all successive generations, from having its ethnicity recorded in census tabulations. Since 1980 the census has reported the number of persons *claiming* foreign

TABLE 1. *Jewish, Italian, and Irish Population of New York City, 1940–1980*

Year	Jewish	Italian	Irish	Total	Percentage of City
1940	1,785,000	1,086,760[a]	467,180[a]	3,338,940	45
1950	1,996,000	1,028,980[a]	456,408[a]	3,481,388	44
1960	2,114,000[b]	857,659[a]	342,381[a]	3,314,040	43
1970	1,836,000	682,613[a]	220,622[a]	2,739,275	35
1980	1,133,100	1,005,304[c]	317,601[c]	2,456,005	35

Sources: Ira Rosenwaike, *Population History of New York City* (New York, 1972); *Socioeconomic Profiles: A Portrait of New York City's Community Districts from 1980 and 1990* (New York, 1993); Federation of Jewish Philanthropies, *Estimated Jewish Population of the New York Area, 1900–1975* (New York, 1959).
a. First and second generation only.
b. 1957 totals.
c. Persons claiming only Irish or only Italian ancestry.

ancestry, which generally yields a higher number of "ethnic" respondents but also introduces a high degree of subjectivity into the process.

Nevertheless, using what numbers are available, it is possible to piece together enough data to arrive at a broad demographic picture. Table 1 reveals the steady erosion of New York's white ethnic population over a period of 40 years, but it also reflects the sustained vitality of those same communities.[4] In 1940 census reports identified some 3.3 million of these white ethnics in New York City proper; thirty years later, that number had dipped to about 2.7 million. This represents a sizeable drop, but in 1970 white ethnics still accounted for over one-third of the city's population and 45 percent of its white population. In reality, they probably accounted for far more, since the census numbers include only first- and second-generation Italian and Irish Americans and ignore hundreds of thousands of New Yorkers from the third and successive generations.

Polling data from around 1960 provide a better measure of New York's population makeup. Roughly 10 percent of city residents identified themselves as Irish and 17 percent as Italian. This translates to 780,000 Irish and 1.3 million Italian New Yorkers and boosts the aggregate number of white ethnics (Jews, Italians, and Irish) living in New York to almost 4.2 million —54 percent of the total population and 63 percent of the white population. Other white New Yorkers included German Catholics, who comprised roughly 10 percent of the city's population, but who forged less cohesive ethnic and religious bonds than the city's Irish and Italian Catholics, and white Protestants, who accounted for no more than 5 percent of New Yorkers.[5]

On the whole, then, it seems that the city's Irish and Italian populations probably diminished at a far slower rate than Table 1 suggests. By 1970 white ethnics may still have numbered as many as 3.1 million. These higher totals square with returns from the 1980 census (Table 1), which asked respondents to identify their ethnic origins and, as a result, found considerably more "Irish" and "Italian" New Yorkers than in 1970.

These numbers are not inconsiderable. They tell a complicated story of diffusion, but also one of continuity. Another way to consider the persistence of ethnicity is to chart regional population shifts over the fifty years between 1930 and 1980. In 1930 over 1.8 million Jews (26 percent of the city's total population) lived in the five boroughs or counties comprising New York City. Each borough reflected its own unique ethnic composition, with Jews accounting for 46.2 percent of the population in the Bronx, 33.3 percent in Brooklyn, and 16 percent in Manhattan, but only 8.1 percent in Queens and 2.4 percent in Staten Island. No suburban population figures exist for 1930 because Jewish agencies did not consider it necessary to count the handful of Jews then living in neighboring Westchester County or on Long Island (Nassau and Suffolk Counties).

By 1957 New York City's Jewish population had climbed to over 2.1 million and constituted a slightly higher proportion of the city's total (27.1 percent) than it had on the eve of World War II. But that year suburban Jews in Nassau, Suffolk, and Westchester Counties accounted for 18 percent of metropolitan New York's Jewish population. Their proportion climbed to 30 percent in 1970 and 33 percent in 1980. Since New York City's Jewish population kept pace in the 1950s and declined by only 13 percent in the 1960s, most of this regional population shift owed to higher rates of growth in the suburbs rather than flight from the city. If New York Jews were not moving en masse to Long Island, neither were they racing across the George Washington Bridge to begin new lives in New Jersey. The proportion of Jews within the greater metropolitan area living in New Jersey held steady, inching up from 11 percent in 1937 to 13 percent in 1968.[6]

Altogether, between 1957 and 1980, the city lost an aggregate of over 980,000 Jews, but only 28 percent of this loss occurred between 1957 and 1970. The most dramatic phase of New York Jewry's flight from the city occurred during the 1970s, when residents left for the suburbs, moved to Sunbelt states such as Florida and California, or, in the case of many older persons, passed away. These figures correspond to a larger study showing that celebrated, historic shifts in American Jewish demography—from city to suburb, from Snowbelt to Sunbelt—occurred more gradually than is sometimes assumed. They also challenge the idea that suburbanization was solely the product of "white flight," inspired by a fear of crime and neighborhood integration. Urban Jews maintained substantial numbers and viable communities even as suburban Jewish communities grew at a quicker rate.[7]

Corresponding data for the Italian community tell much the same story. In 1930 only 10 percent of metropolitan New York's first- and second-generation Italian Americans lived in the suburbs. By 1960 that figure jumped to almost 24 percent. It is more difficult to make a similar assessment of Irish population distribution, since a far greater share of Irish Americans qualified as neither first nor second generation (their grandparents and great-grandparents had been arriving in New York since the 1840s) and therefore eluded the census. But, on balance, Jewish and Italian population patterns demonstrate as much continuity as change.[8]

For the considerable number of Italian, Irish, and Jewish New Yorkers who remained in the city—and, to a somewhat lesser degree, for their suburban counterparts—postwar mobility did not necessarily initiate the immediate erosion of their ethnic communities.

In 1930 roughly three-quarters of all Jews in New York City lived in neighborhoods with populations that were at least 40 percent Jewish. Availing themselves of a massive boom in the construction of apartment buildings and two-family houses, particularly in the outer boroughs (Brooklyn, the Bronx, and Queens), Jews followed the new subway lines to neighborhoods that were actually more ethnically segregated than the places of first settlement commonly portrayed in immigrant literature and film.[9]

This trend toward residential segregation along ethnic lines yielded a sharp rise in the general Jewish index of dissimilarity—measuring Jews against the residual population—from 0.38 in 1920 to 0.58 in 1930.[10] Residential patterns held relatively steady in the Depression years, with the Jewish dissimilarity index dropping to 0.56 in 1940, a relative decline of only 3 percent. Twenty years later, in 1960, the index stood at 0.48, representing a larger (14 percent) though not drastic decrease in Jewish residential concentration.[11] In other words, Jewish residential concentration showed remarkable staying power, even as popular and scholarly writers were announcing the end of ethnicity.

More surprising, in 1960 the Jewish index of dissimilarity for the greater New York metropolitan area was actually 8 percent higher than the corresponding figure for New York City alone. In effect, Jews in the suburbs seem to have clustered together even more than the millions of Jews who still lived in the city proper.

These broader statistical trends were consistent with Jewish neighborhood patterns between 1940 and 1957. At the start of the Second World War, 55.6 percent of all Jews in New York City were still concentrated in fifteen neighborhoods that were at least 40 percent Jewish in population. Almost two decades later, the total number of such neighborhoods held steady but comprised 57.6 percent of the city's Jews—a slight increase. Furthermore, in the ten years following World War II, the proportion of New York Jews residing in neighborhoods with populations that were at least 55 percent Jewish increased by one-third. Altogether, this meant that more than one of every four New York Jews lived in a neighborhood that was over half Jewish in composition.[12] These figures may even underestimate the level of segregation, as residents of larger neighborhoods tended to cluster in smaller areas by ethnicity.

This pattern of ethnic segregation can be seen in the lives of New Yorkers such as Anita and Ruth Rogers. Born in 1942, Anita spent the first decade of her life in Brooklyn, where she lived with her parents and grandparents in a two-family house—a typical arrangement in New York's many prewar, ethnic neighborhoods. Her friends, she recalled, "were mostly Jewish, but mixed. . . . On the block there were some other minorities. There was one Italian family." In 1953 the Rogers clan relocated to the suburban-like community of Far Rockaway in Queens, which Anita described as "all Jewish . . . [or] nearly all Jewish."

Born in 1955, Ruth Rogers was a full thirteen years younger than her sister Anita. Her entire childhood was spent in Far Rockaway, a neighborhood she supposed was "about 90 percent Jewish . . . a little ghetto." Though an overestimation—she was off by about half—Ruth's guess is nevertheless an indication of how she perceived her suburban childhood. Her upbringing was not entirely insular. "We were not separated from other people," she explained. "The neighborhoods abutted each other, so I was not only amongst Jews all the time." But, like Anita, she acknowledged that her visible world bore a distinctly Jewish imprint.[13]

The story of the Rogers family in many ways typifies the postwar demography of metropolitan New York's Jewish and Catholic communities. In New York City proper, as well as in the surrounding suburbs, Italian, Irish, and Jewish families availed themselves of new housing opportunities without fundamentally compromising the residential and social self-segregation that had sustained ethnic neighborhoods in the first half of the century.

TABLE 2. *Indexes of Dissimilarity between Selected Ethnicities and Races,*
Total New York–Northeastern New Jersey Standard Consolidated Area (Above the
Diagonal) and New York Standard Metropolitan Statistical Area (Below the Diagonal)

Ethnic Group	Irish	Jews	Italians	African Americans	Puerto Ricans
Irish	....	0.554	0.455	0.790	0.769
Jews	0.571	....	0.594	0.811	0.781
Italians	0.480	0.605	....	0.789	0.782
African Americans	0.803	0.818	0.805	....	0.660
Puerto Ricans	0.765	0.781	0.778	0.638	....

Source: Nathan Kantrowitz, "Ethnic and Racial Segregation in the New York Metropolis, 1960," *American Journal of Sociology* 74, no. 6 (May 1969): 693.

"I spoke not a word of English when I started school," remembered Jerry Della Femina, an advertising executive in Manhattan. "But then why should I have? Italian was spoken at home. I lived in a claustrophobically Italian neighborhood, everyone I knew spoke only Italian, so it was natural that I didn't know English." Della Femina grew up in Brooklyn—not in the 1920s, but in the 1940s and 1950s.[14]

Like their Jewish neighbors, New York's Italians and Irish continued to segregate themselves residentially throughout the first decades of the postwar period. Data from the 1960 census indicate that the general citywide dissimilarity index for the Irish was 0.37, and for Italians it was 0.39.[15]

Table 2 demonstrates the degree of segregation between Italian, Irish, Jewish, black, and Puerto Rican New Yorkers throughout the entire consolidated census area comprising northeast New Jersey and metropolitan New York City, and in metropolitan New York City alone. Clearly, race and ethnicity were not equally instrumental in determining the character of New York's postwar neighborhoods: African Americans and Puerto Ricans experienced more profound segregation from the city's white residents than the Irish, Italians, and Jews experienced from one another.

Still, certain trends among the city's white ethnic population stand out. The Irish and Italians were more estranged from their Jewish neighbors than from each other (0.480). Furthermore, the data in Table 2 is consistent with a separate sociological study estimating that as late as 1980,

45 percent of Italian New Yorkers lived in identifiably "ethnic neighborhoods," while 18 percent of Italian suburbanites lived in such neighborhoods.[16] These statistical analyses attest to the persistence of residential separation, but they cannot account for the tendency of New York's white ethnics to separate themselves further within mixed neighborhoods.

The Catholic Church played a key role in helping Irish and Italian New Yorkers envision their surroundings in parochial terms. Canon law held that a parish was defined by geographical boundaries. Its parameters were immutable. The strong bond many Irish and Italian New Yorkers felt with their local parishes encouraged them to think of their neighborhoods as distinctly, even exclusively, Catholic.[17]

"We didn't live in New York City, or even the Bronx," recalled John Grimes, the editor and publisher of the Irish Echo from 1957 until his death in 1987. "We lived in Visitation [Parish]. That geographical definition lingered on for years." As a teenager, Grimes attended dances at Friday Good Shepherd—a different parish—where he cultivated a slick, and distinctly Catholic, modus operandi with girls. "After my opening gambit, 'Do you come here often?'—tossed off suavely with each and every partner—I'd move in with, 'Where do you live?,' which was invariably answered by, 'in St. Brendan's,' or 'in St. Philip Neri's,' or the like."

In cities like New York, Catholic papers normally listed apartment rentals by parish rather than by neighborhood, as in a 1965 advertisement in the Echo: "Our Lady of Refuge Parish, 4 rm. furn. apt. with full kitchen & bathroom, 2 or 3 Irish girls, $40 weekly, incl. Gas, elec. TV and washing machine. WE 3-8798."[18]

Catholicism, however, was not the only force influencing New Yorkers to think of their neighborhoods as ethnically or religiously monolithic. Marianna De Marco Torgovnick recalled her childhood in the Bensonhurst section of Brooklyn as distinctly Italian in composition and custom. "Italian Americans in Bensonhurst are notable for their cohesiveness and provinciality," she explained. "On summer nights, neighbors congregate on 'stoops' that during the day serve as play yards for children . . . to supervise children, to gossip, to stare at strangers." To Torgovnick, Bensonhurst was an insular community in which "neighbors are second only to family . . . and serve as stern arbiters of conduct. Does Lucy keep the house clean? Did Anna wear black long enough after her mother's death? Was the food good at Tony's wedding?"[19]

Remarkably, in the late 1950s, when Torgovnick was a young girl, one out of every three residents of Bensonhurst was Jewish, a fact that was not lost on her. "Crisscrossing the neighborhood and marking out ethnic zones—Italian, Irish and Jewish, for the most part," she explained, "are the great shopping streets: 86th Street, Kings Highway, Bay Parkway, 20th Avenue, 18th Avenue, each with its own distinct character." Little wonder that Gloria Wills Landes, a peer of Torgovnick's parents, recalled a completely different Bensonhurst—one that was overwhelmingly Jewish in character and composition.[20] To the outside observer, it may be puzzling that the same neighborhood could appear so ethnically insular to both Landes and Torgovnick. To many New Yorkers, this mentality was normal.

Even as New Yorkers mapped out urban space according to their country or region of origin, class and occupation continued to distinguish New York's white ethnic groups from one another. The Jewish shop owner, the Irish cop, and the Italian bricklayer are stereotypes, but, like many stereotypes, they find some basis in fact. By 1937 Jews owned two-thirds of New York's factories and wholesale and retail establishments. A year later, the Works Progress Administration found Italians represented disproportionately in the building trades. As late as midcentury, Irish Catholics were heavily overrepresented in the city's police and fire departments and held most of the top-brass positions in both divisions.[21] After the Second World War, all three groups experienced appreciable gains in occupational and socioeconomic status. But change occurred gradually.

Table 3 demonstrates the occupational distribution of first- and second-generation white ethnics in the New York–Northeastern New Jersey Standard Metropolitan Area in 1950. Several trends stand out. First, whereas 45 percent of immigrant Jews worked at skilled and unskilled labor (principally, the needle and construction trades), roughly three-quarters of their children qualified as white-collar. By contrast, only 33 percent and 47 percent of second-generation Italian and Irish Americans, respectively, qualified as white-collar. Within the Catholic community's sizable blue-collar ranks, the Irish tended more toward service jobs, while Italians tripled the Irish in semi-skilled labor. Table 3 shows that employment patterns continued to separate Irish, Italian, and Jewish New Yorkers from one another—not only at home, but also in the workplace.

Ten years later, census data for the Northeast revealed only limited change in the occupational profiles of Irish and Italian Catholics (see Table 4). Second-generation Italians made modest but appreciable strides over the course of the decade, increasing the proportion of their workforce engaged in the professions and in skilled jobs and decreasing their presence in semiskilled and unskilled labor, while second-generation Irish men saw a slight drop in unskilled labor and service work. But 64 percent

TABLE 3. *Occupations of First- and Second-Generation New York Males, 1950*
(*All Figures Percentages*)

Occupation	Jewish First Generation	Italian First Generation	Irish First Generation	Jewish Second Generation	Italian Second Generation	Irish Second Generation
Professional, technical, and kindred	9	3	3	19	6	10
Managers, officials, and proprietors	32	13	8	27	10	11
Clerical, sales, and kindred	14	6	13	28	17	26
Craftsmen, foremen, and kindred	16	24	20	10	22	18
Operatives and kindred	23	24	20	12	29	15
Service workers[a]	4	14	23	3	6	14
Laborers	2	14	11	1	9	6

Source: *United States Census of Population*, 1950, "Nativity and Parentage," Table 22.
a. Does not include private household workers.

of second-generation Italians and 56 percent of second-generation Irish Americans were engaged in blue-collar labor, with anywhere between one-third (Italian) and one-quarter (Irish) of the communities' respective workforces engaged in semiskilled or unskilled occupations.

At the same time, the proportion of employed American Jewish men working at white-collar jobs held steady at 75 percent. Importantly, the ratio of Jewish professionals increased from 13.8 percent in the 1940s to 20.3 percent in 1957, while the proportion of Jews employed as managers, officials, and proprietors (35 percent) more than tripled corresponding rates among Irish and Italian Catholics. Even within the white-collar category, Jews gravitated toward more prestigious and high-paying jobs than Irish and Italian Catholics.

Beyond demonstrating the fragmentation of the American economy along ethnic lines, these figures reveal the central role that class played in forming Irish, Italian, and Jewish ethnicity. They also suggest a subtle but important difference between Jewish and Catholic workers. Thirteen percent of Catholic professionals, and half of Catholics in the managerial

TABLE 4. *Occupations of First- and Second-Generation New York Males, 1960*
(*All Figures Percentages*)

Occupation	Italian First Generation	Irish First Generation	Italian Second Generation	Irish Second Generation
Professional, technical, and kindred	4	4	9	12
Managers, officials, and proprietors	9	7	11	11
Clerical, sales, and kindred	7	13	16	23
Craftsmen, foremen, and kindred	26	23	24	19
Operatives and kindred	24	20	24	16
Service workers[a]	14	20	7	11
Laborers	12	10	7	5

Source: *United States Census of Population, 1960,* "Nativity and Parentage," Table 11.
a. Does not include private household workers.

category, were self-employed, compared with a resounding 33 percent of Jewish men who were professionals and 70 percent of Jewish men who were managers. Nationwide, one out of every three male Jewish workers was self-employed—a remarkable figure that probably underestimates the autonomous character of the Jewish economy, since a significant proportion of those Jews engaged in sales probably worked for relatives or simply for other Jews. Catholics, on the other hand, were far more likely to be employees, and no more than 5 percent were self-employed.

This discrepancy contributed in subtle ways to each community's distinct outlook on ideas such as dissent, authority, and intellectual freedom. Self-employed, white-collar Jews enjoyed more leeway in what they said, thought, and advocated than working-class Irish and Italian employees, whose employment status and economic security were not nearly as self-directed.[22]

The continuity in each group's occupational makeup belies popular notions about postwar ethnicity—for instance, that Jews soared from the working class to the professional class in one generation, on the wings of a special commitment to education. Even by 1970, professionals accounted for only 27.2 percent of all employed Jewish men, and it was not until 1980 that this figure rose to 43 percent. While Jews far outstripped non-Jews educationally, commercial opportunities continued to account for the bulk of Jewish economic advancement well into the 1970s.

In 1957 only 28.5 percent of Jewish men had achieved a college or graduate-level education. By 1970 this figure had risen to 36.4 percent— well above educational achievement levels for Protestants and Catholics, but still far below the 64.7 percent figure that Jews achieved by 1980. Ultimately, then, the shift from haberdasher to doctor occurred gradually. The 1970s witnessed an accelerated transformation of the Jewish community's occupational and educational makeup, but in the first part of the postwar period, changes among New York Jews and their Catholic neighbors were modest.[23]

Further enhancing the segregated character of New York's workforce was the anomalous character of its labor unions. Whereas on a national level, the 1930s, 1940s, and 1950s witnessed the advent of industrial unionism—in part an attendant feature of sustained growth in the manufacturing sector— New York's factories on the eve of the Cold War were relatively small and its unions organized more typically along craft lines.

In 1947 the average manufacturing establishment in New York employed only twenty-five workers, a figure almost 60 percent lower than the national average. Non-electrical machine shops in the city employed an average of twenty-eight workers, compared with a national average of eighty-six. Whereas in cities like Detroit, Dearborn, and Chicago, industrial unions represented an expanding universe of semiskilled and unspecialized machinists, organized labor in New York, historian Joshua Freeman has found, reflected the city's bent toward the manufacture of "one-of-a-kind products . . . that were produced in only modest quantities in any particular style, size or version. . . . Firms doing custom or small-batch production—more typical of New York manufacturing—generally had a less developed division of labor, used less specialized equipment, and employed more highly skilled and versatile workers than mass production companies."[24]

In cities like Chicago, industrial unionism in the 1930s may have helped minimize differences between workers of different backgrounds.[25] But New York was not Chicago or Detroit. No single industry or oligarchy of corporations employed the mass of blue-collar workers. New York's unions tended to be organized by craft rather than by shop, which reinforced rather than undermined the segmentation of workers by ethnicity, skill, and function.[26]

Typical of this approach, the powerful International Ladies Garment Workers Union (ILGWU) organized its locals either according to craft (cutters, pressers, etc.) or product (brassieres, dresses, etc.). Taking their cue from the ILGWU, the Hatters, Cap, and Millinery Workers, the Fur and Leather Workers, and the Amalgamated Clothing Workers organized along similar lines. Conforming to the labor activity established by the American Federation of Labor (AFL), other New York unions, like the Painters, Decorators, and Paperhangers, organized their locals according to craft, location, work function, and nationality. As Freeman explains, "the durability of nationality locals testified to the continued salience of ethnicity in working-class New York and the reluctance of union leaders to disrupt important power bases."[27]

Other industrial unions in New York tended to assume a homogenous ethnic character simply by virtue of coincidence and membership restrictions. The famed Transport Workers Union Local 100 was somewhere between one-half and three-quarters native-born Irish and Irish American. The Longshoreman's Union also included large numbers of Irish New Yorkers. By contrast, 90 percent of the American Federation of Teachers' membership was Jewish. In New York City, there was no equivalent of the United Auto Workers of America to discourage ethnic allegiances. The close commingling of ethnic and occupational affiliations blurred the distinction between these categories.[28]

What Irving Howe recalled of the 1930s remained true in the 1950s and early 1960s. "What you believed, or said you believed, did not matter nearly as much as what you were," he reflected, "and what you were was not nearly so much a matter of choice as you might care to suppose. If you found a job, it was likely to be in a 'Jewish industry,' and if you went to college it was still within an essentially Jewish milieu. We did not realize then how sheltering it was to grow up in this world."[29]

In addition to segregation along residential and occupational lines, the social lives of white ethnic New Yorkers were shaped by segregation in the classroom. Thinking back on his formative years, novelist Michael Pearson still recalled the terror of being a fourteen-year-old schoolboy in the Bronx.

In the 1960s, eighth graders in Catholic elementary schools had to apply to Catholic high schools—a frightening process for most of those students. We sent in our applications with our grades and achievement scores and waited. Then it was a matter of waiting for a thick envelope, one that required some effort to pull from the narrow apartment house mailbox. The thin envelopes meant rejection, which for some at St. Philip Neri and other elementary schools meant there was no alternative but public education. *Public school* had the same sound to our ears as *state prison*. At fourteen we believed that going to a public high school meant failure—not a simple failure, either, but a terrible, irrevocable one.

Sweeping in its scope and size, the Catholic school system contributed significantly to the social isolation of New York's white ethnic communities from one another. To many Irish and Italian New Yorkers, Pearson's vivid recollection of "girls in plaid skirts and saddle shoes [and] boys in Oxford shirts and khaki pants"—the very embodiment of "the term BIC, Bronx Irish Catholic"—resonated deeply.[30]

The Catholic school system was the linchpin of a deliberately comprehensive program, dating back to the mid-nineteenth century, that aimed to keep secular culture at bay, imbue Catholic youth with the formal elements of their religion, and insulate the community against the Protestant establishment's manifest disdain for Irish Americans. The architect of New York's Catholic school establishment—and, arguably, of the modern American Catholic Church—was Bishop John Hughes, a fiercely proud native of Ireland's County Tyrone who had a genius for organization and just the tough disposition required to bring order and stability to the city's large community of famine immigrants. "Dagger John" earned the enmity of the city's Protestant elite and the adoration of his fellow Irish when, in the midst of nativist violence in the early 1850s, he armed the parishioners of Old Saint Patrick's Cathedral and publicly warned that New York would burn "into a second Moscow" if its Catholic population were harmed.

Hughes also called for a complete divorce between the city's Catholic population and the common school system when it became clear in 1840 that the Board of Aldermen would bar the church from enjoying funds allotted by the state for the purpose of public schooling, and that the Protestant-leaning organization chosen to administer the common schools intended to use its influence to proselytize among Catholic youth. Tapping into a powerful reserve of ethnic resentment, Hughes told his flock, "We are in the same situation as they were in Ireland from the Kildare Street Society, where for years they tried the fidelity of those who never were recreant to their faith." Three decades later, in 1870, 68 percent of all city parishes had elementary schools, which were attended by 19 percent of New York's school-age population.[31]

By the close of World War II, several generations of "brick and mortar" priests had constructed a sweeping educational infrastructure in cities across the United States. New York was no exception: in 1945 the five boroughs boasted an extraordinary total of 605 parish, diocesan, and privately organized Catholic schools, with a combined enrollment of 274,181 students. Since no precise Catholic population figures filtered by age exist, one can only extrapolate from other surveys the probable share of school-age Catholics captured by the parochial school network. Such estimations reveal that in conjunction with residential and occupational segregation, the city's extensive web of Catholic educational institutions magnified the degree of social isolation between New York's white ethnic groups.

In 1945, 68,914 pupils attended Catholic elementary schools in Brooklyn, accounting for 19 percent of the borough's total school-age (grades kindergarten through eighth) population. Survey results from around that time suggest that roughly 51.5 percent of New York City's white population was Catholic. This means that about 40 percent of Catholic elementary school students in Brooklyn attended parochial institutions. Because so many Catholic children attended parish schools, Jewish children—though accounting for only about 33 percent of all elementary school students in the borough—filled 41 percent of the seats in public grade schools.

These trends only intensified with time: by 1950 roughly half of all Catholic children between the ages of five and fourteen in Brooklyn and Queens attended parish schools. Five years later, in 1955, the total number of these students climbed to 184,143 and accounted for as much as 57 percent of all Catholic students.[32]

In Manhattan and the Bronx—the two boroughs that, in addition to suburban Westchester and Rockland Counties, comprised the Archdiocese of New York—117,059 students were enrolled in parish elementary schools in 1950, representing about 68 percent of Catholic children. Between 1950 and 1960 the share of Catholic children attending parish schools in the two boroughs held steady at about 67 percent.

An additional 85,000 public elementary school students in Manhattan, the Bronx, and the suburbs participated in weekly catechism classes—officially titled Confraternity of Christian Doctrine, or CCD, classes—bringing the total number of primary school students receiving some form of Catholic instruction to over 260,000.[33]

These figures call into question popular jeremiads about American Catholicism, which find that the dislocations of World War II and the late 1940s "undermined the parish-centered, neighborhood focus" of Catholic culture. In fact, between 1940 and 1960, the absolute number of students enrolled in Catholic primary and secondary schools nationwide increased by 219 percent, from 2,369,000 to 5,254,000. New York City's expanding parochial school system was simply one part of a larger, national network encompassing almost 11,000 institutions and one-half of the Catholic elementary school population by the mid-1960s.[34]

In 1961 sociologist Andrew Greeley found that, nationally, 77 percent of self-identified Irish Catholics attended parochial school for at least some (47 percent) or all (30 percent) of their student careers. Only 23 percent reported never having attended a parish elementary or diocesan high school. Italian Americans were a far less "churched" group: 60 percent never attended Catholic schools, while only 8 percent reported attending parish or diocesan schools exclusively during their student careers. As Vincent Panella recalled of his boyhood in Queens in the 1940s and 1950s, "the Catholic Church was an Irish bastion, from the strict priests and nuns down to the rowdy students . . . [while the] public school was the catch basin for the rest of us, Jews and Eastern Europeans, a few Italians, and the few Irish who didn't attend Catholic school."

This discrepancy in group behavior made a distinct imprint on interethnic relations in New York, driving a social wedge between Italian and Irish Catholics but also making it unlikely that most Irish and Jewish children would encounter each other through New York's public schools.[35]

In heavily Jewish neighborhoods, Jewish children were increasingly likely to fill a disproportionate share of seats in the public schools. Because of this trend, third-generation Jews like David Blumberg sometimes thought of their public alma maters as, paradoxically, both Jewish and nonsectarian. As described by Blumberg, Forest Hills High School "was Jewish . . . even though . . . it wasn't really a Jewish school." Edna Rogers, a second-generation Jew who had grown up in East Flatbush thirty years earlier, similarly recalled that when she attended Samuel J. Tilden High School in Brooklyn, "all the young people were Jewish. I don't remember anyone who was not. . . . So I grew up in a completely Jewish environment. I've never really thought about it, but that's how it was." Notably, when Blumberg was a student in the 1960s, the community of Forest Hills was two-thirds Jewish. East Flatbush, however, was only one-third Jewish in the 1930s, when Rogers was a young woman. In effect, a flexible combination of residential segregation and increased Catholic removal from the public school system fostered a great deal of continuity between generations. In retrospect, many Jews continued to perceive public schools as their exclusive domain.[36]

Intensifying this sentiment was the notable preponderance of Jews, and particularly Jewish women, in the professional ranks of New York's public education system. "My daughter, the teacher" served as the rough equivalent of "my son, the doctor" in the popular parlance of Jewish immigrant culture. In the 1920s and 1930s, several developments helped effectively transform public school teaching and administration into a Jewish occupational niche. These changes included the expansion of New York's higher education system, which made a college education attainable for second-generation Jewish women, and Mayor Fiorello LaGuardia's civil service reforms, which broke Tammany Hall's grip on the schools and introduced civil service testing as a prerequisite for teaching.

As early as 1920, Jewish women accounted for 26 percent of all new teachers in the city's public schools; by 1940 their proportion had increased to 56 percent. Although it is impossible to know exactly what percentage of the city's teaching corps was Jewish at any given moment in time, scholars estimate that by midcentury Jews predominated in the city's teaching ranks. This fact had far-ranging consequences. Just as Jewish children were often overrepresented in their local schools, beginning in the late 1920s the Board of Education encouraged teachers to work close to their own neighborhoods. Between 1924 and 1929 the board actually transferred half of its teaching force to facilitate this policy. Public schools in predominantly Jewish neighborhoods thus assumed a particularly Jewish character, among both students and faculty.[37]

The net effect of ethnic population concentration, a comprehensive Catholic education system, the city's neighborhood teaching policy, and Jewish overrepresentation in the teaching ranks was a de facto Jewish school subculture—albeit a secular one—within the city's public school system. Aiding this trend was a tracking system that often placed Italian pupils in "professional," or clerical, classes and Jewish children in academic classes. Even when they attended the same schools, then, Catholic and Jewish students tended to be separated into different classrooms.[38]

Factoring in generational distinctions further sharpens the image of ethnic segregation in postwar New York. A popular tenet of American immigration history holds that "what the son wishes to forget, the grandson wishes to remember." In other words, in their eagerness to become Americans, the children of immigrants tend to forsake all outward manifestations of ethnicity, including religion, while the grandchildren of immigrants, more comfortably at home in America, are free and inclined to return in some fashion to their ethnic roots.[39] Patterns of parochial school attendance challenge this maxim.

Nationwide, Andrew Greeley found in 1961 that third-generation Catholics were far more likely than their parents—who were, in turn, more likely

TABLE 5. *Generation and Parochial School Attendance among U.S. Catholics, 1961*
(*All Figures Percentages*)

School Attendance	First Generation	Second Generation	Third Generation or Later
All Catholic	20	16	20
Some Catholic	21	34	47
No Catholic	59	50	33

Source: Andrew M. Greeley and Peter H. Rossi, *The Education of Catholic Americans* (Chicago, 1966), 38.

than their parents—to have attended parish elementary and secondary schools, either exclusively or for part of their student careers (see Table 5).

Although 70 percent of first- and second-generation Italian respondents nationwide never attended parochial schools, 42 percent of third- and fourth-generation respondents attended parish and diocesan schools either exclusively (10 percent) or for some period of time (32 percent).[40] These nationwide numbers square with a 1969 survey of Italian Americans living in New York City proper. Table 6 demonstrates the tendency of successive generations of New York Italians to integrate themselves into a Catholic school system previously regarded as a bastion of the city's Irish population. These figures indicate that third-generation Italian Americans born in postwar New York were less likely than their parents and grandparents to attend public elementary or high schools.

The steady integration of Italian Americans into the parochial school system was important not only to the general social landscape of white ethnic New York, but also to the growing unity of the city's Catholic culture. The study on which Table 6 is based found that traditional forms of Italian Catholic religiosity—most notably, the tendency to address and give focus to the Madonna and the saints, rather than to Christ—gave way to what might be termed "Irish Catholic" religious culture, with its emphasis on weekly attendance at Mass, financial support of the parish, formalized worship (e.g., learning the catechism), and a primary emphasis on the figure of Jesus Christ.

To the interrogative statement "I pray more to the Blessed Mother and the Saints than I do to God," 57.8 percent of first-generation Italian Catholics replied in the affirmative, compared with 28.8 percent of second-generation and 22.6 percent of third-generation respondents. While 55.1

TABLE 6. *Catholic Schooling among Italian American New Yorkers, 1969*
(All Figures Percentages)

Years of Catholic School Attendance	First Generation	Second Generation	Third Generation
Some grade school	14.9	11.9	7.8
All of grade school	11.9	13.8	21.4
Some high school[a]	2.3	1.4	2.2
All of high school[a]	1.4	4.4	11.9
Some or all of college[b]	2.8	5.5	16.2
All of the above	3.2	3.4	11.5

Source: Nicholas John Russo, "Three Generations of Italians in New York City: Their Religious Acculturation," *International Migration Review* 3, no. 2 (1969): 15.
a. Assumes respondents also attended at least some Catholic elementary school.
b. Assumes respondents also attended some Catholic elementary and/or high school.

percent of first-generation Italians requested at least one Mass annually to honor particular saints, only 15 percent of the third generation sustained this distinctly southern Italian practice. These changes in worship did not indicate a decline in religiosity, since roughly the same proportion of first- and third-generation Italians attended Mass daily or weekly. Instead, the figures point to a shift in worship style. Italians gradually integrated themselves into the fabric of New York's Irish-dominated Catholic culture.[41]

Conceived as a project in conscious self-separation, the Catholic school system emerged by the early twentieth century not only as a successful barrier against Protestant hostility, but also as an inculcator of Catholic faith and form. The integration of Italian American pupils into this parochial school system contributed to a more uniformly churched and doctrinally grounded laity.

Using nationwide data from 1961, Greeley found a significant correlation between parochial schooling and familiarity with doctrinal orthodoxy (see Table 7). While it is difficult to determine whether parochial schooling produced, or was a product of, strong religiosity and familiarity with Catholic practice and creed, clearly a correlation existed between religious education and a grasp of official church doctrine. The steady increase of parish school enrollments throughout the 1940s, 1950s, and early 1960s thus suggests that the Catholic laity became more religiously sophisticated, or at least theologically knowledgeable. How this knowledge translated into

TABLE 7. *Percentage of U.S. Catholics Giving Orthodox Response to Issues of Doctrine and Religious Knowledge by Educational Background, 1961*

Religious/Doctrinal Knowledge	All Catholic School	Some Catholic School	No Catholic School
Jesus directly handed over the leadership of his church to Peter and the popes	89	75	61
There is no definite proof that God exists[a]	80	74	65
Science proves that Christ's resurrection was impossible[a]	73	66	60
God will punish evil for all eternity	62	52	49
Uncharitable talk is forbidden by the eighth commandment	55	47	44
The word we use to describe the fact that the second person of the Trinity became human is "incarnation"	48	38	35
Supernatural life is sanctifying grace in our souls	46	34	27

Source: Andrew M. Greeley and Peter H. Rossi, *The Education of Catholic Americans* (Chicago, 1966), 61–62.

a. A negative response conforms to church orthodoxy.

social and political conduct is another question, but certainly Bishop Hughes's education project reaped some very tangible results by the mid-twentieth century.

The Catholic school system was merely the most conspicuous component of a larger social and cultural network. By the early 1960s, Catholic Charities of New York—serving the Bronx, Manhattan, and several small, suburban counties—provided direct assistance to 20,000 families and over 80,000 individuals annually. At least 350,000 children from metropolitan New York belonged to the Catholic Youth Organization (CYO) and participated in its broad range of after-school and weekend programs: summer camps, boxing leagues, football teams, art classes, swimming lessons, and many other activities. By 1960 the Archdiocese of New York estimated that

40,000 Catholic teens were attending parish and diocesan dances *each week*. Amazingly, that figure excluded Brooklyn and Queens.

For parents and young adults, the church offered a parallel range of social options, such as sodality and Holy Name societies, the Catholic War Veterans, and the Catholic Lawyers Guild. By the early 1950s over 100,000 men throughout New York State belonged to the Knights of Columbus, and their wives joined the group's women's auxiliary. Many lives even began and ended under the watchful eye of the church: its network of twenty-three metropolitan hospitals treated over 150,000 inpatients and about 280,000 outpatients in 1955 alone.[42]

On one level, Catholicism was not entirely comprehensive. National fault lines still existed. Writer Pete Hamill recalled the first lesson that he internalized as an elementary school student at Holy Name of Jesus Parish, near Prospect Park: "I was Irish. At school, kids kept asking: What are you? I thought I was American, but in those days in Brooklyn, when you were asked what you were, you answered with a nationality other than your own." But even those Italian and Irish organizations that were nominally national, rather than religious, often bore a distinctly Catholic mark. Each spring at its annual dinner gala, the Society of the Friendly Sons of Saint Patrick in the City of New York—a fraternal association that went to considerable lengths to include all Irish Americans, both Protestant and Catholic—adorned the dais with "the flag of Eire and on its left the papal (or Cardinal's) flag." Francis Cardinal Spellman, the archbishop of New York, or one of his representatives, normally delivered the opening invocation.[43]

The Catholic Church offered its followers a remarkably comprehensive subculture, one that many New Yorkers happily embraced. Even Catholics who attended public rather than parochial schools, like Doris Kearns Goodwin, were likely to find Catholicism a thoroughly significant if not central part of their lives. "My early years were happily governed by the dual calendars of the Brooklyn Dodgers and the Catholic Church," Goodwin later recalled. "When I was five or six, I would lie awake in bed, listening as the thunder of church bells at midnight announced the coming of the Savior, dreaming of the day I would be permitted to stay up late enough to accompany my sisters to Midnight Mass." Goodwin's autobiography is suffused with memories of endless childhood hours spent at Mass and CCD classes, or wondering at the splendor of St. Agnes, her parish church, in whose "commanding beauty" she took "great pride." As she explained, "So rich were the traditions and the liturgy of my church that I could not imagine being anything but Catholic."[44]

Catholic New Yorkers like George Kelly would later recall that "we did not even know we were part of a Catholic subculture. . . . When we played saying Mass as kids, in a secret corner of our parents' flat, we were only copying the men in the neighborhood we admired most. . . . It was drilled into us from the first day we entered Our Lady of Good Counsel School. We were told to be quiet in church, approach Holy Communion with great reverence, and to confess our sins regularly."[45]

While the vast majority of Catholic New Yorkers dutifully sent their children either to parochial school or to CCD classes, a survey conducted in 1952 revealed that only 28 percent of the city's Jewish school-age youth were enrolled in Hebrew or Sunday schools. Community leaders optimistically noted that roughly 80 percent of city Jews were likely to have attended religious school at one point in time. But even this figure was falsely encouraging, since average synagogue school tenure was only around two years.[46]

The disparity between rates of Jewish and Catholic religious education corresponded to similar differences in formal worship. Although 80 and 78 percent of New York's Irish and Italian Catholics, respectively, attended Mass at least once each week, studies conducted in the late 1950s and early 1960s found that about 6 percent of second- and third-generation Jews in New York attended Shabbat services on a weekly basis. Another 20 percent attended one or more services each month, while the great majority of the city's Jews (70 percent) attended religious services either once each year or "a few times each year"—usually on the High Holidays (Rosh Hashanah and Yom Kippur).[47] While Catholic New Yorkers supported a comprehensive religious subculture, their Jewish neighbors demonstrated a laissez-faire attitude toward religious instruction and formal observance.

Enrollment figures alone do not attest to the relatively weak state of Jewish education in the early postwar period. In contrast to Catholic elementary and high schools, which offered integrative curricula combining secular subject matter with doctrinal and liturgical instruction, most Jewish schools were supplementary. In New York only 11,615 Jewish children attended all-day parochial institutions, the rough equivalent of the Catholic parish or diocesan school. The vast majority of students receiving any Jewish instruction at all attended either Sunday school (a weekly class, usually lasting no more than two or three hours), weekday Hebrew school (ranging from one to four afternoons per week, for as long as two hours each session), or a combination of the two.[48]

In 1944, 60 percent of all Jewish school attendees in New York were enrolled in weekday afternoon classes and another 20 percent in Sunday schools. Three years later those figures stood at 49 percent and 26 percent, respectively. The trend toward fewer hours of religious instruction led Rabbi Israel Goldstein, president of the Conservative movement's permanent synod, the Rabbinical Assembly, to lament that "the greatest failure of the congregational school is that it has still permitted the Sunday school to exist and to flourish. The Sunday school is a snare and a delusion. It is a fraud and a deception. It misleads both Jewish children and Jewish parents into believing that a Jewish education is being imparted when, as a matter of fact, because of its inherent limitations, it does nothing of the kind."[49]

Jewish school attendance was low in part because religious instruction, like synagogue worship, had evolved into a life cycle process. Most Jewish boys did not attend Hebrew or Sunday school until shortly before their thirteenth birthdays, at which time they either became bar mitzvah (in the case of Conservative and Orthodox Jews and some Reform Jews) or were confirmed (in the case of many Reform Jews). In turn, Jewish adults tended to worship regularly on Shabbat only in the years immediately preceding their sons' bar mitzvot. Even then, their rate of synagogue attendance paled in comparison to its Catholic equivalent.

Orthodox Jews were undoubtedly more observant than their Reform and Conservative peers, but only a small minority—probably less than 13 percent—of New York Jews in this period were Orthodox, and fewer still belonged to socially conservative Hasidic sects.[50]

As a child, Simon Rifkind, whose parents were Eastern European immigrants, attended a small yeshiva, or Jewish religious school, in Manhattan. His background in Hebrew language and Jewish texts was formidable, but not uncommon for his generation. Rifkind's two sons, Robert and Richard, attended a much less rigorous Hebrew school until each became bar mitzvah. After their bar mitzvah ceremonies, neither son attended services regularly, and nor did their father. As Robert later recalled, "That really ended my formal Jewish education."[51]

By connecting their worship patterns to life cycle events such as the bar mitzvah and confirmation, New York Jews produced a gender gap in Jewish education. "We continue to get what is to me . . . distressing," Rabbi Ben Zion Bokser told his congregants: "Parents who assume that only a boy is entitled to a Jewish education and not a girl. Don't these people know any better? I am certain that deep within them they do."[52]

Traditional readings of halakha (the Hebrew term for Jewish law) held that only men were required or eligible to perform the act of aliyah (literally, "ascent")—meaning, to climb to the pulpit and read from the Torah.

Since *aliyah* is the primary purpose of the bar mitzvah service, no equivalent ceremony for Jewish women existed until 1922. That year, Rabbi Mordechai Kaplan, a renowned but iconoclastic Talmud scholar at the Conservative movement's Jewish Theological Seminary of America (New York), introduced the term "bat mitzvah" into the Jewish lexicon when he called his daughter, Judith, to read from the Torah. Judith Kaplan's bat mitzvah remained a curiosity until the 1950s, when Conservative and Reform synagogues slowly adopted the ceremony for a variety of reasons—ranging from an ideological commitment to gender egalitarianism (probably not a widespread sentiment) to a more calculated effort to draw a larger number of girls into the Jewish education system. Still, as late as 1955, a majority of Conservative Judaism's Committee on Jewish Law still held that *halakha* either forbade women to perform *aliyah* or permitted it only on special occasions, and, even then, only after the requisite seven men had been called to the Torah.[53]

In this theological climate, religious instruction for girls was neither encouraged nor particularly rigorous. A measure of this imbalance is the fact that, at the close of World War II, girls comprised 33.1 percent of all Jews receiving some form of religious education in New York. Notably, they accounted for almost two-thirds of the student population in weekly Sunday schools, the least stringent instructional program. By contrast, there was no appreciable gender gap in Catholic education. Irish and Italian parents enrolled their children in parochial schools hoping to check the forces of secularism, while formal religion played a less critical role in New York's Jewish subculture.[54]

A survey of 400 Jewish households in Stuyvesant Town, a planned residential community in Manhattan, illustrated this point well. In 1950 the neighborhood's Jewish residents resembled postwar suburbanites more than the tenuously middle-class, first- and second-generation Jews of the Depression era. Over three-quarters were young parents between the ages of 25 and 34 (comprising 47 percent of the local Jewish population) and their children (another 29 percent). Forty-two percent of these well-educated professionals were involved with Jewish organizations. Forty-six percent were fluent in Yiddish, while an additional 25 percent understood it. Yet only 10 percent of Stuyvesant Town Jews belonged to a synagogue, 40 percent had received no Jewish schooling, and another 23 percent had attended only Sunday schools. Stuyvesant Town's new Jewish residents seem to have self-identified as Jews while passing over formal religious observance.[55]

National and citywide studies suggested that second-generation parents in neighborhoods like Stuyvesant Town were doing little more to bolster their children's religious commitment than their parents, in turn, had done for them. In 1959 the Council of Jewish Federations and Welfare Funds, an umbrella organization for Jewish community groups nationwide, found that only 7 percent of children receiving some form of Jewish instruction continued their religious studies beyond the age of fourteen.[56]

The community's relaxed approach to Jewish schooling produced a third generation that was decidedly less proficient in the essential elements of religious Judaism than their Irish and Italian peers were in the theological underpinnings and formal practice of Catholicism. In preparing young Jews to become bar mitzvah or bat mitzvah and to participate in holiday and home observances, synagogue schools focused, of necessity, on Hebrew language instruction. Proficiency in Hebrew enabled Jews to follow and participate in synagogue services and, more fundamentally, to be called to the Torah. In theory, then, a working knowledge of Hebrew was the lowest common denominator of Jewish religious training.

In 1953 the American Association for Jewish Education administered a trial test on basic Hebrew in eleven urban communities, including New York City and Newark, New Jersey. All students taking the test had received the most stringent form of supplementary religious education then available. On average, their classes met three afternoons each week, for a combined total of at least four and a half hours of instruction. As Table 8 reveals, the results gave Jewish education professionals considerable cause for alarm. The sample test queried participants on elementary vocabulary (e.g., simple words such as "dog," "cat," "book," and "room"), basic sentences, and story fragments. The poor performance of advanced (grade 5) students, who were roughly two years away from their bar mitzvot (and the likely close of their religious school careers), suggests that the bulk of synagogue school graduates never attained anything approximating Hebrew language competency.[57]

The weak state of Jewish education reflected the organized community's priorities in the late 1940s and 1950s. In 1947 the Federation of Jewish Philanthropies of New York (FJPNY) —a centralized fund-raising and financial disbursement agency serving the great bulk of New York's Jewish organizations—dedicated just less than 5 percent of its local expenditures to schools or education bureaus, and ten years later this amount had not changed. These figures are somewhat misleading, however, since the vast majority (92 percent) of children receiving Jewish religious instruction attended congregational, as opposed to community (intercongregational or noncongregational), schools. Arguably, the twenty-five Jewish community centers and eleven summer camps funded by the FJPNY performed some educational

TABLE 8. Hebrew Proficiency Test (1953) Average Percentages of
Correct Responses by Grade Level

Section	Grade 3	Grade 4	Grade 5
Vocabulary	37	52	69
Sentences	10	23	40
Paragraphs	38	52	69
Grammar	15	25	43
Stories	26	44	63
Total test	27	42	59

Source: American Association for Jewish Education, "Test on Fundamentals of Hebrew—I,
for Grades 3–6, Elementary Hebrew Schools, 1956," box 10, Tests-Samples Folder, AJHS.

function, albeit of a cultural rather than religious cast. Even so, in the late
1940s these organizations absorbed only 12.5 percent of the FJPNY's budget.[58]

Moreover, since community centers served both adults and children, the
National Jewish Welfare Board (NJWB) found that "Jewish organizations
that serve youth [in New York City] have a maximum of 125,000 members.
Of this number, 54,000 are under 20 years of age. Percentage-wise, this
means that only 7 percent of the entire Jewish population of all ages is
affiliated for social, recreational, and Jewish cultural purposes with a Jewish organization." Only 10 percent of Jewish "youth" (twenty years old and
younger) were so affiliated.

Whereas the comprehensive culture of the Catholic parish—with its
school, community center, and church—reached the vast majority of the
city's Catholics, the scarcity of Jewish community centers and the low rate
of community center membership only further compounded the effect of
low rates of synagogue attendance. The NJWB found that in the West
Bronx, a neighborhood with 300,000 Jews, "there is only one Center—a
synagogue center that has reasonably adequate facilities, and it serves a
tiny fraction of the Jewish population in this area." Flatbush, a neighborhood in Brooklyn with over 100,000 Jewish residents, had "only one reasonably adequately equipped Synagogue Center with very little use," while
areas like the Central Bronx (120,000 Jews), Bronx Gardens (40,000 Jews),
and Pelham Parkway (35,000 Jews) had no such centers. The city's vaunted
YMHAs and YWHAs—notably, the 92nd Street Y on Lexington Avenue—
claimed a total of only 47,000 members.[59]

In effect, the onus was placed on individual congregations to provide the physical and instructional resources for the religious education of Jewish youth, in much the same way that local Catholic parishes were primarily responsible for the construction of physical plants and the employment of teachers—normally sisters and brothers of religious orders—to staff their institutions. Yet diocesanwide collections often supplemented the already considerable resources raised and expended by local parishes in these efforts. Between 1950 and 1955, for instance, the Archdiocese of New York and the Diocese of Brooklyn allotted $40 million for new construction alone. It is unclear how much money the church dedicated each year to operating its vast network of primary and secondary schools, but the figure almost certainly dwarfed the estimated $8.33 million spent by New York's synagogues in 1958 on weekday and Sunday congregation schools, of which the FJPNY provided only 8 percent. Moreover, the bulk of the federation's school spending went to the Jewish Education Committee, a coordinating agency, rather than to the congregations directly. Ultimately, the synagogues and federation combined spent only $80.25 per student.

Although they lagged far behind Catholics in religious observance and education, Jews still did not assimilate at a rapid pace. While city Catholics were building and maintaining a parallel world for themselves, New York Jews constructed a vast philanthropic and political network that became a defining element of postwar Jewish identity.

By the early postwar years, the FJPNY, which conducted the great bulk of the community's fund-raising, had endowed twelve hospitals, eleven family welfare agencies, three homes for the aged, twenty-five community centers, and seventeen summer camps. All told, in the late 1940s New York's Jewish community was raising and spending unprecedented amounts of money each year. In 1946, for instance, the FJPNY—largely through the efforts of 12,000 volunteer grassroots workers—raised $23.5 million, a sum completely separate from the astounding $35 million raised by city Jews for the United Jewish Appeal (UJA). Most of the UJA's receipts were dedicated to overseas agencies like the Joint Distribution Committee, which spent $10 million in January and February alone to aid the Jewish community in prestate Palestine. The New York Jewish community's reputation for fund-raising and philanthropy was well earned, but Jewish education—and the sustenance of Jewish religious knowledge—did not figure highly on the community's priority list.[60]

In the wake of the European Holocaust, the community began to focus on several causes, in particular support for Israel, an emphasis on secular education, and a strong drive for economic and racial "justice" at home—defined by civil rights for religious and racial minorities, an expansion of the New Deal welfare state, and a broader application of civil liberties. These ideas pervaded Jewish philanthropic endeavors, religious school texts, fraternal organizations, and synagogue culture. They came to embody the very idea of Jewish tradition in the mind of New York's otherwise secular Jewish population. In effect, just as it was impossible to separate national origins, religion, and class in the construction of Italian and Irish ethnicity, Jewish identity in the postwar years was not exclusively a matter of religious affiliation. If at first glimpse it seems that synagogue culture and religious observances figured modestly in postwar Jewish identity, in truth, New York Jews fashioned a distinctly political brand of Judaism that accommodated both continued affinity to tradition and religious minimalism.

Throughout the 1950s, synagogue construction in metropolitan New York and the nation at large proceeded at a fever pitch. Between 1945 and 1965, the Conservative movement saw the number of its affiliate congregations jump from 350 to 800 nationally, while the Reform movement experienced an increase only slightly less dramatic, from 334 synagogues to 664. Yet, as one historian has explained, "the notable rise in synagogue affiliation among Jews was not matched by a rise in synagogue attendance."[61] Herein lies the critical paradox: Jews in and out of New York formed and affiliated with religious congregations at unprecedented rates in the postwar years, confirming their continued allegiance to Jewish tradition, but their level and form of religiosity diverged sharply from the brand of Judaism practiced by their forefathers in Eastern Europe.

Most Jews continued to attend services on Rosh Hashanah and Yom Kippur, to send their children to religious school (if only for an average tenure of two years), and to hold or attend Passover seders (a home-based religious service culminating in a festive meal and a practice shared by roughly 90 percent of the community).[62] Clearly, they believed it important to retain a minimal level of observance. By their actions, a majority seemed to find meaning in the *idea* of perpetuating Judaism.

But the pressing question is: how did they understand the central tenets of Judaism? Jews who attended services only on the High Holidays were likely to encounter a wide variety of themes sounded from the pulpit, not the least of which would be a rebuke of the congregation for its lax attendance the rest of the year. They were equally likely to find Jewish tradition expressed through the community's overwhelmingly liberal and politicized outlook. The ideas and messages they internalized on those few occasions when they sat in full synagogue pews, or when they staged Passover seders —and the motifs that their children learned to associate with Judaism in Hebrew school— constituted the core elements of postwar Judaism.

2 Dissent

In *Annie Hall* (1977), his classic satire of postwar Jewish life, filmmaker Woody Allen invested his onscreen alter ego with nearly every imaginable characteristic commonly associated with New York Jews. High-strung, neurotic, overly disputative, and relentlessly overintellectual, Alvy Singer exists in a world built entirely of clichés to which even he subscribes. "The failure of the country to get behind New York City is . . . anti-Semitism," he explains to a friend. "Don't you see? . . . The rest of the country looks upon New York like . . . we're left-wing, Communist, Jewish, homosexual, pornographers. I think of us that way, sometimes, and I—I live here."

Allen's early films often portray the Jewish milieu as excessively chaotic and contentious. *Annie Hall*'s outlandish flashback scenes from Alvy's youth show his family packed tightly around a kitchen table—arms flailing, tempers raging—as, nearby, the Coney Island roller coaster shakes the rafters and drowns out the din of the Singers' ongoing family feud. Conspicuously missing are not only parental authority, but also a substantial reason for the family's arguments. In *Annie Hall*, Jews argue for the sake of arguing.

Throughout the film, Allen's character remains self-conscious of his own vastly overdrawn categorizations. When he meets his future wife at a campaign rally for Adlai Stevenson, he scarcely misses a beat: "Y-y-you['re] like New York Jewish Left-wing Liberal Intellectual Central Park West Brandeis University," he begins, by way of introduction, "the Socialist Summer Camps and the . . . the father with the Ben Shahn drawings, right?"

To his future bride's retort—"That was wonderful. . . . I love being reduced to a cultural stereotype"—Alvy can only acknowledge: "Right, I'm a bigot, you know, but for the left."[1]

Woody Allen's comedy often hinges on the audience's recognition of certain ethnic typecasts. *Annie Hall*'s punch lines assume that viewers already believe that postwar Jews were instinctively a cosmopolitan and argumentative people—that their politics lean leftward and their families are unusually democratic or permissive. By the late 1970s—as New York City's third-generation Jews came of age, and as Allen's career as a filmmaker was on the rise—these ideas were already part of the cultural canon.

Modern popular histories of American Jewry, many written by American Jews and targeted to Jewish audiences, reflect the common assumption that Jews have always been both a "people of the book" and a nation of dissenters. "The masses of Jews are receptive to . . . new visions," explains the narrator of *Image before My Eyes*, an award-winning documentary on Eastern European Jewish culture just prior to the Holocaust. "They are a people who by tradition are readers. They are a people who by tradition discuss and debate. Ideas matter to them passionately."[2]

Joseph Telushkin, an ordained rabbi and author of a popular volume detailing "the most important things to know about the Jewish religion, its people, and its history," informs readers that dissent and antiauthoritarianism are long-standing virtues of Jewish civilization. "It is no small wonder that Israel, the name for both the Jewish people and the modern Jewish state, implies neither submission to God nor pure faith," he writes, "but means wrestling with God (and with men). Indeed, one of the characteristic features of the Hebrew Bible and of postbiblical Jewish literature is the readiness of Jews to argue with God."[3]

To claim intellectual pursuit and political agitation as eternal Jewish values is to read very selectively from the annals of Jewish theology and history. Yet by the early postwar period, many New York Jews readily identified dissent, scholarship, and argumentation as core elements of their secular and religious traditions. They considered it a Jewish imperative to question the status quo and to be skeptical of authority. New York Jews also interpreted their history as having included a long-standing communal reverence for individual rights and prerogatives that would have been unrecognizable to their great-great-grandparents in Eastern Europe.

These ideas were not born in a vacuum. The city's Jewish population was greatly overrepresented in colleges and universities, leading many Jews to believe that theirs was, and always had been, a learned tradition. Much of the community's emphasis on free expression and political agitation owed to the wide-scale democratization of Eastern European Jewish culture in the latter half of the nineteenth century. By the key decades of Jewish migration to the United States (roughly 1880 to 1924), the rupture of traditional lines of authority in the Russian-Polish Jewish community had created a rich but chaotic milieu from which the immigrant ghetto sprang.

Jews who were raised in this environment had every reason to consider dissent and argumentation as staples of Jewish life.

In this sense, the children and grandchildren of immigrant Jews correctly identified secular learning, iconoclasm, and hyperdemocratized public discourse as central to recent Jewish experience. But in claiming that such qualities were timeless virtues of Judaism, they were reinventing their religious heritage to render it compatible with contemporary realities.

I n a sermon delivered for the High Holidays in late 1961, Rabbi Theodore Friedman instructed the congregants of his suburban synagogue that

the Bible . . . is full of men hurling questions heavenwards. Begin with Abraham. God is about to destroy the wicked cities of Sodom and Gomorrah. And Abraham is tormented by a question. "Wilt thou destroy the righteous with the wicked? Shall not the Judge of all the earth do justice?" Then there is Moses. Moved to challenge God's justice when God declares His intention to destroy the children of Israel because of Korach's rebellion, Moses questions, "Shall one man sin and Thou be wroth with the entire congregation?" There are the agonized cries of Jeremiah and the Psalmist. "Why does the way of the wicked prosper?"—"Why are Thou silent O God?" And, of course, there is that whole book of the Bible on whose cover a large question mark might well be printed—the Book of Job. Chapter after chapter, reiterated and sharpened to the piercing point, Job piles up his questions. And beyond the Bible, the Talmud enlarges the image of man, the questioner.[4]

Friedman cautioned the members of his congregation against complacency and urged them to articulate "the questions [that] come from our minds, born of the contradictions we experience all around us—evil mixed with good, joy suffused with pain, ugliness intruding on beauty, death in the midst of life."[5] He understood Jewish religious tradition as a mandate to question authority in the larger interest of promoting social justice.

From the Jewish patriarch, Abraham, who raised his voice against God's designs to destroy even the virtuous in a city flowing with sin, to the prophet Jeremiah, whose lamentations during the first Babylonian exile seemed to register as criticism of divine will, Jewish civilization, according to Friedman, celebrated the social dissenter and petitioner.

Friedman was in good company. Throughout the early Cold War period, Reform and Conservative rabbis regularly instructed their congregants to read Jewish religious texts as a mandate to question authority. In a High

Holiday sermon delivered in the mid-1960s, Rabbi Leon Jick of Westchester County recounted an earlier biblical story about Abraham, whose conversion to monotheism inspired him to raze his father's idol shop. "Abraham . . . was the world's first iconoclast—the first smasher of idols," Jick told his congregants. "This is an appropriate myth to attach to the founder of Judaism—because the religion which he began was an iconoclastic faith. It destroyed the literal, physical idols of paganism. More than this, Judaism smashed intellectual idols. It demolished countless worn-out ideas." Like many of his colleagues, Jick believed that Jews were inherently "an idol-smashing people," and that, "living . . . for centuries as a minority in the midst of societies dominated by authoritarian ideologies, they became . . . the group which challenged absolutism, disrupted uniformity, and proclaimed to mankind in the darkest and most dismal ages that there was more than one way of thinking and acting."[6]

Jick and Friedman were adherents of the Conservative movement, the largest of the three denominational branches of American Judaism. They shared a general belief that Judaism was an evolving religion and that its precepts and modes of worship could be—and had always been—adapted to bring it into harmony with contemporary demands and realities. In locating the roots of Jewish nonconformity in the experience of the Diaspora, they tacitly endorsed the Conservative movement's faith that social and political history played a highly instrumental role in shaping Jewish ethics throughout over 2,000 years of diasporatic existence.

Like their Conservative counterparts, Reform Jews historicized Judaism and acknowledged its gradual but discernible development. They agreed that many elements of Jewish liturgy, custom, and belief were the work of human beings and not of God. Unlike Conservative Jews, however, they more readily discarded formal practices they viewed as archaic and tended to place more stress on the universality of Jewish ethics. Not surprisingly, many Reform rabbis readily agreed with their Conservative colleagues that dissent was somehow a Jewish virtue.

In 1955 Rabbi George Lieberman of the Rockville Centre Jewish Center on Long Island invoked the story of Benedict Spinoza's excommunication by the Amsterdam rabbinate to offer a pointed critique of "the hysteria of the hour" caused by a "certain political bigot" who was terrorizing the country. The reference to Senator Joseph McCarthy was anything but oblique. Lieberman warned that

> there is today a trend toward and demand for conformity. Our psychol-
> ogy is mob-like. . . . Anyone who does not act or speak or think or write

as demanded of him by the emotionalism and fear of the hour, is considered queer, dangerous, radical, un-American. Such a condition prevailed in the seventeenth century of Spinoza. Such a condition is very serious. We may no longer excommunicate people from the Synagogue. But there are other forms of ex-communication equally horrible which are practiced in modern society. Loyalty tests, guilt by association, guilt by blood-relationship, guilt by ideas and intellectual deviation . . . are forms of excommunication.

Lieberman urged his congregation to envision a clear intellectual trajectory from Spinoza's struggle to the 1950s. "The right to dissent," he argued, "the right to be different, the right to believe, and the right not to believe—must never vanish from the heart of man and from the face of the earth under God."[7]

In the context of early Cold War politics, to anchor Jewish ethics to a tradition of intellectualism and dissent was effectively to stake out a firm position on the red scare. In the early 1950s Ben Zion Bokser lamented:

The rest of the world dislikes a stranger. Everywhere throughout the land, subtle pressures are at work to eliminate everything that is strange, everything that is different, and to achieve the unity of sameness. This is one of the ugly characteristics of fascism as well as Communism. But it is unfortunately making headway into our land too. . . . Under the tactics of [Joseph] McCarthy and his stooges, the nation is embarked in a campaign against strangers in its own midst—those who entertain ideas which seem strange.[8]

While most rabbis refrained from making direct political appeals from the pulpit, Bokser situated the culture of McCarthyism in direct opposition to the longstanding tradition of Jewish dissent.

Concern over these issues did not begin or end with the postwar red scare. Toward the close of World War II, Rabbi Samuel Penner of the Jacob Schiff Jewish Center in the Bronx warned his congregants that fascism entailed not only the "glorification of force" and a "tendency [toward] isolationism [and] chauvinism," but also an environment in which "everything is . . . thought out for . . . men." Like his colleagues, Penner believed that free discourse and free thought were among the antidotes to fascism. It was no great leap to suspect that those movements that sought to stifle free speech were themselves neofascist.[9]

These same themes pervaded Jewish liturgy well into the 1960s. In a Rosh Hashanah sermon delivered in 1965, Rabbi Joseph P. Sternstein of

Temple Ansche Chesed (Manhattan) recounted the story of Samuel, who "paid a terrible price" of "ostracism, contempt, ridicule, [and] calumny" for "cherishing ideals which seemed to be anachronistic in the materialistic, mundane world in which he lived." On the surface, Sternstein's lecture was a discourse on the banality of American consumer culture, but in registering a protest against conformity, the rabbi also had another purpose in mind. "Need we be reminded afresh of the old nightmare of the McCarthy hysteria, which insidiously spread its tentacles into the inner texture of our society," he began, "and of the fear which muted trembling lips and quaking hearts? This period is a recollection which will swim again and again from the dark substrata to the fore of our national consciousness with nauseating after effects."[10]

Especially poignant to many rabbis speaking from the pulpit was the biblical story of Jacob, who returns from self-imposed exile to reclaim his patrimony from his brother, Esau. The night before his expected encounter with Esau, Jacob is attacked by an angel, who assumes the form of a man. Jacob successfully pins his adversary to the ground and receives a blessing from the angel. Henceforth, Jacob is known also as "Israel," a word whose Hebrew roots (*Yisra'el*) translate roughly as, "You have wrestled with God and with men and prevailed."

In 1964 Rabbi Benjamin Z. Kreitman of the Brooklyn Jewish Center delivered a High Holiday sermon in which he explained that "the [Talmudic] Sages identify this mysterious stranger as . . . 'the demon or divine genius of Esau.' Jacob was able to avoid a fight with Esau in the flesh, but with the Esau in spirit, the Esau who came to represent the dark forces in human history, he was forced to do battle until the dawn broke. . . . Strange, isn't it, that Jacob, peaceful of nature, is compelled to become *Yisroel*, the bold warrior who does battle with the demon of Esau?"[11]

In Jewish liturgy, the term "Israel" can signify the state of Israel (after 1948) or the nation of Israel, embodying world Jewry across space and time. In emphasizing the etymological roots of this central term in the Jewish vernacular, Kreitman placed in sharp relief what was already a common theme in New York's postwar synagogue culture. Even by virtue of their very name, Jews lived by a divine and historical imperative to wrestle with the angels.

By placing education and freethinking at the core of Judaism, American rabbis were reinventing, or at least simplifying, a long and varied religious history. Still, their widely shared conviction that dissent and agitation lie at the heart of Jewish tradition did not develop in a vacuum but was born of very real circumstances. In the century leading up to the early Cold War era, New York Jews and their Eastern European ancestors had forged a highly democratized culture that celebrated argumentation and dissent. Although the course of events that produced this distinct socioreligious outlook is complex, four general developments help explain the perception that dissent and activism were fundamental elements of Jewish civilization.

First, between the early eighteenth and nineteenth centuries, traditional rabbinical authorities in Eastern Europe faced vigorous challenges to their prestige and the prevailing orthodoxy. Prior to this period of upheaval, most Jews in the region shared a fairly uniform socioreligious culture. Beginning in the late seventeenth century, however, tensions resulting from demographic growth, economic diversification, and geographic mobility gave birth to sporadic antinomian (or nonformalistic) movements within Judaism. The most significant and lasting of these sectarian phenomena was the emergence of Hasidism, a religious persuasion that shared with its shorter-lived forerunner movements a less formal (and more emotive) style of worship, a heightened emphasis on messianism, and the exaltation of charismatic religious leaders.

Although Jewish authorities in northern Poland and Lithuania managed to check the spread of Hasidism in their own communities, the movement's fires burned wild in regions farther south. Even in Lithuania, where the movement eventually foundered, the cost of containment proved high for the rabbinic establishment, which found itself in the unusual position of having to defend its authority against a competing religious ethos. Although many Hasidic sects had reached accommodations with rabbinic authorities and reverted to more formal modes of worship by the beginning of the nineteenth century, they had permanently upset the community's static socioreligious culture, preparing many Jews for the ideological pluralism that would soon become a defining characteristic of the Eastern European diaspora.[12]

Second, in the mid-nineteenth century, secular leaders of the Jewish community in Russia—home to the vast majority of Eastern European Jews after its absorption of Poland in the 1790s—suffered a grave loss of authority. Traditionally, rabbinic authorities supervised the community's religious life, while economic elites governed its civil affairs through the local kehillot, or Jewish councils. Under Czar Nicholas I (1825–55), the Russian Empire abolished in fits and starts this long-standing tradition of Jewish self-governance, culminating in the legal abrogation of the Jewish corporate community, or kehal, in 1844. In its place the czar installed Jewish functionaries, many of whom he drew from the traditional elite, and held them responsible for raising the community's collective tax obligation to the state. The czar also directed these officials to enforce his draconian military draft, which inducted young men for a period of up to twenty-five years, during which they faced degradation and hardships that rendered the practice of traditional Judaism impossible. The draft disrupted family and communal life at all levels and became the object of fear and scorn throughout the Eastern European Jewish community. By the late nineteenth century, the traditional shdatlan, or Jewish political player—because of his unenviable position as tax collector and draft enforcer and Nicholas's dissolution of the kehal—had endured a devastating loss of prestige.[13]

With the religious status quo undermined by sectarianism and the old political elite discredited by its forced collusion with the Russian emperor, Jewish culture devolved into faction and chaos in the late nineteenth century. This erosion of traditional authority set the stage for a third historical development. Beginning in 1881, the czarist regime placed new disabilities on its Jewish subjects, mandating their removal from the countryside and exclusion from occupational sectors that were once mainstays of the Eastern European Jewish economy. In combination with economic transformations emerging from the abolition of serfdom in the 1860s, these new legal disabilities effected a swift urbanization and proletarianization of Russian Jews, who responded to their deteriorating position by constructing a diverse range of political, religious, and social movements to address the community's hardships. Further encouraging the trend toward political pluralism were successive waves of anti-Jewish riots (pogroms) that broke out in Ukraine and southern Russia between the 1880s and 1919.

The forces of proletarianization, urbanization, and anti-Semitism combined to shatter the organic religious community most Jews had inhabited a century earlier and produce a vast spectrum of organizations and political parties, each with its own program to reverse Jewish fortunes in Eastern Europe. Yiddishists, dedicated to cultural autonomy in the Diaspora, vied with Hebrew-speaking Zionists for the allegiance of Jewish nationalists. Bundists, Jewish socialists from Eastern Europe, clashed with a variety of communist factions that placed class identity above ethnic or religious allegiances. Orthodox Jews opposed Zionism, Bundism, socialism, communism, and cultural autonomy with equal fervor. Even within particular parties, different blocs competed for ideological supremacy. Political Zionists allied with Theodore Herzl, for example, battled cultural Zionists loyal to Asher Ginzburg (Ahad Ha'am), and General Zionists allied with Chaim Weizman formed their own faction, whose stated purpose was to oppose the existence of factions.[14] In short, by the era of mass migration to the

United States, Eastern European Jewish culture was rich in variety but more chaotic than ever before. It was from this environment that a generation of immigrants transplanted their culture onto American soil.

The centrifugal direction of Jewish politics gained further momentum from a fourth and final ingredient of Jewish factionalism: the establishment of a democratized religious infrastructure in the United States by a preceding wave of Jewish immigrants. Émigré Jews who came to America from Central and Eastern Europe in the mid-nineteenth century had already established a precedent for American-style Judaism. By the eve of mass migration from Eastern Europe, they had developed, somewhat unwittingly, a democratic religious style that broke with long-standing European conventions. In the absence of conventional rabbinic authority, these Jews had fashioned their religious life according to the congregational model familiar to students of early American history.[15] Voluntary communities of Jews founded synagogues, hired religious leaders, and forged consensus on matters of liturgy and practice. Rabbis served at the pleasure and financial whim of their congregants, who in turn settled all theological disputes by vote or, in many cases, by the secession and reorganization of the minority faction.[16] The democratization of American Judaism preceded the mass migration of Eastern European Jews to the United States between 1880 and 1924 but blended easily with ideas they had already internalized about political and religious pluralism.

By the 1940s most first- and second-generation American Jews who claimed synagogue membership belonged to congregations affiliated with either the Conservative or Reform movements (roughly equivalent to religious denominations). Each movement delegated the composition of its theological and social platforms to a rabbinical synod, members of which served their congregations under contract. In the event of disagreement between clergy and congregation, or between congregation and denominational assembly, members of a particular synagogue could opt to retain the services of a new rabbi, switch affiliation to another denomination, ignore the platform of their parent movement, or any combination thereof. In Conservative and Reform congregations, rabbinic authority was minimal and the atmosphere of the synagogue highly democratic. American Jews were free not only to choose how or how often they would worship, but also to discard, retain, and redefine elements of their religious tradition according to convenience, practicality, and preference.[17]

As a synagogue president in New York told his fellow congregants in 1951, "Unlike many other faiths, the Jewish tradition does not distinguish sharply between the responsibilities of the clergy and those of the laity."

Even the temple officers' most routine tasks were a reminder of the democratic character of the synagogue.

> It has been the historic tradition of our Congregation that the President deliver a report of his stewardship to the annual meeting of the Membership of the Congregation. This has been no idle formality. It has rather been a vital example of the democracy to which our Congregation has been dedicated since the day it was founded. For it is a basic principle of democracy that those chosen to leadership must report frequently and be continuously responsible to the men and women who selected them for their posts. This fundamental principle gains immeasurably in importance today, when the whole concept of democracy is under attack in so many areas of the world.[18]

American Judaism's congregational style only compounded the community's self-consciously democratic culture. Conditioned by over one hundred years of intense factionalism and ideological pluralism, New York Jews at midcentury truly believed that theirs was a religious culture founded on the principle of dissent.

For the vast majority of infrequent synagogue-goers, High Holiday sermons only reinforced their already strong sense that Jews possessed a distinct set of values and mannerisms, and that a person need not necessarily be religious to be Jewish. Writing of his childhood in the Bronx in the 1930s, Irving Howe remembered a community rife with "attitudes of tolerance and permissiveness, feelings that one had to put up with and indulge one's cranks, eccentrics, idealists, and extremists. . . . The Jewish neighborhood was prepared to listen to almost anyone, with its characteristic mixture of skepticism, interest, and amusement."[19]

Aileen Robbins, who grew up in New York in the 1950s, hailed from an outwardly secular Jewish family. As a child, she attended an elite private school that boasted a distinguished, Protestant pedigree and enrolled in ballet, horseback riding, and tap dance lessons. She attended Sunday school for only a few years. Robbins felt like a stranger when she visited her immigrant grandparents each week. "Those were the grandparents who were born in Europe, who spoke with accents, [whose] house . . . smelled like gefilte fish," she explained. "I don't have any pleasant memories of that."

By her own admission, Robbins was always more comfortable around her maternal grandmother, who was "third generation" and possessed "a real sense of not only having been melded into American life but also a certain aristocratic bearing." Her own Jewish identity was ambiguous: "I didn't know whether I was Jewish or not Jewish, and [I] believed in some respect that it was part of my father's upward mobility, social mobility . . . to have . . . me blend even more into a certain class of society by not stressing my Judaism."

But if the Robbins family attempted to forswear all appearances of Jewishness, its success was limited. As an adult, Aileen recalled family meals as having borne an imprint that was, in her mind, nothing but Jewish.

They were all talkers in my house. My father and my sister and I were all talkers, but . . . the only way you could be heard, really, was if you could yell louder than the person who was talking, at which point everybody else would shut up for a little while, but you know, it was just kind of pandemonium in my memory. . . . It was very busy, frenetic—it reminded me of the Woody Allen films, *Annie Hall* or whatever, [in which] parents are arguing but they're not really arguing. . . . [There was] a lot of noise, a lot of stuff going on, and I always felt like I could never really get my two cents in because I was the youngest and I didn't have either the vocabulary or the sheer vocal mechanism to be heard above everybody else.[20]

Like Woody Allen, Aileen Robbins thought of her family's talent for intellectual brawling as a mark—in her case, perhaps the only mark—of its Jewish character.

Emily Koreznick recalled that her father, though not particularly religious, "was the kind of man who loved to argue about things, and that's a good Jewish tradition." Although her parents were both active members of the Jewish community, it seemed to Koreznick that there was something even more immanently Jewish in their manner of speaking, or how they carried themselves. "My family['s] talk was very much one that I think reflects a Jewish personality and attitude," she explained.

I remember arguing very staunchly with [my father at mealtimes]. . . . We would argue very hotly and I was quite allowed to leave my child-parent role for the purpose of these arguments. . . . I remember my brother running for the encyclopedia to prove a point and so forth and so on. So that was lively, sometimes a bit too hostile, but I think that that is also a part of the pattern of Jewish life, that we yell at each other an awful lot. I remember a Christian friend saying "My, how do you Jews carry on with one another!" . . . [T]he Talmud . . . the great book of the

Jewish people, is a book of disputation. They're arguing with one another, they're trying to resolve differences . . . they're bringing in all the differences to put together somehow, and this is just a part of our tradition, I think on the whole a very exciting and stimulating one.[21]

New York Jews like Robbins and Koreznick assumed reflexively that their families' argumentative nature was an outgrowth of their Jewish heritage.

Closely associated with the idea that Jews were naturally argumentative or contrary was a belief that secular scholarship and activism were central to Jewish heritage. Growing up in suburban Rye, New York, in the 1960s, Lisa Goodkind Hathaway attended a few years of Sunday school, but to her and her brothers Judaism "sort of became an object of rebellion . . . for a long time." As she later acknowledged, "We didn't dislike it but we were . . . sort of rejecting it." Years later, because her religious education was limited, Hathaway admitted to "liking" Judaism "superficially. Really, I don't know that much, but what I know, I like, and I also feel a certain connection somehow, [a] cultural and ethnic connection that I feel proud of. Other Jews, the things that I see them doing and standing for, I'm usually proud of." Hathaway believed that Jews were especially likely to be "intellectually curious," that they were "a creative people," and that they possessed an especially heightened "social awareness"—qualities she attributed to "the way they value life and their emphasis on the present rather than the afterlife."[22]

The sense that education and humanitarianism were at the heart of Judaism was not particular to Lisa Hathaway's generation. Ruth Messinger, who grew up on the Upper West Side of Manhattan in the 1950s, also thought of Jews as "learners." Messinger remembered her grandparents, who "came to our house for every holiday," but in whose "very nice, very fancy apartment" there was not "one shred . . . of anything having to do with holiday or religious celebration. What there was instead was an extraordinary respect for learning." In similar fashion, a local chapter of the American Jewish Congress asserted in 1954 that Jews "have brought [to the United States] a tradition of learning, of scholarship, of scientific curiosity . . . a love of the arts and a healthy and growing culture. . . . As Americans and as Jews we take pride and satisfaction that our contributions are so rich and so varied." To local chapter members it seemed intuitive that Jews were by nature intellectually curious.[23]

The idea that a love of learning and uncommon social consciousness were essential building blocks of Judaism reflected an element of ethnic chauvinism. Hannah Hofheimer, who was born in the late 1890s, remarked that she was "proud of being a Jew" because "they have a great many values and total sympathy. They have sympathy for the underdog, they look out for people and they're creative." Speaking of her son and daughter-in-law, who moved from New York to New Hampshire, Hofheimer guessed that although the Jewish community in Portsmouth was small, "most intellectual women are Jews up there."

Marcy Oppenheimer, who grew up in Westchester County in the 1960s, felt "very attached to the Jewish traditions. . . . I mean I'm very proud of . . . the fact that a third of the people at Yale are Jewish . . . and the values of education and family that come from there are now my values. . . . Not that non-Jewish people don't have them, but I think they stress them and manifest them differently." Jean Bennet, who was raised in Scarsdale in the 1950s and early 1960s, believed that "Jews have always stressed education, mostly just to survive, and also because we're just that type of people, and I'm very proud of that. . . . I'm proud of the fact that I read a lot and I'm interested in the world around me and that I have a master's degree."[24]

Given the lopsided ethnic composition of New York–area universities and colleges, it would have been a considerable feat of cognitive dissonance for many second- and third-generation Jews not to discern a connection between their heritage and the ideals of study and reason. As early as the 1930s, Jews comprised between 80 and 90 percent of the student body at City College, Hunter College, and Brooklyn College, over 90 percent at New York University, and 22 percent at Columbia University. And many Jews understood this last figure to be the result of aggressive anti-Semitic restrictions (in 1920, the proportion of Jews at Columbia had been 40 percent).[25]

In 1963 almost half of all Jews in New York City had continued their education beyond high school, compared with 27.5 percent and 18.2 percent of the Irish and Italian communities, respectively. Over half of all Irish New Yorkers and 60 percent of Italians did not finish high school, compared with 35 percent of the city's Jews (only 21 percent among the native born). Inhabiting a small part of the world where most people were either Jewish or Catholic, and where the former were likely to be better educated than the latter, it was natural for Jews to believe that a love of learning was a staple of their heritage. It was this reality that led rabbis like George Lieberman to instruct his congregation's younger members that "the real achievement is not only to be a Reform Jew, but an informed Jew. Judaism emphasizes knowledge. It is a Torah-centered religion. Torah Ora. It is an intellectual light."[26]

Dissent and intellectual achievement were intimately associated in collective Jewish mythology. To be a good Jew, one had to question authority boldly and consistently. To question authority with any success, one had to be learned. In this sense, American Judaism in New York had less and less to do with displays of formal religiosity and more to do with an active embrace of secular values that many ordinary Jews came to identify as uniquely "Jewish."

An important outgrowth of New York Jewry's self-conscious embrace of dissent and intellectual pursuit was its child-centered approach to family life and education. In his acclaimed study of postwar American Jewry, sociologist Charles Liebman argued that Jewish "parents [tended] to emphasize extension rather than distinction in their relationships with their children. Anything that happens to the child also happens to the Jewish parent. . . . [T]he child's strength in the power structure of the family is further enhanced by the parents' dependence on the child as their extension. He is, in the traditional folk formulation, their *nachas* (pleasure). Just as his success and achievement become theirs, so his failure reflects upon them."[27]

Liebman's supposition is consistent with sociological studies conducted in the early postwar years that found that American Jewish parents tended to afford their children a relatively large amount of intellectual latitude from an early age.[28] Far more than their Irish and Italian Catholic peers, Jewish children and teenagers were permitted and encouraged to question their parents' wisdom on matters pertaining to politics, religion, and family governance.

Some scholars traced the "nonauthoritarian" or "antiauthoritarian" culture of the Jewish family to the traditional Eastern European shtetl, where "the raising of questions and the demanding of logical justification for rules, norms, and prohibitions [was] welcomed by adults as an indication of the child's intellectual precocity. . . . Both in the family and later in school life a serious effort [was] made to foster his intellectual exploration. . . . From these experiences the small boy learn[ed] that he [could] attract . . . prestige by asking searching and incisive questions."[29]

It is more likely that attitudes toward authority and obedience were a product of class rather than tradition. A postwar survey of teenagers in New Haven, Connecticut, found that Jewish children enjoyed a far greater amount of "parental regard for judgment," while Italian children enjoyed a higher level of parental "permissiveness in age-related activities." What this meant, in simple terms, was that Jewish parents were more likely than Italians to "encourage" and "respect" their children's opinion in family discussions, to confer with their children about family problems, and to explain or rationalize their rules and expectations.[30] By comparison, Italian American teenagers enjoyed more latitude and less parental meddling than their Jewish peers in their conduct outside of the house—for example, whom they dated, how they spent their own money, or with whom they socialized. When the two sample groups were controlled for class, the distinctions between them evaporated.

In New Haven, as in New York, most Italians worked as blue-collar laborers, while most Jews qualified as white-collar. On average, Jews earned higher incomes and were better educated than Italian and Irish Catholics.[31] To isolate either religion, national origins, or class as the key ingredient of Jewish family culture is to ignore the central role each category played in the creation of ethnicity.

As Deborah Dash Moore demonstrated in her study of interwar New York Jewry, by the 1920s and 1930s "the second generation . . . [had already] constructed a moral community with supports borrowed from American culture, middle-class values, [and] urban lifestyles. . . . In fact, so successful were they in binding middle-class norms to visions of Jewish fulfillment, that their children often could not disentangle the two." To many second- and third-generation Jews, to be middle-class was to be Jewish, and to be Jewish was to be middle-class. The two ideas were often inseparable.

New York Jews fused their ethnic identity to patterns of middle-class consumption, such as eating out, furnishing their homes fashionably, wearing stylish clothing, staging elaborate bar mitzvahs and weddings, and exposing their children to musical instruction, dance lessons, and summer camps. A key feature of the new Jewish identity was its wholesale acceptance of American middle-class domesticity. "The community came together . . . around the ideal of domesticated Jewishness in which home and its inhabitants became the core of a modern Jewish identity," explained historian Jenna Weissman Joselit. "As the burden of cultural continuity shifted from the community to the family, Jewishness itself was redefined." It became "less a matter of faith or a regimen of distinctive ritual practices than an emotional predisposition or sensibility."[32]

With middle-class cultural mores so completely fused to postwar Jewish identity, it is little wonder that many Jews—already tolerant of political and intellectual dissent—readily adopted the child-centered parenting methods popular among many in the postwar middle class.[33] Just as Emily Korez-nick recalled being "allowed to leave [her] child-parent role for the purpose of [family] arguments," Robert Landis, who grew up in suburban Westchester in the 1960s, remembered that "when my family had guests over, the children were never separated from the adult guests. We were always a part of the family[,] so if my mother and father had people over, we were always included, and I thought of their friends as my friends."[34]

Richard Rifkind, a Jewish doctor who raised two daughters in the 1960s, explained his understanding of his parental role in this way:

> I have a client relationship in a sense with my children, that is, it's the way I see medicine. When I have a patient I have two obligations[;] one is paramount and one is minor. The paramount one is that patient's salvation, [and] the minor one, but a real one, is society. I have to find a relationship and that's exactly how I feel towards the kids. My primary goal is their personal happiness and growth. . . . I think Jewish identity should be continued. If it can't be handled in their case, I don't see the history of Judaism as being their total burden."[35]

Ruth Rogers, who grew up in Far Rockaway in the 1960s, recalled that although she had attended a Jewish day school, her parents did not "inflict" Judaism on her—she "was free to make [her] own choices." Rogers's father, reflecting a laissez-faire attitude typical of many Jewish families, explained that "the best . . . that any parent can do, is furnish the children the tools that a parent thinks they ought to [have]. . . . You can't take [grown children] over your knee and spank them: 'You must go to the synagogue. You must do this, you must do that. You can't do that.' . . . All we ever hoped to do was give them the proper education, the proper exposure, to know the Jewish values."[36]

Carole Rifkind remembered that neither she nor her husband insisted on an extensive religious education for their two daughters, who, as they grew older, "were increasingly less interested in going[,] and so just before the bat mitzvah classes would have started [they] just dropped out, and they never had any further education." Carole's daughter, Nancy, appreciated this approach to the faith: "[my] parents' attitude towards the whole thing was—and I really treasure them for this kind of attitude, because it's what I have—[was] that you offer your children Judaism to whatever extent they want it, and you support them in that and maybe even encourage them." Ultimately, Nancy believed, her parents responded correctly to her manifest disinterest in formal Jewish education. "They offered me the choice," she said, "and when I gave them a good enough argument as to why I didn't want it, they let me make that choice."[37]

This breezy attitude toward religious education was part of New York Jewry's general embrace of permissive child-rearing methods. Hannah Hofheimer, whose grandchildren grew up in the 1950s and 1960s, explained that she did not "like a lot of things going on with the young people, but what are you going to do? One of my granddaughters said to me once, you know, 'I'm going to live with'—and she mentioned the boy's name. I didn't say anything, she came and told me. It's accepted." One of Hofheimer's granddaughters, Jean Bennet, later recalled fondly how her grandparents tolerated what were undoubtedly jarring social changes.

> The neat thing about my grandparents is that they didn't like or . . . even understand a lot of things we did, but they never tried to tell us what to do or not to do. In fact, during the 1968 . . . poor people's campaign, there was a big demonstration in Washington and I was very much an activist, and I was going down to it, and it meant I was going to miss a party that my grandparents were throwing. . . . I had a big decision to make, and I decided the only thing I could do [was] to go down to Washington. . . . I called my grandparents to tell them and they were really understanding, they really were. It was good.[38]

On occasion, this hands-off approach could spin out of control. Arthur Rogers, who raised his children in the 1940s and 1950s, explained that neither he nor his wife ever "ask[ed] too much of the children" after they grew up and started families of their own. "We never bother them," he said. "It's their business and their life, and it's okay with me." Their daughter and son-in-law decided in the early 1970s to send their own child to a "progressive school," a decision that did not please the grandfather. "You know what [progressive] means? Well, you can learn how to do finger painting, but you can't read . . . when you're eight years old. I mean, you're a champ at finger painting. . . . And that's what it was with [my grand-daughter]. At eight years old, she couldn't read her name, she couldn't write her name. . . . Who am I to say? I'm dealing with a professional. My son-in-law's a doctor of psychology and I tell him what's right and what's wrong? Obviously not."[39]

Simon Rifkind, a prominent state judge whose grandchildren grew up in the 1950s and 1960s, echoed this same conviction. "I never moralize to my grandchildren," he reflected. "I never give them any didactic sessions or tell them to be good or so on. I expect them to be influenced by the fact that their grandparents and their parents believe in a civilized fashion, that they're interested in civilized activities, that they have a regard for the arts around them and for the aesthetic qualities of life."

One of Rifkind's grandchildren experimented with drugs as a high school student in the 1960s. "My reaction to it was, she'll get over it, as long as it wasn't interfering with her function[s]," explained her father.

"Based on my clinical judgment . . . the best thing to do [was] let her know that I [did not] think [it was] a great idea, that it's probably medically dangerous, that it could be socially dangerous, that there is a certain vulnerability that she placed herself at, having an outlawed drug in her possession, and she ought to know that I didn't think it was a great idea, but I wasn't going to have tantrums on the subject."[40]

Jewish community leaders endorsed and promoted the community's self-consciously democratic approach to child rearing. The Conservative movement's summer camps advised prospective counselors that "kids want to know that they exist and are worthwhile in and for themselves. They know when you are functioning because you are a counselor and when you are relating to them *not only* because you are a counselor." Camp organizers encouraged employees to appeal to each camper's individual aspirations. Among those points they reiterated at each year's training session: "Don't overevaluate or judge a child"; "Be firm and consistent in the areas that call for it. Be flexible in those areas where it really doesn't make a difference"; "Admit to error but don't let your admission excuse incompetence"; "Your acts need not always be reasoned acts, but must always be reasonable and explainable"; and "Lend charm to your bunk. Do the unexpected for them and with them and to them—even break a rule— together!"[41]

Summer camp is, by definition, a child-centered endeavor, but Jewish education experts also took a cue from the public school system and endorsed the child-centered, progressive pedagogical methods then very much in vogue both in New York and nationwide.[42] In 1950 the Brooklyn Jewish Community Council (BJCC), an umbrella group representing 850 social, religious, and ethnic organizations, affirmed that "Jewish adolescents, like adolescents of other faiths in Brooklyn, need a sense of identity and of being wanted and belonging. This feeling of being accepted is paramount. They want to know who they are; what are they doing in Brooklyn and in the World; what are the rules of the game; and how do they fit among people and into things."

Constituent members of the BJCC believed that "in order to [help Jewish children] develop a sense of self-esteem," many synagogues in Brooklyn

> have turned to the adolescents and have given them responsibility for religious practices. By "Youth Centering" the program, adolescents conduct their own Junior congregations and Saturday morning services are conducted by them with a minimum of adult guidance. Many of the synagogues have developed club programs to which the "natural gangs,"

typical of this age group, gravitate. They select their own leadership and plan their own programs. Great emphasis is laid on the democratic process and volunteer or paid leadership is provided to help the adolescents help themselves. These clubs are social-cultural-religious in practice and run the gamut from socials to philanthropic ventures.

While many synagogues initiated "junior congregations" of the sort mentioned by the BJCC, others, like the Van Courtland Jewish Center, assigned Hebrew school students a formal role in the regular congregational services. Under the headline, "Making Youngsters Feel They Belong," the Jewish Education Committee of New York—a coordinating agency for the city's religious schools—explained that Van Courtland's Jewish youth regularly managed the Musaf (additional) services on Shabbat morning and supplied a choir whose members joined the rabbi on the pulpit.[43]

Such unqualified faith in the tenets of progressive education reinforced the culture that Jewish students encountered in the New York City's public schools, whose curriculum goals in the mid-1950s "aim[ed] to promote the general welfare by helping each *individual* to develop his best personal and social competence." In the best spirit of progressivism, the Board of Education affirmed that "the curriculum should be developed as a cooperative project in which the teacher, the supervisor, the parent, the public, and the pupil participate and to which each makes appropriate contributions. . . . Curriculum policies and practices should encourage friendly understanding and democratic relations among supervisors, teachers, pupils, and parents."[44]

Since the overwhelming majority (over 90 percent) of New York's Jewish children attended public schools, the culture they encountered in the course of their secular studies found reinforcement in the synagogue.[45] At the very least, adults in both settings paid considerable lip service to including children and teenagers in decisions that might affect them. Hence, in 1951 Rabbi David Panitz of Temple B'nai Jeshurun (Manhattan) informed adult members of his congregation that "as young Americans who live in a democracy," their children needed "some clear expression . . . that young people will be given a chance to step eventually into positions of responsibility in the community. And since, in a democratic society, each individual should be helped to develop as a dignified personality, with human worth, these youngsters urge greater implementation of democracy."[46]

Other religious leaders even encouraged their adult congregants to *celebrate* the younger generation's rebelliousness. Rabbi George Lieberman told parents in his congregation that their teenage children were "reaching an age . . . when they will dare to shake their fist against heaven. And when they will find fault with everything they see and hear and observe and feel." He counseled adult congregants to embrace this necessary adolescent phase. "This is a part of growth," he assured them. "Yes, wholesome intellectual growth. Not only to accept but also to reject."[47]

And reject they sometimes did. In 1953 the student government organization at Yeshiva University, the nation's most prominent training ground for modern Orthodox rabbis, registered an official protest against the school's administration for planning to combat low attendance at daily prayers (roughly 10 percent) with the threat of expulsion. The students countered that they did not object to participating in religious rites, per se, but they faulted the university for "failing to consult the student leaders when it came to policies affecting them. Had the students been consulted, the administration would have learned that we feel compulsion is no way to solve a religious problem."[48]

Yeshiva's student body was unrepresentative of the community-at-large: the vast majority of New York Jews affiliated either with the Conservative or Reform movements. But the example is instructive precisely because of its exceptionality. Young Jews who attended Yeshiva, many of whom were receiving both their bachelor degrees and rabbinic ordination, were ostensibly among the most observant members of their community. That they chose to attend a modern Orthodox institution is evidence of their religious commitment. Yet they also insisted on individual prerogative and freedom in matters of religious belief and practice, and they willingly challenged university officials in the face of perceived incursions against their intellectual liberties. Conservative Rabbi Morris Goldberg of Congregation Shaare Zedek publicly lauded the students for resisting what he characterized as the university's misguided attempt to "compel" attendance of religious rites.[49]

New York's Jewry's child-based approach to family and education related to the more general conviction that individual freedom was a core Jewish value. A telling example of the intellectual association between youth rebellion, individual autonomy, and Jewish tradition was *Fiddler on the Roof*, a Broadway musical adaptation of the Yiddish writer Sholom Aleichem's short stories. *Fiddler*, which proved wildly popular among New York Jews when it first debuted in 1964, chronicles the everyday trials of Tevye, a poor milkman living with his wife and five daughters in the fictional Russian shtetl of Anatevka around the turn of the century.

Tevye's first test of strength comes when his eldest daughter, Tzeitel, flouts Jewish custom by asking her parents to let her marry a man of her own choosing. Tevye's response is, not surprisingly, irate.

> They gave themselves a pledge. Unheard of, absurd.
> You gave each other a pledge? Unthinkable.
> Where do you think you are? . . . America?
> . . . .
> Tradition—Marriages must be arranged by the papa.
> This should never change.

Ultimately, Tevye realizes he has no choice but to perform the awkward task of breaking off the comfortable marriage he prearranged for Tzeitel and to allow her to wed Motel, a poor tailor.

> They gave each other a pledge—unthinkable.
> But look at my daughter's face—she loves him, she wants him.
> And look at my daughter's eyes, so hopeful.

Tzeitel's success emboldens Tevye's next-eldest daughter, Hodel, who announces her intention to marry the radical socialist, Perchik. When Tevye resists ("I understand. I gave my permission to Motel and Tzeitel, so you feel that you also have a right"), Hodel and Perchik counter: "You don't understand, Papa. . . . We are not asking for your permission, only for your blessing. We are going to get married." Once again Tevye struggles to find the right path.

> I can't believe my own ears. My blessing? For what?
> For going over my head? Impossible.
> At least with Tzeitel and Motel, they asked me. They begged me.
> But now, if I like it or not, she'll marry him.
> So what do you want from me? Go on, be wed.
> And tear my beard out and uncover my head.
> Tradition! They're not even asking my permission.
> From the papa. What's happening to the tradition?

Again Tevye's resolve buckles. "Love," he muses, "it's a new style. On the other hand, our old ways were once new, weren't they?" His strong-willed wife, Golde, complains that Perchik is "a pauper . . . he has nothing, absolutely nothing!" Tevye responds: "He is a good man, Golde. I like him. He is a little crazy, but I like him. And what's more important, Hodel likes him. Hodel loves him. So what can we do? It's a new world, a new world."[50]

The script for *Fiddler on the Roof* managed to juggle two seemingly antagonistic tasks: it sentimentalized the Jewish shtetl while also giving license to the abandonment of long-held traditions and religious tenets. The play's very premise—that without "tradition," Jewish existence was as shaky as a "fiddler on the roof"—invited American Jews to reaffirm their solidarity with past generations (a kind of soft definition of "tradition") even as it sanctioned their abandonment of (hard) religious customs and beliefs.

In a sermon delivered in February 1965, George Lieberman endorsed the play's vision. "I am delighted with it because at last we have something which is authentic, distinctive, and definitively Jewish," he said. "The world of Tevye . . . is gone. That world is no more and, alas, never to return. But the characters of Sholom Aleichem—they still exist. They may live on Main Street and walk down Wall Street, they may wear modern clothes, their occupations have changed. They have telephones and radios and cars. But, alas, some of them are still 'schlemazels,' like Tevye." Lieberman essentially argued that by watching, enjoying, and laughing or crying along with *Fiddler on the Roof*, American Jews in the 1960s could close ranks with generations past and reaffirm their allegiance to Jewish tradition, loosely defined.[51]

Lieberman read *Fiddler*'s central themes correctly: Tevye's embrace of such twentieth-century American ideals as individual happiness and personal fulfillment, and the play's cheerful depiction of Tevye's final decision to move the family to the United States, helped second-generation audiences reconcile their secular, middle-class American lifestyle with a yearning for tradition and continuity.[52]

In Aleichem's original stories, Tevye is far more ambivalent about his daughters' independence. What is more, Aleichem's Tevye rejects America out of hand and relocates to Palestine. As literary scholar Seth Wolitz observed, "A gigantic substitution occurred in the musical. American ideals of individual rights, progress, and freedom of association are assimilated into the Judaic tradition, which is presented as a cultural tradition parallel to the American." The Tevye of 1964 is more comfortable with America than his predecessor of the 1890s because his worldview has been adjusted to reflect the outlook of New York's Jewish theatergoers.[53]

In effect, the musical adaptation of *Fiddler on the Roof* jettisoned the original disquietude in Aleichem's writings, as concern over the breakdown of traditional Jewish life gave way to a celebration of individual fulfillment and happiness.[54] Instead of Aleichem's more meditative political subtext, the musical offered a dialogue on parents and children. The story line suggested that Jewish children had always challenged their fathers and mothers. Such dissent within the family could be difficult. It could even be amusing. But it was timeless, and it was unmistakably Jewish.

3 Authority

Between the 1940s and 1960s, many of the ideological differences between Jewish and Catholic New Yorkers originated with a fundamental disagreement over the definition of good citizenship. Jewish religious leaders used the scriptures to remind their congregants, in the words of one ra[bbi], "history shows us how the idealist with his far-fetched ideas can o[vercome] reality and create new epochs." Just as Joseph, the son of Jacob[, a man] with deep humanistic feelings . . . could not stand on the side, [and look] and say that this is . . . life and . . . there is nothing to be done a[bout it,] contemporary Jews must "realize the value of idealism, of being d[reamers] and visionaries."[1]

By contrast, the Catholic catechism—drilled through daily r[ote] into the memory of every parochial schoolboy and schoolgirl in Ne[w York]— affirmed that "citizens should love their country, respect those who are invested with social authority, pray for them, obey the laws, and conscientiously discharge their political obligations and exercise their political rights." Catholic educators expressed their disdain for "members of the teaching staff in our [public] high schools and colleges who are wedded to foreign ideologies and attempt to spread their subversive opinions among the youth of our nation."[2]

In the 1940s and 1950s, American Catholicism enforced a hierarchical religious culture that promoted obedience of authority, rather than skepticism of it, as a virtue. In parochial schools and local parishes, millions of Irish and Italian New Yorkers learned that religious, political, and social authority derived from the same divine source, and that good citizens and good Christians were expected to subordinate their individual concerns to the interests of the organic community. These ideas were part of a mutually reinforcing triad of national, socioeconomic, and religious mores that encouraged many Irish and Italian New Yorkers to deplore the very dissenting ideal that their Jewish neighbors cherished. Though a reinvention of Irish and Italian ethnicity, this social and political ideology could seem every bit as timeless and inexorable to the city's Catholic community as the dissenting ideal often appeared to New York Jews.

The dual themes underscoring Catholic education in the 1940s and 1950s were an explicit equation of morality and religion and a concerted, almost unconditional endorsement of social, political, and religious authority. Each leitmotif reinforced a Catholic worldview that placed God at the helm of a society that was both organic and hierarchical.

The city's parochial schools, explained one bishop in 1931, existed "chiefly in order to safeguard the spiritual faith of our children; to inculcate thoroughly their duties to their God and to preserve, protect, and promote their eternal salvation of soul." The church's construction and maintenance of so massive an educational infrastructure was overtly ideological in purpose. "We have no desire that our children should join the constantly increasing group in our contemporary school population who are so boldly proclaiming agnosticism and communism," continued the bishop. "We shall never allow them, if we can possibly prevent it, to follow after those who shamelessly profess atheism." In defining Catholic education against secular schooling, the bishop was merely echoing the spirit, if not the letter, of Pope Pius XI's 1929 "Encyclical on Christian Education" (officially titled *Rappresentanti in Terra*, or "Representative on Earth"), which held that "there can be no ideally perfect education which is not a Christian education." He also sounded a theme familiar in official Catholic circles: secularism and communism were of a piece, and that one followed naturally from the other.[3]

Many Catholic educators agreed with Edward James Walsh, the president of St. John's University, who reminded brothers and sisters religious that "teaching in our Catholic schools is . . . genuinely spiritual and supernatural work." He conceded that "there is every appreciation of the need of secular studies according to the approved methods of education, but permeating all the teaching" was the church's mission to acquaint its children with "the only true God and Jesus Christ whom [He] hast sent." In the absence of such firm spiritual moorings, Walsh warned, "materialistic governments" like those in Nazi Germany and Soviet Russia stood to "implant the poison of Godlessness and impurity into young minds and hearts that are unable to protect themselves."[4]

Some church officials, like Rev. Joseph A. Murphy, the pastor of St. Bonaventure's Church in Alban Manor on Long Island, were less diplomatic in their public ruminations on secular study. "Our godless educational systems are producing a copious supply of clever, brilliant, and cultured minds," he told a conference of Catholic educators in 1937, but "it might be well to fashion minds that are somewhat simple, humble, and just, with enough intelligence and mentality to grasp the Ten Commandments and the cardinal virtues and sufficient power and strength to observe them in public and in private. It might be well for our educational system to be a little more concerned with the development of character than the advancement of learning."[5]

An entire generation of Catholic teachers trained in the 1920s and 1930s —the very instructors who staffed parochial schools in the early decades of the Cold War—absorbed this separatist definition of the church's educational endeavor. And teachers entering the profession in the late 1940s learned much the same lesson. "The Catholic Church is unalterably committed to the necessity of Religion as an element in all schools for Catholic children," states the Revised Handbook of Regulations (1946), standard issue in all elementary and high schools in the Diocese of Brooklyn. "She bases objectives and methods on belief in God, the Divinity of the Church, and the Revelations of Christ. The aim is thus Divine. Though comparison with public schools may show us below their standard in size of buildings, number of units, and value of equipment, we are leading in the aim of making citizens for both earth and heaven."[6]

That same year, Mother Mary Williams, principal of St. Francis de Sales School in Patchogue, Long Island, affirmed that "our main purpose in education is the formation of a Christian character and . . . the ultimate purpose of our life on earth is to know, love, and serve God." This same idea found a voice two years later, at Brooklyn's annual, diocesanwide pedagogical conference, when a teacher at the St. Thomas Aquinas School in Flatlands (Brooklyn) reminded his colleagues of their responsibility to devise a general "curriculum with Catholic moral and social thought underlying every subject." Even in preparing mathematics and science courses, he explained, teachers must remember that "we cannot divorce our conscious acts, even in the sciences, from the moral law."[7]

By design, then, Catholic institutions of learning consciously infused religion into every aspect of a student's education. A typical first grader attending parochial school in the Diocese of Brooklyn began her day by facing the class crucifix and making the sign of the cross, then reciting the Our Father and Hail Mary and joining in a special grade prayer. Her morning session ended several hours later with another sign of the cross, an Angel of God, a Hail Mary, and a grade prayer. Upon returning from lunch, yet another sign of the cross, grade prayer, and Hail Mary were prayed, and at the close of the day a similar regimen was followed.

But this form of organized worship was only the most basic practice reinforcing the church's dicta that "religion is the most important subject in the Syllabus," and that the overriding purpose of a Catholic education was "to impress essential religious truths indelibly upon the mind of the pupil; these are, the purpose of life, the existence of God and the Holy Trinity, the life of Jesus Christ, the Judgment, and the duty to know, love, and serve God. To make Religion the motive power in the lives of the public so that they may live in accordance with the Commandments of God, the Precepts of the Church, and the spirit of the Evangelical Councils."[8] In fact, school officials injected religious themes even into those subjects that fell ostensibly under the category of secular study.

In their oral skills lessons, first-grade students attending parochial schools in the Archdiocese of New York discussed topics such as "our Blessed Mother and our Guardian Angel" and "How God Made the World" along with "Salute to the Flag," "what each member of the family does," or the "danger of playing with knives and matches." The Diocese of Brooklyn instructed its fourth-grade English-language classes to emphasize "much reproduction of information gained from Bible and Catechism stories."

Even art classes contributed to the church's essential mission to foster in students a broad religious consciousness and convey the belief that the material world was filled with outward signs of God's presence and grace. "Through a course in Elementary Art . . . there is begotten and nurtured an interest in our impressive surroundings," claimed education officials in the Diocese of Brooklyn. By cultivating their students' aesthetic sensibilities, teachers could better inspire them to "see God in all the works of his Beautiful Hand." By comparison, the New York City public school system stated that the mission of art class was to develop "individuality, confidence, and a respect for one's own art expression" and to increase "awareness of the wide range of art media and their possibilities for personal expression."[9]

To be sure, parochial schools offered the full gamut of secular subjects. Students attending high school in the Diocese of Brooklyn followed a course of study that included Latin and religion but also English, biology, physics, algebra, plane geometry, French, world history, American history, and civics. Catholic schools did not shirk their mandate to prepare students for the secular world.[10] But they instilled in Catholic children, from a very early age, an understanding of the world that placed religion—and, more importantly, God—at its center. By comparison, Jewish children, almost all of whom attended public schools and received minimal supplementary religious instruction, spent their formative years in a highly secular environment. This difference produced subtle but important distinctions.

Children attending Catholic elementary schools learned basic vocabulary from specially revised "Dick and Jane" readers. Both versions made frequent use of the personal pronoun, but the revamped Catholic edition tended to transfer agency from its human characters to the supernatural realm.[11] While the secular series placed its two lead characters at the center of all action and reaction, the Catholic series rendered them more passive and made God its most instrumental personage.

On a more vital level, Catholic and Jewish students in New York absorbed different lessons about their world. "Just as we stress the duty of obeying all commandments without exception," explained one woman religious at an annual teacher's conference in 1933, "so in our civic life our children are made to realize their obligation of observing all laws without exception. We, in our limited capacity and lesser knowledge, may not see the need for new legislation, but those in command usually can be relied upon to enact only such measures as will promote the general welfare."[12]

The idea that obedient individuals made good citizens pervaded Catholic pedagogy throughout the 1920s and 1930s, when the generation of teachers who served in the city's parochial schools throughout the early Cold War era took their formal training. In 1936 a teacher from the St. Catherine of Alexandria School in Brooklyn reminded her diocesan colleagues that

> without religion and morality, good government is impossible. Loyalty and devotion to superiors is inculcated by the loyalty and devotion to God Almighty. Just as we stress the duty of obeying all Commandments without exception, so in our civic life our children realize the obligation of observing all laws. Since the beginning of Catholic schools, we have impressed the principle of deep respect for authority. Adherence to any government is temporary, without this principle. . . . *Dissension and hatred will shatter to the ground unity and strength of a nation, and its original status can never be replaced in its niche.* The democratic philosophy for which our pioneer patriotic fathers fought, is being assailed from alien sources.

This teacher clearly had events in Spain and Mexico on her mind when she warned that "to maintain the unity, peace, and happiness of our nation, it is necessary to inculcate the abhorrence for communistic radical principles and agitators." The job of the Catholic educator, she continued, was to ward off "antipathy and skeptical attitudes toward our public officials," attitudes that naturally resulted in "political discrepancy" and threatened to "break . . . the nation."[13]

This idea enjoyed great staying power. Ten years later, in 1946, Sister Mary Madeline of the Blessed Sacrament School in Jackson Heights (Queens) asserted that "just as the keeping of the Commandments indicates our love for God, so does obedience to law characterize the good citizen. . . . [The American Catholic] will obey his country's laws because he knows that legitimate authority receives its power from the Divine Ruler Himself."

Like many of her colleagues, Sister Mary Madeline believed strongly in the mandate to inspire Catholic children with a sweeping appreciation of hierarchy and authority, stretching from home to the Church and the state. "The obligations of citizens should certainly be included in religious lessons connected with the study of the Fourth Commandment," she asserted, "and should be emphasized with the same forcefulness that accompanies the teaching of duties towards parents and teachers." Importantly, Sister Mary Madeline's mandate to her fellow teachers was in perfect step with Pope Leo XIII's encyclical "On Christians as Citizens" (*Sapientiae Christianae*, January 1890), which affirmed that "hallowed . . . in the minds of Christians is the very idea of public authority, in which they recognize some likeness and symbol of Divine Majesty, even when it is exercised by someone unworthy. A just and due reverence to the law abides in them . . . from a consciousness of duty."[14]

The culture of parochial schools socialized students from an early age to respect religious, parental, and civic authority and to conceive of the world as naturally hierarchical. Such a worldview necessarily discouraged religious or political nonconformity. Education officials in the Diocese of Brooklyn envisioned one of their primary objectives as helping "our students to understand that unwillingness to serve, inattention to the courtesies of life, crude unconventionality, roughness, slovenliness, far from being liberty, is [sic] the most cruel of servitudes—selfishness."[15]

Children learned that "when passing the Church, Priests, Brothers, and sisters, boys raise their hats" and "girls bow their head[s] and say an aspiration." Such displays of deference accorded with one of the most basic refrains of the *Baltimore Catechism*: "God is everywhere," and Catholics must treat God's house and his representatives on Earth with due respect. Consequently, the obeisant culture of the parochial school did not begin or end with its students. "Every teacher shall have a direct concern in awakening and maintaining respect for Priests, Brothers, and Sisters," the Diocese of Brooklyn instructed its educators.

Salutation of these [religious authorities] on public streets or in buildings is to be taught. The Church fears a loss of much influence where any loophole is open for anti-clericalism or indifference to Church authority. . . . Loyalty demands that all Community matters be kept within convent walls. Priests shall be addressed by their highest title. They shall have their full name (correctly given) used in all correspondence with them and their Christian names never abbreviated. Correct spelling of the names of the Clergy and of parishes should be stressed in every room by class or home room teacher.

Stressing a common theme in Catholic social thought, the diocese reminded its teachers that even small challenges to clerical authority posed a grave danger to the unity of the Catholic culture. This stress on preserving an organic religious community was applicable to civil affairs as well, and in fact, deference to religious and political authority were parts of the same whole in church teachings.[16]

Official guidebooks instructed first-grade teachers in the Archdiocese of New York that "many of the accidents that befall children are due to ignorance of danger on the part of the little victims. The aim of every lesson should be to impress safety by obeying the laws made for the protection of all." In their history lessons, second graders learned to exhibit "obedience, loyalty, [and] trust in God," qualities that prepared them for good "citizenship." Good citizenship, in turn, hinged on "cooperation" with officials of the police and fire departments, and support of the army and navy," while "good government . . . encourages respect and decency, punishes law breakers, encourages religion, and encourages good organizations [such as the] Boy Scouts, Girl Scouts, [and other] clubs." Fourth graders studying English in the Diocese of Brooklyn learned to value "school loyalty" and "good citizenship," which rested on "obedience, self-control, and courtesy." Seventh graders learned that boys and girls had a "special place and duties in the home," each distinct from the other, and that the proper attitude one should convey at the dinner table was "cheerful, quiet, and gracious." Eighth graders were beseeched to "avoid . . . anything that would attract attention to the individual or the group" and to respect public authorities such as the "Board of Health, Sanitation Department, Fire Department, [and] Police Department."[17]

Above all, then, Catholic educators adopted a pedagogical approach that emphasized the virtue of obedience to authority, whether it be parental, religious, or civic. The most glaring demonstration of this ethos was the use of corporal punishment, a practice very rarely inflicted in public schools but tolerated in Catholic institutions. Anecdotal evidence suggests that Catholic educators availed themselves freely of the right to use physical force as a means of disciplining students. Michael Pearson's memories of a seventh-grade teacher famous for her facility with a "wooden paddle, eighteen inches long, six inches wide, and two inches thick" are fairly standard fare in the popular genre of Catholic school "war stories."[18]

By 1946 church officials appeared conflicted about their continued sanction of corporal punishment. The Diocese of Brooklyn "strictly for[bade] any teacher under any circumstance" to strike a student. But it added that "persistent violations of this regulation shall be brought to the attention of the Community Supervisor and in the case of lay teachers to the Pastor," suggesting that the rule was not hard and fast. Furthermore, "where parents in written permission allow and the Pastor approves, corporal punishment may be inflicted by the Principal on certain rare occasions and within the bounds of reason and kindness." Diocesan officials endorsed a "middle course"—neither "a complete abolition of corporal punishment nor" a situation whereby "the teacher [was] allowed to inflict it under any provocation."[19]

Catholic memoirists tend to recall beatings as simply another fact of life in their parochial school years. In a semiautobiographical account of his boyhood in the late 1940s and 1950s, the novelist Dennis Smith remembered the time that his teacher disciplined him for striking another student: "My head is hurting from where he knuckled me, but I know it is going to hurt even more as Sister is about to give me a whack with the pointer across the back of my pants. I wish I had corduroy pants instead of these thin gabardines. Here I am standing on the bare wood-slat floor, eyes closed, biting my teeth together as hard as they will go, my hands flat against the chalky blackboard, leaning over for all the class to see, as the thin pointer comes down and goes shwitt across my shiny pants." When Smith protested that "[Dennis] Shalleski hit me first," his teacher retorted, "So next time don't hit back. Turn the other cheek. Think about what Jesus said in the Sermon on the Mount, and pray for anyone who you think is mean."[20]

Corporal punishment was the most extreme manifestation of the Catholic school's overarching emphasis on discipline and social order. "School was an unending series of competitions," Michael Pearson later recalled.

Who had memorized the catechism best, which team answered the most questions in history and therefore could be dismissed first from class at the end of the day, who wore honor roll pins, who sat in the first row and who in the last[?] . . . It was the competition that they taught us, the necessary discipline to win, an affection for the rules of the game, a love of the game itself. The rules associated with church were fairly simple. If you did not go to mass on Sunday, you had committed a mortal sin. If you died with a mortal sin on your soul, you went to hell, and that meant an eternity of burning lakes, unquenched thirst, unending screams. . . . No matter how unfair we might have felt it would have been to end up with murderers and slave traders because we had skipped church and perhaps been struck down by a city bus as we headed for the park to play touch football, we knew that hell is where we would have ended up. So, throughout grade school, few of us dared to miss mass on Sunday.[21]

Like hundreds of thousands of Catholic children who attended New York's parish schools in the 1940s and 1950s, Pearson inhabited a world replete with rules that governed the limits of the individual's prerogatives within the larger religious and social community. Students were reminded constantly that every transgression invited its own consequences.

It was this ethic of sinning and repentance that writer Pete Hamill described in his memoirs of a Brooklyn childhood in the 1940s and 1950s. "I didn't care much about the Holy Ghost . . . the Blessed Trinity or the Original Sin," he explained. "But I did understand the catechism's definition of a mortal sin; it had to be a grievous matter . . . a mortal sin was a felony."

In his autobiography, John R. Powers put the matter in even sharper relief. Writing of his high school science and religion teacher, Powers remembered that Brother Sofreck's preferred method of teaching religious ethics was to "resort to terror tactics," like the time he challenged students to hold their hands under a burning match. "If you feel like committing a mortal sin," he began, "just light a match and stick your finger in it. . . . If you like it, if it feels good . . . go ahead and commit that mortal sin. Commit all the mortal sins you want. You'll just love it in hell. There, your entire body will be engulfed for all eternity."[22]

Doris Kearns Goodwin's memories of a Catholic childhood are decidedly more sweet. Still, she recalled that when learning the catechism in CCD class, "each question had a proper answer. The Catholic world was a stable place with an unambiguous line of authority and an absolute knowledge of right and wrong. . . . We learned to distinguish venial sins, which displeased our Lord, from the far more serious mortal sins, which took away the life of the soul. . . . Lest we feel too far removed from such a horrendous deed, we were told that those who committed venial sins without remorse when they were young would grow up to commit much larger sins, losing their souls in the same way that Herod did."[23]

Catholic pedagogy was the complete antithesis of the principles guiding New York City's public education system from the 1930s until the late 1950s. Historian Diane Ravitch has found that by the early years of the Depression, "the language of progressive education and modern psychology had captured the bastion of the New York City school system. The schools fulfilled the progressives' demand that they take on the problem of 'the whole child' by enlisting an army of psychologists and social workers." Progressive education, and its postwar spin-off, "life adjustment education," ideally attempted to cater to each individual child's particular needs. In reality, because many schools lacked the resources to practice progressive techniques, lifestyle adjustment education often entailed an overreliance on standardized tests and academic tracking, both of which allowed educators to steer pupils toward subject matters deemed appropriate for them.

But on a more fundamental level, progressives took their cues from the philosopher John Dewey, whose education formula placed the individual child at the center of the learning process. Teachers in New York public schools were taught to embrace a child-centered pedagogical approach that Catholic education officials openly spurned. As one student of Catholic schooling has concluded, mention of Dewey "did not engender much admiration at meetings of Catholic educators."[24]

Those steeped in New York's Catholic culture believed that the excesses of progressive education—particularly, its focus on child-based, experiential learning—were symptomatic of the secular world's disregard for civil and religious authority. A columnist for the *Brooklyn Tablet*, the official organ of the Brooklyn Catholic diocese, complained in 1951 that the public schools had created a "generation of youth so egocentric that neither respect for God or neighbor is holding it in check. . . . For 16 years students have been allowed to become a law unto themselves, intellectually speaking. As a result, we have social and moral chaos of varying degrees all through the country today." Blaming the "progressive experiment" for social ills like juvenile delinquency and intellectual lassitude, the writer "urge[d] a return to the traditional method."[25]

Official Catholic pedagogy considered the religious character of parochial schools a natural antidote to any erosions of public trust and authority. In 1948 Father Robert Gannon, the president of Fordham University, asserted that "the old theory which is presupposed in the [United States]

Constitution and the Declaration of Independence rests on the fact that there is a superior law which tests the laws of [humankind], and that there are objective standards for weighing the validity as well as the expediency of new legislation." Gannon told his Catholic audience that popular trends in public education and constitutional law "ignore[d] the existence of God as the source of all authority" and robbed "God, the Author of Natural Law," of "His rightful place beside the judge."[26]

Around the same time, Father Joaquin Garcia, superior of the Vincentian Fathers of St. John's University, told graduating seniors and alumnae that secular universities were producing a generation of "modern men . . . for [whom] there is no God, no moral law, no restrictions of any kind, no accountability to any one, no future life, or judgment." Such rhetoric reflected the Catholic hierarchy's insistence that religious and civil authority were seamless—an understanding that stood in contrast to the ideas shared by many New York Jews.[27]

In January 1949 grave diggers at the city's Catholic cemeteries demanded a reduction of their work week, from 48 hours to 40 hours, plus time-and-a-half pay on Saturdays. Their negotiating position met with firm opposition from Francis Cardinal Spellman, the staunchly anticommunist archbishop of New York who some later commentators wryly dubbed the "Archbishop of the Cold War."

Because New York Catholics were a highly unionized population, Spellman was normally cautious in his relations with organized labor. But the cemetery workers' local was affiliated with the Food, Agricultural, and Allied Workers, a Congress of Industrial Organizations (CIO) affiliate whose national leadership was allied with the Communist Party. When the cemetery workers voted to strike, Spellman publicly denounced them as communists—a charge that stung the workers, most of whom counted themselves as devout Catholics—and allowed over 1,000 unburied bodies to pile up in archdiocesan graveyards. He then pressed seminarians from St. Joseph's into service as scabs and personally escorted them past the strikers.

The young students, most of whom had been raised in working-class families, were wracked with guilt over Spellman's order. A handful left the seminary rather than breech a sacred community standard: never cross a picket line. Others quietly handed the tips they received from families of the deceased over to the striking cemetery workers. But the students faithfully carried out a directive that many of them considered wrongheaded and cruel. In the last measure, the image of seminary students working as strikebreakers—literally digging up the earth and burying corpses—was powerful enough to overcome the community's allegiances to organized labor. Without the support they needed from other unions and Catholic leaders, the striking grave diggers voted to go back to work.[28]

The image of rabbinic students at Yeshiva University in 1953 asserting their right to pray when and where they chose stands in stark contrast to the picture of Catholic seminarians, many from working-class families, rolling up their shirtsleeves and crossing picket lines.[29] Yeshiva University students had been raised in a culture that permitted and even celebrated dissent. St. Joseph's seminarians grew up in a culture that cherished obedience to authority. It is hard to imagine Yeshiva students crossing a strike line at the behest—or instruction—of a university president. It is equally difficult to imagine students at St. Joseph's disobeying an archbishop.

The church's concerted efforts to impress upon young Catholics a respect for authority and hierarchy were consistent with a longer sequence of institutional, theological, and popular developments over the preceding century. Whereas the nineteenth and twentieth centuries saw an end to the stasis and order that once characterized Ashkenazic Jewry (the Jewish civilization that emerged in Europe over the preceding centuries), the same epoch witnessed the "churching" of Italian and Irish Americans. In effect, as Jewish political and religious life grew ever more fractious, American Catholic culture emerged more cohesive and insular.

Although the popular image of Catholic Ireland (and, by extension, Irish Catholic America) is an enduring fixture of film and literature, a stringently religious culture rooted in parish and home developed relatively late. Even in the 1840s and 1850s, the successive waves of refugees who fled Ireland to escape the potato blight hailed from a country still noted for its rampant indifference to formal religion and grossly inadequate ecclesiastical infrastructure.[30]

Only in the aftermath of the famine did Catholicism take firm root in Ireland, around the same time that the church emerged as a dominant cultural force in the Irish American diaspora. Under the concurrent direction of two extraordinarily talented archbishops—Cardinal Paul Cullen in Ireland (1849–78) and Bishop John Hughes in New York (1838–64)—the Irish church undertook a vast expansion at home and in the United States, establishing the spiritual and physical foundations of what became, by the late nineteenth century, the predominant cultural institution in both Eire and the American diaspora.

Cullen extended the church's ecclesiastical presence, enforced strict discipline among clergy, and successfully made Catholicism an instrument to alleviate the pain and suffering of postfamine Irish life. Hughes turned the church into an emotional and political bulwark against Protestant nativism, which was achieving ever more violent levels in the years prior to the American Civil War. By the early twentieth century, Irish Catholic immigrants arriving in the United States were more doctrinally conservative than their forerunners and found in the American church a well-established, thriving institution. The story of Irish and Irish American Catholicism in the twentieth century is therefore one of ascendance—of centripetal rather than centrifugal movement.[31]

These developments did not occur in a vacuum. Around the time of its modern ascendance in Ireland and the United States, the Catholic Church was effecting a sweeping ecclesiastical revolution from above. In 1869, while engaged in a fierce struggle against the expansion of European liberalism, Pope Pius IX (the pontiff who had suffered temporary exile from Rome during the revolutionary upheavals of 1848) assembled a meeting of the world's bishops—the first such gathering since the Council of Trent 300 years earlier—and secured their endorsement the following year of a new article of faith: the doctrine of papal infallibility. This dogma was central to the church's nineteenth-century revival, a key component of which was a new embrace of Thomism, or principles associated with the thirteenth-century theologian Thomas Aquinas. In the face of a massive, transatlantic liberal offensive, Pius IX and other church leaders embraced a medieval worldview for global Catholicism—generally labeled ultramontanism—that asserted the predominance of the corporate community over the autonomous individual, formal worship and experiential religious rites over interior dialogue and inquiry, and centralization over regional or national distinction (a creed known as anti-Gallicanism).

By the late nineteenth century, the church demanded at all levels—from the halls of the Vatican to the smallest town parish—unflinching deference to hierarchy, more uniformity and less localism, and a clamp on religious democratization. The church culture that Hughes, Cullen, and their successors helped create reflected Catholicism's new discipline and was in harmony with the ultramontane revival.[32]

It had not always been so for American Catholics. In the years prior to the great Irish migration, America's small Catholic community infused its religious culture with the republican and democratic principles of the Revolution. Leading laypersons like John Carroll, and prominent clerics like his cousin, Bishop John Carroll of Baltimore, espoused a form of Enlightenment Catholicism that emphasized reason, tolerance, ecumenicalism (such as it existed in the early nineteenth century), and persuasion. Instead of concentrating on the formal acts of devotion and piety that came to define Catholic culture after the 1840s, most American Catholics in the early republic embraced a more low-key observance that concerned itself with interior dialogue. People "owe to God an inward worship," read a popular religious pamphlet, "because this is the only worship which is suited to the nature of God, who being a spirit desires to be worshipped in spirit and truth. . . . Exterior, without inward, worship would be a mere farce and mockery."[33]

In keeping with the political and social legacies of the Revolution, early American churches tended to be architecturally understated—even ordinary—when compared with the Gothic style preferred in Europe. Under the trustee system that governed a handful, though certainly not all, of the early dioceses, lay parishioners conducted parish affairs, oversaw parish finances, hired (and occasionally dismissed) priests, participated in church services, and reached democratic consensus on matters pertaining to liturgy and practice. It was a style of Catholicism that in many ways resembled nothing so much as a Congregational Church in Boston.

According to Matthew Carey, a leading member of Philadelphia's Catholic community during the late eighteenth and early nineteenth centuries, even the anemic, prefamine church in Ireland was structured so that "too frequently the relations between the pastor and his flock partake of the nature of extravagantly high-toned authority on the one side and servile submission on the other." By contrast, in America the "people never will submit to the regime in civil or ecclesiastical affairs that prevails in Europe. . . . The extreme freedom of our civil institutions has produced a corresponding independent spirit respecting church affairs, to which sound sense will never fail to pay attention."[34]

All of this changed in the mid-nineteenth century, when American Catholicism turned away from the trustee system and toward a centralization of authority under the bishops and prelates. A new generation of laymen and laywomen—most of them immigrants from Europe—effectively rejected Enlightenment Catholicism for the more rigid precepts of ultramontanism and Tridentine Catholicism. The formal system of observance that had emerged from the sixteenth-century Council of Trent, Tridentine Catholicism enforced the subordination of the laity and the authority of the hierarchy, mandated a passive role for parishioners in both worship and church governance, and introduced a two-part system of worship based on regular attendance at Latin Mass and participation in any number of devotions, normally conducted in the vernacular. Devotions to the Sacred Heart, benedictions of the Blessed Sacrament, and recitations of the rosary replaced biblical exegesis as a common expression of piety, just as the church's emphasis turned away from Enlightenment humanism and toward a new emphasis on the figure of a suffering Christ.

In cities like New York, by the mid-nineteenth century each parish was its own corporation, its five-person board of directors selected and chaired by the archbishop. Parishioners exercised no input or oversight of financial or religious matters. This system endured for over one hundred years, until the introduction of lay councils after Vatican II. As one scholar of Catholic life observed in 1952, "It is evident that the lay people in the Catholic parishes are not stock-holders, or members in any way of this corporation. They contribute the money and the properties which the corporation administers [but] the two lay members of the Board are not their elected representatives. Viewed in this legal light, the American urban parish is neither a spontaneously organized social structure not a mass-controlled organization."[35]

In 1949 Gretta Palmers, a columnist for the *Catholic News*, the official weekly newspaper of the Archdiocese of New York, noted with amusement that clerical authorities in the Protestant churches were grappling with lay resistance to official doctrine and social policy. Referring specifically to the case of John Howard Melish, an Episcopalian minister whose activities as chair of the National Council of American-Soviet Friendship raised the ire of his diocesan superiors, Palmers noted that "the much-mooted Melishes of Holy Trinity [Episcopalian] Church in Brooklyn have flatly defied the authority of their Bishop, who has ordered the Rev. John Howard Melish to surrender his pulpit. They have also defied their own vestrymen and have appealed for an injunction to remove them." Ultimately, Palmers marveled at the power vacuum in the Protestant churches. Such insubordination would never be tolerated, she implied, in a Catholic parish.[36]

Much of the popular acquiescence to this more rigid and hierarchal style of worship owed to the arrival of several million European immigrants between 1840 and 1924. Though claiming diverse religious backgrounds, these immigrants generally hailed from regions where Catholicism was organized—or was being reorganized—along more authoritarian lines, and where ultramontanism was on the ascendant. In this respect, they shared more in common with each other than with the upwardly mobile, English-speaking Catholics who had built America's first dioceses.

For the great multitude of Catholic peasants who were violently displaced from the land, and particularly so for the famine wave of Irish immigrants who literally endured the horrors of starvation, pestilence, and coffin ships, the image of a suffering Christ—introduced time and again in sermons bearing titles such as "Joy Born of Affliction"—surely resonated deeply. "Meditate on your suffering Jesus," a New York clergyman told his congregants in 1854. "Let us place ourselves, now, my very dear brethren, by the side of him who is suffering for us in the Garden of Olives. Let us contemplate him in his agony and covered with blood, and ask ourselves, who is this sufferer?"

The notion that suffering was an essential step toward salvation served as a great measure of reassurance to subsequent waves of immigrants—Irish and non-Irish alike—who made the transatlantic journey over the course of the late nineteenth and early twentieth centuries. Having fled a world of diminishing opportunities in Europe only to endure the human toll of industrial capitalism in America, millions of Catholics turned gratefully to the imposing, Gothic cathedrals that arose everywhere throughout the United States after 1850.

Quite unlike the Catholic churches of the early Republic, these new cathedrals prominently featured dark representations in oil, wood, and marble of Christ's last moments on earth. Critics decried them as "endless pantomimes of pain," but the Catholic laity embraced them nevertheless. They found meaning in emotional rituals like the stations of the cross, a communal prayer involving fourteen wood carvings or paintings that depict key events in Christ's crucifixion. This same attraction to representational suffering incited popular enthusiasm for devotions to the Sacred Heart, which revolved around images of the bleeding heart of Christ punctured by a crown of thorns.

Protestant elites viewed this culture of affliction and otherworldliness as a fatalistic distraction from the critical work of social reform on earth. Many, such as radical reformer and theologian Theodore Parker, voiced their concern. Parker complained that Catholic immigrants "seemed to have the idea that their sufferings in this life, if rightly endured, would be considered as a sort of penance, in consideration of which they would gain eternal life in the world which is to come." But Parker was missing the point. For the average Catholic immigrant, who lacked fundamental economic and political agency over his life and who continued to suffer the intense hostility of native-born Americans, the comforts of Catholic revivalism offered a way to find meaning and consequence in everyday adversity and to assert at least a modicum of control over one's destiny, even if this control was limited to the afterlife.[37]

Just as Catholic immigrants found inspiration in the idea of redemptive suffering, they accepted religious centralization and hierarchy—and a doctrine that privileged community over autonomous individualism—as a realistic answer to the everyday trials that came their way in industrializing America. Like their Protestant and Jewish neighbors, Catholic citizens in the late nineteenth century experimented with a variety of reform remedies —some collectivist, others aimed at recovering the individual autonomy once enjoyed in the bygone days of the free labor economy. Catholics joined the Farmer's Alliance and the Knights of Labor and championed utopian movements that offered refuge from the growing sense of confusion, dependency, and powerlessness. But above all, it was the church that offered ordinary Catholics new moorings in an uncertain world. Long after the Populists and Knights of Labor passed from the scene, America's ascendant Catholic subculture offered parishioners some degree of comfort and control—not just against the vicissitudes of economic change, but also against the intense legal, physical, and cultural abuse that Catholics suffered at the hands of native Protestants.[38]

From the burning of Boston's Charlestown Convent in 1834 and the Know-Nothing upheavals of the 1850s, to the ever-present "No Irish Need Apply" signs of the 1890s and the Ku Klux Klan revival of the 1920s, immigrant Catholics faced the brunt of Protestant rage and anxiety, and they reacted accordingly.[39] The popular acceptance of a more formal, passive, and hierarchical form of Catholicism reflected a partial rejection of America's liberal, democratic inheritance—an inheritance that seemed to hold no place for Catholics. In a world that robbed them of much political, social, and economic autonomy, many laypersons could find wisdom in Pope Leo XIII's 1888 encyclical declaring, in the best Thomistic tradition, that "the true liberty of human society does not consist in every man doing what he pleases," but rather, it "supposes the necessity of obedience to some supreme and eternal law."[40]

The expansion of the Catholic parish and education system after the 1850s introduced successive generations of Irish and Italian Americans to the formal modes of worship and fundamental ideals of the Catholic revival. In a remarkable trickle-down process, a never-ending cascade of expatriate theologians—trained in Europe's most conservative seminaries —arrived in America to teach successive generations of Catholic clergy essential Thomistic dogmas. These dogmas, in turn, seeped into every school textbook and church sermon throughout the country.

At newly founded Catholic universities, lay teachers learned how to place the wisdom of medieval theology in a modern-day context. The same Catholic collegians at Fordham University who would one day serve as schoolteachers, principals, and Catholic polemicists read texts like The Thirteenth: Greatest of Centuries and studied from ethics textbooks that claimed "truths that spring necessarily from the very nature of man and of human society, never change." Ultimately, the vast infrastructures of the Archdiocese of New York and the Diocese of Brooklyn ensured that the ecclesiastical and theological revolution begun in Rome would permeate quickly and endure for decades to come—barring unforeseen social upheavals that were beyond the church's power to control.[41]

Not all Catholics took instantly to religious centralization. Italian immigrants who arrived en masse in the late nineteenth and early twentieth centuries practiced a variety of Catholicism marked by widespread anticlericalism and casual observance of certain rites and sacraments—particularly, Communion and penance. They also tended to place more emphasis on the figure of the Virgin Mary than on the suffering Christ. Unlike most Irish Catholics, Italians also prayed for divine intercession from local saints, whom they credited for earthly deeds, and preferred a religious style that was more emotive and participatory than Tridentine Catholicism. Their most exciting and popular rites—saint's day festivals—normally took place outside of the church, under the direction of nonclerical authorities.

But Italian Catholicism, if not in accordance with some of the formal strictures of Tridentine Catholicism, was ultramontane in its own way. It deemphasized personal agency and placed supreme faith in divine intercession (in this case, saintly mediation), and it celebrated respect for authority (in this case, divine, rather than clerical, authority).[42] These similarities may have helped many Italians reach an accommodation with the American church. By the eve of the Cold War, traditional elements of Italian Catholicism were waning, as the children and grandchildren of immigrants were increasingly likely to attend parochial schools and to adopt the principal forms of the Irish-dominated American Church.[43]

Catholicism was a central component of Italian and Irish identity in the first decades of the twentieth century, but it intersected with national origins and class to forge a comprehensive ethnic worldview. The church's newfound attention to hierarchy and authority reinforced—and, in turn, was reinforced by—social mores already fixed in nineteenth-century Irish and Italian secular culture, and in working-class American life.

In his transatlantic study of the Irish diaspora, Kerby Miller found that "in the broadest terms . . . the Catholic Irish were more communal than individualistic, more dependent than independent, more fatalistic than optimistic, more prone to accept conditions passively than to take initiatives for change, and more sensitive to the weight of tradition than to the possibilities for the future." Irish Catholics who emigrated to the United States in the late nineteenth century hailed from "a socioeconomic framework in which the concept of individuality was less sharply defined and hence less important than in contemporary Protestant frameworks."

Traditional Irish culture, according to Miller, was fundamentally "hierarchical, communal, [and] familial." Its families were tight-knit, but also "authoritarian and patriarchal." Furthermore, the privileged position accorded in Irish culture to the "authoritative" family was largely "analogous" to Catholicism, which was also "fundamentally" collectivist. "Even in the realm of behavior," according to Miller, "Catholicism provides a framework which—while it intensifies personal responsibility to obey God's laws as interpreted by the church—limits the field of individuality." With the consolidation of its authority and spread of its influence in the late nineteenth century, the church emerged as an institution well suited to Irish ethnic mores.[44] When leading American clerics argued that "the social unit is the family[,] not the individual," their words found resonance among Irish immigrants who were already predisposed to believe it.[45]

In his original analysis of Gaelic, Miller even found that "the Irish language itself reflected and reinforced an Irish world view which emphasized dependence and passivity." Unlike English, whose construction is largely active, Gaelic tends more toward the passive voice. For instance, the English phrase, "I met him on the road," translates in Irish to "he was twisted on me on the road." Instead of the English, "I am sad," the Irish variant translates roughly to "I have been subjected to sadness." Such interpretive nuances led Miller to conclude that "traditional Irish culture was composed of three interlocking subsystems—secular, religious, and linguistic—supporting a world view which valued conservatism, collective behavior, and dependence and which limited individual responsibility in broad areas."

The same was true of traditional Italian culture. Sociologists agree that first- and second-generation Italian American families were unusually insular and patriarchal. Parents—particularly fathers—held sway over their children. Extended family relationships, particularly among siblings and cousins belonging to the same "peer group," assumed an importance second only to the individual's relationship to God. Saint's day festivals, which were integral to first- and second-generation Italian culture, functioned as religious dramas in which the participants reaffirmed the community's unwavering support of paternal and maternal authority. Ethnographers also agree that Italian American communities were cohesive in a way that may have appeared overly conformist and stifling to outsiders, but which inspired a sense of mutuality and commonality among their inhabitants.[46] All of these widely shared social principles were highly compatible with modern church teachings that stressed the organic and hierarchical character of the community and the precedence of family and community over the autonomous individual.

These values represented a departure from the Jewish community. Certainly every Jew was not a freethinker; neither did Irish and Italian Catholics submit mindlessly to all authority figures, be they paternal, civic, or religious. But the culture of Italian and Irish American Catholicism—its teachings, its official mores, its family arrangements—stressed obedience and community, while Jewish theology and secular culture paid considerable tribute to individuality, intellectual freedom, and dissent.

Just as religion and national origins were mutually reinforcing ingredients of Italian and Irish ethics, class was also an important component of Catholic ethnicity. Catholic skepticism of progressive or "democratic" education techniques reflected the community's general attitude toward child rearing. Unlike the city's Jews, who tended to allow their children an unusual amount of intellectual and personal freedom, many Irish and Italian New Yorkers governed their families according to a model that contemporary sociologists labeled "autocratic" or "authoritarian."

The terminology that many commentators used to characterize Catholic families in the 1940s and 1950s was freighted with negative meaning. As the debate over federal aid to education got mired down in a secondary dialogue over state financing for parochial schools, liberal critics of the Catholic church maintained that secular and Catholic understandings of child rearing and pedagogy represented "two totally different philosophies." Whereas public schools encouraged a "recognition of values achieved on the basis of experience" and reinforced the "democratic companionship" presumed to govern most non-Catholic families, parish schools demanded unthinking repetitions of the catechism and encouraged an unchecked, "authoritarian submission" to clerical and parental authority.[47]

These value-laden characterizations notwithstanding, sociologists writing about Italian Americans in the 1940s and 1950s found that a powerful combination of traditional folkways from the Mezzogiorno—the region south of Rome that delivered 80 percent of Italian immigrants to America—and working-class ideas about child rearing created a distinct outlook on home life. Though progressive models of child rearing and schooling had been enormously popular among middle-class families since the 1920s, most working-class families tended to resist the child-centered, indulgent approach to parenthood and education that was favored in the public schools and in mainstream parental-advice literature.[48] This was certainly true of working-class Italians.

In his study of Boston's West End in 1962, Herbert Gans determined that "the predominant method of child rearing is punishment and reward. Children are punished when they misbehave, and rewarded—though not always—when they are obedient. In the West End, children come because marriage and God bring them. . . . The major method of family planning seems to be ex post facto. . . . The fact that children are not planned affects the way in which parents relate to them, and the methods by which they bring them up." Gans characterized Italian working-class culture as "adult-centered." While middle-class families tended to be "child-centered"—"parents subordinate adult pleasure to give the child what they think he needs or demands"—working-class families like those he encountered in the West End were "run by adults for adults, where the role of children is to behave as much as possible like miniature adults."

Although Gans acknowledged the striking similarities between child-rearing practices in the Mezzogiorno and the West End—including the early transition between childhood and adulthood and the paternal author-ity structure—he attributed the essential characteristics of Italian American family life to socioeconomic status. "West Enders raise their children im-pulsively, with relatively little of the self-conscious, purposive child rearing that is found in the middle class," he explained. "Parents tell their children how they want him [sic] to act without much concern about how he re-ceives their message. They do not weigh their words or methods in order to decide whether these are consistent with earlier ones." Such patterns, according to Gans, characterized working-class families generally.[49]

Other studies appeared to support Gans's findings. George Psathas's survey of teenagers in New Haven, Connecticut, found that Jewish parents permitted their children more intellectual freedom but kept closer watch over their extracurricular activities, while Italian parents brooked little dis-sent at home but demonstrated considerable "permissiveness in age-related activities"—that is, what their children did outside of the home. In effect, Jewish families were child-centered because parents indulged their sons and daughters and encouraged their intellectual growth; Italian American families were adult-centered because parents expected children to comply with domestic rules but left them free to run the streets when away from their authority. Critically, when Psathas controlled for class, distinctions between the two groups disappeared.[50]

A similar study of 954 families in four northeastern states, including New York, found that Jewish parents were far more likely than their Italian counterparts to encourage values like "achievement" and "independence" in a child; or, more simply, they "expect[ed] him to be self-reliant and, at the same time, grant[ed] him relative autonomy in decision-making situations where he [was] given both freedom of action and responsibility for success or failure." Ultimately, the report acknowledged that its findings were as much a function of class as national origins: "There are relatively more middle class than lower class subjects among Jews . . . than among Italians."[51]

In 1960 almost two-thirds of second-generation Italian New Yorkers worked at blue-collar jobs, and only 16 percent qualified as professionals, managers, or proprietors.[52] The city's Italian subculture was overwhelmingly working-class, in much the same way that the Jewish community was overwhelmingly middle-class. Class status did not merely reinforce ethnicity among New York City's Italian residents; it was a *critical component* of Italian ethnicity.

Folkways carried to America from the Mezzogiorno were also instrumental in shaping the second- and third-generations' outlook on child rearing. Studies of New York Italians in the 1940s and 1950s found a stubborn adherence to old forms of domestic wisdom. In Southern Italy, popular maxims held that *i figli si devono domare* (children must be tamed), *bisogna inculcare nei figli timore e rispetto* (it is necessary to inculcate fear and respect in our children), *mazza e panella fanno I figli belli* (a stout stick and bread turn out good children), and *chi non ubbidisce mamma e tana, fa la morte di un cane* (those who disobey their mother and father will die like a dog). Economic, social, and political conditions in America undoubtedly blunted the rough edges of Italian folk culture. But scholars like Leonard Covello and Michael Eulo found that second- and third-generation Italians in New York held tight to a vision of family that placed children in a decidedly subservient position to their parents, particularly their fathers.[53]

"My father was the supreme authority, my mother a much weaker second-in-command," Vincent Panella recalled of his childhood in Queens in the 1940s and 1950s. "Neither was a companion with whom intimate fears or feelings could be shared. On those occasions when my father tried to engage me on such delicate subjects as sex and fighting, the circuits slowly shorted. He could not be an autocrat and an equal." In the world where he grew up, Panella learned that his "father's way was the right way and the only way. Like his father, he was feared. Like his father, he didn't reveal his emotions."[54]

Sociologist Jonathan Rieder found that many of these same attitudes still held sway among the working-class Italians he interviewed in Brooklyn's Canarsie section in the early 1970s. "Among the most cosmopolitan Jews," Rieder reported, "parenting was sometimes seen as a self-conscious task with an ultimate aim, and children as bundles of possibility who required an unhamper[ed] environment to flourish as individuals." Not so for Italians, who "stressed the timelessness of human nature and the corollary need to hedge in that restive individuality with a web of communal rules." The result was that Italians from Canarsie "often claimed that all desirable traits in children stemmed from a single source, respect for and obedience to parents." Hence, the dockworker who told Rieder that "you must obey the family rules and have strict discipline, because human nature is strange. If kids can take an inch, they'll take a foot"; and his neighbor, who claimed that "respect for parents" was the key "from [which] comes all the other things you want."[55]

The body of sociological literature on Italian family mores finds no substantial parallel for Irish Catholics. One study conducted in 1960 found that Catholic adults in the midtown section of Manhattan (known as "Hell's Kitchen") were more reluctant than their Jewish neighbors to embrace modern child psychiatry. When posed with the same question—"Let's suppose some friends of yours have a serious problem with their . . . child's behavior. . . . The parents ask your advice. . . . What would you probably tell them to do?"—over half of all Jewish respondents proposed psychotherapy, compared with 24 percent of Catholics. These results may be consistent with the Catholic subculture's aversion to indulging unruly children. And since midtown Manhattan was heavily Irish, the results might also suggest a convergence of opinion between the city's two largest Catholic contingents. But either assumption is tenuous without more evidence.[56]

Individual memoirs suggest that working-class Irish families, particularly those that identified closely with the church, entertained many of the same thoughts on child rearing. George Kelly remembered that "the Catholic ethos dominated [his life] and the various segments of the community reinforced each other. You never came home with a complaint about what they did to you in school because you would find yourself in trouble all over again. And, if for some reason the cop on the beat picked you up, he did not take you to jail, but upstairs to your mother."[57] In Kelly's world, the artifices of familial and community authority overlapped, and both bore a distinctly Catholic mark. Elders, parents, police officers, nuns, priests, and teachers all essentially derived their power from the same source, and they worked in concert with each other to see it preserved.

Dennis Smith recalled the same synergy between home, school and church. Once, when he admitted over dinner that his teacher had paddled him as punishment for twisting a classmate's ear, his mother answered the confession by "reach[ing] for the strap. I freeze, because I know I can't run. . . . The strap is a piece of belt an inch wide and a little more than a foot long. It has a slit at the end which opens to fit over the back rung of the kitchen chair." Clearly the instrument saw frequent service in the Smith household. When young Dennis continued to deny culpability, his mother replied simply: "Don't correct me. You have no control. You have to learn to control yourself or you'll never get out of trouble."[58]

I f Italian and Irish Catholic institutions stressed obedience of authority and the subordination of individual to group interests, there were always cracks in the armor, and these cracks grew wider in the 1960s. As increasing numbers of Catholics attended secular universities, and as a more general, nationwide revolt against authority threatened to pervade Catholic life, prominent spokespersons like New York City Police Commissioner Stephen Kennedy renewed the call for vigilance. "The home is truly the basic unit of society," Kennedy told a national group of Catholic collegians in 1958. "Here a child learns to obey or disobey, he learns right from wrong. He is either responsive to training or grows rebellious to all authority, whether it be that of parent, police, or even priest."

"In a Seminary, you are subject to authority and thus you know the meaning and value of obedience," he continued. "Such obedience is comparatively easy, for the authority is unchallenged." But outside of its "holy, secluded" walls, the absence of total discipline tempts individuals to pursue "pleasure with little regard for the laws of God or man." In a society devoid of the seminary's attention to deference and hierarchy, "many do not care whether an act is right or wrong, as long as it seems useful at the time. The result of constant tension, pressure, and anxiety . . . one world crisis after another, wild and erotic music, and excessive drinking have dulled the sensibilities of people to the point where they are no longer shocked by brutality nor repelled by grave offenses against moral law."[59]

A few years later the dean of Fordham's law school, William Hughes Mulligan, sadly reported to attendees of the Society of the Friendly Sons of Saint Patrick's annual dinner gala that "there's no peace and tranquility on today's college campus. . . . When I was a law student and a young teacher, we were living in the age of the divine right of deans." But this was no longer so. "The first signs of trouble appeared a few years back," Mulligan explained, "when the doctrine became popular in academic quarters that the administration of a college should be directed by the faculty with the dean, becoming, in effect, the presiding officer of a learned debating society."

Traditionalists like Mulligan could tolerate the new imperative to "share authority with the faculty," but they were "hardly prepared for the newest phenomenon, the claim for equal partnership by the student body." The dean regretted that university life—once a mainstay of corporate community—was falling prey to the forces of democratization and capitalism. "The sit-ins, the boycotts, the mass demonstrations of students are prompted not only by the reluctance of most normal students to attend classes," he claimed, but are based "on the theory that the student's voice must be heard because he is . . . paying his way." Ultimately, Mulligan hoped that "perhaps a shave, a haircut, a bath, and a larger sized pantaloon would go far to solve the unrest."[60]

The St. Patrick Society's dinners brought New York's Irish elite together several times a year. Assuming that keynote speakers catered their message to the audience, it is little wonder that honorees like National Baseball Commissioner Bowie Kent Kuhn earned warm applause when he reminded listeners that "baseball is a game of rules. Baseball lives by rules, the way our society should." Strictly speaking, Kuhn was referring to a minor controversy over Babe Ruth's career-long home run total, which stood at 714 but might have been bumped to 715 were the commissioner to apply retroactively new rules governing grand slams. But Kuhn's political message was more significant than his decision's influence on baseball history: "The Babe is going to be governed by the rules of the society in which he played ball. . . . I think that if the Babe were alive today he would say: Thank God for the Commissioner; I will take my 714."[61]

Even in the early postwar era, the limits of Irish and Italian Catholic obedience were clearly on display. Surveys conducted in the 1950s revealed that over half of Catholic women nationwide practiced some form of birth control, in direct conflict with the church's proscriptions against artificial contraception. As the years wore on, the discordance between official doctrine and popular conduct only grew.

A survey of Catholic women in 1955 found that 57 percent practiced birth control, including 30 percent who used methods of contraception explicitly forbidden by the church. Striking as these figures may have been, the same study also revealed that Catholic women, even when controlled for education and income, were far less likely than Jewish and Protestant women to use birth control and, when they did turn to contraception, tended to do so later in their marriages. By 1965, however, 77 percent of Catholic women admitted to using contraception, including 53 percent who reported using methods that were in conflict with church teaching.[62]

Quiet dissent was evident in other places, as well. In 1951 Cardinal Spellman ordered a pastoral letter read at St. Patrick's Cathedral and at all parishes in the Archdiocese instructing city Catholics to boycott Roberto Rossellini's controversial motion picture, *The Miracle*. The film's lead character is a religious fanatic who comes to believe that Saint Joseph has seduced her. Spellman won considerable support from Catholic lay groups.[63] Members of the city's many Holy Name Societies protested outside Manhattan theaters ("Don't be a Communist—all the Communists are inside!"), while the New York Chapter of the Catholic War Veterans (CWV) produced 1,000 picketers, some of whom carried signs denouncing *The Miracle* as an "Insult to Every Woman Not to Mention Child." Five years later, Spellman resorted to the unusual measure of speaking directly from the pulpit at St. Patrick's, where he denounced Elia Kazan's film, *Baby Doll*, for its alleged sexual abandon. Again, the CWV and other lay groups supported the archbishop, while Catholic priests stood guard at neighborhood theaters, pen and paper in hand, ready to take down names of wayward parishioners attempting to see the film.[64]

Spellman's power play backfired: the studios responsible for *Baby Doll* and *The Miracle* could not have bought better publicity. Both films—especially *The Miracle*—enjoyed a boom in ticket sales after the archbishop's interdictions piqued the curiosity of local audiences. One study showed that, on average, ticket receipts in Catholic neighborhoods were no lower than in other areas.

Nevertheless, the reaction of Catholic lay groups is telling. When the archbishop called for a ban in 1953 of a United Artists release, *The Moon Is Blue*, over 4,000 Catholic residents of suburban Dutchess and Putnam Counties (each part of the archdiocese) presented a petition to the Poughkeepsie Common Council, calling for a law banning "immoral shows and motion pictures" within the town lines. In nearby Elizabeth, New Jersey—part of the Archdiocese of Newark—the Knights of Columbus and other Catholic lay groups pressured theater owners and the city government into temporarily banning the film, pending a hearing before the state courts.[65]

By comparison, grassroots members of Jewish lay and religious groups steadfastly opposed measures aimed at limiting public access to art and entertainment, a stand consistent with the community's zeal for the idea of intellectual freedom. While a storm of controversy raged over *The Moon Is Blue*, members of the Rabbinical Assembly of America—the Conservative clergy's official, permanent synod—denounced the "vigilantism of some religious and patriotic groups who have taken it upon themselves to intimidate booksellers and librarians and movie exhibitors [in an] unwarranted infringement upon the rights of Americans to read legally published works and to see licensed movies."[66]

Community members had at least one occasion to put their money where their mouths were. When the film *Oliver Twist* was released in 1948, the BJCC complained that "the character, Fagan, as portrayed in 'Oliver Twist' amounts to antisemitic stereotyping. . . . This portrayal is all the more regrettable because it could have been carried off in a non-defamatory manner without impairing the value of the Charles Dickens classic." But the BJCC also asserted "the right of a distributor to distribute any picture he chooses. We further recognize the great danger to civil liberties and to democratic government inherent in censorship and suppression which are particularly pronounced in the present climate of opinion[,] and we feel that attempts to interfere with free expression through the arts are likely to encourage an ever-heightening control over men's minds, culminating in a state of regimented thought and expression characteristic of a totalitarian society." Even crude anti-Semitic caricature was protected speech, the BJCC concluded, and its members "therefore strongly urge[d] against picketing or similar display in connection with the picture." In any event, "such demonstrations, as experience has shown, [would] serve only to increase attendance."[67]

Not all Jews agreed with this position. The New York Board of Rabbis bitterly opposed certification for *Oliver Twist*, and in response, the film was ultimately pulled out of wide circulation. On this question, the rabbis were out of step with their congregants, but perfectly in step with the city's Catholic archdiocesan newspaper, which maintained that "while fanning the fires of racial prejudice is deplorable at any time, it is particularly inappropriate and even dangerous now."[68]

The question of censorship, like the question of birth control, complicates the sharp dichotomy between the Jewish and Catholic subcultures. Those New Yorkers who most clearly identified with the Catholic subculture were likely to endorse a conservative social creed that assigned less importance to individual choice than to community interests. Many who identified most strongly with New York's Jewish subculture self-consciously placed the individual's rights ahead of the community's and beyond any formal political or social restraints. Yet in practice, New York's Irish and Italian Catholics often quietly ignored authority figures.

This important caveat notwithstanding, many Irish and Italian New Yorkers placed a high rhetorical and theoretical premium on organic community and authority, and this emphasis produced very real differences with their Jewish neighbors. Even on matters about which there was some semblance of agreement between each side, agreement often proved elusive.

In a typical anticommunist philippic delivered before the New York Chapter of the Knights of Columbus, Cardinal Spellman foretold the dire "consequences [of the] Soviet, atheistic peace" that American communists promoted. Spellman told a convention of the Knights of Columbus that "to live, to love, if need be to fight and die for God's glory, our country, and our brother should be the self-command of every American citizen and patriot, as, with avowed allegiance to his faith, his flag, and his fellowman, he aspires to become the inspiration of his own generation and the salvation of generations of Americans yet unborn."[69]

On the surface, Rabbi Israel Goldstein, spiritual leader of Manhattan's Congregation B'nai Jeshurun, agreed with Spellman that "Communism and Religion are in a contest for the soul of mankind." Yet while the archbishop directed his concern to communism's incursions against "faith," "flag," "fellowman," and "country"—each a symbol or embodiment of organic community—Goldstein used his Yom Kippur sermon to argue that "religion believes in the worth of the individual, considers the Moral Law to be binding upon nations as well as individuals. . . . Communism glorifies the state and suppresses the individual, is cynical about morality when it conflicts with the interests of the state. . . . We have seen enough of Communism in practice as well as in theory to know that it is the 'False Messiah' of our time, which undermines men's souls while it enslaves their bodies."[70]

Both authorities viewed communism as God's violent adversary, but Goldstein emphasized its violation of the individual's free will, while Spellman took aim at its crimes against national and religious communities. Goldstein's address was as much a critique of the authoritarian state as it was a homily against communism; Spellman's speech rooted American "freedoms" and the "American way of life" in the "privilege of being citizens of our republic." Certainly Goldstein did not forswear allegiance to the republic or the state, just as Spellman did not beseech his listeners to submit blindly to either. Yet each clergyman's focus was distinct from the other's. The Catholic Church encouraged its followers to think of America as a hierarchical and organic society, with God at its helm. Jewish religious leaders spoke of America as the realization of individual freedom.

This distinction was often at the heart of Catholic-Jewish tensions. For Jews, "fascist" conformity was the greatest menace to democracy; it violated the individual's sacred right to free conscience. To many Catholic New Yorkers, "Godless communism" threatened to fray the delicate bonds of community and nation. This subtle distinction was a major source of tension in the early Cold War era.

4 Fascism

In 1949 a seventh-grade social studies teacher from Brooklyn named May Quinn found herself at the center of a gathering political storm. Quinn was hardly a stranger to controversy. Six years earlier, a dozen of her public school colleagues had filed an official complaint alleging that she promoted "intolerance and un-Americanism" in her classroom. Quinn stood accused of ridiculing Jewish students and teaching that Hitler had achieved positive goals in Germany. In an attempt to clear her name, she sued her fellow teachers for libel and lost, whereupon the local school superintendent suspended her without pay and relayed her case to the Board of Education. Ultimately, the board absolved her of serious charges and reinstated her with a fine of two months' pay, but not before the city's supportive Irish Catholic community made her a cause célèbre.

The Holy Name Society of the parish church near Quinn's school charged that the accusations against her originated with "a subversive or Communistic group now operating in this part of the city," while the King's County (Brooklyn) Board of the Ancient Order of Hibernians saluted Quinn's "loyal Americanism" and lambasted her prosecutors. Meanwhile, local and citywide Jewish groups united unsuccessfully to demand that Quinn be dismissed from her teaching post.[1]

After the board's decision, Quinn disappeared from the radar screen for a few years. In December 1949 school officials censored her again for telling students that "Negroes were happy before they knew about racial discrimination" and suggesting, "I would not go where I was not wanted." These statements sparked a virtual firestorm of public controversy that pitted the city's Catholic and Jewish communities against each other.[2]

At issue was not just ethnic wrangling over coveted public teaching positions or simple neighborhood scuffles of the sort long familiar to New Yorkers. More fundamentally, Jews were "demand[ing] an education free of fascism," and Catholics were outraged by "Communists [who] need reinforcement from Russia to oust Miss Quinn."[3] This highly charged rhetoric exposed the deep cultural divisions that drove much of early Cold War politics in New York. Many Catholics and Jews viewed the world as sharply bifurcated, with democracy locked in an epic struggle against either communism or fascism.

In the years immediately following the second Quinn controversy, the *Brooklyn Tablet* (a Catholic publication) explained to its readers that anti-Semitism was a stock "communist slogan" invoked to sully the reputation of "anti-Communists" like the "Catholic public school teacher, Miss Mary A. Quinn." The *Tablet* was the official organ of the Diocese of Brooklyn; its intensely anticommunist editor, Patrick Scanlan, spearheaded a defense committee for Quinn that raised $10,000 in small contributions from the paper's readership.[4]

While Catholic supporters of Quinn labeled her critics as communists, Jewish activists—particularly local chapter members of the Jewish War Veterans (JWV) and the American Jewish Congress (AJCongress)—worked to convince the larger New York community that Quinn was "a symbol of the broader issue of proper democratic teaching in the schools."[5]

When protesters squared off outside Public School 220 in early 1950, their placards reflected a fundamental division between many devout Catholics, who understood the controversy as a case of communist aggression against American unity, and many Jews, who viewed Quinn as an agent of an incipient "fascist" threat to American democracy.[6]

Scholars are of two minds about whether ethnicity was a driving force behind early Cold War domestic politics. In the early 1950s leading sociologists and historians like Richard Hofstadter attributed anticommunist extremism to a sense of "status anxiety" shared by working-class Catholics and "old family, Anglo-Saxon Protestants."[7] Subsequent studies sought to discredit the idea that Catholics were exceptionally conservative or ardent in their opposition to communism.[8] Similarly, while political observers once speculated that anticommunism might have served as a cover for Catholic anti-Semitism in the late 1940s and early 1950s, more recent scholarship takes a skeptical view of this notion, reminding readers that leading anticommunist politicians like Joseph McCarthy scrupulously avoided appeals to religious prejudices (indeed, McCarthy's chief adviser, Roy Cohn, was Jewish) and that most Jews were no less opposed to communism than Catholics or Protestants.[9]

Studies that minimize the ethnic dimension of anticommunist politics in the early Cold War era may give too much focus to political elites like McCarthy and Cohn at the expense of examining political culture at the grassroots level. In metropolitan New York, ethnicity greatly influenced the debate over anticommunist politics. At the heart of that dialogue were fundamental disagreements about citizens' proper relationship to public authority and conflicting fears about which totalitarian ideology most imperiled American democracy—the fascist threat to individual liberties or the communist threat to national unity.

This theoretical and rhetorical difference led to early political divisions between Jews and Catholics. In the aftermath of World War II, many American Jews came to believe that United Nations–style internationalism and a fortified welfare state were vital antidotes to European-style fascism. Though modern scholars tend to believe that American Jews were disinclined to discuss the Holocaust before Adolf Eichmann's arrest and trial in 1960–61, many New York Jews actually dwelled on it much earlier and considered it a clarion call for New Deal–style liberalism.[10]

By contrast, a considerable number of New York Catholics demonstrated a strong distrust of liberalism. Compared with most white Americans, Irish and Italian New Yorkers were highly sympathetic to unions and racial minorities. But their general skepticism of political dissent, as well as the church's long-standing ideological war against international communism, led a great number of Catholic New Yorkers—sometimes a majority—to disavow some of the city's vibrant liberal coalition. Certainly conservatives held sway in the city's leading Catholic institutions. By 1948 it was not surprising that a columnist for the *Catholic News* would openly denounce key elements of President Harry Truman's Fair Deal—"socialized medicine; increased federal housing; federalized education; federal power industry; the extension of the TVA idea . . . federal control of employment services; the repeal of the Taft-Hartley Act; federal subsidies to agriculture; continued heavy taxation"—as "socialism."[11]

Complicating Catholic politics in Cold War–era New York was the city's anomalous political landscape. Because a brand of "Popular Front," antifascist politics persisted longer in Gotham than throughout the rest of the country, the city's strongest voices for racial and economic equality were often tinged by past affiliation with the Communist Party. This proved a major obstacle to many Catholics, whose disdain for communism and radicalism often took precedence over their support for the rights of racial minorities and the working class.

Jews and Catholics in New York City clung to the political lexicon of the Depression era long after other Americans abandoned it for the new language of the Cold War. They continued to disagree about which totalitarian ideology—fascism or communism—posed the greater threat to the United

Catholic supporters of May Quinn, ca. 1949–50. (Brooklyn Jewish Community Council Papers, American Jewish Archives, Cincinnati, Ohio)

Jewish opponents of May Quinn, ca. 1949–50. (Brooklyn Jewish Community Council Papers, American Jewish Archives, Cincinnati, Ohio)

States. Because of this conflict, in metropolitan New York the New Deal electoral coalition of Catholics and Jews, apparently strong in the 1930s, broke down easily and frequently in the postwar years, revealing deep layers of ideological discord between the city's Jewish and Catholic communities.

Voting data specific to New York City are hard to come by for the early Cold War period. Prior to the 1960s, news outlets did not conduct polls that revealed the racial, ethnic, or religious breakdown of election results. Consequently, researchers are forced to rely on what political scientists have dubbed "ecological" voting studies—that is, analyses of returns from sample election districts containing a preponderance of a given ethnic group.

Technically, these surveys are of limited value and accuracy. They do not permit precise analyses of group behavior, but only of voting patterns within certain predominantly Jewish, Irish, or Italian neighborhoods. With this caveat in mind, diverse ecological studies nevertheless suggest that the storied New Deal political coalition between Irish and Italian Catholics on the one hand and Jews on the other began disintegrating long before race became a central issue in local or national politics. Even before the Cold War era, the city's ethnic groups began to display marked political differences (see Table 9).

Although Franklin Roosevelt enjoyed the overwhelming support of white ethnic voters in 1932, by 1940 he struggled to break even in the city's Irish and Italian districts; by comparison, his share of the vote in heavily Jewish election districts increased over time.

These ecological studies suggest that while New York Jews demonstrated overwhelming loyalty to the New Deal, a significant minority of Irish Catholics and an outright majority of Italian New Yorkers may have bolted Roosevelt's coalition in 1940—the latter partly in response to the president's outspoken opposition to Benito Mussolini's fascist regime.[12]

The intricacies of New York state politics disguised some of the growing political discord between the city's Jewish and Catholic voters. In 1936 David Dubinsky, head of the largely Jewish International Ladies Garment Workers Union, and Alex Rose, a leader of the United Hatters, Cap, and Millinery Workers International Union (also predominantly Jewish), created the American Labor Party (ALP), a third party that existed only in New York State and offered Jewish leftists an opportunity to support prominent Democrats like Roosevelt and Governor Herbert Lehman without having to pull the regular Democratic lever. In 1942 a schism within the ALP resulted in the formation of the center-left Liberal Party.

TABLE 9. *Electoral Support for Franklin Roosevelt in New York City by Ethnic Group* (*All Figures Percentages*)

Year	City	Irish	Italian	Jewish
1932	66.4	75.7	80.5	72.2
1936	73.5	72.8	78.7	87.5
1940	60.9	56.0	42.2	88.5
1944	62.0	49.5	41.0	87.0

Sources: Ronald H. Bayor, *Neighbors in Conflict: The Irish, Germans, Jews, and Italians of New York City, 1929–1941* (Baltimore, 1978), 147; William Spinrad, "New Yorkers Cast Their Ballots" (Ph.D. diss., Columbia University, 1955), 14.

Thus, until the ALP disbanded in the early 1950s, New York City Jews enjoyed two alternatives to the regular Democratic line, and they frequently took advantage of this opportunity. Voting studies suggest that in 1938, running as the candidate of both the Democrats and the ALP, Lehman garnered 30 percent of his Jewish votes on the ALP ticket. These same studies suggest that in 1941 almost three-quarters of all Jews casting votes in the city's mayoral election supported Republican incumbent Fiorello LaGuardia, but that most did so by pulling the ALP, rather than the GOP, lever. LaGuardia, who was at sharp odds with the Republican Party's national leadership, enjoyed wide support in the Jewish community because of his aggressive support of the New Deal and his outspoken opposition to European fascism. It did not hurt that his mother was Jewish and that he delivered campaign speeches in Yiddish.[13]

Because many candidates continued to run on multiple tickets in the 1940s and 1950s, Jewish and Catholic voters sometimes supported the same candidate without actually endorsing the same political party or platform. This quirk of New York's system helped mask many of the fault lines that lay beneath the New Deal coalition.

Voting patterns in the 1940s suggest that Catholics favored Democratic machine candidates in local elections but were increasingly likely to support Republican candidates in statewide and national elections. By contrast, Jews voted overwhelmingly for Democrats in statewide and national elections, but in municipal elections they split their votes between the Democratic Party, Liberal Party, and ALP. This meant that Democratic candidates—especially those running in local elections—could not reasonably expect to win a majority of the Jewish vote without also earning the nomination of either the ALP or the Liberal Party.

In his bid for a fourth term in 1944, Roosevelt won 87 percent of the vote in heavily Jewish districts, but only a slim majority (55 percent) of those Jewish votes came on the Democratic Party line; 45 percent of his supporters in Jewish neighborhoods voted for Roosevelt on the ALP and Liberal Party tickets. By contrast, FDR garnered only 49.5 percent and 41 percent of the vote in heavily Irish and Italian districts; about 80 percent of Roosevelt's supporters in Irish and Italian neighborhoods that year cast their votes for the incumbent president by endorsing the regular Democratic ticket. Because the New Deal coalition in New York City often operated outside of the Democratic Party—Republican-Liberal Mayor LaGuardia controlled the city's federal patronage throughout most of Roosevelt's presidency, while Tammany Hall remained aloof from the White House—votes on the Democratic line did not necessarily indicate support for New Deal policies.

These figures point to two trends. First, over half of all Catholic voters in New York may have broken away from Roosevelt by 1944; and second, almost half of all Jewish voters who endorsed Roosevelt considered themselves either too liberal or too independent to ally themselves with New York's Democratic Party. Either pattern bore ominous implications for the long-term stability of the city's liberal coalition. Even when Jews and Catholics voted for the same candidate, they often could not bring themselves to support the same line.

Subsequent state and municipal elections confirmed both trends. In 1945 Democrat-Labor mayoral candidate William O'Dwyer garnered almost half of the vote in heavily Jewish neighborhoods, but over one-third of his supporters in these areas endorsed him on the ALP line. Put in other terms, only a third of voters in Jewish neighborhoods proved willing to support the regular Democratic line. By contrast, O'Dwyer won the endorsement of 63 percent and 72 percent of voters in heavily Irish and Italian neighborhoods, respectively. Almost all of his support in these election districts came on the Democratic line.[14]

In 1949 O'Dwyer ran for reelection solely as a Democrat. Newbold Morris ran on the Republican and Liberal lines and left-wing Congressman Vito Marcantonio ran under the ALP banner. Studies suggest that only 41 percent of New York Jews voted for the Democrat O'Dwyer, while 20 percent supported Marcantonio and 37 percent cast their ballots for Morris. In sum, O'Dwyer's share of the Jewish vote may have fallen by about 16 percent, a drop largely attributable to his loss of the ALP's endorsement. No figures for 1949 exist to confirm the assumption of most contemporary political professionals that O'Dwyer won a resounding victory in Irish precincts, but it seems likely that few Irish New Yorkers cast their votes either for Marcantonio, who was widely regarded as a communist "fellow traveler," or for Morris, who, like Marcantonio, opposed federal assistance to parochial schools. That year, Marcantonio and O'Dwyer split the vote in heavily Italian neighborhoods almost evenly (40 percent for each candidate), a phenomenon owing more to "Marc's" personal sway with Italian voters than to the community's endorsement of his radical political platform.[15]

Subsequent election returns confirm that the ALP's strong showing in Italian neighborhoods that year should be read as a measure of Marcantonio's popularity rather than as a ringing endorsement of his politics. In 1950, 48.9 percent of voters in heavily Italian districts supported Republican Thomas Dewey in his reelection campaign for governor, while only 39.5 percent cast ballots for the Democrat-Liberal candidate, James Lynch. By contrast, Lynch won over 71 percent of the vote in Jewish districts. Dewey's strong showing in Italian areas suggests that Italian votes for Marcantonio the year before had been cast out of personal, not political, loyalty.[16]

No citywide returns exist to shed full light on trends in Irish voting after the late 1940s, but one neighborhood study suggests that many Irish New Yorkers were forming an incipient electoral coalition with their Italian neighbors, one that placed them at ideological odds with New York's Jewish voters. In the predominately Jewish neighborhood of Borough Park in Brooklyn, Roosevelt garnered 96 percent of the popular vote in 1944; in Bay Ridge, a predominantly Catholic neighborhood, he finished behind the Republican Dewey by 4 percent. In the 1948 presidential election, 28.1 percent of voters in Borough Park supported former vice president Henry Wallace, a left-wing candidate who ran on the ALP line, while 60.3 percent supported Truman. The same year, Wallace garnered only 4.9 percent of the vote in Bay Ridge, against 50.3 percent for Truman and 44.8 percent for Dewey. The political lesson appeared to be that a liberal candidate could still squeeze out a victory in Bay Ridge, if only by a slim margin, but a left-wing candidate stood no chance whatsoever.

Four years later, in 1952, Borough Park voted overwhelmingly (84.3 percent) for Democrat Adlai Stevenson for president, while in Bay Ridge, Dwight Eisenhower earned 70.2 percent of the vote against a mere 29.5 percent for Stevenson.[17] These figures suggest that a majority of Irish Catholics in New York were breaking away from the Democratic Party in all but local elections.

This same wisdom was not lost on contemporary observers. In the immediate aftermath of the 1956 presidential election, the New York Times reported that Eisenhower ran well in areas of Queens where "voters of

Italian ancestry predominated. He likewise made a substantial improvement [over 1952] . . . in other areas where voters of Irish and German ancestry were found in large numbers. The President carried all but two of the thirteen Assembly districts in Queens. The two he lost were areas where there is a large Jewish population." A similar outcome was found in Brooklyn, where Eisenhower won "areas heavily populated with people of Italian, Irish, German, or Scandinavian ancestry"; and in neighborhoods in northern and eastern Bronx, where "there are large groups of citizens of Italian and Irish origin."[18]

These studies were consistent with national surveys that revealed an emergent conservatism among a significant portion of the Catholic electorate. The national percentage of Catholic respondents identifying themselves as politically "liberal" dropped from 46 percent in 1944 to 21 percent in 1948, back to 34 percent in 1954, and down again to 26 percent in 1957. The portion of Catholics identifying themselves as conservative rose as high as 32 percent in 1954. By comparison, the percentage of Jewish respondents identifying themselves as liberal increased steadily, to a high of 79 percent in 1955.[19]

Scholars agree that American Jews were an especially loyal, if small, segment of the postwar liberal coalition.[20] In the turbulent political atmosphere of the early Cold War, their almost reflexive liberalism featured a tolerance of political dissent, strong support of social welfare measures, a faith in internationalism, and a commitment to dismantling legal and social barriers based on race, religion, or ethnicity.

What historians do not agree on are the causes of American Jewish liberalism. Some have located its roots in traditional, religious Judaism.[21] Others have argued convincingly that "the traditional Jewish political attitude is one not only of conservatism but also of fundamental detachment," noting that the small segment of the postwar American Jewish community that continued to adhere to traditional forms of Judaism also tended to be more politically conservative. Accordingly, these scholars argue that, since the French Revolution, Jews have pragmatically cast their lot with the forces of liberalism and revolution, or, alternatively, that Russian and Polish Jews who immigrated to the United States in the late nineteenth and early twentieth centuries carried with them a distinct brand of Eastern European radicalism that transmuted over several generations into a more moderate, liberal outlook.[22] Still others have claimed that Jewish liberalism in its postwar context was largely a matter of self-interest, particularly as it pertained to campaigns against discrimination and prejudice.[23]

Most compelling is the argument that the American Jewish community's affinity for left-wing politics originated in czarist Russia. "The spread of industrialization in Eastern Europe . . . together with discriminatory acts of the Czarist government, created considerable economic suffering for the Jews," according to Arthur Liebman. "They responded to their new situation and exploitation by waves of strikes, violence, and sabotage." By the late nineteenth century, "upon their arrival in the United States, large numbers brought with them a sympathetic orientation to radical ideologies such as socialism, Socialist-Zionism, and anarchism. Many also brought with them first-hand experience in labor, radical, and socialist movements."

In New York, which was unquestionably the nerve center of the immigrant community, almost 40 percent of gainfully employed Jews worked in the needle trades, whose "exploitative and arduous [working] conditions . . . created a constituency for socialism and reform." Indeed, Jewish culture in the years leading up to the Great Depression was rife with socialist and radical politics. Boasting a circulation of almost 150,000, the socialist newspaper *Forverts* (or *Jewish Daily Forward*) was the largest foreign-language daily in the country; it also captured almost 40 percent of the Yiddish print market.

Edited by the skilled journalist Abraham Cahan, the *Forverts* helped school countless immigrants in the maze of American customs and habits while also encouraging their continued devotion to trade unionism and socialism. Aiding in this process were organizations like the Arbeiter Ring (Workman's Circle), a fraternal society that claimed 60,000 members by 1918 and drew a large portion of its membership from former Bundists, and the Jewish People's Fraternal Order, a liberal-left group whose membership still stood as high as 50,000 in 1950.

All told, for reasons owing largely to the radicalization of Eastern European Jews prior to their departure for the United States, the sons and daughters of Jewish immigrants grew up in a milieu that celebrated not merely political pluralism, but also unionism, socialism, and radicalism. Each ideal was inseparable from the other. As Irving Howe recalled of his early years, "the Jewish labor movement, ranging from the garment workers unions to the large fraternal societies and small political groups, had established a tradition of protest, controversy, and freedom, so that even when [various communist factions] violated this tradition, it still exerted an enormous moral power in the Jewish community and provided cover for left-wing parties."[24] In effect, Jewish radicalism both relied on and reinforced the community's embrace of intellectual freedom.

Between 1920 and 1945 first- and second-generation Jews in New York transferred their political allegiance to the Democratic Party in presidential elections and to the Democratic, American Labor, and Liberal Parties in congressional and local contests. Legal and political assaults after World War I had effectively destroyed the Socialist Party as a viable electoral option. In 1921 the New York State Assembly refused to seat five Socialist legislators from New York City; the following year it gerrymandered Socialist Congressman Meyer London out of his heavily Jewish district in Manhattan's Lower East Side. In local races, Republicans and Democrats formed fusion tickets to defeat Socialists like Baruch Charney Vladeck, a Jewish alderman from the Williamsburg section of Brooklyn.

In the absence of a strong Socialist alternative, many New York Jews began turning in the 1920s to the Democrats who, under the leadership of Governors Al Smith and Franklin Roosevelt, incorporated a range of liberal welfare measures into their political agendas. Smith's combination of urban liberalism and ethnic tolerance made the party a more attractive vehicle for political involvement to a large part of the city's Jewish population. But it was Roosevelt who solidified the Jewish community's incipient ties to the Democratic Party. Because he ushered in the modern American welfare state, and for his unshakable opposition to worldwide fascism, Jews living in Depression-era New York claimed Roosevelt as their political icon. As Edward Fogel recalled of his formative years in Brooklyn, voting was "easy because everyone was for Roosevelt. The question is, were you a Communist or were you not, a socialist or not. . . . Everybody of that milieu, I'd say, certainly talked about it and flirted with it one way or another." Fogel remembered that even communists voted for Roosevelt.[25]

By the 1940s Jews were the city's staunchest supporters of Roosevelt and his disciples and, more generally, of an expanded welfare state and internationalist foreign policy. Moreover, in the early years of the Cold War, many New York Jews were convinced that Judaism and contemporary liberalism were not only compatible, but inseparable.[26] They believed that their fate was tied, and had always been tied, to the success of progressive political movements everywhere, and while the overwhelming majority of Jews did not count themselves as socialists or communists in the years after 1930, children and grandchildren of the ghetto took pride in the community's erstwhile radical culture. They saw New Deal and Fair Deal liberalism as a pragmatic adaptation of long-standing political traditions.

number of Rabbis in metropolitan New York used their Rosh Hashanah and Yom Kippur homilies to trumpet a closely allied set of values. Ben Zion Bokser told his congregants that "the great men of Jewish history earned their laurels by being meddlers. Abraham was born into an idolatrous world. He began his career by challenging, by denouncing, by interfering. Moses, too, made his mark by refusing to leave his world alone and minding his own business." Though agitation for agitation's sake was a worthy goal—"the way out of stagnation is through challenge, through interference"—Bokser also went a step further. Throughout history, he claimed, "the trait of meddling with evil . . . becomes a passion with the Jew. . . . Every movement of protest against social abuse has received vital reinforcement from the Jewish community." Jews must demand "better working conditions, better housing, a fair wage, decent treatment for the sick and aged." They should continue to "giv[e] vital support to the struggle against racial and religious prejudice" and "meddl[e] with the abuses of the economic system." Turning again to the Old Testament—this time to the Prophets, rather than the Torah[27]—Bokser directed his congregation's attention to "Jeremiah, [who] summed up his mission in words that became part of the Jewish mind: 'See I have set thee this day over the nations and over the kingdoms, to root and pull down, and to destroy and overthrow, to build and to plant.'" Bokser reiterated that Jeremiah's self-stated "mission was to build, to plant a better world, *but he had to begin by disturbing the old, by challenging the old to make way for the new.*"[28]

The themes of free political expression, social democracy, and minority rights pervaded Jewish religious culture, explaining why New York Jews believed they were faithful to their heritage despite their overall minimal engagement with formal religion. This merger of Judaism and liberalism at the grassroots level helped sustain New York Jewry's great self-contradiction: widespread, professed dedication to a religion few claimed to practice formally. Thus, New York Jews like Ruth Messinger almost reflexively explained their commitment to liberal causes as an outgrowth of Jewish tradition. In her capacity as a community leader in the 1970s, Messinger frequently had to answer reporters' inquiries about the origins of her "strong degree of social concern [and] willingness to talk about . . . increasingly unpopular issues that have to do with protection of poor people and minorities. . . . My instinct is always to say, 'Because I'm Jewish.' That is not a useful answer to most reporters and not exactly the way I want it written up, but that is very much the way I feel."[29]

Typical of this blending of political and religious traditions was a sermon delivered by Rabbi Israel Mowshowitz of the Hillcrest Jewish Center

(Queens) on Rosh Hashanah in 1961. He recounted the biblical story of Joseph's release from prison. "Certainly this did not refer to a physical prison," he explained. "There are prisons far more confining and oppressive than those built with brick and mortar. . . . Joseph was confined in a self-imposed prison." Mowshowitz suggested that Joseph, aside from his literal incarceration,

> had to come out of yet another prison, the prison of prejudice. Joseph had a strong compulsion to find fault with his brothers. . . . He thought of them as competitors and looked at them with the microscope of criticism in order to expose their every weakness. . . . Poor Joseph. . . . He thought he would grow at the expense of his brothers. He meant to build himself up by tearing his brothers down. He did not give himself the opportunity to draw close to them, to learn to understand them, and to share life's hopes and dreams with them. He was a prisoner of his own prejudices.

Mowshowitz bemoaned the tendency of prejudice to "bind" and "confine" humans. "We do not like a race or a people or an individual when we see them afar, and therefore we conspire against them. . . . One of the tragedies of our time is that prejudice has enslaved the minds of millions." Prejudice was "costly . . . irrational, [and] criminal," and it "robs man of the opportunity to broaden his understanding and enrich his life." Subtly wedding the theme of intellectual cosmopolitanism to a moral imperative to blot out race and religious hatred, Mowshowitz called on his congregants to break "through the prison of prejudice."[30]

Even more than the High Holidays, Passover became the lowest common denominator of religious observance among many Jews. Celebrated in the spring, the holiday's focal point is the family seder, the climax of which is the reading of the biblical story of Israel's liberation from Egyptian bondage.[31] In the immediate aftermath of the Second World War, Jews could hardly have missed the holiday's added meaning: the Holocaust brought into sharp relief the Jewish community's stake in the struggle for civil rights at home and peace abroad.

"The Seder, the Passover observances, and the Prayer Book all keep alive the memory of the event known as 'the going out of Egypt,'" explained a typical postwar synagogue newsletter. "This has become one of the greatest Jewish doctrines. It declares that God is on the side of the slave and the oppressed. Tyranny may flourish for awhile, and may even appear all-powerful. But God hates the oppressor and sooner or later overthrows him. Egypt seemed unconquerable, but it fell before God's punishment."[32]

In 1945 Rabbi Jacob Pressman of the Forest Hills Jewish Center in Queens reworked the traditional parable of the four sons, a reading familiar to most Jewish families who observe Passover. According to custom, seder attendees take turns reciting an allegorical review of the wicked son, who cares nothing for Judaism; the simple son, who does not comprehend the holiday's meaning; the son who is too young even to ask questions of the seder leader; and the wise son, who appreciates the seder's role as a living historical drama, with freedom at its center.

In a newsletter published for members of his synagogue then serving in the armed forces, Pressman proposed a new approach to the story, given the "universal trial" humankind confronted in the waning days of World War II. He urged the community to devote itself to educating the uninformed son of "the precarious position of the remnant of our people who survive in Europe" and to "remind him of his glorious past and his equally promising future, which is bound up so intimately with the success of the United Nations cause." Pressman also honored the "wise son [who] fights the current battle as an American and as a Jew. He knows what he is fighting for in both instances. He does not enjoy the fight, but he knows that in fighting for freedom and democracy he is fighting for life itself." The wise son was a "modern Moses, daring to lead the world out of its wickedness of ignorance, hate, and mistrust. . . . He has learned that only in the freedom of ALL people—Jews, Chinese, Negroes, Indians—can there be an assurance of freedom for ANY people."[33]

On the grassroots level, lay Jews echoed their rabbis in finding contemporary meaning in the historical drama of Passover. In April 1946 an officer of the JWV, Manhattan Post No. 1 wrote that "two world-shaking wars [have been] fought to make the victory for human freedom complete. But victory for what? Victory to go back to the internal prejudices and dissensions [sic] that mock and divide us? Of course not! Our boys in the armed forces did not die for dear old Intolerance. They sacrificed their young lives to keep America true to her ideals." The post commander reminded his colleagues that "the celebration of Passover . . . emphasize[d] the great moral responsibility which rests upon each and every [Jew] . . . so that life and living in this great country of ours will be a truly happy experience for all." Jewish war veterans, wrote the officer, had fought to secure for all Americans "the right to live, worship, and work in full freedom, with equal opportunity for all—regardless of race, color, or creed."

In an edition of its monthly newsletter dated April 1946, the same JWV post found new meaning in the Passover holiday. "Our ancestors have secured . . . freedom under the most abject conditions of oppression and servitude," the bulletin announced. "It was almost as hopeless to emerge from the yoke of the Pharaoh of ancient days as it looked for a while from the tyranny of the erstwhile Fuhrer of our own time." The lesson the veterans drew from recent history was that Jews must be forever vigilant in the pursuit of universal freedom. "The religious implications . . . are similar. . . . Freedom from slavery must be won."[34]

The essential lesson of Passover, explained Rabbi Seymour Fenichel a decade earlier, was that "the Jew is told not only to despair of freedom, but also . . . never to lose the quality of sympathy and never to treat our fellowmen without mercy." Rabbi Morris Goldberg of Temple Shaare Zedek in Manhattan reminded his congregants that on Passover, "we . . . dedicate ourselves to the unfinished tasks of our ancestors. In this way, we prove that the past has meaning for us of the present. . . . A people is judged by the way it honors the individuals of the past."

Writing in April 1954, only nine years after the end of the Holocaust and one month before the Supreme Court's ruling in *Brown v. Board of Education*, Goldberg's message to his congregants was clear. "The MOSES of history is the constant leader whose life and experience made us realize the value of freedom. . . . We are all [God's] children and the Almighty plays no favorites. Pesach [Hebrew for Passover] directs us to think of freedom as everyone's desire. Just as no nation could live 'half slave and half free,' so the world must now recognize that all men must be free. 'Let my people go,' is still the message today, even as it was in the days of Moses."[35] Drawing on both Moses and Lincoln, Goldberg not only brought Judaism and Americanism into harmony. He also drew an explicit connection between Passover and the postwar drive for civil rights.

The still-nascent civil rights movement offered the most obvious application of biblical wisdom to contemporary politics. But in the 1940s and 1950s Jewish leaders also urged their coreligionists to broaden the definition of "freedom." As Rabbi Israel Levinthal wrote in April 1954:

What the Rabbis wanted to teach us is that true freedom does not touch just one, but every aspect of life. Political freedom, the right to express one's will at the polls, is an essential phase of freedom, but not enough. There must be economic freedom—freedom of opportunity to earn a livelihood; social freedom—freedom from all hate and prejudice; religious freedom—freedom to worship as one sees fit; intellectual freedom—freedom to think as one wills and to express these thoughts as one sees fit, so long as these thoughts do not endanger the ethical and moral life of the people.[36]

Levinthal wove an expansive definition of freedom to include economic rights, racial and religious tolerance, and the familiar theme of intellectual liberty. In the early 1950s such rhetoric was unquestionably a confirmation of the liberal agenda—a commitment to full employment, civil rights, and the expansion of the welfare state.

However blunt his endorsement of Fair Deal liberalism may have been, Levinthal was a paragon of self-restraint when compared with his colleague Samuel Penner, the spiritual leader of the Jacob Schiff Jewish Center in the Bronx. "Jews should take a definite stand on the side of Liberalism," Penner told his congregants on the eve of Passover in the late 1940s. "Whatever pertains to the extension of human freedom, to the widening and deepening of human life, should be the particular care of the Jew. It is a grave error for the Jew to align himself with the forces of reaction, of obscurantism of any kind." According to Penner, the shared historical ordeal of the Exodus rendered Jews a "living argument for freedom, and simply because in our day we are lumped together with the foremost exponents of obscurantism as objects of discrimination we must identify ourselves with these forces."[37]

New York Jews consistently demonstrated their racial liberalism at the voting booths and in their rhetoric, but on a personal, day-to-day basis, interest politics often canceled out high-minded ideology. In predominately black neighborhoods like Harlem, African Americans paid considerably more on average for food, rent, and clothing than white New Yorkers. Because Jews owned two-thirds of all retail establishments in the city and were prominent in the rental market as developers and building owners, they were chiefly responsible on an individual level for exploiting black customers who had little choice but to pay artificially high prices and rents. As early as 1935, when a riot erupted in Harlem, and again in 1964, black New Yorkers leveled their anger at local Jewish shop owners and landlords and exposed a deep breech between two communities that seemed, on the surface, to share a common interest in open housing and employment laws.[38]

From a purely theoretical perspective, however, New York Jews tended to embrace civil rights and, more generally, liberalism with greater enthusiasm than other white groups. In commemoration of Passover in 1949, the Flatbush Yeshiva, a day school for children from Orthodox homes, sponsored an exhibition titled "Slavery and Freedom." According to the Jewish Education Committee (JEC), "one of the objects on display was a model of a kibbutz in colorful clay, under the theme of *Freedom*. Another was a replica of a concentration camp, under the theme of *Slavery*. *Haggadahs* were displayed in many languages." In coupling "freedom" with an Israeli agricultural collective and "slavery" with Nazi Germany, the school's administrators drew directly on the Holocaust, Jewish socialism, and Zionism for political inspiration; none of the three strains of thought operated independently from the others. The pairing of Holocaust and Zionist themes was probably not uncommon. Another display of art by Jewish children, staged the year before, featured "drawings and paintings from Bergen Belsen . . . [to] emphasize the Nazi horror and stress the theme of hope and desire for Palestine."[39]

Students in most New York Jewish schools were likely to learn that internationalism, as best manifested in support for the United Nations, was a linchpin of Judaism. "A number of Jewish schools joined in the celebration of United Nations Day," crowed the Jewish Education Committee (JEC) *Bulletin* in November 1950. "They stressed the continuous striving for peace which has characterized Jewish tradition and has been reflected in Jewish history and literature throughout the ages." The JEC recommended that all schools build some kind of commemoration into their schedules. Possibilities included the performance of a short sketch titled " 'Isaiah and the United Nations' . . . a fantasy in the form of a dream in which appropriate quotations from Isaiah are introduced into a mythical session of the United Nations Assembly."[40]

Teaching students that internationalism was somehow a tenet of Judaism was commonplace in postwar Jewish culture. Certainly it was a lesson that adult members of the community seemed to appreciate. In 1954 the Scarsdale Chapter of the AJCongress–Women's Division declared October a "commemorative period in which we reaffirm our unswerving belief in the principles of the United Nations Organization. We know that the only answer to recurring war is negotiation; and that the only instrument for negotiation that exists in the world today is the United Nations Organization."[41]

More pointedly, the *Brooklyn Jewish Center Review* ran an article in 1946 explaining that the Jewish biblical Prophets "introduced an entirely new and revolutionary concept, Universalism, into the ancient world. They viewed the entire universe as . . . the creation . . . of one single, and therefore universal, God." And "since all men are children of this universal Creator . . . they are brothers. . . . Accordingly, all warfare and strife among these nations must be condemned as fratricide." Jewish universalism therefore mitigated against violence, a sentiment that Isaiah advocated "most vociferous[ly]" when he wrote: "And they shall beat their swords into plowshares. . . . Nation shall not lift up sword against nation, neither shall they learn war any more." The essayist reminded his readers of a midrash (rabbinical commentary) containing "this lofty exegesis: 'God said to Moses: Wage war' (on [the monarch] Sihon, Deuteronomy 2:24). But Moses did otherwise. He sent emissaries of peace." Here again, a religious leader was celebrating an act of biblical dissent, committed in the interest of humanitarianism and cosmopolitanism.[42]

The sermons and seders in which Jews participated were not the source of their liberalism, though for some, these religious rites may have been a source of inspiration. More often they were a reflection of the community's widely shared political persuasion. Nonliturgical sources reinforce the idea that Jews thought of dissent and liberalism as appropriate themes for discussion in religious and cultural settings.

In the late 1940s and 1950s, the Brooklyn Jewish Center sponsored a monthly lecture series that brought controversial political figures together to debate questions of public concern. In 1949 Eleanor Roosevelt—to many, the "First Lady of liberalism"—delivered a speech on "the accomplishments and failures of the United Nations," while former vice president Henry Wallace gave a talk titled, "Where I Stand." The Brooklyn Jewish Center also provided a stage for liberal senator Wayne Morse of Oregon and former congresswoman Helen Gahagan Douglas of California, each a bête noire of the anticommunist rank-and-file. The center sponsored a roundtable discussion on "socialized medicine," including in its program speakers in favor of and opposed to the concept.

At roughly the same time, the *Brooklyn Tablet*, speaking for the Diocese of Brooklyn, ran an exposé that deemed "socialized medicine a menace to society" and dismissed as "sheer nonsense" the notion that "there is a rank injustice in 'guilt by association.' . . . The old proverb that a man is known by the company he keeps is founded in truth and common sense." Francis Cardinal Spellman told an enthusiastic convention of the Knights of Columbus in 1950 that "if we are to continue to be the world's treasure-house of liberty . . . we must stand sentinel against imminent dangers . . . bred and spread by faithless, God-hating Communists and Communist sympathizers who are using their freedom to destroy our freedom." This, the same year that the Brooklyn Jewish Center staged a debate on the McCarran Act of 1950, which required that "subversive" groups register with the Justice Department and denied entry visas to aliens who once advocated communism.[43] Only a small minority of Jews in New York attended the center's lecture forum. Yet the willingness of a major Jewish cultural institution to host debates on controversial subjects, and to open its doors to speakers so reviled in much of the Catholic community, suggests a fundamental difference between Jews and their Italian and Irish neighbors.

Secular Jewish organizations felt at special liberty to isolate political conservatism as inimical to Jewish interests and values. The Scarsdale Chapter of the AJCongress–Women's Division dedicated one of its regular Wednesday morning discussion groups in 1954 to investigating "the menace of reactionary thinking in this country." The meeting's organizers posed the ominous question: "Do you think that you know everything about McCarthy and his cohorts? You don't! Come and learn more!"[44]

The AJCongress, founded after World War I, was by far the most liberal of the three major Jewish "defense" agencies, a trio of groups dedicated to combating libels and disabilities directed at Jews and other minorities. In the wake of the Holocaust, the AJCongress stepped up its efforts and collaborated with the American Jewish Committee (AJC) and the Anti-Defamation League (ADL) to conduct a vigorous assault on racial and religious prejudice. The legal arm of the AJCongress—the Committee for Law and Social Action (CLSA)—hired seven civil rights attorneys in 1945 and filed suits against universities, landlords, realtors, and employers known to discriminate against minorities. Among its most prominent targets in New York were Columbia University and New York State's nine medical schools, all of which imposed quota ceilings on Jewish admissions, and the Stuyvesant Town housing project in Manhattan, which was closed to African Americans. Although the AJCongress represented the left wing of the organized Jewish community, it fell squarely within the liberal consensus, and its politics reflected the community's outlook.[45]

Like their colleagues in Scarsdale, members of the Brooklyn Chapter of the AJCongress–Women's Division understood radical anticommunism as hostile to the broad liberal agenda they pressed in the name of Jewish values and interests. At a banquet in 1954, members of the chapter performed a musical skit that reflected the Jewish community's overriding hostility toward Joseph McCarthy.

> Gotta protest, against McCarthy
> Gotta write postcards regularly
> Chairman of CLSA, fights bigotry.[46]

> Oh, Joe McCarthy, oh Joe McCarthy
> I'm so blue since they changed Dave to Private Shine
> Though he calls me twice a day
> In the army he must stay
> Like the other boys he's made to toe the line.[47]

> Oh, Mr. Cohn, oh Mr. Cohn
> We're not ordinary people, you and I

Are your red-rimmed eyes still wet
We'll make Shine a Colonel yet
We'll use pressure, Joe McCarthy
Plenty pressure, Mr. Cohn.

Oh, Joe McCarthy, oh Joe McCarthy,
You're a master when it comes to treachery,
Tell me, in our bag of tricks
Are there photos we can fix[48]
While we wave the flag and sing "Oh, can you see?"

Oh, Mr. Cohn, Mr. Cohn
Don't you fret, you underestimate this Joe
All my power I will muster
Filibuster, Joe McCarthy
Points of order, Mr. Cohn.[49]

In their parody, the young women of the Brooklyn Chapter probably singled out Roy Cohn for special treatment because he was Jewish. More to the point, they revealed an unspoken conviction that battling anticommunist political forces was simply an extension of their fight against bigotry.

I n the late 1940s and 1950s, religious and secular leaders in the American Jewish community turned to the social sciences to explain contemporary events. In particular, they developed a complex understanding of prejudice as being "unitary," which means that racism, anti-Semitism, and all other forms of bigotry stemmed from the same sociological and psychological roots. To combat one without targeting the others was scientifically unsophisticated and practically futile, according to this outlook. All forms of prejudice were equally menacing to democratic institutions.

Driving these perceptions was a series of academic inquiries into the roots of bigotry, commissioned by the AJC and titled *Studies in Prejudice*. Particularly influential was *The Authoritarian Personality* (1950), a volume drafted by a team of social scientists headed by Theodor Adorno, a leading member of the Institute of Social Research (ISR) in New York. Essentially the reincarnation of the famed Frankfurt School, the ISR brought together many leading left-wing Jewish intellectuals who had fled Germany in the 1930s.[50] While muting their Marxist tendencies and concentrating primarily on the psychological ingredients of fascism and bigotry, the authors of *The Authoritarian Personality* and other volumes in the *Studies in Prejudice* series identified economic insecurity as a prime motivator behind all forms of group hatred. In *Dynamics of Prejudice: A Psychological and Sociological Study of Veterans*, ISR scholars Bruno Bettelheim and Morris Janowitz stated that "the economic goals of social action are . . . clear: An adjusted annual wage to do away with fears of seasonal employment, stabilization of employment, and an extension of social security. In the absence of comprehensive and successful attempts in that direction, it remains doubtful whether programs oriented specifically toward interethnic issues are at all relevant for changing interethnic relations."

The prescriptive sections of *Studies in Prejudice* essentially read like a page from Truman's Fair Deal manual. Each championed a modest expansion of the welfare state and the encouragement of economic growth, rather than a substantial redistribution of resources. But they also stressed that interreligious and interethnic dialogues were secondary in importance to the moderation of economic inequality.

Bettelheim and Janowitz's study also concluded that persons most susceptible to the lure of intolerance were likely to hold established social institutions, like the federal government and the university system, in contempt. This finding lent credence to a suspicion among Jewish community leaders that McCarthyism and fascism shared common derivatives. A telling example of this intellectual association was Rabbi Israel Levinthal's warning in 1952 that McCarthy's tactics—"the method of the smear . . . the half truth . . . innuendo . . . twisting the meaning of words"—were no different from the means employed by Joseph Goebbels in Nazi Germany.[51]

It is nearly impossible to determine how widely known or correctly understood the *Studies in Prejudice* series actually was. Certainly its main themes enjoyed some dissemination among the American reading public in 1950, when the *New York Times Magazine* ran an article about *The Authoritarian Personality*. Moreover, social science and academic expertise enjoyed something of a popular renaissance in the early postwar years. From Gunnar Myrdal's study of race prejudice in 1944 to John Kenneth Galbraith's critique of American materialism in 1958, social and economic studies reached an increasingly broad audience.[52] Statements like those of Rabbi Louis Levitsky—that "antisemitism is but one aspect of hate, and . . . it can be lessened only to the extent to which hate in general is reduced"— suggest a certain popular familiarity with the themes underscoring the *Studies in Prejudice* publications. Significantly, Levitsky's larger point was that in order to ensure "that what happened in Germany will [not] happen here," American Jews must throw themselves into the work of interfaith relations.[53]

The tendency of prominent New York Jews to turn to the social sciences

—albeit in a popular, diluted format—to develop a framework for addressing contemporary political and cultural issues stood in sharp contrast to the inclination of leading Irish and Italian Catholics to view current affairs through the prism of faith. Whereas Jewish activists thought of bigotry, violence, and conflict as emanating from economic inequality, poor education, or political instability, many of their Catholic counterparts endorsed a religious dichotomy between right and wrong that left little room for scientific reasoning.

In 1949 a columnist for the *Catholic News* assailed the increasingly common tendency to define certain forms of asocial behavior, like drunkenness and compulsive gambling, as diseases rather than sins. "Next will come cheating and thieving," he scoffed. "And lying. And sloth, and lust, and anger, even the anger that results in manslaughter and murder." In a world where God's law gave way to the vagaries and moral relativism of social science, "there will be neither 'good' nor 'bad,' 'right' nor 'wrong.' Human actions will be in harmony with or at variance with social advantage." Turning to the very questions that vexed the ISR, the columnist worried that

> to push the modern theory so far may seem to be an exaggeration. Perhaps it is a reductio ad absurdum. But in all soberness I must say that if gambling is now to be classed as a form of sickness along with alcoholism, I cannot see why we should limit the psychological theory to only those two forms of delinquency. Why shouldn't we include, for example, the two greatest offenses of the Nazis and Communists, lynching and cruelty? If a man is a congenital liar or has instinctive tendencies to cruelty, how can we blame him? Why should we try him in court, condemn him and execute him? Perhaps the keepers of Buchenwald and Dachau and Saschsenhausen were sick men and hence not criminals. . . . How are we to know that vice and crime are not really forms of sickness?[54]

The *Catholic News* columnist exaggerated the point a little: most advocates of social science sought to explain and avoid violence, rather than pardon it. But the Catholic position on sin, which was above all a theological problem, stood in sharp contrast to the increasingly popular tendency among Jews to think of hate and violence as social problems, with roots in everyday experience. As previously stated, popular scholarship holds that the Cold War muted the Jewish community's discussion of the Holocaust, and American Jews were generally reluctant to discuss the tragedy before the 1960s. However, New York Jews were enthusiastically liberal even prior to their internalization of the "authoritarian personality" interpretation of prejudice and hatred, and the Holocaust, far from being a taboo subject, only strengthened their political convictions.

At a Chanukah ceremony in Manhattan in 1955, participants lit candles in "honor of the vivid memory of the heroes of the Warsaw ghetto [whose] courageous struggles against the brutal Nazis will be remembered for ages," and in commemoration of "the hardy group of Jewish pioneers who landed on American shores . . . and whose struggle for religious freedom, for civil rights, are now part of American history." Jews did not have to state explicitly why mention of the Holocaust was relevant to a discussion of American civil rights. The connection was obvious.[55]

Jews on the grassroots level were also outspoken in their criticism of the American government's lax efforts to de-Nazify Germany. In April 1950 local chapters of the AJC, AJCongress, ADL, JWV, Brooklyn Board of Rabbis, Jewish Labor Committee, and National Council of Jewish Women sponsored a public meeting to "give sober consideration to Nazi re-emergence in Germany. . . . We in Brooklyn have the opportunity of giving leadership to the entire Nation in meeting the question which faces us: Germany—Democracy or NAZISM?" Predictably, the conference identified key liberal institutions as antidotes to fascism's resurgence in Germany: "democratic elements such as the labor movement . . . cooperatives . . . social welfare agencies and municipalities under effective popular control [will] facilitate the re-education of the German people . . . in a spirit of democratic and peaceful cooperation." To de-Nazify Germany thoroughly, then, the United States must "democratize the economy and curb the concentration of economic power in cartels and trusts."[56]

Prominent rabbis like Israel Goldstein of Manhattan's Congregation B'nai Jeshurun used the High Holidays to address the "horrible, unspeakable crimes which have been committed against the Jewish people by the Nazi regime." In a sermon delivered for Rosh Hashanah in 1952, Goldstein posed the rhetorical question:

What should be the Jewish response [to Germany's repentance] at this season of forgiveness? I doubt if it is possible psychologically and emotionally for those whose dear ones have perished in the Nazi crematoria or who themselves have been subjected to the ordeals of the Nazi concentration camps, to forget and forgive. . . . The decisive questions will be: Will Chancellor [Konrad] Adenauer dismiss the erstwhile Nazis and war criminals whom he has permitted to hold high office in his government? Will there be a real effort to reeducate the German youth? Will antisemitism really be prosecuted? Will restitution and reparation to the Jewish people be in some reasonable proportion to the huge Nazi plunder of Jewish wealth and property? . . . It is too early to adopt a policy of "forgive and forget."

Goldstein was not alone in confronting the question of German guilt. He was in good company, joined by leading Jewish organizations of nearly all political vantage points.[57]

Another indication of Jewish consciousness of the Holocaust in the early postwar years was the community's overwhelming support of, and fascination with, Israel. The rise of fascism in the 1930s sounded the death knell for respectable anti-Zionist elements within organized Judaism, but the unprecedented surge in fund-raising, first for the Yishuv (the Jewish community in prestate Palestine) and then for the Israeli state, can be understood only in the context of European Jewry's near destruction. New York Jews were raising astounding amounts of money each year for the UJA, which dedicated most of its proceeds to the Jewish Joint Distribution Committee, which in turn focused on aid to Palestinian Jewry and to displaced Holocaust survivors in Europe. All told, after 1948 American Jews were raising at least $200 million annually for the UJA.[58]

Rabbis and community leaders explicitly invoked the Holocaust in their fund-raising drives for the UJA. The spiritual leader of Manhattan's Congregation Shaare Zedek, for instance, reminded his congregants that "many more Jews could have been saved from Hitler if we had given enough [money] and in time. This time we must not be too late. We must see to it that the UJA has the funds to . . . strengthen Israel as a haven for the persecuted and the homeless, and to step up all of its worldwide life-building work. Don't let Jewish lives be lost for lack of funds."

Schoolchildren especially were encouraged to think of the Holocaust and Israel's birth as closely related episodes in Jewish history. Throughout New York, pupils at religious schools "adopted" and raised funds for sister and brother schools in Europe, part of a program whose educational element focused on "the problems which face Jews as an aftermath of the war and the Jewish accomplishments in Palestine." A summer program in Manhattan divided campers into groups, each of which researched and presented information on "a Jewish population of a European country in the nineteenth and twentieth centuries. Through the medium of folk song, dance, stories, etc., the groups reconstructed the life of the Jews, and a somber life it was indeed. The children then followed these European Jews to a happier and freer life in Palestine."[59] Above all, the generation of

Jewish children who filled religious schools after 1945 learned in some-times subtle, but often candid ways that the community's liberalism and commitment to Israel were two parts of the same whole.

The union of secular values and Judaism developed as self-prophecy. Because many Jews placed special emphasis on free thinking, intellectual pursuit, and liberalism, and because their level of religious observance was minimal, they came to believe that Judaism's core value system was a mandate to learn, to argue, and to build a humanitarian society. Rabbis only reinforced this politicized form of religious minimalism when they used their pulpits to extol the virtues of dissent and liberalism on those few occasions when they had a sizable, captive audience.

5 Communism

For several days in the late summer of 1949, national attention turned to Peekskill, New York, a small town forty miles upstate from Manhattan. There, a predominately Catholic mob twice ambushed a benefit concert featuring the renowned left-wing political activist and virtuoso, Paul Robeson. The event was intended to raise money for members of the Communist Party who were awaiting trial on charges of violating the Smith Act.

Four days before the scheduled performance, the *Peekskill Evening Star* ran a blistering editorial complaining that "every ticket purchased for the Peekskill concert will drop nickels and dimes into the till basket of an Un-American political organization." The paper's editor urged that "the time for tolerant silence that signifies approval is running out. Peekskill wants no rallies that support iron curtains, concentration camps, blockades, and NKVDs [a violent wing of Joseph Stalin's Soviet government], no matter how masterful the décor, nor how sweet the music." Leading citizens took up the paper's challenge. Hundreds of protesters blocked a road leading to the picnic area where the concert was to take place. Some members of the mob hurled anti-Semitic and racist invective at the concert attendees—most of whom were Jewish or black, and from New York City—and succeeded in manufacturing enough chaos to cancel the event.

A week later, Robeson returned—this time protected by 2,500 left-wing, bat-wielding union members—to perform before an audience of 20,000 supporters. The concert went off without a hitch. At the show's conclusion, the police directed the city-bound spectators up a windy, gravel road, where a mob several hundred strong awaited them from the overhang. Folksinger Pete Seeger, who also performed that day, later recalled that members of the crowd yelled "Go home you white niggers," "Kikes," and "Go on back to Russia," while some of the younger rioters smashed the fleeing vehicles with small boulders and dragged concert attendees from their cars, beating some of them unconscious.[1]

The fallout from the Peekskill riot was complex. Left-wing activists like

Henry Wallace and Robeson described the event as evidence that America was rife with "fascist" potential.[2] Some national Jewish groups like the ADL and the AJC revealed the limits of Jewish freethinking and quickly distanced themselves from the Robeson forces, fearing that criticism of the riot might compromise their place in the broad anticommunist political coalition. On a grassroots level, however, New York Jews seemed much more enraged than their national leaders. The Brooklyn Jewish Youth Committee issued a strong protest against the riots, which it compared to earlier events in Nazi Germany. Other local groups also expressed their opposition to the riots, including the Brownsville and East New York Jewish Community Council and both the Brooklyn Division and Brooklyn Women's Division of the AJCongress—an organization whose national office was on record as being firmly opposed to communism and other brands of "totalitarianism."[3]

Though their stridently anticommunist organization had initially spoken out against Robeson, the local JWV condemned both the first and second riots. In the week between Robeson's two scheduled appearances in Peekskill, the JWV's Westchester County commander threatened any member who had participated, or planned to participate, in the first wave of anti-Robeson violence with an official "court-martial" and ouster. "The lynch spirit evidenced, the mob violence practiced . . . the innocent people hurt and the property damaged must find nothing but revulsion in real Americans who are opposed to any form of wool-hatters, black shirts, or 'super'-Americans," he told the press, invoking the specter of homegrown fascism to emphasize his point.[4]

To many local Jews, including committed anticommunists, the riots seemed to pose a threat to free thought and expression. Leading Catholics could not have disagreed more strongly. Firsthand reports from Peekskill— a community that fell under the auspices of the Archdiocese of New York— indicated that members of the Catholic War Veterans (CWV) had played a disproportionate role in fanning the flames of the riot. It was an assumption the organization did little to discredit when its local chapter commander dismissed accounts of the riot as fictitious and labeled the concert attendees and their supporters "godless, ruthless, and vicious."[5]

Predictably, the *Brooklyn Tablet* weighed in heavily against the Robeson forces and, focusing on communism's illegitimate challenge to established authority, branded the concert an "active conspiracy to overthrow our government." Editor Patrick Scanlan echoed the official line of the Brooklyn diocese and New York archdiocese and denied "that the Peekskill affair was in any way the result of anti-Semitism or anti-Negro prejudice."

At the heart of the paper's argument was the familiar Catholic stance toward authority and dissent: "It is part of the Communist strategy to create a distrust of public officials by distortion and magnification of incidents such as these," argued one columnist, "and also to bring about incidents to harass those officials and distract them from their functions of serving the community."[6]

In the wake of the first riot, the more temperate *Catholic News*, published by the Archdiocese of New York, implausibly charged that "the disturbances at Peekskill Saturday night . . . would never have been precipitated if Communists and their sympathizers from New York had not invaded the area: the immediate cause of the trouble obviously was the determination of the Reds to turn a peaceful demonstration by veterans' organizations into a riot." After the second riot, the newspaper repeated the claim that communists had "provoked" violence, "disorder," and "chaos."[7]

Peekskill brought into sharp relief the key distinction between New York's Catholic and Jewish subcultures. Although both groups were largely inimical to communism, their opposition stemmed from different sources and, consequently, assumed different levels of intensity. Whereas Jews tended to fear the encroachment of totalitarian authority on individual liberties, many Catholic voices, like the journalists for the *Catholic News*, tended to fear that communists would break the bonds of organic community by driving "a wedge between clergy and laity, to alienate them from one another. Just as unswerving loyalty is expected of a citizen by his country in a time of great national danger, so is such loyalty from Catholics to their Holy Father, their Bishops, and their priests required especially today."[8] Communism was first a foremost a challenge to Catholic solidarity, and it required a swift and steady response. That response, in turn, made liberalism a suspect creed in New York's Irish and Italian communities.

On the surface, New York's Catholic citizens were likely supporters of the postwar liberal bloc that most of their Jewish neighbors supported. The vast majority of Irish and Italians were semiskilled or unskilled workers whose economic interests lay with the left wing of organized labor, and both groups knew enough of ethnic and religious bigotry to find meaning in the Cold War–era assault on racism pioneered by leading left-wing and liberal activists.[9] Furthermore, Catholic doctrine was very clear on two points: first, that capital had certain material and moral obligations to labor; and second, that racism was a violation of Christian doctrine. Yet by the early 1950s, significant numbers of Catholic voters broke with the liberal coalition and endorsed conservative Republicans in national and statewide elections.

Many of these Irish and Italians were not opposed to core elements of the New Deal welfare state, the rights of organized labor, or the nascent civil rights movement. But they refused to join hands with liberal activists whose relationship with the communist and socialist Left seemed to them far too cozy. Catholic conservatism, which was on the ascent in the 1940s and 1950s, derived much of its strength from the growing perception that American liberalism was tainted red, and that the communist menace stood to undermine deeply cherished notions about community and both religious and civic authority.

One of the great ironies of Catholic anticommunism is that it derived much of its theological and intellectual strength from the same textual sources that inspired left-wing Catholics involved with the small but influential Catholic Worker Movement. Whatever else they disagreed on, conservative Catholic clerics like Francis Cardinal Spellman and radical laypersons like Dorothy Day and Peter Maurin shared a common affection for Pope Leo XIII, who issued an encyclical in 1891 that ultimately anchored official *and* dissident Catholic social philosophy for the better part of the next seven decades.

Rerum Novarum (Of New Things), known also as "On the Conditions of the Working Class," censured both communism and classical liberalism for their violation of core Catholic values. It was the opening volley in the church's century-long struggle against atheistic communism, as well as its much weaker complaint against unfettered market forces. As Charles R. Morris has explained, "basic Catholic principles [held] that there is an externally ordained social order that humans can understand rationally through natural law. Society is organized in a hierarchy, running from the Church through the State and through subsidiary associations like labor unions down to the family." According to this worldview, "society is an organism; each component is bound by a complex of duties and obligations to every other." Catholic doctrine thus held that "individuals derive their identity from a thick web of social relations" and that "the modern tendency to elevate the rights of individuals" was "at variance" with Christian reality. *Rerum Novarum* flayed both communism and classical liberalism for their inherent materialism and focus on the individual.

In theory, *Rerum Novarum*—with *Quadragesimo Anno* (In the Fortieth Year), a companion encyclical issued by Pope Pius XI in 1931 as a reiteration of Leo XIII's well-established social principles—demanded that capital recognize the reciprocal nature of its relationship with labor. Employees were entitled to decent working conditions, free time for family and religious pursuits, and, most importantly, a "family wage" adequate enough to keep mothers out of the workplace and provide households with a dignified standard of living. In return, workers were enjoined to respect their obligations to employers, execute their duties faithfully, disavow violent confrontation, and strike only when absolutely necessary. Both encyclicals demanded that government respect the rights of labor and capital in kind, that the worker not be unduly deprived of his earnings by excessive taxation, and that the factory or shop owner not be deprived of ownership and direction of his enterprise.[10]

In reality, the church both in Europe and the United States placed disproportionate stress on the anticommunist element of the two social encyclicals—especially in the 1930s and 1940s, when Depression-era politics and Soviet expansion forced a widespread reappraisal of Catholic social philosophy. Catholic officials grew consistently outspoken in their opposition to communism and socialism and noticeably muted in their criticism of capitalist excess. In the United States, the Association of Catholic Trade Unionists (ACTU) was founded in the 1930s as an organization dedicated to aiding in the development of labor unions and promoting a quasicorporatist ethic among unionized workers. In effect, its mission was to advance a Catholic social program that protected the dual rights of labor and capital. But by the mid-1940s, in cities like New York, the ACTU had effectively evolved into an anticommunist watchdog agency that worked to discredit left-leaning labor unions.

So, too, with official church spokespersons and organs, particularly diocesan newspapers, whose denunciations of communism grew louder as their criticism of capital grew softer. In 1949 a columnist for the *Catholic News* voiced bitter opposition to a massive strike by longshoremen and stevedores, arguing that such actions produced "joy in the Kremlin. Nothing gives Stalin and his incorporated murderers such satisfaction as a good big expensive strike in America. These strikes of ours are, in these crucial days, a crazy way of settling disputes. They may add up to disaster. . . . If these lunatic proceedings continue, the American way of life will come to an end. We shall be forced into some sort of socialistic or totalitarian form of government in which a dominant political power will tell both labor and management where they head in and where they head off."[11]

As they lined up squarely against communism, these same Catholic leaders and institutions voiced growing concerns about Roosevelt's New Deal, whose statist approach to governance seemed to them to smack of socialism. They grew more determined in their opposition to economic liberalism as the 1940s wore on. Such concerns led Father John Flynn, the president of St. John's University, to warn in 1950 that for "the present government program of nationalizing things like credit, education, agriculture, medicine, and welfare organizations, a great amount of federal tax is required." Increased federal taxation, Flynn added, was placing America "on the road of totalitarianism and nationalization that we are apparently bent on following." Despite the considerable dividends the postwar welfare state promised to deliver to working-class Catholics, the specter of communism compelled leading clerics like Flynn to align themselves with the conservative cause.[12]

The church's animus toward communism dated back to the nineteenth century but intensified in the 1930s, when Spanish Republicans (or Loyalists) opposed to General Francisco Franco's fascist army slaughtered upwards of 7,000 members of the clergy, subjecting some to highly symbolic acts of torture like eye gougings, crucifixions, and burnings at the stake. Members of the Roosevelt administration and leading American liberals voiced support for the Spanish Republicans and also lent encouragement to the left-wing, anticlerical Mexican government, which was engaged in a long-running conflict with conservative Catholic rebels. Though neither the Spanish Loyalists nor the Mexican government was under communist control, communists were closely allied with both—especially with Spanish Republican forces, who received material aid from the Soviet Union.

Many American Catholics came to believe that the church was under communist siege and that Popular Front liberals at home were little more than communist dupes. According to this view, increasingly widespread in Irish and Italian communities, liberals applied a hypocritical standard in denouncing the violent excesses of Italian and Spanish fascism even as they winked at brutal anti-Christian campaigns perpetrated by communists and fellow travelers. In 1946 public opinion polls revealed that 46 percent of Catholics nationwide viewed General Franco unfavorably, while 14 percent viewed him favorably and 40 percent had no opinion one way or the other. This hardly signaled resounding Catholic support for Spanish fascism, but it contrasted sharply with corresponding opinion in the Jewish community, where only 2 percent viewed Franco favorably and 78 percent viewed him unfavorably.[13]

As late as 1948, the Brooklyn Tablet ran a biting political cartoon that depicted the forces of "International Diplomacy" enjoining Uncle Sam not to extend material assistance to Franco's Spain. "No, Sam. . . . [S]he's not a democracy," explains the bespectacled representative of International Diplomacy—a clear jab at presidential candidate Henry Wallace's supporters, who placed more faith in negotiation than armament. In turn, the drawing describes Spain as "communism's oldest and most steadfast foe." Three years later New York's *Irish Echo* reprinted an editorial arguing that "Americans who suggest we should toss our great weight against Christian Spain are either Communists, fellow-travelers, native-born pinks, lovers of Moscow or . . . unfortunate psychopathics." In effect, by the late 1940s, the Roosevelt and Truman administrations' foreign policies had made New Deal and Fair Deal liberalism a suspect creed among many Catholic spokespersons. Examples from the *Tablet* and the *Echo* articulated these misgivings.[14]

For many Catholic leaders, anticommunism also offered a new form of relief from the condescension—real and imagined—they suffered over the years from Protestant cultural and political elites. This was especially so for Irish Catholics, who had long bridled at the disdain with which they had met since the very first wave of famine immigrants arrived on American shores in the mid-nineteenth century. Like other newcomers to America, most Irish émigrés left Eire in search of economic stability, for want of political freedom, or to join family and friends. But in its songs, literature, folklore, and politics, the Irish American disapora continued to envision itself as an exilic culture. According to this rendering of history, the Irish were victims of criminal acts on the part of English and American Protestants, designed to drive them from their homeland.[15]

The potato famine itself became the central theme of this narrative. Though many historians agree that the blight owed mostly to a lethal combination of outmoded agriculture, overpopulation and natural disaster, and the stubbornly laissez-faire economic policies of the British government, for generations of Irish Americans it would be remembered as a deliberate, would-be genocide perpetrated by willful English neglect. Many Protestant elites in the United States made it all too easy for Irish immigrants and their children to draw sweeping connections between the Anglo-American establishment and the English establishment. Nineteenth-century American journals caricatured the Irish as apes, little different from African slaves. Slanderous tracts like the *Awful Disclosures of Maria Monk* portrayed the Catholic Church and its adherents as sexually depraved, subversive, and generally maniacal.[16]

Even for the New York Irish of the early Cold War period, memories of "No Irish Need Apply" signs in shop windows, the virulently anti-Catholic, million-member American Protective Association of the 1890s, the reincarnation of the Ku Klux Klan in the 1920s, and Al Smith's political tribulations in 1924 and 1928—dutifully passed down from grandparents to grandchildren, in much the same way that second-generation American

Jews continued to "remember" the injustices of czarist Russia—encouraged a continued association of all things "establishment" with all things Protestant and British. The suggestion that Catholics, particularly those of Irish descent, might be unfit for democratic citizenship lingered well into the postwar period. As far back as 1869, no less a political firebrand than Elizabeth Cady Stanton warned that, by virtue of their religious affinities, Catholics could not "take in the grandeur of the American idea of individual rights. . . . The human mind is ever oscillating between the extremes of authority and individualism; and if the former—the Catholic idea—finds lodgment in the minds of this people, we ring the death knell of American liberties."[17]

Almost eighty years later, in 1948, the Nation—a prominent, left-wing journal founded by Stanton's reform-oriented colleagues in the twilight hours of the Civil War—ran a series of articles by Paul Blanshard on the American Catholic Church. Blanshard recycled the old charge that Catholics were parochial and intellectually backward—a menace to democracy unless otherwise disentangled from the grip of an autocratic church that was "perfectly willing to compromise with democratic forms of government so long as its own special areas of power are respected." While his series was technically an exposé of the church as an institution, it implicitly indicted all American Catholics as slaves to an antidemocratic religious institution.[18]

The Cold War supplied Irish Catholics with a long-awaited opportunity to turn the tables on the Protestant "establishment." Anticommunism had been a central theme of American Catholicism for a half-century, but after 1947 it became a defining American creed, as well. Establishment figures in the state department and academia suddenly found themselves on the defensive, forced to explain to an unbelieving public how the Soviet Union developed its atomic bomb, why China fell to the communists, and exactly how so many state secrets were apparently finding their way to Moscow.

Catholic anticommunist credentials were unimpeachable. Not so for the New Dealers, Fair Dealers, and Popular Fronters who, many Catholics thought, always seemed to enjoy looking down their noses at Irish America. Daniel Patrick Moynihan, a product of New York's Irish community, famously observed that "the Irish achieved a temporary advantage from the McCarthy period. . . . In the era of security clearances, to be a Catholic became prima facie evidence of loyalty. Harvard men were to be checked: Fordham men would do the checking."[19]

In the early Cold War period, the Irish Echo consistently singled out Secretary of State Dean Acheson for especially harsh criticism in its op-ed pages, as when it claimed in 1951 that "his honey-combed Red Department prepared the ground for red aggression in the Far East [and his] bitter anti-Irish policy plays into the hands of the Soviets in Western Europe." In 1954 the *Echo* accused the "Democratic party, or certain sections of it," of having "entered into a pact with the British government to sabotage American foreign policy in the interests of Britain and Russia." To those Irish Americans who were both ardently anticommunist and intensely interested in the fate of the "six counties" (Northern Ireland), the pro-British disposition of leading liberals only brought into sharper relief the apparent difference between loyal Catholics and traitorous Protestants.[20]

Debates over foreign policy in the 1930s had in many ways precipitated a growing Catholic resentment of high-ranking Protestant officials in the 1940s and 1950s. Many Irish Americans viewed Roosevelt's war policy as patently Anglophile, while many Italians deeply resented the president's condemnation of Italy's attack on France ("The hand that held the dagger has plunged it into the back of its neighbor"). Cold War geopolitics only reinforced a sense shared by many Irish and Italians that liberals were elitists and, perhaps, bigots. These grievances would ultimately lead many Catholic Americans to embrace a "politics of revenge" against liberals and Democrats, to borrow a phrase from political scientist Samuel Lubell. That revenge was anticommunism.[21]

Also contributing to the intensification of Catholic anticommunism was the Soviet Union's repression of Christian churches in Eastern Europe. In midwestern cities like Chicago and Detroit, both home to large numbers of immigrants from behind the "iron curtain," a close political identification with eastern bloc countries probably accounted for a substantial part of the Catholic animus toward communism. This was less the case in New York City, where the vast majority of Catholics were Irish, Italian, or German in origin. Still, Catholic institutions encouraged New York parishioners to show solidarity with their aggrieved coreligionists in Europe.[22] Headlines from a six-week run of the *Brooklyn Tablet* indicated this acute sensitivity to Soviet religious oppression: "Mockery of Court Trial in Yugoslavia Is Described in Report on Bishop Cule's Case," "Statistics Show Success of Reds: But Church in Hungary Lives On," "Romania Church Life Strangled: Support of Communism Demanded; Nuns in Fear of Starvation," "Reds in Romania 'Retire' Bishops and Abolish See," "Hungarian Reds Jail More Clergy," and "Cardinal Prays; Reds Attack Him."[23]

Of the four general phenomena feeding Catholic anticommunism in the 1940s and 1950s—Catholic social theology, international conflicts, anti-establishment resentment, and the repression of Christianity in Eastern

Europe—theology is often given short shrift. Many Catholics firmly believed that their prayers and devotions contributed measurably to the battle against Soviet tyranny, an idea that Pope John XXIII drove home when he called members of Catholic sodalities the "shock troops of this army" against communism and credited them with the "salvation of souls through prayer, through vital action, and through the example of all the virtues." Using similar language, a leader of the New York State Ancient Order of Hibernians proclaimed a "fundamental struggle throughout the world between the forces of Christ and Communism."[24]

The marriage of religion and anticommunism was particularly evident in popular devotions that developed around "Our Lady of Fatima." Many Catholics believed that in 1917 the Blessed Virgin Mary appeared before three children in the Portuguese town of Fatima and said: "I come to ask the consecration of Russia to my Immaculate Heart. . . . If [Catholics] listen to my request, Russia will be converted, and there will be peace. If not, she will scatter her error through the world, provoking wars and persecution of the Church." The Blessed Mother's anticommunist prescription required that Catholics say the rosary each day for the conversion of Russia, and that on the first Saturday of five successive months they take Communion. Not all Catholics diligently followed these requirements, leading at least some to understand World War II and the Cold War as a result of their failure to heed the Blessed Mother's word.[25]

In the late 1940s Pope Pius XII encouraged popular devotions and pilgrimages to Fatima. Fulton Sheen, an American bishop and host of a popular television show in the 1950s, was so convinced of the authenticity of the story that he made ten trips to Fatima and thirty to Lourdes, the French town that was the site of the first modern-day Marian appearance in 1858. In 1950 a farmer's wife in Wisconsin reported seeing the Virgin Mary, who requested that she pray for Russia. Over 100,000 people from across the country trekked to her farm to await a second apparition. *Scapular* magazine, a popular Catholic periodical, enrolled a million American Catholics in its "Blue Army of Fatima." Members pledged to pray for the Soviet Union and keep "First Saturdays." Catholic intellectuals were no less effected than the rank-and-file. "Our Lady herself has told us at Fatima that 'we must pray the Rosary,'" explained clergy members at Notre Dame to their students. "She promised the conversion of Russia if we said the Rosary. Will any student belittle the Russian threat?"[26]

New York Catholics were every bit as fervent about Marian devotions as their coreligionists across the country. In November 1945 between 25,000 and 30,000 Catholics turned out spontaneously for an evening vigil near the Grand Concourse in the Bronx to witness nine-year-old Joseph Vitolo Jr. kneel at the spot where he claimed to have seen the Virgin Mary's apparition several days earlier. On this particular occasion, Mary's entreaty was apolitical: she asked simply that Joseph pray, with no particular mention of the Cold War.[27] But the episode revealed the deep religiosity that ran through New York's Irish and Italian communities, which manifested itself in a spiritual cosmology that viewed history and politics as inextricably bound up with everyday devotions.

Hence, in 1948 some 7,000 New Yorkers turned out to venerate a statue of Our Lady of Fatima at the Catholic Monastery Church of the Immaculate Conception in Jamaica, Queens. The following January, thousands of city Catholics attended devotions at St. Patrick's Cathedral, where Rev. Charles McManus ordered the continual recitation of the rosary from 1 P.M. until 7 P.M. in honor of Our Lady of Fatima. The event was intended to secure the release of Joseph Cardinal Mindszenty, the famed Hungarian bishop then imprisoned by the Soviet puppet state. In 1954, 20,000 people attended outdoor services at Fordham University for a recitation of the rosary and consecration to the Virgin Mary. There, they heard Cardinal Spellman declare that the miracles at Lourdes and Fatima were proof that the "century of Mary will prevail in history over the century of Marx."[28]

More dramatically, in October 1954 over 50,000 worshippers braved a cold autumn rain to attend a tribute to the Virgin Mary at the Polo Grounds. One thousand schoolgirls formed a human rosary that spanned the entire length of the field on which the New York Giants baseball team normally played to sellout crowds. Inside the rosary were reproductions of five shrines where the Virgin Mary was said to have made appearances, including Our Lady of Fatima. Participants heard Rev. Robert Gannon decry the "bewildered sophistication" and "empty, pointless paganism" of modern life and herald the "white-hot purity of Mary."[29]

It is impossible to know with any certainty whether, or to what extent, participants in Marian ceremonies accepted the church's official interpretation of such occasions. In his work on popular venerations of Saint Jude, historian Robert Orsi has found that the millions of Catholic women who offered prayers and devotions to the saint did so with diverse and often complex motivations that owed much to their individual efforts to reconcile religiosity with American identity. Orsi's study is a reminder that elite and popular actors often assign different meaning to the same events. Yet on one level, Marian venerations may very well have reinforced a popular worldview that regarded human actions as key components of a divine drama.[30]

If millions of ordinary Catholics would only follow "God's blueprint for permanent peace," Rev. Harry J. Wolff declared at a Mass at St. Patrick's Cathedral—if they heeded Mary's warning at Fatima "to do penance" and committed themselves to "prayer and sacrifice for the conversion of sinners and the return of people to God"—then the threat of world war could be averted. So intensely spiritual was Catholic cosmology that Wolff, a member of the cathedral staff, did not raise eyebrows when he repeated the popular myth that God caused the sun to revolve around the earth on 13 October 1917, in confirmation of the Blessed Mother's message to the three children at Fatima. The "scoffers, atheists, and cynically curious" who doubted this supernatural intervention only stood as proof that "in our enlightened century many so-called intellectual giants proved themselves to be spiritual pygmies by deliberately and scoffingly ignoring the message and challenge of Fatima." Wolff drove home the political implications of the miracle of 1917 when he reminded worshippers that "unless men repentantly turned toward God, godless communism would propagate its diabolical hatred through the scourge of war and enslavement of peoples. The history of the last twenty years certainly bears bloody testimony to the truth of Mary's predictions."[31]

When Italian and Irish New Yorkers joined the Blue Army of Fatima or participated in mass devotions, they were actors in a high political drama with divine origins and a divine script. In this sense, their understanding of the Cold War stood in sharp contrast to that of their mostly secular Jewish neighbors, who turned to the social sciences rather than God to understand and address the creeping influence of totalitarian ideology around the world.

Throughout the 1940s and 1950s, fear of communism pushed many Irish and Italian New Yorkers to the political right. This process first involved a rejection of anything resembling economic radicalism. In 1949 some 57,000 Catholic schoolchildren from Brooklyn marched down Flatbush Avenue to commemorate "Loyalty Day," a Catholic counter-holiday staged annually on May Day. There they heard Rev. Ralph J. Garvey reaffirm the community's emphasis on deference and obedience. "The security of American ideals rests in God," he announced, "God known, God respected, God obeyed." Ridiculing the competing May Day pageant staged by the left flank of organized labor, Garvey told the children that "right here on these streets . . . this morning we have seen something more than a demonstration of patriotic devotion. We have seen a challenge flung into the teeth of those who would destroy our American way of life and over-throw our American form of Government!"

As international tensions mounted in the early 1950s, American anti-communism grew more strident and less subtle. Garvey was encouraging Catholic schoolchildren to believe that patriotism came in one package, and that all opposing ideologies were inherently subversive. Ironically, Catholic spokespersons like Garvey were deft at appropriating the Left's anticapitalistic vernacular. Garvey warned the students that the May Day celebrants, "these propagandists of atheistic Communism . . .) would have us think of man as just so much mud in motion, as just so many soulless cogs in an economic machine." Such thinking was wrongheaded, he argued, because it held that "the soul as well as the body of man belongs to the all-powerful state and that human beings have no rights except those conceded for its own purposes by the police state." Rather than stake out a middle ground that rejected the presumed excesses of capitalism and communism alike, official Catholic spokespersons in the 1940s and 1950s zeroed in on the latter and all but ignored the former.[32]

In 1949 the *Brooklyn Tablet* conceded that "it would be . . . foolish to lay all of our economic ills at the door of the Reds." Industry also bore some of the blame for postwar labor strife. But communists had a "large and busy hand" in promoting the "series of crippling strikes and industrial tie-ups" that wracked American labor relations in the years immediately following World War II. The *Tablet*'s religion columnist believed that church officials had an obligation to remind their parishioners of the "duties of the employers and the employed" alike: "The employed should manifest towards their employees such sentiments as love, respect, service, obedience and honesty. They must also show a proper regard for the reputation and property of their employers. I wonder just how many workingmen realize these obligations or try to fulfill them."[33]

The church provided its working-class constituents with alternative expressions of labor solidarity. In 1951, eighty-eight parishes in the Diocese of Brooklyn, representing almost 30 percent of the total, staged special Labor Day celebrations. The diocese distributed 50,000 copies of the National Catholic Welfare Conference's statement on "social justice" and urged parish priests to draw special attention to the clause urging "recognition of our common responsibility to cooperate under God, establishing the rule of social justice in American economic life." The church unequivocally asserted that "working people . . . possess a God-given dignity" that no employer was entitled to violate, but its emphasis on cooperation and moderation contrasted sharply with the city's more combative labor movement.

At the same time, the church carefully proscribed non-Catholic forms of labor politics. Many Irish and Italian Catholics followed the church's lead and rejected New York's left-wing and liberal allies of organized labor, particularly the Liberal Party and ALP.[34] Catholic prelates like Cardinal Spellman, and church organs like the *Catholic News* and *Brooklyn Tablet*, regularly scored leading left-wing unionists as communists or fellow travelers and suffered minimal damage to the continued allegiance of their mostly working-class Catholic parishioners. Still, they often had to tread lightly in their dealings with organized labor. When Spellman broke the cemetery strike in 1949, he went to great lengths to emphasize that he was a supporter of unions, in principle. "I feel I am doing something for proper organized labor," he told followers. "Just because a union exists doesn't mean it is a good union. Because a strike is called doesn't mean it is a good strike. Several labor leaders have contacted me and confirmed my belief in this."[35]

The story of the Irish-dominated Transport Workers Union (TWU) is a case in point of the church's balancing act. From its inception in the early 1930s, the TWU withstood considerable opposition from Catholic Church officials, who used their sway with the rank-and-file to discredit the union's officers, many of whom were communists or fellow travelers. The TWU's 30,000 members consistently endorsed their left-wing officers out of personal loyalty and respect, but as Joshua Freeman has established, "The heavily Irish Catholic New York transit workers [had] always . . . been somewhat uncomfortable with the leftism of their leaders." In 1949, under intense pressure from the church and regular workers, TWU chief Mike Quill—probably a onetime party member himself—expelled communist officers and members. Similar purges, resulting in part from pressure among rank-and-file workers, saw such predominantly Catholic unions as the National Maritime Union and the United Electrical Workers cut off their left-leaning factions. These local developments were part of a national pattern. In 1949 the CIO expelled communist-led unions representing 900,000 workers. In New York, as in other parts of the country, the church assumed a leading role in proscribing anything but conservative trade unionism.[36]

Local politics intensified the aversion to liberalism that increasing numbers of Catholics came to exhibit at the polls. In New York City, more than in other parts of the country, communists and fellow travelers played a critical and lasting role in the development of liberal and left-wing politics after World War II. Popular Front–style politics persisted in fact, if not in name, well into the 1950s, despite the political ravages of McCarthyism. Freeman has found that, "while the defeat (and self-destruction)" of the Communist Party after 1949 "transformed working-class New York in numerous ways, much didn't change. The Communist Party itself all but disappeared . . . but onetime CP members and sympathizers, and the worldview they shared, continued to influence working-class New York for decades to come. . . . Nowhere did left-wing and left-leaning ex-Communists have more influence than in New York."[37]

Because one-time communists and fellow travelers enjoyed a strong position in New York's liberal-left coalition, many Irish and Italian Catholics proved consistently wary of liberal institutions and public figures. Irish and Italian voters largely refused the overtures of ALP and Liberal Party candidates, even though their unions were often strongly allied with both parties. They also demonstrated considerable skepticism toward Democratic candidates running for statewide and national office—notably, Herbert Lehman and Adlai Stevenson. Ironically, New York's "labor" candidates drew more support from the city's increasingly white-collar Jewish population than its highly unionized, working-class Italian and Irish neighborhoods.

The Catholic reaction to postwar liberalism was not abnormal. Between 1949 and 1954, most major American institutions—such as labor unions, universities, public schools, entertainment groups, publishing companies, and government services—effected a general purge of communists and those suspected of being communists. New York's Irish and Italian voters were no more enthusiastic in their endorsement of anticommunist politics than the country at-large. If anything, it was Jewish voters who were iconoclasts, given their high tolerance of the American Left. But in New York particularly, the survival of Popular Front politics made liberalism a less viable political option to many Catholics who considered themselves conservative on communism.

Ironically, this resistance to left-liberalism drove the Catholic Church and many of its Irish and Italian devotees to reject the city's most articulate and genuine proponents of civil rights. On one hand, Catholic doctrine was unambiguous: racism was a violation of Christian doctrine, since Christ resided in all human beings, irrespective of race, when they took the Eucharist. Cardinal Spellman took several opportunities to ratify this doctrine publicly, including a speech he delivered before 30,000 Catholics in 1945. He decried bigotry and celebrated American GIs who "may dislike one another's personalities, attitudes, beliefs, and actions, but nevertheless patriotism lifts them above disunion." The archbishop affirmed that "real Americans [fight] the spread of bigotry," a sentiment he reiterated in 1959, when he famously reminded the U.S. Civil Rights Commission that antidiscrimination "is what the Church has always and must always believe and teach."[38]

But in the 1940s and 1950s, rooting out communism was the central concern of the church and of many of its followers; this state of affairs precluded widespread cooperation with left-wing civil rights activists, many of whom were Jewish.[39] In the late 1940s New York City's strongest and most vocal opponents of American racism tended to be members of the ALP and Liberal Party, the former including backers of Henry Wallace's failed bid for the presidency in 1948. In the minds of many Irish and Italian Catholics, these individuals were communists or fellow travelers, and their advocacy of black rights was surely a cynical ploy to disrupt social harmony.

In 1948 Patrick Scanlan, the influential editor of the Brooklyn Tablet, assured readers that "much of the shouting about discrimination against one or another racial [or] religious group is deliberately instigated and encouraged by the Communists and others who seek to further their own ignoble ambitions by creating disunity and conflict." Scanlan beseeched Catholic citizens to "recognize the 'tolerance racket' as a snare"—a cheap ploy to "promot[e] distrust and hatred among neighbors." That year, as Wallace braved hostile and sometimes violent southern audiences to take his egalitarian message into the heartland of Jim Crow, the Tablet launched vicious attacks not only on the candidate and his supporters, but on such diverse organizations as the National Association for the Advancement of Colored People, the (New York) Jewish Welfare Board, and the AJCongress, whose cooperation with "Red-front groups" like the Youth for Wallace Committee greatly offended the Catholic officialdom.[40]

The Tablet attacked the Southern Conference for Human Welfare and its prominent supporters— Wallace, Melvyn Douglas, Harold Ickes, and Dorothy Parker, "big names and radical minds," all—and agreed with the House Committee on Un-American Activities (HUAC) that the group was "perhaps the most deviously camouflaged Communist front organization" in the nation. In warning Catholics that the Southern Conference "displayed consistent anti-American bias and pro-Soviet bias, despite professions . . . of love for America," the Tablet played directly into the hands of conservative southern Democrats, some of whom dominated HUAC. These staunch defenders of Jim Crow were heavily invested in discrediting the Southern Conference, whose leadership included early civil rights stalwarts like Virginia Durr and Clark Foreman, and whose primary activities included marshaling opposition to the poll tax, fighting antilabor legislation in southern legislatures, and publicizing brutal attacks against African Americans.[41]

Neither the Tablet nor its readership supported Jim Crow. In fact, Catholics consistently registered a more liberal position on race relations than other non-Jewish whites. National polls in 1947 revealed that 58 percent of Catholics supported the Interstate Commerce Commission's ban on segregated transportation, compared with 53 percent of northern Protestants and 67 percent of Jews. In 1957, 63 percent of Catholics expressed support for open housing and employment laws, compared with 57 percent of northern Protestants and 66 percent of Jews. Many devout Catholics instilled in their children a firm sense of racial and religious justice. "A bigot is a hater," writer Pete Hamill recalled his mother saying. "A bigot hates Catholics. A bigot hates Jews. A bigot hates colored people. It's no sin to be poor, she said. It is a sin to be a bigot. Don't ever be one of them."[42]

Conservative Catholic newspapers went to great lengths to avow support for civil rights. In 1949 the *Irish Echo* called "Jim Crowism the most repulsive of social and civil blandishments on [the] national escutcheon," an "ugly impairment of the rights and privileges guaranteed in the United States Constitution to all American citizens." Finding parallels between the plight of African Americans in the United States and Catholics in Ireland, the newspaper claimed that "in Ireland there is a counterpart to Jim Crowism . . . which lives and flourishes with the consent and support of the British Government[:] the subordinate puppet Parliament of Britain at Stormont [Castle]." Dean Acheson and the Democratic Party were not the only subjects fit for comparison to Great Britain. If in fact the *Echo* gave accurate voice to the concerns of conservative Irish Americans, it was not race liberalism that many Catholics opposed, but rather liberalism's apparent collusion with communism.[43]

Each summer over 1,000 black and white children attended integrated summer camps sponsored by the CYO and its parent, the New York Catholic Charities. The program's organizers "decided to test its sincere belief that among boys and girls, 14 years or younger, there is no natural race prejudice," explained the camp's director. "We have never had a fight at the camp over race." Between 1942 and 1957 over 20,000 children benefited from the camps.

The Brooklyn Catholic Youth Organization (BCYO) also won kudos from the diocese for its repeated attempts to force the American Bowling Congress to integrate its leagues. Catholic leaders emphasized the harm that racism did to the anticommunist cause. "The eyes of the world are turned to the United States," warned the BCYO's spokesperson, "to see if our principles of democracy are working in practice. Imperialism is a thing of the past. Will the millions of people in Africa, India, and China turn to a democratic form of government or to something else?"[44]

Clerics like Monsignor Raymond Campion told the Brooklyn Catholic Interracial Council that "the freedom we boast as every American's precious right and heritage is at this moment largely denied to our Negro fellow Americans." Campion lamented that Catholic activists dedicated inadequate effort to fighting communism by making democracy more attractive to black Americans.

> It has been estimated that there are over half a million graduates from Catholic colleges in this country. This is a tremendous potential force for leadership in applying Christian principles to our social problems. This great group certainly outnumbers the convinced Communists who are devoted to propagating hate, misery, and destruction. Yet the record shows Communists are more active and better organized for their destructive program of promoting human misery than are today's Catholics in leading us on the constructive way to a better social order and happier life.[45]

But the Catholic Church's war against racism took a second seat to its epic struggle with communism. In the 1940s and 1950s many of the strongest advocates of racial equality in New York were often tinged by past and present association with the Popular Front. Accordingly, the church often restricted itself to small battles, like its campaign to integrate indoor bowling and outdoor lawn tennis.

It was this ordering of priorities that informed the *Tablet*'s review of the 1948 presidential election: "two [additional] parties came into the field—the States Rights Party and the Progressive Party—the first launched to divide Mr. Truman's supporters and the second a project formulated by the Communists . . . to divide the whole nation." By the paper's estimation, Wallace posed a threat to national harmony; Strom Thurmond's candidacy, at the helm of an avowedly racist ticket, was a matter of political infighting.[46]

Likewise, though his staunch defense of Jim Crow clearly violated church doctrine, Rep. Martin Dies of Texas, a leading member of HUAC, earned praise in 1950 from the Diocese of Brooklyn, whose official newspaper announced on its front page that "time has confirmed his warning of [the] menace of Communism." When George Smathers unseated Sen. Claude Pepper in Florida's Democratic primary that same year, the *Tablet* cheered, claiming that "since the war, [Pepper] became a human microphone for Soviet Russia's cause." The Diocese of Brooklyn saluted the "people of Florida" for endorsing "a candidate . . . who stated he was against both Communism and Socialism," and it marveled that "labor leaders—not the average members—should champion a man whose pro-Soviet views" were well documented.[47]

Scanlan and his editorial staff ignored Pepper's long-standing defense of organized labor (clearly one reason he enjoyed backing among CIO leaders); they also made no mention of his support for federal anti–poll tax and antilynching legislation. Neither the *Tablet* nor the Diocese of Brooklyn opposed these measures. Quite to the contrary. But to the *Tablet*'s editorialists, Pepper's affiliation with Wallace overshadowed his consistent demonstration of political conscience, just as Smathers's uncompromising opposition to communism eclipsed his crude appeal to white supremacist sentiment during the Florida primary race. It seems likely that Brooklyn's diocesan newspaper spoke for those Catholic voters who disliked Jim Crow but hated Joe Stalin more.[48]

Certainly the position of the *Brooklyn Tablet* was not necessarily shared by all or most Irish and Italian New Yorkers. The paucity of Catholic primary sources makes it difficult to determine how pervasive Scanlan's opinion was in Catholic neighborhoods. But certain clues suggest that the weekly paper was not only influential, but also a useful gauge of the community's more conservative elements. The *Tablet* boasted a paid circulation of about 160,000 and was also required reading in all diocesan high schools. Its staunch anticommunist appeal probably reflected the more general culture of the Cold War church, whose pews were filled to peek capacity nearly every Sunday. As Jerry Della Femina later recalled, "There were no sermons to speak of. These were the salad days of 1947, 1948, and into the 1950s, the days of that hero of the Church, Senator Joseph McCarthy. McCarthyism was on its way and if we didn't heed the message, Godless Russia was going to swallow us up. Every Sunday we said a prayer for the conversion of Russia. . . . The priest was constantly sending out letters about atheists, communists, Godless atheists, Godless communists, and occasionally a socialist, although nobody could figure out the distinction."[49]

Pete Hamill later remembered that, although the red scare was somewhat understated at his high school—most likely a result of the "Jesuitical irony and skepticism [that] generally prevailed" there—it "dominated" his neighborhood. Even at school, one could always find palpable indicators of the church's position. "I do remember seeing a Catholic comic book that showed communist mobs attacking St. Patrick's Cathedral. And there was an extended discussion of a papal encyclical called *Atheistic Communism*. . . . In the *Daily News* [New York City's working-class newspaper, whose readership was heavily Catholic] there were frantic warnings about pinkos, fellow travelers, New Dealers, and liberals. And even in Regis [Hamill's school]

. . . I started to hear a lot of favorable talk about the junior senator from Wisconsin, Joseph McCarthy."

The defection of so large a portion of the city's Catholic electorate from the liberal bloc also suggests that the *Tablet* and the church may have spoken to, and for, many Irish and Italian New Yorkers who felt serious misgivings about postwar liberalism and the Democratic Party. Hamill recalled the mood at his high school in September 1950, when it seemed everyone had an older brother or acquaintance serving in Korea. "Almost everybody thought that communism had to be stopped. At the same time, they were attacking Truman and Acheson, blaming them for the war. I tried to make sense of this. If it was important to be fighting the communists, and Truman and Acheson were fighting them, why were they wrong?"[50]

Leading political figures also sensed a growing rift between liberalism and Catholicism—particularly among the Irish. In 1949 George Combs, a high-ranking Democratic Party operative in New York City, explained in a private interview that "Catholicism . . . has become nearly a state religion for the Irish. It's more than religious faith. It has become an expression of transplanted nationalism. Consequently, the Irish here are much more devoted and faithful to the Church and very much more militant in their attacks on anyone who seems to oppose it than are, for example, the Polish Catholics or the Italian Catholics." Combs revealed that many Irish voters opposed Democrat Herbert Lehman's bid for the U.S. Senate because he had sided with Eleanor Roosevelt in her very public confrontation in 1949 with Cardinal Spellman over federal aid to education. Roosevelt and Lehman opposed earmarking any funds for parochial school students, while Spellman and the Catholic hierarchy supported it. Irish voters seemed quick to avenge the church against perceived grievances from the left.

More surprisingly, Combs also confided that "a few [Irish Catholics], although this is not yet a substantial defection, are also against Mayor O'Dwyer," in part because of his association with Eleanor Roosevelt and Lehman, but primarily "because he has flirted with the left wing of the A.L.P." The incumbent mayor stood to lose "Irish and Catholic supporters [because of] his coquetry with the American Labor Party," under whose banner he ran in 1945 but not in 1949. "Years ago, here in New York," Combs explained, "the Irish and the Jewish people stayed together politically. . . . That's all gone. I think it's largely ascribable to the Fascist growth in Europe. So there is a dangerous, disheartening, and rather tragic cleavage now between our Irish friends and our Jewish friends—and I am afraid that is going to deepen as time goes on." Election returns from the late

1940s and early 1950s suggest that Italian voters, too, were defecting from the New Deal coalition in similar force.

Not all New York Catholics left the liberal fold. Speaking again of the Irish, Combs believed that

> the union and labor people have been trained in paths of very much more liberal, progressive thought than was true five, six, or ten years ago. The Roosevelt tradition, the Roosevelt philosophies, were inculcated in the laboring class of the Irish. . . . Generally, Irish labor is just about as progressive in its outlook as Jewish labor or any other element in the labor picture. When you begin going up the scale, however, into middle class Irish and more prosperous, you will not find that to be true. They are beginning to represent a somewhat reactionary point of view and vote substantially in accordance [with their] economic brackets and also tend to support those who are most strongly supported by the Church. So you have this very unfortunate cross-current and the thing may get exacerbated as time goes on.[51]

No polling data exist to verify or challenge Combs's suspicion that only middle-class Irish Catholics—and, by extension, Italian Catholics—left the Democratic fold. But his interview testifies to the growing rift within the Catholic community, whose conservative wing was on the ascendant in the 1940s and 1950s.

Aside from the *Tablet*'s pages, which featured weekly tributes to McCarthy and equally reflexive attacks on his enemies, scattered evidence abounds that Irish and Italian activists supported the Wisconsin senator. When a Senate Foreign Relations subcommittee headed by Maryland senator Millard Tydings denounced McCarthy in mid-1950, the Long Island Chapter of the Knights of Columbus, meeting in Brooklyn, jumped to his defense and demanded an investigation of Tydings.[52]

McCarthy's most famous endorsement by New York's Catholic establishment came in 1954, just after the "Army-McCarthy hearings," when the senator attended a special Mass at St. Patrick's Cathedral for the Holy Name Society of the New York City Police Department. Cardinal Spellman made a dramatic entrance at the ensuing Communion breakfast, where he clasped the senator's hand and beamed for the crowd. Later he told reporters that McCarthy was "against communism and he has done and is doing something about it. He is making America aware of the dangers of communism." Less high-profile events also point to the support McCarthy enjoyed from New York's Catholic establishment. In 1950 the Long Island Chapter of the Knights of Columbus excoriated Democratic senator Millard Tydings of Maryland for his recent denunciation of McCarthy's tactics. Four years later, with McCarthy's career on a virtual free fall, Harry Rapp, a columnist for the *Echo*, called McCarthy the "most important Red hunter in the country . . . we want 100 percent Americans who consider this country first." The Catholic Action Committee of St. Nicholas of Tollantine Parish in the Bronx pressed ahead with its local anticommunist crusade, persistent in its support of McCarthy well into the late 1950s.[53]

Even after McCarthy's career met an inglorious end in the mid-1950s, the Catholic Church continued to honor the Wisconsin senator annually with a Mass at St. Patrick's. When McCarthy died in 1957, the *Irish Echo* saluted him as "a great American" in its weekly editorial. "He showed unqualified devotion to his country by fearlessly exposing those who would subvert the American way of life to the political and economic positions emanating from the Red Russian regime," reported the *Echo*. "The Senator became the pray of critics who had less conscience than duplicity in their bones." Occurring in the same decade as the deaths of Sen. Pat McCarran and Sen. Robert Taft, McCarthy's passing led the paper's editors to believe that "God must be Angry . . . Almighty God must have lost his patience with the U.S.A."[54] A special memorial Mass at St. Patrick's drew a capacity crowd of 2,000 mourners, including leading representatives of the CWV, the New York State Board of the Ancient Order of Hibernians, the Knights of Columbus, and the Irish Counties Association.[55]

Unlike their Catholic institutional counterparts, New York's organized Jewish community seemed less concerned by the specter of communism than by perceived threats to free speech and discourse. Certainly this was true of the Brooklyn Jewish Youth Committee (BJYC), an umbrella group representing 20,000 young Jewish adults who belonged to a variety of religious and secular Jewish groups in Brooklyn. Between 1947 and 1949, the BJYC struggled over the membership application of the Jewish People's Fraternal Order (JPFO). The JPFO was a national affiliate of the International Workers Order, a fraternal organization that the U.S. government had designated a communist front shortly after World War II. The BJYC's constitution excluded all partisan organizations and stipulated that constituent groups have an expressly "Jewish" program. Delegates hotly debated whether the JPFO should be disqualified on either count, and while they acknowledged that "some of the leaders of the Jewish Peoples Fraternal Order are reputedly members of the Communist Party," they affirmed that this fact "would be no grounds for rejection unless their program indicated a similar conviction for the entire group and active participation in a political party program." A special subcommittee reported back to the

BJYC's executive committee that "much of the program of the J.P.F.O. is on a positive line. . . . The problems we must face at this time are: whether or not the J.P.F.O. is primarily a political group and as an integral part of a non-Jewish organization, is the J.P.F.O. eligible for membership."

Ultimately, the executive committee voted 13 to 12, with one abstention, to favor membership for the JPFO, a recommendation that the BJYC Annual Meeting rejected by a more decisive vote of 33 to 24. The same delegates also denied membership to Betar, a youth affiliate of the right-wing Revisionist Zionism movement in Israel. Notably, the BJYC's adult advisory committee observed that in the matter of the JPFO's membership application, "the people who were in favor of acceptance felt that [the BJYC] was being influenced by current hysteria. On the other hand, the members who were in favor of rejecting this organization felt that . . . there had been no red-baiting and that the Executive Committee was not influenced by hysteria; and that the JPFO was not a Jewish organization." If on no other point, the BJYC's delegates agreed that prospective member organizations should be judged exclusively on their dedication to Jewish programming and their disavowal of partisan politics. This position was wholly consistent with the community's aggressive acceptance of political pluralism and intellectual freedom.

Even those BJYC delegates who voted against the JPFO felt obliged to establish that they were not opposed to working with individual communists, or with members of a group that might include communists. Not so the Catholic *Brooklyn Tablet*, which dismissed as "sheer nonsense" the idea that "there is a rank injustice in 'guilt by association.' . . . The old proverb that a man is known by the company he keeps is founded in truth and common sense."[56] Viewing the world as an organic and hierarchical community, many Catholics naturally believed that one's associates were a good indication of one's character and affiliations.

Events like the Peekskill riot in 1949 were in many respects homegrown affairs. Because the marriage of left-wing and liberal politics endured longer in metropolitan New York than in the country at large, the reactionary posture of many Irish and Italian Catholics may have been an exceptional case. Put otherwise, the very real and lasting political relationship between liberals and leftists may have pushed many New York Catholics further to the right than their coreligionists in other cities, where the Popular Front suffered a more decisive defeat after 1949.[57]

Another side effect of New York's uncommon political culture—one brought into equally sharp relief by the Peekskill affair—was the sometimes unholy marriage between anticommunism and anti-Semitism. In a city whose Jewish population leaned decidedly toward the left, it is little wonder that numerous elements on the Catholic Right veered close to painting all the city's Jewish residents red and unpatriotic.

In 1948 the Knights of Columbus issued an anticommunist tract that began with the story of a movie magnate "who had skyrocketed from a pants-pressing emporium to control of a mammoth picture-producing corporation." The education-starved mogul naturally falls prey to a slick communist intellectual, who flashes about "big woids" and slogans like "materialistic interpretation of history," "economic determinism," "bourgeois morality," and "the Iron Law of wages." The rest of the booklet was dedicated to explaining and exposing communist argot. The opening story line seems to have been merely a gratuitous jab at immigrant Jews.[58]

In 1950 the Nassau County (Long Island) Council of Catholic Workmen met at Holy Name of Mary Church to hear a lecture on the communist threat. Audience members learned that "there are about 500 Communists teaching in New York City schools now" and that the city was host to "55,000 party members" and "an estimated 500,000 fellow-travelers who are willing to go along with Communist causes." Neither charge was aimed explicitly at Jews, but it was little secret that public schoolteachers and leading left-wing unions (the TWU excepted) were overwhelmingly Jewish. Along similar lines, the CWV of New York denounced the New York Teacher's Union as communist controlled, taking aim at a labor organization whose composition was almost entirely Jewish.

More pointedly, in 1947 Archbishop J. Francis A. McIntyre announced that the Archdiocese of New York was squarely opposed to the Austin-Mahoney Bill, then under consideration in the New York State Legislature. With Jewish groups providing some of its strongest backing, Austin-Mahoney proposed banning racial and religious discrimination in both private and public schools. The archdiocese opposed the bill primarily because it feared inordinate state police powers, but for good measure it denounced the proposed law as "formed after a Communistic pattern . . . it will permit further encroachments on the parental function of education. That is what we mean by the infiltration of Communist ideas."[59] The archdiocese's opposition to Austin-Mahoney demonstrated the increasing tendency of Catholic officials to characterize their political opponents—who were often Jewish—as communists. The end result was that these Catholic leaders made red-baiting Jews something of a habit.

Whereas anti-Semitism was a marginal opinion in Catholic politics, on the other side of the spectrum was a sizable, politically effective minority of

Irish and Italian voters in the 1940s and 1950s who remained committed to the Democratic Party or continued to ally themselves with left-wing and liberal labor unions. In the 1950s over 1 million New Yorkers were dues-paying union members, a large portion of whom were Irish and Italian Catholics. Many of their unions—like the International Ladies Garment Workers Union, the International Brotherhood of Electrical Workers, the United Electrical Workers, and the American Federal of State, County, and Municipal Employees—were deeply involved with the ALP and Liberal Party. Along with other, more moderate and conservative craft unions, these organizations helped make New York City a true labor town. Workers in New York averaged fewer hours per week than the national average, earned higher wages than their counterparts in unorganized states and cities, and, through their unions, compelled the municipal government to enact a sweeping array of measures that provided access to hospital care, medical checkups, middle-class housing, and free university education to working-class residents. However conservative their rhetoric and ideology were at times, Italian and Irish voters overwhelmingly supported candidates who pledged to sustain the city's informal labor compact. In this sense, interest politics often balanced or outweighed ideas.[60]

In other cases, sizable numbers of Irish and Italian New Yorkers broke politically with their ethnic communities over both ideology and substance, revealing persistent ideological pluralism within the Catholic community. Since its inception in the early 1930s, the TWU drew its leadership, and about half of its membership, from a generation of Irish immigrants who came to the United States in the 1910s and 1920s.[61] Veterans of the struggle for Irish independence, many TWU figures, like president Mike Quill, had belonged to the Irish Republican Army (IRA) and seen service in the guerrilla war against British occupying troops. In the United States they held to their faith in radical activism; some among their ranks also continued to harbor serious anticlerical leanings as a result of the church's opposition to the IRA.

Ignored or opposed by conservative Irish institutions like the Society of the Friendly Sons of Saint Patrick, the Ancient Order of Hibernians, and the Knights of Columbus, the TWU enjoyed critical support from the Communist Party. In return, many union leaders adopted the party's social platform and continued, even after their split with the party in 1949, to steer Catholic transport workers toward the left. Most rank-and-file members of the TWU were both practicing Catholics and supporters of the ALP and Liberal Party well into the 1960s. They moved easily between the radical labor milieu and the more conservative, Irish immigrant subculture. Their example points not only to the diversity of opinion in New York's Catholic community, but also to the flexibility of conservative Catholics who may not have admired Quill's politics but who nevertheless invited him to serve as master of ceremonies at Hibernian lodge dinners or as grand marshal in the annual Saint Patrick's Day parade.[62]

Another prominent Catholic politico was Vito Marcantonio, the radical congressman from the working-class neighborhood of Italian East Harlem. Throughout his long congressional career (1935–37, 1939–51), the church excoriated Marcantonio with unusual fervor. Although "Marc" never actually joined the Communist Party, he toed its line consistently on the House floor. In foreign affairs this stance translated to an agonizing series of policy flip-flops: voting against war preparedness between 1939 and mid-1941; vigorously supporting armament and militarism after Hitler's invasion of the Soviet Union in June 1941; and then, opposing Harry Truman's containment policies in the late 1940s.

Like other communists and fellow travelers, Marcantonio also championed a broad civil rights agenda. In the late 1930s he served as chairman of the International Labor Defense—the Communist Party's legal affiliate, which provided high-profile assistance to the Scottsboro Boys in Alabama— and during World War II he emerged as the most outspoken congressional proponent of a permanent Fair Employment Practices Committee and anti-lynching laws. In the late 1940s he even refused to support Rep. Graham Barden's bill providing federal aid to public education, principally because it "abett[ed] the . . . perpetuation of Jim Crow and segregated school systems." (The Catholic Church also opposed the Barden Bill, but its opposition was aimed at the legislation's prohibition of aid to parochial schools and more or less ignored the race question.)[63]

No matter how intensely Catholic elites in New York denounced Marcantonio, his constituents continued to return him to Washington. His biographer has concluded that "Italian Harlem knew Marcantonio's left-wing political beliefs and associations." They voted for him anyway, even as they turned to more conservative candidates in other electoral contests. On one level, Marcantonio championed a broad agenda that many working-class Italians favored—tenants' rights, rent control laws, low subway fares, the right to bargain collectively, an expansion of Social Security. But "more impressive" to Italian Harlem "was Marcantonio's conformity in most major ways to its lifestyle." He never moved more than ten blocks from his boyhood home in East Harlem. He shared the community's folkways, values, and mores.

When Marcantonio died in 1954 at the age of 51, Cardinal Spellman denied him a Catholic burial Mass, but tens of thousands of his constituents defied the archbishop and filed through a small Harlem funeral home to pay their last respects. Neither the church nor anticommunist political figures enjoyed anything approximating complete control over the Italian community.[64]

Still, by the late 1950s Italian Harlem was turning rightward, as were many Irish neighborhoods. In the fall of 1960 political observers were astonished to learn that the Catholic vote was very much up for grabs, notwithstanding the presence of John F. Kennedy—a third-generation Irish American—on the Democratic presidential ticket. "If Jack Kennedy thinks he has the Catholic vote in his back pocket," said an Irish Catholic political activist from the Bronx, "he's wrong." A Catholic priest told reporters, "There are a good many of the clergy who would rather not vote for Kennedy," while a Catholic advertising executive confessed, "I just don't know what I'll do. I want to vote for Nixon . . . but if the Protestants keep kicking my church around, I may change."

In a series of interviews with city Catholics, the *New York Times* found that most shared a deep concern about "communism, both at home and abroad —with most thinking the Republicans are better at opposing it than the Democrats." Explained a Catholic state assemblyman: "Nixon's kitchen debate with Khrushchev, the Hiss case, Lodge in the United Nations, the way the Democrats attacked Senator McCarthy, the talk about recognizing China—they all add up to a picture of Republicans who are tough on Communists and Democrats who are soft."

Though Kennedy claimed unimpeachable anticommunist credentials, most of the Catholic voters who spoke with the *New York Times* viewed him as no more credible on the issue than the rest of his party. Some of them mentioned Kennedy's offhand comment that "whoever was elected President by the Democratic party would ask Governor [Adlai] Stevenson to serve as Secretary of State." A Catholic Democrat active in party affairs noted that Stevenson, a two-time Democratic presidential nominee and outspoken internationalist, "might be good for some Jewish votes, but it isn't going to help us with the Catholics." It was an observation confirmed by a city Catholic who remarked, "Why that effete, incompetent intellectual. I voted twice against him, and if you think I'd vote for anyone who would make him Secretary of State, you're crazy."

Possibly more damning, still, was the fact that some city Catholics doubted whether Kennedy was sufficiently ethnic. Far too rich to be lace-curtain Irish, and certainly not working-class Irish, Kennedy struck more than a few New York voters as inauthentic. "What kind of Catholic is he?" asked an indignant office worker. "He never went to a Catholic school in his life."[65]

6 Race

In December 1966 the liberal Catholic magazine *Commonweal* announced that white "backlash" had come to Brooklyn. Only a month before, New York City voters had approved a binding referendum that eliminated the Civilian Complaint Review Board, a commission established by Mayor John Lindsay to hear official charges of police misconduct. In no borough were the results more lopsided than in Brooklyn, where working-class citizens plainly rejected the board.

"It would be wrong to dismiss the vote on November 8th . . . as a local aberration in a city characterized by George Wallace as home of the 'Communist-Socialist-Beatnik Conspiracy,'" explained writer James J. Graham. "The size of the anti-Board tally, especially among normally liberal Jewish voters, and on an issue much less sensitive than open housing, for instance, dramatically demonstrated that whites in big cities are ready to call a halt to Negro advances too close to home." The editorial page of the *Nation* agreed, informing its readers that, "like Proteus, the white backlash has many shapes. One is the measure on the New York City ballot giving the voters the opportunity to abolish the Civilian Review Board." Obliterating the board signaled nothing less than "a rebuke to civil rights groups and a setback for the whole civil rights movement."[1]

New York City's review board controversy came three years after President Kennedy began receiving scattered reports from Democratic Party operatives of a certain "back-lash" brewing in northern cities against his proposed civil rights initiative. (This was probably when the term first entered America's political lexicon.) National opinion surveys in mid-1963 revealed that 41 percent of all voters felt the president was moving "too fast" on integration; 42 percent opposed Kennedy's legislative package, the substance of which President Lyndon Johnson ultimately signed into law a year later as the Civil Rights Act of 1964. Six months before Kennedy's assassination, White House insiders believed that the administration's new push for civil rights had cost the Democratic Party 4.5 million white voters.

These estimates led even the president to worry: "This issue could cost me the election," he told civil rights leaders.[2]

Three years later, in the wake of a curiously strong showing by Alabama governor George Wallace in several northern presidential primaries, liberals began to worry that working-class racism might rend the fabric of the celebrated New Deal coalition. The same day that New Yorkers went to the polls to defeat the Civilian Review Board, a former B-grade actor named Ronald Reagan trounced incumbent governor Edmund "Pat" Brown in California's gubernatorial election. Brown's defeat owed largely to the defection of conservative Democrats allied with Los Angeles's law-and-order mayor, Sam Yorty. Frightened by the Watts riot of 1965 and embittered by Brown's support of open housing policies, these voters turned to Reagan, whose campaign appealed subtly but unquestionably to their racial fears.

Thus it seemed to the *Nation* that events on each coast were of a piece. A week before the election, its editorial page worried that "even a symbolic victory for the backlash in cosmopolitan New York City would contribute to the growing sentiment nationally, the more so if Ronald Reagan should win the gubernatorial election in California. For the results would be interpreted as meaning that backlash had prevailed in the country's two largest states." Indeed, by the end of the decade, New York City's white ethnics— both Jews and Catholics—would earn a reputation for reaction and backlash that rivaled even their counterparts in Boston, Detroit, and Los Angeles. The police referendum was widely regarded as the opening volley in a white campaign to roll back mounting civil rights advances.[3]

Volumes have been written about the hazy phenomenon known popularly as white backlash. Initially, liberal scholars and writers rebuked working-class whites for their intransigent opposition to busing, affirmative action, and, on occasion, the antiwar movement. These observers tended to decry any political position not in accordance with their own as patently racist and reactionary. Thus, opponents of court-mandated busing in Boston were no better than members of the White Citizens Council in Mississippi, Jewish teachers in New York betrayed their group's self-serving hypocrisy when they clashed with black community leaders over decentralized school districting, and white Democrats who defected to the Republican Party were using crime and civil unrest as a convenient mask for their own racism and parochialism.[4]

It was not long before public intellectuals began to acknowledge that backlash came in several varieties, and that considerable economic and social pressures were indeed making life increasingly difficult for the "hardhats" and "ethnics" who were abandoning the liberal creed. Following the 1968 elections, when Wallace and Richard Nixon pried away enough former Democrats, North and South, to deny Hubert Humphrey the presidency, Garry Wills advised readers that the "desire for 'law and order' is nothing so simple as a code word for racism; it is a cry, as things begin to break up, for stability, for stopping history in mid-dissolution. Hammer the structure back together; anchor it down; bring nails and bolts and clamps to keep it from collapsing. There is a slide of things—a queasy seasickness."[5]

Similar accounts followed. If scholars were not sympathetic to backlash voters, they were at least empathetic. Many pointed out that urban crime rates had in fact skyrocketed in the mid-1960s, and that backlash voters were probably not exaggerating when they complained of a rise in random muggings and rapes. While welfare rolls swelled between 1965 and 1970— and with them, well-published cases of welfare fraud—blue-collar workers saw the combined effects of hyperinflation and "bracket creep" in taxes eat away at their incomes and savings. Moreover, there was a certain hypocrisy to middle-class liberalism. Many of the white (and black) parents who opposed Judge Arthur Garrity's busing order in Boston were truly concerned that their children might have to endure long commutes and violent conditions. They resented suburban liberals who sent their children to lily-white schools—schools that enjoyed immunity from cross-district busing arrangements with the inner city, by virtue of the Supreme Court's decision in *Milliken v. Bradley* (1974). These same working-class voters watched with indignation as college-educated liberals denigrated the American war effort in Vietnam, a conflict that many of the young, antiwar protesters avoided through the student deferment system.[6]

Recent scholars have taken a longer view of the subject and determined that backlash long predated the culture wars over affirmative action and busing in the late 1960s. As early as the first decades of the twentieth century, working-class whites in cities like Detroit and Chicago employed a variety of legal and extralegal means to prevent African Americans from climbing the social ladder to middle-class comfort and respectability. Driving these struggles were debates over neighborhood integration and, somewhat less frequently, equal opportunity in the workplace. Much of this new scholarship once again situates race consciousness at the center of white backlash.[7]

The New Deal welfare state expanded opportunities for second-generation white ethnics, helping to increase and stabilize industrial wages and allow more workers to realize the dreams of home ownership and college education for their children. But, as Gary Gerstle has explained, "discrimi-natory federal housing policies had led white homeowners to believe that they had a right to live in racially exclusive neighborhoods. The many southern and eastern European ethnics in the ranks of white homeowners had only recently been accepted as 'white' and were determined to protect that skin privilege at all costs."[8]

New York departs somewhat from this pattern. Since most New Yorkers rented their homes or apartments, residential integration—though often a point of serious contention—was a less combustible issue than in cities where high rates of home ownership raised the economic and emotional stakes for white ethnic voters. Moreover, for reasons owing largely to New York's historic diversity and cosmopolitan culture, white voters proved more sympathetic to the civil rights movement, and to African Americans generally, than did whites in other northern cities. Still, as the 1960s wore on, soaring crime rates and urban blight fostered a growing ambivalence—even hostility—toward integration on the part of many Jews and Catholics. Critically, though they arrived at the same skeptical position on civil rights and integration by the late 1960s, Jews and Catholics continued to embrace different political agendas and ideals.

Public opinion surveys reveal two important details about New York race relations in the late 1950s and 1960s. First, most white New Yorkers did not think or care very much about the civil rights move-ment until the mid-1960s. And second, events in the mid-1960s in-spired a widespread skepticism of integration on the part of many white voters, Jewish and Catholic alike. Nevertheless, white New Yorkers main-tained a cosmopolitan outlook on race relations even while they soured on race liberalism. They were far more tolerant of everyday interactions with black Americans, and far less likely to view citizenship in racial terms, than their white counterparts throughout the North.

In a private study conducted for Mayor Robert Wagner in 1959, pollster Louis Harris listed "minority and race problems" as the tenth-most-important issue in municipal politics out a total list of fourteen problems. Taxes, the rental market, schools, unemployment, the subways, welfare fraud, traffic and parking, juvenile delinquency, and street and road repairs were all of greater concern to the public than race relations. "In 1957 we labeled [minority and race problems] 'important but minor' and repeat the phrase now," Harris told Wagner. Even most black New Yorkers had other worries on their minds. Only 20 percent named race relations among the top three concerns facing the city.[9]

When Harris polled city Democrats two years later, in 1961, civil rights still figured low on their priority list. While 56 percent of the sample voluntarily named "crime and law enforcement" as "issues of concern," only 9 percent mentioned race relations. A mere 5 percent of Jewish and Italian respondents volunteered a favorable position on integration. Even black Democrats worried more about other issues. When asked to identify the most urgent problems facing New York, 45 percent said crime, 62 percent said the housing crunch, and 39 percent said the "economic bite," while only 21 percent said "integration." The results did not suggest that New Yorkers opposed racial integration but that they did not count it among their top political priorities.[10]

There are two explanations for the seeming indifference of most New Yorkers, black and white, to the very issue that would soon occupy center stage in local and national politics. First, although the civil rights movement earned unprecedented media attention in the mid-1950s—the combined effect of the Supreme Court's decision in *Brown v. Board of Education* (1954), Emmett Till's murder in Mississippi (1955), and the Montgomery bus boycott (1955–56)—the final years of the decade saw no comparably newsworthy events.[11] It was not until the early 1960s, when young students in the South began ratcheting up pressure on the white establishment, that newspapers and television networks restored attention to the black struggle for equality. New York was no exception to the rule.

Second, relative to other places, New York offered African Americans a fair amount of social and political equality. Black New Yorkers faced no barriers at polling places, and as their numbers increased, so did their clout in local and national government. By the 1950s it was standard practice among city Democrats to nominate a black candidate for Manhattan Borough president; blacks served on the city council and in the state legislature; and every two years, Harlem voters sent the fiery minister Adam Clayton Powell Jr. back to the U.S. House of Representatives, where he ultimately served as chairman of the Committee on Education and Labor.

Black New Yorkers enjoyed full access to subways and buses, stores, restaurants, and other places of public convenience. The city university system was fully integrated, and in 1948 the state passed and began strictly enforcing the Fair Educational Practices Law, which forbade racial or religious exclusion in nonsectarian private universities and colleges. Since few New Yorkers of any race owned their own dwellings, discriminatory banking and real estate practices posed a less visible and immediate problem than in cities like Detroit and Chicago, where most whites owned their own homes and fought hard to keep their neighborhoods lily-white.

New York had not always stood out as a relative bastion of racial inclusion. The explosion of the city's black population—from 6 percent of all residents in 1940 to 20 percent by the late 1960s—forced New Yorkers to confront longstanding arrangements that had gone unquestioned for decades.[12] Though New York had passed a comprehensive civil rights law in 1872—a rare statute that prohibited segregation or discrimination in places of public accommodation—the act went largely without enforcement until the 1940s, when rising sensitivity to the injustice of racial and religious bigotry fueled a series of high-profile cases that pressed the city government into action. With prosecutors more likely to bring criminal charges and ordinary black citizens emboldened to file civil suits against noncompliant companies, it became increasingly expensive for businesses to afford the luxury of a lily-white clientele.

When the Hotel Knickerbocker was forced to pay a $100 fine to the city and $250 in civil damages—roughly equivalent to $3,600 in current dollars—for refusing to accommodate William Bowman, a black organizer for the United Auto Workers, it abandoned its discriminatory policies. For smaller businesses like O'Gara's Bar and Grill in East Harlem, the cost of telling black customers "we don't serve Africans here"—$300 in court-imposed fines—was steep. The same was true of a barber shop that refused service to Linwood Carrington ($110 in civil court fines) and the apartment building that would not permit Claude Marchant access to its elevator. In 1949 a local civil rights group headed by Telford Taylor, the former chief prosecutor in the Nuremberg war crimes trials, surveyed the East Side of Manhattan—from 34th Street to 59th Street—and found that 42 percent of restaurants discriminated against black customers. Two years later, in the face of an all-out legal assault, that number dropped to just 16 percent.[13]

This is not to say that rampant, institutionalized inequality did not persist into the 1960s. New York's neighborhoods—and, as a result, its schools—were deeply segregated. Black New Yorkers faced endless barriers to fair and decent rental housing, the highest-paying industrial jobs were mostly inaccessible to minority workers, and police brutality against African Americans and Puerto Ricans became an ever more volatile issue as the 1950s wore on. But prior to the civil rights revolution of the mid-1960s, black and white New Yorkers appear to have focused on these issues as discrete problems. For the 1 million black southerners who relocated to New York in the 1950s, Harlem and Bedford-Stuyvesant were not the Garden of Eden, but they offered a vast improvement over Jim Crow.

By 1963 race relations appeared more prominently on New York's political radar screen. In a survey conducted in Manhattan's 8th Assembly District a month prior to President Kennedy's assassination, pollster Oliver Quayle found that 71 percent of all likely voters believed "Negroes should have more equality in New York"; only 1 percent answered that blacks should enjoy "less equality." Turning to national politics, a resounding 93 percent of likely voters supported Kennedy's proposed civil rights package, including its controversial component section barring segregation in places of public accommodation.

The 8th Assembly District was almost as diverse as the city. Although situated within the famous "silk stocking" congressional district, whose wealthy voters routinely sent liberal Republicans like John Lindsay to Congress, the area also included large numbers of Irish, Italian, and German Catholics and Jews—some of them well off, but many of them working-class or middle-class. Quayle confessed that he was baffled by the neighborhood's firm commitment to civil rights, a sentiment that seemed to cut across ethnic and political boundaries. "The 8th A.D. of New York has shown the most 'decent' attitude on the race question we have found in some 15 states since the outbreak of the Negro Revolution of 1963," he wrote. "Whether voters are Republican or Democratic they are for integration."[14]

Five years after Quayle conducted his poll, white attitudes toward the civil rights movement changed drastically. By 1968 most of the city's white ethnic voters believed that the march toward black equality was moving "too fast," an opinion shared by 59 percent of Jewish and Irish respondents and 62 percent of Italians. Only 7 or 8 percent of each group felt that the civil rights revolution was proceeding "too slow." Why this sudden reversal?[15]

For many working-class people, New York became a difficult place to live in the 1960s. At the same time the city's manufacturing sector was experiencing a long-term decline, hundreds of thousands of nonwhite migrants arrived by plane from Puerto Rico and by bus and rail from the rural South. In conjunction with a housing market that systematically discriminated against people of color, these economic and demographic transitions created vast pockets of urban blight in northern Manhattan and north-central Brooklyn. The subsequent escalation of violent crime rates, welfare dependency, and neighborhood decay robbed white New Yorkers of their sense of personal safety and stability. Black and Puerto Rican newcomers had it far worse. They enjoyed fewer opportunities for upward mobility than white immigrants who preceded them. But as the 1960s wore on, fewer white ethnics were able to appreciate the complicated dynamics driving the black ghetto's growth.

In the decades immediately following World War II, New York City's industrial base experienced a slow but steady decline, as firms relocated to nearby suburbs or to other states where unions were weaker and wage scales lower. Gotham's loss of industrial jobs was due partly to federal policies that favored the Sunbelt over the Rustbelt in the awarding of defense and research contracts. Generous government subsidies that encouraged the development of green-field sites, and the natural, climatic draw of coastal towns in Florida and California, also helped effect a swift reorientation of national resources from north to south, and from city to suburb. In the 1950s alone, the South's share of defense spending doubled, while California saw its portion of defense contracting jump from 13.2 percent in 1951 to 21.4 percent in 1958. At the same time, the South's inflexible resistance to organized labor made it a haven for expanding businesses that preferred right-to-work states over AFL-CIO strongholds like New York, Michigan, and Pennsylvania. Such were the motivations behind American Safety Razor's decision in 1954 to move its plant—and with it, 1,400 skilled jobs—from Brooklyn to Virginia.[16]

Federal defense spending and union-busting accounted for only part of New York's economic restructuring. Because its land mass was relatively small, New York City's capacity for industrial expansion was limited. Companies that sought to expand their operations found that Gotham was lacking modernized roads and rail connections, which resulted in higher shipping costs.[17]

In some cases, industrial workers also found their jobs made obsolete by virtue of mechanical innovation. New York's longshoremen are a case in point. At its height in 1944, the Brooklyn Naval Yard employed 71,000 workers, who were involved in every aspect of transporting, packing, and moving millions of tons of cargo each month. By 1965 less than 7,000 workers remained. The introduction of commercial jet carriers after World War II made cargo ships increasingly outmoded, and Brooklyn's antiquated docks and rail lines were inadequate for new methods of shipping (like containerization, a process by which boxes of freight were packed in large metal containers and then loaded and unloaded by crane). Once a mainstay of New York's urban economy, the city's waterfront subculture disappeared almost overnight. Its decline was one chapter in the story of postwar New York's economic shake-up. In 1946, 41 percent of Gotham's labor force worked at blue-collar jobs. By 1970 that figure had declined to 29 percent, nearly matched by the 27 percent of New York workers who held secretarial and clerical jobs.[18]

New York's industrial decline coincidentally overlapped with the migration of several million black southerners to points north in the decades following World War II. In the postwar years, the city's African American population skyrocketed, from 460,000 in 1940 to almost 1.7 million in 1970. Altogether, black New Yorkers boosted their share of the city's population from 6 percent to 21 percent.[19]

The convergence of these demographic and economic forces did not bode well for black employment, but it was not the sole, or even the primary, cause of rampant poverty in the city's African American neighborhoods. Long before black in-migration picked up speed, organized labor had cooperated effectively with employers to keep all but the least desirable jobs lily-white. In 1942 African Americans accounted for a mere 0.4 percent of the 60,000 Brooklyn dockworkers employed in well-salaried shipbuilding and yard jobs. In 1950 blacks comprised only 7,530 (or 1.5 percent) of the nation's 496,320 skilled machinists, 34,860 (3.9 percent) of its 898,140 unionized carpenters, and 3,090 (1.0 percent) of its 302,340 trained electricians. By extension, the number of skilled black workers in New York was negligible.

Because New York was a labor town, and because AFL-CIO locals were thoroughly segregated, black migrants to Gotham would have faced a tough labor market even in regular times. But the city's steady loss of skilled and semiskilled jobs stiffened competition and further denied black New Yorkers access to the same well-paying, industrial employment that helped earlier immigrants climb their way to middle-class status and comfort. Without this economic ladder, black migrants clustered in low-paying service jobs—hospital orderlies and home health care workers, for instance—or found themselves excluded from the workforce entirely. In 1961 the citywide unemployment rate was 5 percent, but for African Americans it hovered around 10 percent. In those few industries that minority workers actually managed to penetrate (like the needle trades), interregional competition forced unions to bargain down wage levels and benefits in order to discourage factories from relocating to other states.

The result of these structural dilemmas was a growing income gap between the city's old and new residents. In 1960 the average New Yorker earned $6,091 annually, while the average nonwhite New Yorker earned only $4,437. The median income for black workers in the New York metropolitan area was only 70 percent of the corresponding median for white workers. The income gap between black and white workers in New York was more pronounced than in other cities like Detroit and Chicago, where industrial unions in the automobile, steel, and meatpacking industries effected something closer to wage parity for workers of different races. At the same time, black New Yorkers were largely immune in the late 1960s and 1970s to the aftershock of major layoffs in the industrial sectors. As troubling as the unemployment rate for blacks may have been in New York (10 percent in 1961), it paled in comparison to corresponding figures in Chicago (17 percent), Cleveland (20 percent), and Detroit (39 percent).[20]

Widespread housing discrimination worked to compound the effects of New York's segregated economy, but it did so in a fashion that departed from patterns established in other northern cities. Throughout the 1950s and 1960s, fewer than 20 percent of dwellings in New York were owner occupied; the vast majority of white and black New Yorkers rented their houses or apartments. The absence of widespread home ownership did not suggest anything approximating equality in the rental market, however. In 1948 the U.S. Supreme Court declared restrictive covenants to be nonbinding and illegal, and in 1958 the New York State Legislature enjoined landlords from discriminating against prospective tenants on grounds of race or ethnicity, but resistance at the grassroots level—among homeowners and property agents—effectively restricted African Americans to a handful of neighborhoods and barred them from all but the worst rental properties.

Federal mortgage policies made matters worse. Beginning in the 1930s, most American mortgages were underwritten by the Federal Housing Administration (FHA), a government agency that insured banks against losses from homeowners who defaulted on their loans. The FHA insured these mortgages in return for securing the banks' pledge to provide home loans at low interest rates and to spread interest payments over the term of the mortgage, to require only a small down payment for the purchase of a home, and, finally, to allow homeowners at leastfifteen and as many as thirty years to pay back their loans. At minimal expense to the federal government and with only the pledge of default insurance, the FHA therefore freed up unprecedented levels of capital and helped create a postwar social order in which 60 percent of American families owned their own homes.[21]

In deciding whether or not to insure a mortgage, the FHA used maps devised by another government agency, the Home Owners Loan Corporation (HOLC). Throughout the 1930s, the HOLC "redlined" entire neighborhoods in north-central Brooklyn, designating areas like Brownsville, Williamsburg, Greenpoint, Bushwick, and Flatbush unfit for real estate investment. Ironically, though these areas would soon house New York's largest black ghetto, anchored by Bedford-Stuyvesant and encompassing most of north-central Brooklyn, the HOLC's initial cause for declaring them off-limits to federal mortgage insurance was their strong concentration of "undesirable" white ethnics. Jewish Brownsville earned a poor "D" rating because its residents were a "Communist type of people, who agitated 'rent strikes' some time ago." Greenpoint received a similar ranking by virtue of its high concentration of Poles—"frugal" and "home loving" people, but a poor investment nonetheless.[22]

HOLC maps helped arbitrate Gotham's postwar racial boundaries. Since areas that carried the stigma of a low rating were effectively closed off to new investment and, hence, to new construction and renovation, private builders gravitated to less-developed areas in Staten Island, southern Brooklyn, and Queens, where they built tens of thousands of owner-occupied and rental units in the decades following World War II. Between 1950 and 1957, when Manhattan, Brooklyn, and the Bronx registered population declines, Queens reported a 14 percent increase and Staten Island a 10.6 percent increase. Returning armed service members moved their families to newly constructed, modern apartment complexes or, less frequently, used the GI Bill to purchase new homes in the outer boroughs. But black service members were denied these same opportunities. As late as 1948, over 85 percent of new subdivisions in Queens, Nassau, and Westchester Counties carried restrictive covenants barring black homeowners. Even after 1948, developers and lenders continued to discriminate against prospective black home buyers, whose very presence in a neighborhood would effectively eliminate the prospect of government mortgage insurance for other homeowners in the census tract.[23]

African Americans faced similarly dim prospects in the rental market. The FHA's logic assumed that African Americans drove down housing prices and thereby jeopardized real estate investments by their mere presence in a neighborhood. Consequently, not only did private lenders refuse to provide black New Yorkers with mortgages to buy homes in new urban and suburban developments outside the Harlem and Bedford-Stuyvesant ghettos, they also balked at underwriting investments in integrated communities, thereby encouraging landlords to restrict black renters to certain neighborhoods. Denied any funds for necessary capital improvements or new construction, these neighborhoods faced a certain future of decay and blight.

The pervasiveness of housing discrimination in New York was made painfully obvious by a highly public and embarrassing controversy that dogged the city's power elite throughout 1947. Having convinced the United Nations (UN) to establish its permanent home in Manhattan, the city found that an overwhelming number of delegates and consulate employees were having trouble securing apartments; landlords simply refused to rent to people of color. Ultimately, the UN was compelled to lease an entire apartment complex—Parkway Village in eastern Queens—to house nonwhite employees and delegates.[24]

Because new apartment complexes and housing developments were generally off-limits to people of color, most of the city's black and Puerto Rican migrants gravitated to areas with preexisting concentrations of minority residents. In Brooklyn, the Bedford-Stuyvesant ghetto swelled from 65,166 just before World War II to 137,436 in 1950. At the same time, the white population of Brooklyn declined sharply: between 1940 and 1960, 340,000 whites left the borough for new housing developments in Queens and Staten Island and suburban communities outside of the city. Much of this new flight was voluntary and had nothing to do with the expansion of New York's black population. Many returning GIs were simply eager to avail themselves of housing opportunities otherwise unavailable in Brooklyn. But their departure led naturally to the ghetto's physical expansion. Between 1940 and 1970, the ghetto's epicenter—that is, the mass of census tracts with a black population of 80 percent or greater—expanded threefold and swallowed up the northern third of Brooklyn. Neighborhoods that once played host to thriving white ethnic communities, but which the HOLC had long declared unfit for new investment, quickly became part of the greater Bedford-Stuyvesant slum.[25]

It was almost inevitable that landlords would conspire to manipulate market forces to their own advantage. The problem was that many black New Yorkers were cash poor. Without access to high-paying, skilled jobs, many African American migrants could scarcely afford to pay market-level rents. Their saving grace was welfare. By the late 1960s, over 1 million New Yorkers, the majority of them black and Puerto Rican, were welfare recipients. Their benefits accounted for one-quarter of the city's budget, or $6 billion—above and beyond the equally staggering amount provided by the state and federal governments.[26] Welfare rent stipends were below market rates, but they provided cash subsidies to landlords in central Brooklyn who were eager to replace a diminishing population of white renters. These same landlords quickly found a way to turn substantially better profits off of their new welfare tenants.

Until 1966, when Mayor Lindsay won approval of a municipal income tax, the bulk of New York's revenues derived from a fairly substantial levy on real estate. The status quo was fairly simple: most city voters did not own real estate, so naturally the tax burden fell to the relatively few who did. Landlords in Bedford-Stuyvesant and Harlem, and in nearby, transitional neighborhoods, found it was more profitable to consolidate and subdivide their properties than to maintain all of them. A landlord with three holdings in central Brooklyn did better to abandon two of his buildings and carve up the third: he could thereby default on two-thirds of his property tax bill, sharply reduce maintenance and utility costs, but still gross the same revenue.

Because their housing options were severely limited, many black New Yorkers had no choice but to rent cramped apartments in these dangerously overcrowded, subdivided buildings. The result was that vast areas of Brooklyn and northern Manhattan became wastelands. Boarded-up, empty buildings dotted every block, attracting drug dealers, vagrants, prostitutes, and vandals. Those properties that remained viable quickly deteriorated; they housed far too many tenants, and landlords typically neglected upkeep costs. The community's physical infrastructure simply crumbled. Furthermore, since black New Yorkers were forced to contend with an artificially tight rental market and an artificially depressed job market, the average family in Harlem paid 45 percent of its monthly wages in rent, compared with 20 percent for the average white Manhattanite.[27]

On the rare occasions when African Americans were able to purchase homes in New York, they often did so under the disadvantageous terms of "blockbusting"—a process whereby unscrupulous real estate agents created a panic among white homeowners by spreading rumors of a large influx of black homebuyers, purchased the houses of frightened white residents at below-market rates, and resold the same homes at above-market rates to black families who had little choice but to buy into an artificially inflated housing market. In 1963 the National Community Relations Advisory Council (NCRAC), a leading Jewish civil rights agency, found that blockbusting was especially prevalent in central Brooklyn neighborhoods like Crown Heights, Bushwick, East New York, and Park Slope, and in Queens neighborhoods like Cambria Heights, South Jamaica, Hollis, and Elmhurst. The NCRAC reported that blockbusting posed a special problem for Jews in two respects: many of the real estate agents responsible for blockbusting in Queens and Brooklyn were Jewish, and most of the white neighborhoods where these real estate agents operated were heavily Jewish. From a purely pragmatic viewpoint, blockbusting was destabilizing local Jewish communities; from a political perspective, it was driving a wedge between black and Jewish New Yorkers; and from a moral perspective, it revealed an appalling level of opportunism on the part of many Jewish real estate agents.[28]

Neighborhoods in central Brooklyn and northern Manhattan did not transform themselves overnight from ethnic enclaves to black ghettos, and for white residents of areas like Brownsville, Williamsburg, and Flatbush the changeover was often jarring. Many Jewish and Catholic New Yorkers came to equate vagrancy, vandalism, sexual permissiveness, and violence with black culture. They looked around and saw boarded-up homes; overcrowded, filthy apartments; out-of-work men; single mothers; and, above all, crime. Impressionistically, at least, these generalizations seemed compelling. As early as 1960, 40 percent of public housing residents in New York were black. One-quarter of the city's black households were headed by women (compared with less than 10 percent of white households). The rate of "illegitimate" births among black women was between fourteen and fifteen times higher than that among white women. And 60 percent of all first-time female admissions to city prisons, and 40 percent of all first-time male admissions, were black.[29]

It became increasingly common for white New Yorkers to view the African American community with a strong measure of cultural disdain and fear. As early as 1964 surveys revealed that 46 percent of city Jews believed the civil rights movement was proceeding too quickly, against 45 percent who believed it was advancing at the right pace or not quickly enough. Among Catholics, 39 percent of Irish respondents and 25 percent of Italians believed the movement was advancing at the right pace or not quickly enough, compared with 61 percent of Irish voters and 58 percent of Italians who thought it needed to "slow down." At the same time, a majority of black New Yorkers also informed pollsters that the civil rights movement needed to "slow down," highlighting the complex meaning behind such issue surveys.[30]

Nevertheless, the slow crawl away from overt racial liberalism turned into a steady march by the decade's close. Polling conducted in 1968 revealed that fewer than 20 percent of Italian and Irish Catholics, and only one-third of city Jews, believed that African Americans faced wage discrimination. A slight plurality of Jews, and a resounding majority of Irish and Italian Catholics (54 percent and 63 percent, respectively), believed that black New Yorkers did not suffer discrimination in the rental market.[31]

As sociologist Jonathan Rieder observed in his penetrating study of Italian and Jewish Brooklynites in the early 1970s:

The slums of Brownsville give it an unruly appearance. . . . When whites looked north across Linden Boulevard, the chaos transfixed them. Memories of the old immigrant neighborhoods forced them to compare . . . the Brownsville they knew from their youth and what they encountered now. Like archeologists of moral life, they peeled back the layers of time and read signs of vice and virtue in the crumbling build- ings. One Jewish craftsman mused, "I can't help thinking of the immi- grants, I mean, they tried to make a living, they sacrificed so the next generation could have a better life. They gave their family values. Don't shit where you eat. My grandfather lived in Brownsville, and look what they did there!"

The structural roots of the black ghetto were invisible to most white New Yorkers; they saw only the aftereffects of economic stagnation and housing discrimination. It was easy to believe that "lower-class blacks lacked industry, lived for momentary erotic pleasure, and in their mystique of soul, glorified the fashions of a high-stepping street life."[32]

Residential segregation was particularly slippery in New York because most whites could honestly claim, and actually believe, that they were not party to it. Unlike in cities where homeowners' councils used violence and political coercion to keep their neighborhoods lily-white, most whites in New York were renters and did not exercise direct control over discrimina- tion in the housing market. In fact, in a number of high-profile cases in the late 1940s and 1950s, white renters in Manhattan, Queens, and the Bronx actually organized to encourage building owners to open their develop- ments to middle-class black families. In a perverse sense, private- and public-sector discrimination afforded white New Yorkers the luxury of their race liberalism long after white residents of other northern cities embraced the politics of backlash. Not forced to live the reality of integration, the city's white population could honestly endorse the abstract idea of civil rights at little expense to themselves.[33]

Although most white New Yorkers did not necessarily appreciate the complex roots of urban decay, their fears and resentments still had some basis in fact. The city's crime rate skyrocketed in the 1950s and 1960s, a phenomenon many attributed—not without reason—to the growth of the black ghetto. Chronic poverty and substandard housing had created a breeding ground for urban vice. In 1966 alone, the number of reported burglaries citywide increased by 96.4 percent, the number of robberies by 89.9 percent, and the number of rapes by 22.1 percent. Altogether, the felony rate jumped 59.9 percent. It became axiomatic that entire parts of the city were off-limits to law-abiding citizens. Even public transportation seemed increasingly dangerous. In 1965 the rate of "serious" crimes re- ported on the subways—robberies, muggings, and armed assaults—in- creased by 52 percent.[34]

New York reeled from one gruesome crime after another, like the murder of Charles Gallagher, a physics professor at Columbia University who was found dead of a gunshot wound in Central Park. *Time* magazine remarked that Gallagher's murder was a reminder that the park, "a sunny sanctuary for birds and bird watchers like Charles Gallagher during the day, [has] long been a junglelike hideout for muggers, holdup men, and perverts after dark." Even more chilling was the murder of Bertha Haas, a sixty-eight-year-old Bronx widow who was beaten, raped, and strangled to death inside her own apartment building.[35]

Such tragedies had a cumulative effect. A survey conducted in 1966 revealed that almost half of all white Brooklynites felt unsafe when walking outside after dark; 40 percent reported staying home on occasion and foregoing a social engagement because "it was too unsafe" to go outdoors; and 74 percent were "somewhat concerned" or "very concerned" that their homes might be burglarized. And by the decade's close, opinion polls showed that 41 percent of city Jews, and 48 percent of Catholics, believed that blacks "breed more crime" than other groups. Roughly one out of five white New Yorkers, Jewish and Catholic alike, admitted they would feel "personal concern" if a black person crossed the street and began walking toward them.[36]

On its own, the rising crime rate cannot account for the swift erosion of white ethnic support for the civil rights movement. By the close of the decade, over 40 percent of the city's Jews, and about half of its Catholics, believed that blacks had "less ambition" and "looser morals" than whites. Almost one-third of all Jews, 48 percent of Italian Catholics, and 42 percent of Irish Catholics felt that African Americans wanted "to live off a handout." When asked whether black Americans had "less native intelligence than whites," 22 percent of Jewish respondents, 27 percent of Irish respondents, and 42 percent of Italians replied in the affirmative. Crime was clearly just one piece of the puzzle. So, too, was the depressed state of New York's black community. Equally important was the "rights revolution" that almost tore New York apart at its seams in the mid-1960s. It aggravated the visual impact of ghetto culture and eroded white support for integration, a trend that cut equally across the Jewish, Italian, and Irish communities.[37]

The evolution of the civil rights movement, from its early faith in the gospel of integration to a growing embrace of Black Power, is a familiar story. By the mid-1960s, African Americans in both the North and South were increasingly sympathetic to various strains of the community empowerment ideal expressed alternately by Malcolm X, Stokely Carmichael, and James Forman. Certainly these more radical spokespersons for separatism did not command the allegiance of all or most African Americans, but some of their fundamental beliefs resonated with New York's ghetto residents; namely, that segregated black institutions were not inherently inferior and that people of color were owed a comprehensive set of rights to redress historic economic and social grievances.

These developments were part of a larger pattern, a rights revolution that emboldened women, gays and lesbians, students, American Indians, and poor people to demand a greater share of the American dream in the 1960s and 1970s. In New York, two phenomena came to embody all that was radical about the national rights revolution: the welfare advocacy movement, which catered principally to black and Hispanic persons on public assistance; and the intensely divisive battle over local control of public schools, which seriously undermined New York Jewry's long-standing sense of affinity with black America.

The welfare system as it existed in the 1960s was a thorny affair. Charles R. Morris, who served as director of New York City's welfare programs in the second Lindsay administration (1970–74), explained that "there were separate programs for the permanently disabled, the aged poor, and the blind, for one-parent families with dependent children, for two-parent families with children . . . and a catch-all program of 'home relief' for people who fell through the net." Further complicating matters, no standard level of support cut across individual programs. "Grant levels varied from program to program, and in Aid to Dependent Children (ADC), the single biggest program, grants were built up from detailed tables that accounted separately for rents, heating requirements, the food requirements of children of different sexes at different ages, clothing needs at various times of the year, school expenses, and myriad other details of daily living."[38]

Under this patchwork arrangement, welfare benefits were arbitrary and caseworkers played an endless game of "let's-make-a-deal" with their clients, trading benefits or threatening reprisals in return for behavioral changes. A caseworker might demand that a welfare mother sever ties with an unemployed boyfriend by using either the "carrot" (an extra clothing allowance) or the "stick" (the threat of diminished benefits). In either event, the system was capricious and oftentimes excessively coercive.

In 1964 New York activist Frank Espada, who later served as Lindsay's director of community organization, discovered that most welfare recipients were legally entitled to larger benefits packages than they were actually receiving. He began organizing the poor—educating them about their statutory rights, encouraging them to challenge their caseworkers—and was soon joined in his efforts by community organizations that were funded by the federal Office of Economic Opportunity. A year later George Wiley, a senior staff member with the Congress of Racial Equality (CORE), became the first director of the National Welfare Rights Organization (NWRO), an advocacy group that drew half its national membership of 100,000 from New York City. The NWRO fused CORE's confrontational style to Espada's entitlement strategy.

In 1966 the new movement garnered widespread media attention when Frances Fox-Piven and Richard Cloward, two radical public policy scholars, published an article in the *Nation* arguing that the only long-term solution to institutional poverty was the destruction of the welfare system. By aggressively enrolling poor people and pressuring caseworkers to maximize stipends, the NWRO could force the government to its knees and compel congressional enactment of a more progressive, minimum-income entitlement program. What Fox-Piven and Cloward were proposing was nothing less than a groundbreaking expansion of American rights and privileges and a massive, downward transfer of private wealth.

Activists in New York responded enthusiastically to NWRO's program, and they gained critical support from sympathetic members of Lindsay's administration—notably, Mitchell Ginsberg, the commissioner of social services who provided Spanish interpreters, babysitters, car fare stipends, and night hearings for the tens of thousands of welfare recipients who lined up to seek increased benefits from their caseworkers. By 1968 Ginsberg estimated that New York was augmenting its welfare rolls by between $10 million and $12 million each month.

Emboldened by their success, clients and their advocates began plying a more confrontational strategy of sit-ins, demonstrations, and public disturbances. The result was widespread turmoil and systematic strain, just as Cloward and Fox-Piven had intended. By the end of Lindsay's first term in 1969, the city's welfare caseload had doubled. Total spending for public assistance jumped from $400 million to $1 billion ($2 billion when Medicaid was factored in), one-third of which came directly from municipal coffers. The *New York Times* reported that "demonstrators have jammed the [welfare] centers, sometimes camping out in them overnight, broken down administrative procedures, played havoc with the mountains of paperwork, and have . . . thrown the City's Welfare program into a state of crisis and chaos."[39]

While the welfare explosion rattled New Yorkers of all backgrounds, Catholics were probably more sensitive to the fiscal implications of the city's liberal antipoverty initiatives. As early as 1959, when newly elected governor Nelson Rockefeller inaugurated the first ever state income tax, Irish and Italian voters exhibited a low threshold for public sector expansion. It caused pollster Louis Harris little surprise that the governor's approval rating bottomed out at 16 percent among city Jews, who had voted overwhelmingly for his Democratic opponent, Averill Harriman, just six months before. But only 31 percent and 18 percent of Irish and Italian New Yorkers, respectively, gave Rockefeller a favorable rating in 1959—a marked drop-off in the space of half a year. Many opponents of the new administration in Albany probably agreed with an Irish businessman in Queens, who told Harris, "I don't like anything about Rockefeller. . . . He's a millionaire with a millionaire's disregard for money. When I saw his tax program I was sorry I voted for him."[40]

Two years later Harris reported that 20 percent and 35 percent of Irish and Italian Democrats, respectively, volunteered that city taxes were too high, compared with only 7 percent of Jewish Democrats. The difference between these ethnic groups was probably more pronounced than Harris's survey suggested, since a large number of Catholic voters were Republicans and, hence, more likely to oppose taxes. Several years later, in 1965, a private poll conducted for mayoral candidate Abraham Beame showed over 20 percent of Catholic respondents voicing unprompted concern over high taxes, compared with only 6 percent of Jewish respondents.[41]

It is not entirely clear why some New Yorkers were more troubled by taxes than others, though higher rates of home ownership among Catholics may have made the city's property and real estate levies unpalatable to many Irish and Italian voters. Catholic voters also resented what they considered a double-tax burden: in addition to financing their parochial schools, Catholics also helped carry the cost of the city school system, though few of them made extensive use of it. Any incipient tax revolt was only bound to gain traction in 1966 when Lindsay, left by his predecessor to contend with a large budget shortfall, won legislative approval of a citywide personal income tax. Coming right on the heels of the welfare explosion, and less than a decade after the imposition of New York State's first income tax, the new levy aggravated Italian and Irish voters whose threshold for public sector expansion was already low.[42]

At the same time that the city's welfare system was spiraling out of control, tensions between the teacher's union and black community activists in Brooklyn and Harlem seriously undermined long-standing Jewish support for integration and black empowerment. New York's African American community had long been at odds with city officials, who consistently resisted demands that local districts be gerrymandered to remedy the extensive, de facto segregation that characterized the public schools. Black leaders rightly pointed out that private- and public-sector discrimination in the housing market had created racially homogenous and unequal school districts throughout the city. In the mid-1960s civil rights activists committed a sudden about-face: reflecting the movement's new embrace of community empowerment and separatism, black leaders in Harlem and Brooklyn began demanding that they be permitted control over public schools in their own neighborhoods, rather than accept creative integration of the citywide system. The activists claimed that the schools were badly neglecting black and Puerto Rican children and that at the heart of this failure to educate students of color was a deep-seated racism and cultural insensitivity on the part of white teachers and administrators.[43]

There was some truth to these charges. A study conducted in 1955 revealed that 8 percent of all elementary and junior high schools in New York City had student populations that were at least 85 percent black and Puerto Rican. Located in segregated neighborhoods, these schools tended to be old, poorly maintained, and staffed by relatively inexperienced teachers who had not yet accrued enough seniority to apply for transfers to schools in more desirable neighborhoods. The same study found that per-pupil expenditures in these predominately black and Puerto Rican schools were equal to expenditures in majority-white schools, but this fact was of little comfort to parents who believed their children were being relegated to the same Jim Crow standards they had fled in southern states such as Alabama and Georgia.

By 1968 the share of city schools with over 90 percent minority student populations grew from 8 percent to 28 percent of the total number of schools. Yet the situation was neither as dire nor deliberate as many black activists and their liberal white supporters maintained. Because they fell along neighborhood lines, grade schools and junior high schools were considerably more segregated than high schools, which drew students from a wider geographic radius. In 1960, out of thirty-two high schools in Brooklyn and Queens, seven schools had student populations that were between 22 percent and 54 percent minority. In 1964 eleven high schools were at least 20 percent minority, and by 1970 only three high schools in both boroughs had less than 10 percent minority students.

The rapid desegregation of outer-borough high schools owed to a massive demographic change. In the 1960s alone, the city lost a net total of 617,127 white residents and gained a net total of 702,903 black and Puerto Rican residents. Because many Catholic children attended parish and diocesan schools, by the early 1960s the city's public school population was

40 percent minority. With black families moving to New York en masse, and with over 40,000 white students leaving the public school system each year, it became virtually impossible for education authorities to manipulate school populations, had they wanted to.[44]

With so many black students now living in Brooklyn and Queens, gerrymandered segregation was out of the question. Yet, with so many white students leaving the system, the trend toward segregation was unstoppable. In effect, the kind of willful segregation that many black parents suspected the Board of Education of creating simply did not exist. The city's population was in tremendous flux, and what segregation did exist in the public schools owed to pervasive segregation in residential housing. In 1960 the citywide index of dissimilarity (introduced in Chapter 1) for African Americans was 84.4 percent, representing an almost total level of segregation.[45]

This level of residential segregation was not, strictly speaking, "de facto," in the sense that it evolved from an accident of residence rather than state policy. On the contrary, residential segregation owed to a powerful combination of state and private institutional policy. In this sense, it was somewhat ironic, and certainly unfortunate, that the bitter school wars that racked New York in the 1960s pitted black parents and community activists against the predominately Jewish teachers' union, rather than against the banking sector, the real estate industry, or the federal housing bureaucracy.

By the late 1960s some 50 percent of all public school students in New York were black and Puerto Rican, but 90 percent of the teaching and administrative employees were white, and as many as two-thirds of these were Jewish.[46] As grassroots activists began gathering momentum for a community control scheme, they grew increasingly casual in their use of such terms as "educational genocide" and intellectual "colonialism," reflecting a growing consensus among movement leaders that their cause was at one with anticolonial struggles in the "third world." Such vitriolic attacks on a predominantly Jewish teaching force were bound to result in a conflagration, as indeed they did.[47]

Partly in response to black activists' demands, in 1967 the Board of Education created three trial districts in a tentative move toward decentralization.[48] The arrangement called for the election of community school boards in Harlem, lower Manhattan, and central Brooklyn; these official committees were empowered to work with district "administrators" (the equivalent of district superintendents), but neither the New York City Board of Education nor the state legislature ever outlined in adequate detail the limits of local control. Black activists in Ocean Hill–Brownsville—one of the three trial districts, situated between Bedford-Stuyvesant and Browns-ville—assumed they would enjoy complete autonomy over staffing, curriculum, and administration. But the city was bound by contracts it had signed the previous fall with 57,000 members of the United Federation of Teachers (UFT).

Part of the initial misunderstanding owed to the popular conflation of decentralization and community control—two similar programs born of very different motivations. City bureaucrats who studied the state's complex school funding formula discovered in the mid-1960s that the city stood to gain upwards of $100 million annually in additional funding if it treated each borough as a separate school district. Black activists, on the other hand, touted decentralization primarily as a strategy to devolve power to the community level and, hence, increase community control. While the two ideas were not mutually exclusive, black parents were working from the assumption that the new experiment was designed mainly to accord them more control over their children's schools, whereas municipal and school officials generally understood the project as a method of maximizing the city's intake of state education funds.[49]

Parents and community leaders in the Ocean Hill–Brownsville district selected Rhody McCoy, an eighteen-year veteran of the city schools, to serve as administrator. An enthusiast of Malcolm X's teachings, McCoy was also deeply embittered by his career failings, which he attributed to the racist culture of New York's public school system. Though for many years he refused to take civil service tests required of all teachers and administrators, he remained convinced that his slow advancement up the occupational ladder was a matter of race prejudice. To be sure, McCoy's experience working with poor and troubled youth, and his educational credentials (degrees from Howard University and New York University), rendered him a good fit for the job, but his confrontational style ultimately helped undermine the entire experiment.

From the start, McCoy tested the limits of city officials. He hired Herman Ferguson, a vice principal from a neighboring district, as one of his new school principals. Only months before, Ferguson had been indicted on charges of conspiring with radical black activists to assassinate moderate civil rights leaders Whitney Young and Roy Wilkins. (He was ultimately convicted of the charges but jumped bail in 1970.) In a controversial article outlining his vision of black community schooling, Ferguson called for classes in martial arts, "instruction in gun weaponry, gun handling, and gun safety," and loudspeakers that would softly play Malcolm X speeches as a constant backdrop against the school day.[50]

In mid-1968, McCoy transferred nineteen teachers and administrators, all but one of them Jewish, out of Ocean Hill–Brownsville. The mass transfer violated school board policy, as well as the legally binding contracts the city had signed with the UFT, which stipulated that no employee could be involuntarily reassigned by a district superintendent without a formal hearing. McCoy rendered his position all the less tenable when he warned, "Not one of these teachers will be allowed to teach anywhere in this city. The black community will see to that." Since two of the teachers in question were local UFT representatives, the statement probably violated federal and state laws prohibiting the intimidation of labor organizers. It was a challenge that no responsible union could accept. When the district's teachers went on strike as a show of solidarity with their colleagues, McCoy took steps to transfer them all out of Ocean Hill–Brownsville, setting the stage for a major escalation of hostilities.

The local community board and the UFT agreed to submit to binding arbitration that summer. The charges against the teachers and administrators proved entirely baseless, and retired civil court judge Frances Rivers, who adjudicated the disagreement, reinstated all nineteen defendants. (The case against one teacher rested entirely on hearsay evidence that he criticized the decentralization scheme at a private holiday party the preceding December. Rivers dismissed the charges as a violation of the accused's First Amendment rights.) But days before the 1968–69 school year began, McCoy announced that he had replaced all 350 UFT members who had gone out on strike the previous spring.

The end result was a series of three major, citywide teachers' strikes that crippled New York's public school system until November 1968. Twice throughout the standoff, the school board sought to end the walkout by entering into binding "consent letters" with the UFT, agreeing to honor the due process clauses enshrined in teachers' contracts and official board policy. But pressure from virtually every major establishment in the city— including the mayor's office, the Ford Foundation, and the *New York Times*— led the board to back down from its pledge each time.

Throughout the strike, and for years after, UFT leader Albert Shanker suffered intense abuse from his erstwhile allies on the left. Much of the criticism stemmed from the union's decision to highlight some of the more vulgar instances of anti-Semitism and racism emanating from the Ocean Hill–Brownsville community and from the district administrative staff. Shanker distributed 500,000 copies of an anonymous leaflet that was left in employees' mailboxes at Junior High School 271, which labeled Jewish teachers "middle east murderers of colored people" and "bloodsucking exploiters," and accused them of "brainwashing" black children into "self-hatred. . . . The idea behind this program [community control] is beautiful, but when the money chargers heard about it, they took over."

Leading newspapers and liberal spokespersons lambasted Shanker for disseminating the flyer and contributing to the divisive atmosphere, but many rank-and-file teaches felt that the UFT leader raised an important point. McCoy administered his district recklessly, allowing firebrands like Less Campbell, a leader of the Afro-American Teacher's Association, to intimidate white teachers and post anti-Semitic invective on student bulletin boards. The morning after Martin Luther King's assassination, Campbell addressed a student assembly at Junior High School 271, sharing such bits of wisdom such as: "If whitey taps you on the shoulder, send him to the graveyard," and, "Don't steal from a brother. Don't steal a comb. Steal what you can use." Jewish teachers in Ocean Hill–Brownsville were routinely assaulted and threatened with physical violence. The radical leader of Brooklyn's CORE chapter, Sonny Carson, reported with great satisfaction that he and a group of community activists had once surrounded Shanker and forcibly refused to let him leave the room. If McCoy and his allies took umbrage at charges that they were anti-Semites or racists, they did little to disabuse Jewish teachers of this suspicion.

All of this occurred against a backdrop of mounting violence and intimidation targeting city teachers and school administrators, before, during, and after the Ocean Hill–Brownsville crisis. The 1966 school year saw 213 attacks against public schoolteachers, and the 1967 school year saw 224 attacks. By the eve of the 1968 school strike, many members of the UFT feared that black community activists were targeting them for violence or turning a blind eye when their children lashed out at white teachers. "We don't say that anybody should beat up anybody," said Margaret Campbell, chairman of the Parents Organizations of District 13, Bedford-Stuyvesant, "but we also say that nobody should [be made to] feel that they have to beat someone. This system has made people feel like this. While we don't condone it, we're in a position where we cannot condemn it, knowing the root causes."

When black parents in Harlem—one of the neighborhoods vying for participation on the community control scheme—forced the resignation of Stanley Lisser, the white, Jewish principal of I.S. 201, a *New York Times* reporter visited the school and declared it in a state of "bedlam." Representatives of the Ford Foundation agreed, describing the building as an "armed camp. Vandalism was rampant; children roamed through the halls. Pieces of school tiling were ripped up. . . . Seriously undermanned, several of the staff were observed standing in the hallways with yardsticks to protect themselves."[51]

In the wake of the Six-Day War of June 1967, New York Jews were already acutely sensitive to the unholy marriage of violence, anticolonial rhetoric, and anti-Jewish incitement emanating from prominent voices in the black community. In June 1967 the Student Non-Violent Coordinating Committee had run a scurrilous article in its summer newsletter asserting among thirty-two "points of information" that "Zionists conquered the Arab homes and land through terror" and that "the famous European Jews, the Rothschilds . . . were involved in the original conspiracy . . . to create the 'State of Israel.'" The bulletin also featured a cartoon of Israeli defense minister Moshe Dayan, complete with dollar signs plastered to his epaulets, and an outstretched hand bearing a Star of David and a dollar sign, tightening a noose around the necks of Egyptian president Gamal Abdel Nasser and boxer Muhammad Ali (Cassius Clay).[52]

Later that fall, at the New Politics Convention in Chicago, militant radicals turned a gathering of left-wing and liberal activists, originally drawn together in hopes of fielding a third-party challenge to Lyndon Johnson, into what the New Yorker dismissed as "an incendiary spectacle." The black caucus demanded and received half of all committee assignments and floor votes and unconditional agreement to its platform, including a condemnation of the "imperialistic Zionist war." Many Jewish attendees stormed out of the general session, although as one observer remarked, "Walking out of the New Politics Convention didn't mean much, because the people who walked out kept walking back in, so they could walk out again." The assembly dissipated into various radical caucuses and ended, in the words of another journalist, as "a Lewis Carroll production of Marat/Sade."[53]

When leading proponents of community control suggested that black children were being "slaughtered through educational genocide," or, more pointedly, that "we have no intention of returning to the old ways of educational genocide perpetuated by the Board of Education and the United Federation of Teachers," many city Jews took seriously Shanker's warning that there was more at stake in the Ocean Hill–Brownsville crisis than just a labor contract.[54]

Moreover, New York Jews were not inventing from whole cloth the dread specter of black anti-Semitism. Polling conducted in 1968 revealed that 49 percent of African Americans in New York believed that "Jews are irritating because [they are] too aggressive"; 39 percent thought Jews were "too ambitious for their own good"; 71 percent of city blacks thought that "between money and people, Jews will choose money"; and only 21 percent believed that Jews were more loyal to the United States than to Israel.[55]

Complicating matters, most of the city's influential personalities and institutions lined up behind the community control experiment, including the Ford Foundation, the Rockefeller Brothers Fund, the banking industry, the *New York Times* editorial page, corporate liberals like McGeorge Bundy, and left-wing intellectuals like Dwight Macdonald, Jason Epstein, and Paul Goodman. Community control was a small price to pay for Manhattan's moneyed elite, who wanted desperately to avoid the same fate that befell south-central Los Angeles and that would soon befall Detroit, Newark, and dozens of other cities. Epstein placed this position in sharp relief when he informed readers of the *New York Review of Books*: "If the children of the ghettos are trapped in a dance of death, their dancing partners are the holders of the city's mortgages, the owners of its utilities, and the rulers of its commerce. For the ideologists of Black Power to talk of coalitions with the working class is besides the point. Their appropriate allies are the city's power elite."

With the lines thus drawn, it was the Jewish "working class"—in this case, middle-class teachers and school administrators—whose parochial concerns stood in the way of black progress and urban peace. This was an odd political configuration for a city in which Jewish-dominated unions and labor parties had long allied themselves with civil rights groups. Perhaps with this history in mind, proponents of community control—particularly John Lindsay—felt obliged to overstate their case and make the UFT into a northern equivalent of the White Citizens Councils. Speaking to a television audience just months before the Ocean Hill–Brownsville crisis, the mayor blamed opposition to black educational advancement on "a storm of opposition from the very middle class . . . who were fearful of decentralization. . . . I had the impression from the mail and the telegrams we received that the opposition to decentralization had to some extent succeeded in frightening the middle class in our community. That decentralization meant black power, black control. And then somehow some kind of iron-fisted violence on top of it all."[56]

No person came in for a worse drubbing than Shanker, whose name was dragged through the mud without mercy by the city's liberal spokespersons. Jimmy Breslin, the cantankerous left-wing columnist, wrote that Shanker was "an accent away from George Wallace . . . the worst public person I have seen in my time in the City of New York." I. F. Stone rushed to Lindsay's defense, informing readers that the mayor "suddenly finds himself the mayor of a Southern town. The Mason-Dixon line has moved north, and the Old Confederacy has expanded to the outer reaches of the Bronx." Murray Kempton dismissed Shanker as a "goon." A writer for *Ramparts* magazine impugned the entire membership of the UFT when he suggested that "white middle-class New York teachers may quietly vote for George Wallace."[57]

These charges were unfair. There was a serious, principled case to be made against the way in which decentralization had been carried out. Like many of his rank-and-file union members, Shanker—a longtime supporter of the black civil rights movement who had marched with protesters in Selma, Alabama—had been raised in a self-consciously urban milieu that valued the ideals of liberal cosmopolitanism. He feared community control and supported a centralized education system for the same reason that he opposed states rights and supported federal civil rights laws. "We don't happen to believe that the little old hometown is a warm, nice place," Shanker explained. "We think that the smaller the area, the more provincial, the more bigoted, the more narrow; that the smaller the group, the more homogenous, the more there's an appeal to a primitive type of tribalism." In Shanker's mind, the extremists who co-opted the community control experiment in Ocean Hill–Brownsville more or less confirmed these fears.[58]

Further complicating matters, many of the communities contending with the teachers' union were in the throes of a sudden demographic transition. They had recently been Jewish neighborhoods but, in the short space of ten years, had become overwhelmingly African American. By the time of the school crisis in 1968, only 40 percent of Ocean Hill–Brownsville residents had lived in the neighborhood for more than five years; just 18 percent of the district's parents had been born in New York, compared with 51 percent who had been born in the South and 21 percent in Puerto Rico.

By contrast, many of the striking teachers had grown up in central Brooklyn—Brownsville, Flatbush, and East New York. They knew its streets better than some of their students did and had returned to teach at the very primary and secondary schools they attended as children. The parents of some of the striking teachers still lived on the periphery.[59] In neighborhoods like Brownsville, which had a long tradition of Jewish radicalism, Jews had even worked closely with black leaders to smooth the transition to an integrated and, later, predominately black community.[60]

The Ocean Hill–Brownsville crisis was not just about race. It was about communities in competition for resources. This, too, had a longer backstory than liberal spokespersons may have appreciated. Throughout the late nineteenth and early twentieth centuries, Jewish, Irish, and Italian New

Yorkers had fought tooth and nail over access to municipal jobs, control of the school system, and power within the Democratic Party and the city government. In the postwar era it was easy to forget how acrimonious and violent interethnic relations had been as recently the 1930s and early 1940s.[61] In this context, many white ethnics understood African Americans as just one more group that delivered large numbers of migrants to New York, achieved critical mass, and began clamoring for power and resources. Just as city life had pitted Irish against Italian, Italian against Jew, and Jew against Irish, the addition of a large black population created new competition for entry into niche industries and control over city government.

When black parents claimed that their children were often consigned to manual and secretarial education classes, they probably did not realize that the same was true of many Italian students who attended public rather than Catholic schools in the 1940s and 1950s.[62] This history lesson was of little consolation to black New Yorkers, who justifiably bristled at the suggestion they wait in line for economic and educational resources. But the political backstory was more complicated than most supporters of the decentralization plan appreciated.

Racial resentments and fears flowed both ways, and the city's welfare and school wars explain a good part of the white reaction against race liberalism in the late 1960s. By the close of the decade, 42 percent of Irish New Yorkers, 45 percent of Jews (a plurality), and 44 percent of Italians (also a plurality) thought their black neighbors aspired "to tear down white society." Roughly one-quarter of respondents in each community were simply "not sure." Approximately 19 percent of all Jews and 29 percent of white Catholics rejected "integration" in favor of a "separate society" for whites and blacks. Fewer than half of all Catholics and two-thirds of Jews continued to profess support for an integrated city.

It would be a mistake to confuse white misgiving about integration for indiscriminate racism. In 1968 only 1 percent of Jews, and 2 percent of "non-Jewish" backlash voters—the overwhelming majority of whom were Catholic—admitted they would feel uncomfortable if a "black sat next to [them] at a lunch counter"; by comparison, 12 percent of white voters nationally responded in kind. Among New Yorkers, 2 percent of Jews, and between 4 and 5 percent of non-Jewish backlash voters, volunteered that they would feel ill at ease if a black person "used the same restroom" or "sat next to [them] at a movie theater." Fourteen percent of all whites nationally admitted to the same discomfort. On the whole, white ethnics in New York seemed considerably less troubled by routine, physical interactions with African Americans than the white population in other parts of the United States.[63]

Journalist Jim Sleeper has ventured that everyday race relations in New York were unusually casual in part because the city's network of "public transit, schools, hospitals, libraries, parks, and museums . . . offered a social interaction different from the sort found elsewhere: a city of walkers and subway [riders] instead of drivers; of brassy, better-educated workers; of intellectual development possible without the sums of money usually needed to cross the threshold of higher education."[64]

Indeed, Gotham was a city like no other in America; it afforded its citizens unparalleled opportunities to brush shoulders and lock horns. As late as 1990, when Sleeper wrote his acclaimed book on New York liberalism, the city still claimed 30 percent of the nation's public transit riders. In the late 1960s, roughly around the time of the Ocean Hill–Brownsville crisis, the City University of New York (CUNY) boasted ten senior colleges, eight community colleges, and a graduate center. No other city in America, then or now, provided so comprehensive an educational network for its citizens. In 1970 almost 200,000 New Yorkers were enrolled in CUNY's various branches, half of them full-time—and not one of them paid a dime in tuition or fees.

Historian Joshua Freeman reached essentially the same conclusion as Sleeper, claiming that "the cosmopolitanism, energy, and sophistication of New York's working-class population was a major force in the city's post–World War II success." Because most New Yorkers rented small apartments instead of spacious homes, they walked the streets and rode the subways—which cost only fifteen cents until the mid-1960s—to "escape [the] parochial bonds" of their ethnic neighborhoods. Not only was Gotham overflowing with "museums, libraries, jazz clubs, concert halls, street festivals, parks, demonstrations, debates, theater, and the city colleges," but, equally important, "the proximity of so many ethnic and racial groups made the city an arena for the creation of hybrids whose innovations recast local, national, and even world culture."[65]

New York has always been "a merchant metropolis with an extraordinarily heterogeneous population," as Nathan Glazer and Daniel Moynihan described it in 1963. By virtue of its diversity, compressed size, and classic status as a "global city," its residents were probably more accepting of diversity in practice than other people in other places.[66] This does not mean that racial and ethnic prejudice did not exist. They did, as opinion polls consistently revealed. But white racism in New York was inconsistent

—inspired by specific concerns and resentments, not a comprehensive ideology or a way of life.

By the mid-1960s, these concerns and resentments boiled over. But they never assumed primacy in the complex world of New York politics. Even as Jews and Catholics developed a similar skepticism of integration and a fear of their black neighbors, they continued to embrace different styles and substance in city politics.

7 Reaction

Throughout the 1960s, social upheaval in New York drew Jews and Catholics closer together in their position on race relations. Both groups began the decade as wholehearted supporters of integration and ended it as skeptics of its social value. It would follow naturally that the city's Irish, Italian, and Jewish voters might forge a united electoral block—that "silent majorities" within each community might come together to form a cross-ethnic backlash constituency. But this did not happen.

Many of the patterns established in the 1940s persisted into the 1960s. On the local level, when the opportunity presented itself, Jewish voters tended to back reform candidates of any party, while Irish and Italian voters split their votes between the GOP and the regular Democratic machine. In statewide and national elections, Jews tended to back Democrats by 3-to-1 margins; Catholics continued to split their votes more evenly, though they moved steadily closer to the Republican Party. In effect, most Jews clung stubbornly to their liberal heritage, while the conservative wing of the Catholic community continued gradually to outpace the growth of liberal Catholicism. Thus, the breakdown of race relations between white and black New Yorkers did not cause a substantial defection by Jewish Democrats; neither did it cause a sudden, fundamental political turn among Irish and Italian voters, who had been casting their lot with Republicans in ever greater numbers since the early 1940s.

Yet, at the same time that the liberal coalition suffered further Catholic attrition on its right flank, a small but unusually influential minority of young Jewish New Yorkers turned against their liberal inheritance from the left. Gravitating in highly disproportionate numbers to radical groups like the Students for a Democratic Society, these third-generation Jews—raised in a culture that celebrated the idea of dissent—aggressively rejected every last vestige of adult authority. Far from being shocked or hurt by their children's defection from the broad, postwar liberal consensus, many of their parents stood firmly by their sides. By the early 1970s, extremes of two dynamically opposite ethnic cultures—one rooted in spirituality, hierarchy, and authority and the other rooted in secular humanism and dissent— came very close to burning down the political house that Franklin Roosevelt had built.

I n 1961 Mayor Robert Wagner Jr. broke publicly with the regular Democratic organization, bringing to a climax two years of wrangling with Tammany Hall's controversial leader, Carmine De Sapio. Wagner, who was running for a third term in office, found himself in a tight electoral spot. Substantial portions of the Catholic community had already defected to the GOP; those Italian and Irish voters who still supported Democratic candidates with any regularity tended to favor the machine over the new reform clubs that were contesting the old leadership for control of the party.

In a private survey conducted for the mayor's campaign that March, pollster Louis Harris found that "the Catholic vote is not in good shape, and, with the exception of the Italians, now appears ripe for voting Republican in this fall's election. The Irish, who were also not with Kennedy last fall, now seem ready to leave the Democratic party in droves in this year's municipal election. . . . The Italians at the moment are evenly split. A real fight will have to be waged for their favor in this year's election."

Harris developed an end strategy that departed sharply from the old Democratic orthodoxy. It was no longer feasible to build a coalition of working-class Catholics and middle- and working-class Jews. Almost two-thirds of the Irish supported Wagner's likely Republican opponent, Louis Lefkowitz; the Italians were evenly split. Instead, Harris suggested a new electoral combination of African Americans and Puerto Ricans, who "seem[ed] to be almost invulnerable to Republican attack," and Jews, who had leaned "heavily Democratic in the city for many years and [who were] proving to be more solidly that way with each passing year."[1]

Before he could stitch together a new liberal coalition of Jews, blacks, and Puerto Ricans, Wagner first had to win the Democratic primary against his machine opponent, Arthur Levitt. In August 1961 Harris found that black and Puerto Rican primary voters backed Wagner 3-to-1; Irish Democrats preferred Wagner by a comfortable margin of 60 percent to 40 percent; Jews backed the incumbent mayor 55 percent to 45 percent; and Italian Democrats narrowly preferred Levitt by the same margin.

These numbers obscured underlying electoral trends. Harris's poll was targeted only to Democrats. Wagner's strongest Catholic supporters tended to be union members—particularly, municipal employees who revered the mayor's father, the late senator Robert Wagner, who authored organized labor's "bill of rights" (the National Labor Relations Act of 1935). These Irish and Italian Democrats also admired the mayor for recognizing municipal employee unions. It is little wonder that Wagner faired exceedingly well with Irish unionists and held his own with Italian workers. Critically, however, these voters represented the minority of Irish and Italian voters who still backed the Democratic Party. In sharper terms, Wagner only enjoyed the support of about a quarter of the city's Catholic electorate.

Jewish Democrats were split between Wagner and his primary opponent, but virtually every Jew signaled his or her intent to back whomever the Democratic nominee was in November. Harris counseled his client to bolster his standing with Jewish Democrats in the mayoral primary by playing up his split with Tammany. "The Jews will respond best of all to the bossism issue," he wrote, "and will vote almost unanimously against De Sapio, if the issue is cast this way." The surest way to achieve this goal was to press Eleanor Roosevelt and Herbert Lehman into service; both party elders were wildly popular among New York Jews and were aligned with the reform movement. But this strategy also drove a further wedge between Wagner and his waning Catholic base.[2]

Ultimately, Wagner swept the Democratic primary and won handily against Lefkowitz in November. He followed Harris's advice to the letter. The mayor carried Jewish primary voters by raising the pitch of his anti-Tammany rhetoric, and in the general election he built a coalition of blacks, Puerto Ricans, Jews, and staunch Catholic unionists—the latter, a minority in the Irish and Italian communities, but an important part of the new liberal realignment.

Amid Wagner's decisive primary victory in 1961, De Sapio lost his seat as district leader to a candidate fielded by the Village Independent Democrats (VID), downtown Manhattan's reform club. No longer a member of the New York County Democratic Committee, the erstwhile party boss was ineligible to serve in Tammany's top position. In 1963 De Sapio staged an unsuccessful attempt to win back his old seat on the County Committee and wrestle control of the party from the reformers. His primary opponent was a young VID activist named Ed Koch.

Polling conducted for the reform Democrats that spring shed further light on the split between Catholic and Jewish Democrats. Only 8 percent of Jews in the first assembly district—an area encompassing Greenwich Village, with its combination of working-class Catholics and upwardly mobile Jews—backed De Sapio, while 67 percent supported Koch. Among

Italians, 85 percent supported De Sapio, 10 percent were undecided, and 5 percent backed a third candidate. One-third of Irish Democrats preferred Koch, while 56 percent supported De Sapio. Jewish voters clearly had no use for Tammany Hall; Italian voters felt equally hostile toward the reformers; and Irish Democrats leaned heavily toward the machine, though a strong minority contingent allied itself with the party's liberal, Jewish reform wing.

Polling revealed that De Sapio and Koch loyalists shared some concerns. Roughly two-thirds of each group volunteered a position in favor of more affordable housing for middle-class renters and apartment owners. But De Sapio's supporters were far more worried about escalating crime and tax rates than Koch voters who, in turn, were far more keen on education and civil rights initiatives. The two sides were not necessarily at an impasse over core issues, but they held to different ideas about which battles the Democratic Party should fight with the most vigor.[3]

New York's 1965 mayoral race brought some of these divisions into sharper relief. That year, Democrat Abraham Beame, the city controller, faced off against Congressman John V. Lindsay, the young, handsome, and Ivy-educated establishment candidate of the Republican and Liberal Parties. Also in contention was William F. Buckley Jr., the pugnacious editor of the National Review who carried the banner for the newly formed Conservative Party. Buckley possessed a doctrinaire hatred of government and the welfare state, matched only by a keen intellect and sharp tongue. He was smart enough to realize that his was a spoiler's campaign. His chief objective was to punish the Republican Party for its moderation by stealing enough GOP votes to deny Lindsay a victory.

Buckley tailored his message to disaffected Italian and Irish voters who were aching for a restoration of stability in a city that seemed to be spiraling out of control. Warning of a society "in which order and values are disintegrating [and] the wrath of the unruly falls with special focus on the symbols of authority, of continuity, of tradition," he decried an era "infatuated with revolution and ideology." Speaking before an overwhelmingly Catholic audience of New York City police officers, the conservative candidate held that the "principal agents of revolution" aimed for nothing less than the destruction of the church, with its "unyielding devotion to eternal truths which resist the plastic manipulations of the willful revolutionaries."

In front of the same audience of city law officers, Buckley lambasted black protesters in Selma, Alabama, for provoking a police response—prompting the New York Herald Tribune to lead with a damning headline, "6,000 N.Y. Police Applaud a Defense of Selma Cops"—and, on other occasions, he told supporters that "we cannot help the Negro by adjourn-ing our standards as to what is, and what is not, the proper behavior for human beings." Lindsay's assistant press secretary scored Buckley for making an "opaque highbrow appeal . . . to certain lowbrow prejudice," and many liberal-minded observers agreed that Buckley was simply partak-ing in good, old-fashioned race-baiting. Yet in fixing his target on alleged black lawlessness, Buckley was able to confine the debate to familiar tropes about law and order, and obedience and authority, which resonated sharply in New York's working-class, Catholic communities.[4]

Isolated incidents on the campaign trail suggested that Buckley was hitting a nerve. Campaigning in working-class neighborhoods in Brooklyn and Queens, Lindsay withstood two months of violent heckling that re-minded him "of some of the worst moments of history." When a backlash voter in Coney Island jabbed Lindsay's chest with the sharp end of a Buck-ley sign, the candidate's wife, Mary Lindsay—every bit the classic Protestant patrician as her husband—slapped the protester across the face. Jim Car-berry, one of Lindsay's speechwriters, recalled that several days after the Coney Island incident "an Irish-looking kid, apple-cheeks and pale skin and blonde hair and a little beefy" stepped up to shake the candidate's hand. Just as he began to extend his arm, Lindsay noticed that the young man was wearing a Buckley pin and concealing a thumbtack in his palm. Toward the end of the month, Lindsay was greeted by jeers of "Bum!" and "Communist!" as he road through Ridgewood, a predominately German and Irish Catholic section of Queens.[5]

In the weeks leading up to the election, internal Democratic Party poll-ing showed Buckley gaining significant ground among Catholics, roughly 18 percent of whom supported the Conservative Party candidate. Lindsay's aides believed that "the Irish as a group are basically politically conservative and are opposed to Lindsay's liberal image."[6] The results only partly sup-ported this notion. On election day, about 10 percent of Irish votes ul-timately went to Buckley, another 50 percent to Beame, and 40 percent to Lindsay, who became New York's first Republican mayor in two decades. Among Jews, roughly 57 percent cast their lot with Beame and 43 percent with Lindsay (mostly on the Liberal Party line). Italians proved the most receptive to the Conservative Party's overtures: 20 percent voted for Buck-ley, 41 percent for Lindsay, and 39 percent for Beame. Buckley's gambit failed. Instead of siphoning votes from Lindsay, he appeared to chisel just deeply enough into the Democratic Party's Catholic base.[7]

On the face of things, these results seem inconclusive: each major ethnic constituency split its votes. Moreover, Lindsay's liberal record made it difficult to characterize his support. Were Jewish voters backing Lindsay because he was liberal, while Irish and Italian voters backed him because he was a Republican? Ultimately, two important trends emerged from the contest. First, an outright majority of Catholics voters—about half of the Irish and over 60 percent of Italians—rejected the Democratic nominee. They did so because the community's conservative wing continued to gain strength by the mid-1960s. Most Catholics now fell somewhere between the center and right end of the political spectrum. The year before, conservative presidential candidate Barry Goldwater had won about 40 percent of New York's Italian vote and 55 percent of its Irish vote—this in the wake of John Kennedy's assassination and in an election cycle that saw Democrats sweep national and state elections.

Second, Jews voted almost to the last person for the Democratic and Liberal Party candidates. Critically, when Jews voted for Lindsay, most of them did so by pulling the Liberal Party lever; when Catholics voted for Lindsay, they did so by pulling the Republican Party lever. Lindsay's Catholic and Jewish voters probably endorsed him for different reasons: the former, because he enjoyed the backing of Old Left stalwarts like Alex Rose and David Dubinsky; the latter, because he was a Republican. Lindsay had earned a reputation for his strong advocacy of civil rights in Congress, but it may not have been apparent to his Irish and Italian supporters that he was further to the political left than virtually any other politician in New York. When he ran for reelection four years later, having shown Gotham his true political colors, Lindsay lost virtually all of his Catholic support.

Chris McNickle, author of a detailed ethnohistory of New York politics, concluded that Lindsay's coalition in 1965 was "unusual. A variety of groups had given him support, but each for different reasons. It would make maintaining a coalition challenging." In fact, Lindsay's original coalition crumbled almost overnight.[8]

H istorians and journalists have long considered New York's 1969 mayoral race a classic case of white voter backlash. That year, Lindsay lost his bid for renomination by the Republican Party, mostly because Italian and Irish voters—who accounted for almost half of all registered Republicans—swung overwhelmingly to his right-wing primary opponent, state senator John Marchi of Staten Island. That fall, Marchi ran on both the Republican and Conservative Party lines. Lindsay saved himself from political oblivion by securing the Liberal Party's nomination. And after a fractious, five-way primary, the Democrats nominated city controller Mario Procaccino, a product of the machine whose politics were far more moderate than history has recorded. Otherwise perceptive scholars have mislabeled Procaccino as a "right-wing," "law-and-order" Democrat— pejorative terms meant to identify him as a backlash candidate. But this assessment is wrong.[9]

Running in a crowded primary field that included such liberal heavy-weights as former Mayor Wagner, Bronx borough president Herman Badillo, and novelist Norman Mailer, Procaccino carved out his own political space by articulating in no uncertain terms the fears and resentments of middle- and working-class voters. Most conspicuously, he promised to crack down hard on crime. Locked in a tight race for front-runner, Badillo and Wagner each tried to outposition the other as the only viable alternative to backlash and racism. This strategy needed a demon, and that demon was Procaccino.

"If the voters are to have a choice among only arch-Conservative [John] Marchi, moderate Republican Lindsay, and a conservative Democrat like Mr. Procaccino," Wagner declared days before the primary, "then they will have no choice at all." A Procaccino victory, he continued, would be nothing less than "a disaster for liberalism." For his part, Badillo accused the former mayor of trying "to out-backlash Procaccino." On election day, Procaccino squeaked past his two rivals. Had either of them dropped out of the race, the other would almost certainly have won; had Mailer not taken 35,000 votes, Badillo probably would have emerged the victor.[10]

In fact, Procaccino was not a backlash candidate. Except for his willing-ness to engage in a frank discussion of urban crime, he bore almost noth-ing in common with Philadelphia's Frank Rizzo, Los Angeles's Sam Yorty, Boston's Louise Day Hicks, or Newark's Anthony Imperiale. To be sure, Procaccino was an obtuse, even bumbling politician whose lack of polish and sophistication made him an easy target to define and criticize. His short, thin frame, pencil-thin mustache, and beady, bespectacled eyes made him an instant favorite among caricature artists. While Lindsay deliv-ered inspiring oratory and Marchi poised himself as an intellectual's con-servative, Procaccino shouted, flailed his arms, and strayed hopelessly off message. Editorial writers relished his every rhetorical gaffe, as on one occasion when he told an audience in Harlem, "My heart is as black as yours," or when he informed reporters that his running mate, Francis X. Smith, was a man who "grows on you like cancer." Lindsay's retinue of Ivy League–educated political aides thought their Bronx rival was a light-weight: "What's a Mario Procaccino?" went one of the many jokes circulat-ing around Gracie Mansion.[11]

Procaccino announced that it was time to stop "coddling criminals" and called for reining in the "relief chiselers" who had brought the municipal budget to its breaking point. In the most popular line of the entire campaign, he dubbed the mayor and his supporters "limousine liberals." But he also deliberately positioned himself as a "moderate liberal." Rather than throw people off welfare, he would raise the minimum wage in order to make low-scale jobs more attractive than public assistance. He proposed a massive public works and job training program, to be funded by siphoning federal antipoverty money away from Community Action Programs that were "not producing, from which the poor don't really get money or other help." The idea was probably infeasible, but it was consistent with New Deal–style welfare policies that provided permanent relief for the "deserving poor" and temporary aid to those who could ultimately fend for themselves. As the candidate himself explained, "There are 40,000 persons on welfare who can work or can be trained for jobs. When I am the Mayor, these people will either work or become trainable or off welfare they'll go."[12]

Procaccino pledged to establish a cooperative daycare system for welfare mothers, enabling as many relief recipients as possible to undertake publicly financed career training and job placement. He even blasted the mayor for opposing a program to help wean drug addicts off heroin by providing free access to methadone. And he courted the favor of prominent city liberals assiduously, if sometimes ineptly: "I'm the same progressive Democrat today that I was 25 years ago when LaGuardia appointed me [to city government]," he told members of his party.

Procaccino especially bristled at charges that he was playing the race card. "If you think my record is that of a bigot," he protested, "you're out of your . . . cotton-picking mind." He denied that he was a "law-and-order" candidate, pointed to his support for a stronger black and Puerto Rican presence in the state's delegation to the 1968 Democratic National Convention, and claimed that he was happy to concede the backlash vote to John Marchi.

Above all, Procaccino excoriated his opponents for their elitism. "I've got the help of the little people on my side," he proclaimed, taking aim at his favorite targets—wealthy, white leftists. "I don't have the select few. I don't have those people that live in penthouses and who send their children to private school, and who have doormen, and who don't ride the subways. I have the people who sweat as they go into the subway." He also argued, to little avail, that it was wrong and even bigoted to assume that African Americans somehow opposed tougher sanctions on criminal behavior. Black New Yorkers, he said, "want law and order more than anyone else."[13]

Of the three mayoral candidates, only Marchi came close to representing the forces of backlash, though even he bore little resemblance to right-wing incendiaries in other northern cities. Introspective and courtly, he was the most understated of the entire field and was never considered a serious contender for the office. But he was deeply committed to the Goldwater wing of the Republican Party. The *Brooklyn Tablet*—no longer under Patrick Scanlan's tutelage, and far more liberal than it was in the 1950s—described the Staten Island senator, and his political ideology, with measured skepticism: "Refer to the John Birch Society and he will tribute them as God-fearing, patriotic men. Bring up the [college] campuses and he scowls his displeasure at a minority of 'brutalitarians' who would deprive the majority of an education. Ask him and he tells you that . . . he would use whatever force necessary to quell any disturbance on any campus in the City." The *Tablet* compared Marchi to an old-school parish priest. "He is at the front of the classroom, on his pulpit, defining, with Thomastic exactness, what is law and what is order," the editors wrote. "Listen to it. . . . Pray on it. John Marchi is your candidate for law and order. John Marchi is your candidate to bring the city together again. [But] no one raises his hand and suggests that championing law and order at the same time that he hopes to bring all the people together in this city would be a little less miraculous than multiplying the loaves and the fishes." Yet even a conservative candidate like Marchi, who openly embraced the term "law-and-order," bristled at the suggestion his was a "reactionary" movement.[14]

The mayoral candidates offered New Yorkers a healthy degree of ideological variety. On the left stood Lindsay—vice chairman of the National Advisory Commission on Civil Disorders (the Kerner Commission), unabashed ally of the Black Power movement, promoter of big government and Lyndon Johnson's Great Society, more at home in Harlem than in white, outer-borough neighborhoods. In the center was Procaccino—a product of the Democratic machine, a moderate by local standards who, in any other city, might have been considered very liberal. And on the right, Marchi—a member of Buckley's Conservative Party, an opponent of the New Deal welfare state, a foreign policy hawk, a champion of unmitigated police force. The distinctions between Marchi and Procaccino were significant, but Lindsay's campaign made a concerted and ultimately successful effort to paint both candidates as equally conservative. The reasoning behind his strategy was as old as New York City itself: ethnic politics.

Lindsay's advisers understood that their candidate was in deep trouble. Internal campaign polls in the early summer showed the mayor trailing Procaccino by fourteen points. Indeed, there was much about the incumbent administration to criticize. Police reports showed that "crimes against persons" more than doubled over the course of the decade. At the same time, Lindsay made his national reputation by walking the streets of Harlem and Bedford-Stuyvesant, dispatching aides and resources to ghetto neighborhoods, and placing black and Puerto Rican street criminals on the city's payroll to keep them from stirring up trouble during the "long, hot summers" of 1966, 1967, and 1968. Whether this approach should be credited for the relative calm that persisted in the streets of New York City is debatable. To many white voters, it seemed that the mayor cared far more about black radicals and violent criminals than middle-class and working-class taxpayers.[15]

Especially to members of the police and fire departments—mainstays of the Irish and Italian ethnic communities—Lindsay's New York could seem like a grim place to live and work. Between 1965 and 1969, the number of fire alarms requiring a departmental response increased from 68,000 to 240,000—partly a consequence of decaying infrastructure and arson in the urban ghetto, but also a result of the sharp upswing in false alarms, which rose from 18,000 per year in 1950 to 72,000 in 1969 even as the number of personnel held steady. This meant that by 1970, first responders in the Bronx answered almost twenty-three alarms per day. Firefighters viewed the surge in false alarms as an indication of deteriorating civic virtue and were incensed that the mayor's office regarded the problem merely as a political nuisance.

Lindsay also made enemies in the police department by breaking the "Irish mafia's" grip on the top brass. "One of the nice things about the Police Department," observed a high-ranking officer, "not only for me but for all of us, was that one was continually running into men who had once been schoolmates. A lot of us from Good Shepherd later would end up in the Police Department. . . . The brotherhood that ran all through the Police Department was very deep, and caused by a number of things, but one of them was this, that it bound all of us up in the lives we had in the city."

For better or worse, Lindsay changed the fortunes of many police officers when he appointed Sanford Garelik, a Jewish veteran of the New York Police Department, as chief inspector (the department's second-ranking job); Lloyd Sealy, a black officer, as assistant chief inspector; and Howard Leary, an Irish Catholic—but a Philadelphian—as commissioner. That all three men were regarded as either ethnic or geographic outsiders was bad enough to many city cops. Even more egregious, in their opinion, the Lindsay administration imposed a strict nonengagement policy meant to avoid the kind of violent clashes between rioters and police that were wracking other cities. Officers were routinely pulled back from riot scenes and told to hold their fire, even at the risk of personal injury. When 6,000 New Left activists descended on Grand Central Station at midnight on 22 March 1968, Garelik and other top brass literally had to restrain their officers while a band of yippie protesters vandalized the building's interior and spray painted obscenities on the marble walls and columns. Such incidents did not endear the mayor to the city's Irish and Italian communities, which placed a high premium on order and authority.[16]

Lindsay also performed dismally at the everyday tasks that compose the core of a big-city mayor's responsibilities. With patrician airs, he dressed down municipal labor leaders, who responded with a stultifying series of public sector strikes: the subway and bus workers in 1966, the teachers in 1967 and 1968, and the sanitation workers in 1968. The garbage strike left 10,000 tons of waste piled up in the streets each day; rats and stray cats and dogs swarmed over the mounting heaps of refuse and juvenile delinquents set scores of trash fires. Further problems for Lindsay came in early 1969, when his administration botched the city's emergency response to an unexpected winter blizzard, leaving most thoroughfares in Queens under more than a foot of snow for as long as two weeks.[17]

By the kindest assessment, Lindsay was an energetic and charismatic leader possessed of hopelessly inadequate management skills. He gave black and Puerto Rican New Yorkers a long overdue seat at the table and directed more resources to traditionally underprivileged and underserved communities. He also appealed to white New Yorkers' sense of justice, pluralism, and tolerance in a way that set him apart from other urban mayors. But he made no effort to conceal his disdain for working-class ethnic communities, which he regarded as parochial and even tribal. In 1965, when a reporter asked William F. Buckley which issue resonated most clearly with his supporters, the conservative candidate replied, "Mr. Lindsay's pretentiousness."[18]

John and Mary Lindsay worked hard to inject a sense of style in the mayor's office. They entertained visiting artists and intellectuals, attended the opera and ballet, and were photographed almost weekly in black tie and evening gown. But if these attributes made them the darlings of wealthy, cosmopolitan Manhattan, they made them anathema to many working-class Catholics who recognized in the Lindsays the same Protestant elite that had always refused to give the Italians and Irish a fair shake.

Nancy Seifer, a young Lindsay aide responsible for repairing relations between Gracie Mansion and white ethnic New York, found that the people running the city administration were hopelessly limited in their perspective. "There was a whole world out there that nobody at City Hall knew anything about," she complained. "The guys around Lindsay didn't know what a neighborhood was. If you didn't live on Central Park West, you were some kind of lesser being."

A cab driver summed up white ethnic frustration with the mayor when he told journalist Jack Newfield, "I can't stomach Lindsay. If you're colored, you're all right with him. If you're white, you got to obey the law." Pete Hamill, a popular city columnist, thought it really boiled down to a question of competency. "Lindsay doesn't really care much about Brooklyn, not about the white working class," he wrote, "and the white working class of Brooklyn was perceptive enough to understand that. The white working class will probably never relate to John Lindsay and his St. Paul's moralizing. They would tolerate him, I suspect, if the machine he runs would only function. But unfortunately, in his hands, it has functioned only sporadically."[19]

By early 1969 it was clear that the mayor was in deep political trouble, for reasons both within and outside his control. Lindsay's staff brought pollster Louis Harris to Gracie Mansion for a series of intensive strategy sessions. Harris's advice was simple. The mayor clearly had the black and Puerto Rican vote sewn up. Together, these two groups accounted for 30 percent of the population, but only 21 percent of registered voters—not nearly enough to secure a victory. Lindsay would almost certainly lose heavily among German, Irish, and Italian Catholics, who comprised roughly 35 percent of the electorate. The key to the election, then, was the Jewish community: 25 percent of the city's population, Jews also cast 30 percent of all votes in city elections.

According to Harris, Jews were deeply ambivalent at best—and at worst, hostile—toward Lindsay. To win reelection, the mayor would have to woo Jewish Democrats away from Procaccino—a fact that was not lost on the city controller or his staff. "What we're really talking about this year is the Jewish vote," one Democratic campaign official told the *New York Times*. "Most of the other vote is locked in. Is an Italian going to vote for Lindsay? How much of the Negro vote can we [Procaccino] possibly get?" The mayor's surveys found that middle-class Jews in Brooklyn and Queens were particularly dissatisfied with the administration's poor performance on crime, his ineffectual reaction to the 1969 winter blizzard, and his seeming disregard for outer-borough communities. But what alienated the Jewish community most of all was the mayor's strong show of support for Rhody McCoy and his blistering criticism of Al Shanker throughout the Ocean Hill–Brownsville controversy.[20]

Lindsay had made virtually no effort to serve as a good faith broker between the various adversaries. He baldly accused the UFT—90 percent of whose membership was Jewish—of demanding "illegal reappraisals" against the community school board, and he publicly charged Shanker with uttering "unfounded smears" against black parents and activists. Many Jews considered Shanker's charge of black anti-Semitism considerably well founded. In the strike's aftermath, Jewish leaders told the mayor's aides that their constituents "wish[ed] to be assured that all people, regardless of race or religion, will have their interests protected by the City authorities." More particularly, Jewish community members insisted that "persons presently on the public payrolls who are members of militant groups and who teach racial or religious hatred in any form [should] be removed with appropriate protection and due process"—a clear reference to teachers like Les Campbell, who routinely spewed antiwhite and anti-Semitic invective.[21]

Even members of the New York City Chapter of the American Jewish Congress—the Jewish community's most liberal mainstream advocacy group—felt that "the city has been particularly insensitive to Jewish interests." They complained that federal antipoverty funds were being targeted exclusively to black and Puerto Rican neighborhoods and missing the elderly, Jewish poor in neighborhoods like Williamsburg. In the wake of the widespread property damage and looting that befell Jewish shops on the evening of Martin Luther King Jr.'s assassination, "not even a statement was made [by the administration] to show sympathy for" Jewish store owners. "The inference was that, again, the real interests of Jews were ignored." Independent sources confirmed what the mayor's Jewish friends were telling administration officials. A survey conducted by Oliver Quayle in the spring of 1969 showed Procaccino besting Lindsay by a 2-to-1 margin among city Jews. The conservative columnists Rowland Evans and Robert Novak marveled at the results: "Astonishingly, sentiment among supposedly liberal Jews and supposedly conservative Catholics is indistinguishable," they wrote.[22]

When middle-class Jews from the outer boroughs began to cry foul, they were not necessarily indulging in baseless paranoia. For all his progressive instincts on matters relating to race and poverty, Lindsay frequently betrayed an attitude just shy of anti-Semitic. Early in his tenure, the mayor tried to restore alternate-side parking regulations—which required car owners to move and repark their vehicles twice a week—on Rosh Hashanah and Yom Kippur. Jews took strong exception to the proposal, which violated the city's long-standing cancellation of parking regulations on weekends and holidays. Under intense fire, Lindsay backed down. On another occasion, aides overheard him say, "It's about time I got rid of the white middle-class Jewish establishment that has run New York for so long." To Lindsay, Jews were neither a progressive force in city government nor a boon to civic culture. They were just one more entrenched, white ethnic power bloc—like the Irish police and the Italian sanitation workers —that stood in the way of liberal reform and efficient city government.

"I don't understand why people call me an anti-Semite," Lindsay complained to Werner Kramarsky, one of his top staff members. "Practically everybody around me is Jewish." This was a fair point. Lindsay's administration was top-heavy with young, Jewish liberals. But the mayor failed to understand the distinction between these well-educated, third-generation Jews and their parents, who lived in Brooklyn and Queens and still worked as schoolteachers, wholesalers, accountants, and dentists. When Kramarsky offered that Lindsay did not fundamentally understand the Jewish community, his boss "hit the roof."

Kramarsky was onto something, however. In September 1968, when Lindsay asked the heads of leading Jewish groups like the Anti-Defamation League, American Jewish Committee, and New York Board of Rabbis to "control" Albert Shanker, he simply did not appreciate how reviled the figure of the *shdatlan*—Yiddish for political fixer—was in collective Jewish memory. This may have been especially the case in the 1960s, when leading intellectuals like Hannah Arendt, who reached a wide reading audience, indicted Jewish community elites in wartime Europe as overaccommodating and even unwitting accomplices to Nazi ghettoization policies. When one of the rabbis present at the meeting asked Lindsay whether he had called on Cardinal Spellman to manage Mike Quill during the transit strike, the mayor replied angrily, "You Jews have made me use up all my Negro credit cards."

Even during the 1969 election season, Lindsay let slip his distaste for middle-class Jews. When a supporter approached him on a campaign swing through Fresh Meadows in Queens and told him he was a "wonderful man," the mayor pointed to nearby hecklers and replied, "And you're a wonderful woman, not like those fat Jewish broads up there." Journalists from the Associated Press and WNEW Radio recorded the mayor's off-color comments but decided against releasing them for public consumption. The *New York Times* did the same: a reporter later noted that Arthur Gelb, the paper's metro editor, "could be tough, but he was never malicious. You don't kick a man when he's down."[23]

In order to pry Jewish votes away from Procaccino, Lindsay followed his pollster's advice and took a two-part approach. First, he swallowed his pride and issued an endless stream of mea culpas to middle-class Jews in Queens and Brooklyn. He apologized for his conduct during the school strike, for his slow response to the blizzard, for his tendency to downplay black anti-Semitism, and, more generally, for his inattention to the outer boroughs.

Second, he undertook a deliberate campaign to cast Procaccino as an agent of reaction and backlash. The New York City election, Lindsay claimed, might very well be American liberalism's last great stand. The mayor pressed liberal Democrats into service to accuse the city controller of racism and conservatism. He argued directly that Procaccino was playing to people's fears and baser instincts, the same way that Richard Nixon and George Wallace had the year before.[24] The "whole thesis of our campaign," admitted Lindsay's trusted adviser, Richard Aurielo, "was to try to appeal to the Jewish consciousness in terms of the minorities. . . . We had to bring back some of the Jews who were not angry at the blacks."[25]

When Procaccino accused Lindsay of placing convicted criminals on the public payroll—a charge that was technically true, since the city bankrolled a community action program that employed ex-cons—the mayor pulled an old trick out of his campaign bag and dismissed the charge as a "Joe McCarthyite shotgun smear." It was a remark that was certain to enrage many Catholics and that could not possibly have been designed to win broad appeal among any bloc of voters except Jews. Hours later, the mayor appeared at the Moshulu Jewish Center in the Bronx, where an audience 1,200 strong gave "generous applause" when he promised to make New York a "center of liberalism and compassion." Phrased that way, New York Jews could not help but approve.[26]

Lindsay also played up his opposition to the Vietnam War, going so far as to lower the flag above city hall to half-mast during antiwar moratorium demonstrations in October. Both of Lindsay's opponents accused him of employing a "diversionary" tactic to steer the public's attention away from his record in office. Marchi spoke out even more forcefully than Procaccino, who also opposed the war, claiming that the mayor had "planted a dagger in the back of every American serviceman in Vietnam."

But Lindsay's plan was well conceived and deliberate. Harris had informed Liberal Party operatives that Jewish voters, who had long supported international cooperation and demilitarization, almost uniformly opposed American involvement in Vietnam. Playing to this critical demographic group, Lindsay called for an immediate truce and political "dissent . . . the highest form of patriotism." He also told protesters that "those that charge this [demonstration] is unpatriotic do not know the history of their own nation and do not understand that our greatness comes from the right to speak out."[27] It was central to his overall strategy to appeal to Jews by painting Procaccino as a carbon copy of Marchi—a reactionary, through and through—and to associate his own campaign with the politics of dissent and antiauthoritarianism.

In these efforts, Lindsay enjoyed considerable help from editorial writers, columnists, entertainment celebrities, and prominent liberal Democrats who alternated between painting Procaccino as a dangerous reactionary and a political clown. Appearing at a Lindsay fund-raiser, Woody Allen launched into a standup routine that imagined Procaccino lounging around in his living room "in his undershirt, drinking beer, and watching Lawrence Welk on television." Another quip popular among the self-styled learned classes held that Procaccino planned to replace the rugs at Gracie Mansion with linoleum, and that "Mario is so confident he's going to be elected mayor that he's bought a giant pink flamingo for the front lawn of city hall." A perceptive observer noted that "Italians especially . . . must wonder where contempt for class leaves off and prejudice against Italians begins. People who would not dream of telling Negro jokes regale each other with Italian jokes. . . . If I were Italian I might imagine that the humorous liberals are not conspicuously partial to Italians."

But Lindsay's supporters were not courting Italian votes—they were courting Jewish votes. And Jews, they believed, would gravitate naturally to the candidate who postured as more intellectual, middle-class, and progressive—if only they would bother to see the contrast. Much of the city's liberal establishment pitched in to sell Lindsay's message. Even before he won his party's nomination, the New York Post wrote Procaccino off as "short and square with a thick moustache and pin-stripe suits . . . like the caricature of an Italian ward heeler, so much so that many who demand a degree of dignity in a public figure find it hard to take him seriously." At the same time, the Post's editorial page warned that Procaccino was the "frenetic voice of the reactionary Democratic bloc."[28] The charges were unfair, but they stuck. On election day, the mayor carried roughly 44 percent of the Jewish vote, enough to win the election (see Table 10).

While newspapers tended to credit Lindsay's victory to his wide margins among African Americans, Puerto Ricans, and wealthy white liberals in Manhattan, in fact he would still have won had all the votes in Harlem, Bedford-Stuyvesant, Brownsville, South Jamaica, and the South Bronx been thrown out. As Andrew Hacker has noted, "The appearance of strong support arose from high percentages but exceedingly low turnouts. Receiving 76 percent of the votes in Brownsville looked impressive until it

TABLE 10. *1969 Mayoral Election Results by Ethnicity (All Figures Percentages)*

Ethnic Group	Lindsay	Procaccino	Marchi
Jews	44	44	12
Irish	26	26	48
Italians	15	55	30

Source: "Poor and Rich, Not Middle-Class: The Key to Lindsay's Re-Election," *New York Times*, 6 November 1969.

emerged that only 13,377 people had voted there. Lindsay would appear to have done much more poorly in Little Neck [a Jewish neighborhood in Queens] where his share was 32 percent, yet because the turnout in Little Neck was 49,925, his 32 percent there brought him more actual votes than his 76 percent in Brownsville."[29]

Put otherwise, a small but critical number of liberal Irish and Italian Catholics, and almost half of the Jewish electorate, formed Lindsay's critical election coalition. His was a narrow victory among middle-class voters, owing in no small part to a successful scare campaign that tapped into long-standing Jewish fears of the political right.

With the longer view in mind, what stands out about the 1969 election returns is their continuity with patterns established during the preceding two decades. Bearing in mind that the political center in New York City had always been—and continues to be—several degrees to the left of the national center, Jews split their votes between the moderate and left-wing alternatives, while most Catholics divided between the moderate and right-wing alternatives. These trends were long in the making and did not suggest a radical electoral realignment inspired by white backlash. To be sure, some of Marchi's and Procaccino's support owed to simmering racial antagonisms. But much of it did not.

Many Jews who backed Procaccino believed they were balancing pragmatism and liberalism as best that circumstances would allow. One such voter was Rose Shapiro, who served as president of the New York City Board of Education—the first woman ever to fill that post—during the better part of the 1968 teachers' strike. As a young girl, Rose had immigrated from Russia with her parents. She grew up in a fairly observant Jewish household, but her family was also deeply committed to socialism. Both Rose and her husband Morris were active members of the Socialist

Party and onetime confidantes of Norman Thomas. Throughout the 1930s, Morris Shapiro served as second chair to defense attorney Samuel Liebowitz in the famous Scottsboro trials in Alabama. He later served as assistant corporation counsel under Mayor Fiorello LaGuardia and, later, as director of Jacob Javits's first congressional campaign. Throughout the 1950s and 1960s, Morris continued to play a central role in the state Liberal Party.[30]

When their children began attending the city's public schools, Rose became an active member of the PTA, the United Parents Association, and her local community school board. Mayor Robert Wagner appointed her to the Board of Education in 1965, and in May 1968 she was elected president. Rose had opposed decentralization and community control from the start, but her chief complaint about John Lindsay was not so much his schools program as his callousness. As she later recalled:

> We didn't have . . . friction [on the board] until Lindsay came in. When Lindsay came in he was determined to run the Board of Education and I was determined not to let him run the Board . . . so we had a conflict. The whole decentralization issue was introduced and Lindsay . . . set up a committee to reorganize the whole school system and put the power in the hands of the community boards. . . . So they tried three experimental districts, each one failed, and that's when the anti-Semitism and all began. Each one failed. . . . I said, "I'm not against parents being active, I'm a living example of that kind of activity. I worked my rear end off in Harlem getting parents to come out and join the Parents Association. That's not the answer to this problem. [Community control was] a political answer to an educational problem and Lindsay [was] counting on that so that he [could] have the support of the black and Puerto Rican community." It was as simple as that.

Though Lindsay helped remove Rose Shapiro from the Board of Education in 1969, by early fall he realized that hers was an important voice in the Jewish community. Despite endless appeals from the mayor's aides—Shapiro later recalled that they "begged" her for an endorsement—she took to the synagogue circuit to denounce the mayor and urge that Jews reject his reelection bid.[31]

Morris and Rose Shapiro were precisely the sort of voters whom John Lindsay had alienated by late 1969. They rejected him not because he was a race liberal—on that score, the Shapiros had far better credentials than even the mayor. Instead, they opposed him because he seemed entirely indifferent to the concerns of liberal Jews who were otherwise favorably disposed to many of his programs and ideas.

Just as many Jewish supporters of Mario Procaccino were not apostles of white backlash, many Catholics who voted for John Marchi did so out of deeply held convictions about law and order—not out of an obsessive opposition to integration. A good example of Marchi's core supporters was Joe Kelly, a thirty-one-year-old elevator mechanic who participated in the famous "hardhat" demonstrations in mid-1970. For two weeks that spring, construction workers in downtown Manhattan—"hardhats," as the newspapers dubbed them—marched in support of the Nixon administration. They carried banners calling Lindsay a "communist" and a "faggot"; they rained kicks and blows on antiwar protesters; they even heckled and attacked a few innocent passers-by who seemed to fit the counterculture profile. It was a brutal display of conservative rage, made more surreal by the approving cheers of nearby brokers and secretaries from Wall Street. The mini-riots culminated on 20 May, when 100,000 longshoremen and tradespeople marched on city hall, chanting "USA, allaway," singing patriotic songs ("You're a Grand Old Flag," "God Bless America," "Yankee Doodle"), and waving American flags.[32]

Kelly was one of the hardhat protesters. He lived on Staten Island in a brand new, $40,000 home with his wife and two daughters. A Marchi voter the year before, and a supporter of William F. Buckley's mayoral bid in 1965, Kelly proudly informed a New York Times reporter that "no one's more Establishment than I am." As the interviewer reported:

Joe Kelly is proud, confident, and outspoken in the old American style. He is almost mythically proud of his flag, his country, the establishment, and eager to end the Indochina war by striking more aggressively, though the deaths of young soldiers and innocent civilians saddens him. He is determined to be on guard against Communism and to crush it wherever it threatens his nation. Joe is convinced that a subversive conspiracy of teachers, influenced by foreign powers, is brainwashing the students to Communist beliefs. Distressed by the hippie life-style of so many youths, he is also furious at student radicals who burn and shut down schools which his taxes pay for. . . . He's a stalwart charter member of Richard Nixon's silent majority, a devout Roman Catholic and fiercely loyal to his President, whose office he regards with almost holy respect.[33]

These were the ideas that Kelly was imbued with as a child while attending elementary and high school at St. Peter's, a parish on Staten Island in the Diocese of Brooklyn. Drawing a powerful correlation between tenets of the Catholic catechism and the American political system, Kelly explained that "the Pope to the Catholic Church is the same as the President is to the American people. He's the one who decides. He's infallible when he speaks of religion. . . . I'm not saying Nixon is infallible. But he's Commander in Chief of the armed forces. He's in charge." Patrick Scanlan himself could not have put the matter in sharper relief.

It is little wonder that the Lindsay years drove Kelly to a breaking point. For someone reared on fixed ideas about authority and culture, New York in the late 1960s probably seemed like Rome before the fall: welfare moochers violently asserting their right to larger public stipends, street hoodlums running a glorified protection racket on the mayor's office, black militants running roughshod over schoolteachers and public officials, escalating crime rates, and neighborhoods in decay. Or so it all seemed to Joe Kelly. "[You can] do what you want in Lindsay's city," he fumed. Even "burn the schools."

Many backlash voters like Kelly were far from pristine on matters of race and civil rights. When asked whether he would mind if a black family moved onto his block, Kelly did not have to think twice. "I had to bust my backside for five years to get that down payment for that house," he explained, echoing conventional wisdom that racial integration was likely to drive down neighborhood property values. "I am not interested in seeing that all go down the drain." Yet Kelly's racism was inconsistent—not an obsession, nor even particularly well thought out. "They're here to stay, entitled to [stay]," he said of new black and Puerto Rican members of his AFL local. Like many other New Yorkers, Kelly drew sharp lines between home and workplace. To labor beside African Americans and Puerto Ricans was acceptable, but neighborhoods were to be protected at any cost. Ultimately, though, Kelly's racial fear was only one among many resentments that drove him to support Buckley, Nixon, and Marchi.

On the other hand, it was undeniable that race played a part in the 1969 elections. As Lindsay campaigned in working-class, predominately Catholic areas of Queens and the Bronx, he was greeted by jeers and cries of "Nigger lover!"[34] Race politics in New York were usually more subtle than this. Shortly after the mayoral election, Lindsay's office announced plans to raise 840 units of low-income housing in the suburban-style Queens neighborhood of Forest Hills—a predominantly Jewish area with a roughly equal number of renters and homeowners. The city's designs met with almost instantaneous opposition. Residents complained that the construction of three high-rise public housing buildings—each twenty-four stories tall—would destroy the integrity of their community. They especially feared the blight and violence that seemed to ensue naturally from the infusion of a high-poverty population in an otherwise stable, middle-class neighborhood.

Many Forest Hills residents were "refugees" from neighborhoods in Brooklyn (Crown Heights, Brownsville, and Flatbush) that had fallen victim to ghettoization. They were less than eager to see their new homes slip into the same malaise. Moreover, they suspected that cynical calculations were at play. Jews had a reputation for fleeing neighborhoods at the first sign of decline; Catholics had a reputation for fighting integration—sometimes violently.[35] "We do not wish to prevent the betterment of any minority group, but why is it always at our expense?" complained one community member. "Is it because the City knows that when it comes to these things the 'liberal' Jews among us develop an unwarranted guilt complex and won't fight City Hall?" Within months, a group calling itself the Queens Jewish Community Council (QJCC) arose to fight the development plan. The New York City Board of Rabbis lent its support to the community group, though not without internal dissension. Several prominent rabbis—among them, Ben Zion Bokser of the Forest Hills Jewish Center—vocally supported the scattered-site housing plan.[36]

The Lindsay administration handled the situation with typical clumsiness. It claimed that 40 percent of the tenants would be elderly, a statistic meant to assuage fears of increased crime and violence. In fact, 40 percent of the units were to be reserved for senior citizens, but only 14 percent of the development's occupants would be elderly. When this information became public, trust quickly broke down between both sides. The city also continued to oppose the screening of potential project residents for arrest records or history of drug use. Lindsay's aides had long maintained that such practices placed an undue burden on the poor.[37]

A young lawyer named Mario Cuomo served as mediator between the city and the Forest Hills community. Initially he was skeptical of the Jewish residents, observing:

The theme generally is that the low-income housing project results in decay and eventual destruction of the surrounding middle-class community. The evidence for this is usually quite meager. . . . But the conversation is undiminished by the failure of specific proof. . . . One story of a mugging at a project—whether true or not—will overcome in their minds any array of statistics. The syllogism is simple: Welfare and Blacks are generally responsible for a great deal of crime; there are

Welfare and Blacks in projects; there will be a great deal of crime in and around the project. And then, too, there is a quick projection from the problem of crime—however real, however fancied, or exaggerated—to all other middle-class complaints: taxes, education, etc. All of these may be legitimate, but this coupling of them with the crime problem results eventually in an indictment of the project for all the sins against the middle class.

Indeed, there was little love lost between Cuomo and the QJCC. But even he came to admit that the situation was complex. "It seems clear to me that the influx of welfare families will bring with it a threat of increased crime," he conceded, several days later. "That has been checked out in several sources and is a matter of almost common experience. . . . But if it is true where does that leave us? Is it better to keep these families and their crime in the ghetto, where crime is already rampant?"[38]

Angry letters poured into Rabbi Bokser's office. They revealed an almost singular focus on the threat of crime and violence, seconded by the fear that yet another Jewish neighborhood might fall to ruin. Bokser's neighbors were furious with the city and with their apostate community leader. Absent from their dispatches were the overt expressions of racism and meditations on declining property values so common in other cities where white homeowners' councils tried to slow the tide of integration. But the shouts of protest bore unmistakable similarity to race-based housing revolts in other northern cities. "You said that the people who oppose the low-income project are driven by meaningless fear," wrote one angry resident to Bokser. "You intimated that the people of this community do not want the project because many of its residents will be black. Well, I can tell you that the people of this community *are afraid*. . . . [T]o the average, hard-working, law-abiding resident of Forest Hills, low-income housing means one thing—CRIME. We are not afraid of having people with black skins, green skins, or purple skins move into the community."[39]

The unusually low rate of home ownership in New York City rendered the influence of anti-integration homeowners' councils fairly moot. Even in Queens—next to Staten Island, the most suburban of the five boroughs—almost 60 percent of all housing units were renter occupied.[40] A study of new Queens residents in the 1940s and 1950s has found that homeowners' and renters' groups frequently coalesced to fight for better infrastructure and public services; in this sense, New York's quasisuburbanites were political almost from the start.[41] But resisting black home ownership does not seem to have figured into their political activities—at least not until the

Forest Hills controversy. Notably, opposition to low-income housing in Forest Hills in the early 1970s drew on both renters and homeowners. Theirs may have been a struggle to preserve the neighborhood's class character as much as its racial homogeneity, but the end logic of the anti–public housing campaign was the perpetuation of segregated communities.

"People have a right to be alarmed by the influx of such a large number of low income residents," wrote Rabbi Harry Halpern to Bokser. "I know that in schools where there has been considerable busing there are numerous cases of threats against children who will not give their money to those who wield knives." Rabbi Joseph Sternstein, who served as spiritual leader of Manhattan's Congregation Ansche Chesed before the surrounding neighborhood slipped into decline, explained: "I have served . . . an inner city temple . . . and I was in the thick of many . . . controversies . . . and had my family exposed to the conditions of the city. . . . I can tell you personally that if you don't want Queens Blvd. to be transformed to upper Broadway, where Jewish women cannot walk down streets unmolested, you will reverse your position on this Forest Hills project."[42]

It only complicated matters that the city's small number of black homeowners often voiced some of the very same concerns in their opposition to scatter-site public housing. In Baychester, a neighborhood tucked away in the northeast corner of the Bronx, the local chapter of the NAACP went so far as to oppose the city's construction of the Boston-Secor Houses, a low-income housing project championed by Mayor Lindsay. "People say, 'You're prejudiced against your black brothers,'" lamented a local black homeowner. "But I'm not prejudiced against my black brother. I know what it took for me to get here and I say he can do the same. If his son's a junkie, I don't want him stealing my TV. Does that make me a racist?"[43]

Sociologist Jonathan Rieder found a far cruder variety of backlash among Italian Americans in Canarsie, a blue-collar section of Brooklyn that was the scene of violent resistance to school busing and residential integration in the early 1970s. Rieder explained that these working-class New Yorkers were likely to assert their right to preserve neighborhood integrity at any price. But even hard-liners tended to distinguish between "blacks," for whom they readily acknowledged respect, and "niggers" or "trash," whom they defined as the enemy. As one Italian resident explained: "The neighborhood was totally destroyed as soon as the blacks moved in. Buildings started burning down, and we had more crime. My sister and two of my little cousins went trick or treating one night, and about six or seven niggers ripped them off. . . . I'm not saying it's all blacks. It's just that people have blacks living right next to them, and sure, they're nice people. In my old neighborhood we used to have blacks who were nice people and we were friends and everything." Like the residents of Forest Hills, Canarsians seemed transfixed by the crime and violence that burned a hole in most of the neighboring areas of Brooklyn—areas from which many of them had fled only a few years before—and, despite their attempts to qualify such fears as color-blind, associated African Americans with urban blight and decay.

One homeowner noted: "It's the minority's right to move where they want. I wouldn't mind if a colored family moved next door if they were upstanding and fine like me. Educated and intelligent blacks, why not? They are people. Color shouldn't have any place there. But I don't want trash who will frighten me. My problem is walking in the streets and seeing people who I don't know whether they are going to bother me. There is no reason to walk in fear."[44] Critically, these attitudes were shared by an almost equal portion of the city's Jewish, Italian, and Irish communities, suggesting a racial polarization that pitted black and Puerto Rican residents against their white neighbors.

But even as white New Yorkers came to share many of the same racial concerns and animosities, they parted ways at the polls. The powerful combination of religion, national origins, and class continued to divide Jews and Catholics from each other, especially on election day. Exit polls in 1968 indicated that 87 percent of city Jews voted for Democrat Hubert Humphrey, down only slightly from 1964 totals, when 92 percent supported Lyndon Johnson. In heavily Catholic backlash areas, Humphrey eked out a slim majority (52 percent), while Nixon received 41 percent and George Wallace 7 percent of the vote.[45]

Four years later, when Nixon ran for a second term, the New York Times reported that the president "overwhelmed [George] McGovern in areas of predominantly Roman Catholic voters," while Jews continued to vote Democratic, though in somewhat diminished numbers. Exit polls suggested that McGovern won 66 percent of the Jewish vote nationally but a whopping 85 percent among New York City Jews. Nationally, Nixon won 58 percent of the Italian vote, compared with 68 percent of New York Italians who supported the incumbent president. Nationally, 53 percent of Irish voters backed Nixon.[46]

By the early 1970s, over half of all Irish New Yorkers—but only 16 percent of Jewish New Yorkers—identified themselves as "conservative." Half of all Jews considered themselves "liberals" and another 27 percent "moderates," compared with just 13 percent of Catholics who identified as "liberals."[47]

In effect, patterns dating back to the 1940s persisted long into the postwar period. Most New York Jews clung stubbornly to political liberalism, long after many of them abandoned liberal positions on integration and urban race relations.[48] The Catholic community continued to divide sharply between moderate and conservative factions. It was still possible for a candidate like John Lindsay, whose administration was openly hostile to Jewish interests, to court Jewish voters by conjuring up their traditional fears of political reaction and conservatism. Similarly, many Catholics reared on the culture of conservative anticommunism in the 1940s and 1950s found themselves drawn to backlash candidates in the 1960s who promised a return to law and order and a renewal of public authority. The end effect was a slow but steady disintegration of the city's New Deal coalition of urban Jews and Catholics.

But Catholic backlash voters did not pose the sole threat to the New Deal bloc. As Allen Matusow has noted, however "ephemeral" the New Left might have been, "the movement had significant consequences" for postwar liberalism. "Confronted by the rage of their own children, mainstream liberals moved left. Those who did not—the Johnsonian liberals of the Democratic party, the corporate liberals of the new left demonology—lost their capacity to shape events. The young Americans throwing rocks at the Pentagon and chanting, 'Hey, hey, LBJ. How many kids did you kill today?' were one reason why Johnson, as he entered the election year of 1968, was staggering toward political extinction."[49] Prominent among those young protesters were a small but vocal minority of Jewish youth who took their dissenting heritage to its logical conclusion, and their Irish and Italian peers, who began exposing the generational cracks in New York's Catholic subculture.

8 Upheaval

Americans living in the late 1960s witnessed a general unraveling of authority in virtually every area of life—from the church to the classroom, and from the dinner table to the political convention. Many of these social and political disturbances pitted parents against their children. Consequently, scholars have devoted a great deal of attention to the dynamics of generational conflict, alternatively blaming or crediting any number of causes—including progressive child rearing, middle-class affluence, and the disconnect between the rhetoric and reality of Cold War liberalism—with turning the baby boomers against their elders.[1] Historians have noted that the general revolt against authority played out differently according to class, race, gender, and region.[2] But in New York, as elsewhere, ethnicity also played a central role in determining how the struggle between parents and children evolved.

If the city's liberal coalition was bleeding white (mostly Catholic) voters on its right flank, it also faced a strong challenge from the left. Whereas many Italian and Irish voters could no longer support a political persuasion that seemed inimical to the values associated with their ethnic upbringing, many young Jews took their parents' dissenting ideal to its logical conclusion and joined the ranks of the antiliberal New Left. Prominent voices in the Jewish community roundly condemned these prodigal sons and daughters for their radical approach to social and political reform, but the parents of Jewish activists, who raised their children to question authority and to view themselves as autonomous individuals, often lent a surprising degree of support to the student movement's rejection of Cold War liberalism.

Young Irish and Italian New Yorkers also grappled with the social and political challenges of late 1960s. But their rejection of adult authority was more complicated. It broke with a long-standing consensus in the city's Catholic community about the importance of authority and the organic, divine order of community. Encouraged by theological developments within the church and by the same demographic pressures and sociopolitical events that spurred non-Catholics to action, these Italian and Irish protesters challenged some of the most cherished ideals of their upbringing and incurred a much greater wrath from their elders than their Jewish counterparts.

The contrast between two student uprisings—one at Columbia University in 1968 and the other at Fordham University in 1969–70—spoke volumes about the persistent influence of ethnicity in determining how different communities responded to the revolt against authority. At the same time, the reaction to these events also revealed shifting circumstances that would soon undermine the city's once-cohesive white ethnic communities.

In late April 1968, just weeks before the end of the academic year, upwards of 700 white and black students at Columbia University staged a takeover of five campus buildings, including Low Library, which housed the offices of President Grayson Kirk. The original protests were inspired by the campus chapter of Students for a Democratic Society (SDS), whose newly elected leader, twenty-year-old college junior Mark Rudd, galvanized left-wing opposition to three university policies: the administration's decision to build a new gymnasium in Morningside Park, a run-down public commons bordering nearby Harlem; the university's participation in the Institute of Defense Analysis, a research consortium involving leading American universities and the Department of Defense; and, finally, the administration's alleged disregard for student opinion.[3]

The previous fall Rudd—whom Daniel Bell, a prominent Columbia sociologist, described as "a tall, hulking, slack-faced young man with a prognathic jaw and blue-gray eyes so translucent that his gaze seems hypnotic"— had wrestled control of the Columbia SDS chapter from its so-called "Praxis Axis," a relatively moderate wing that favored abstract intellectual discussion over the more direct confrontation methods favored by Rudd's "action faction." True to his colors, Rudd set off the spring showdown with a dramatic and incendiary public letter addressed to Kirk. "If we win," Rudd announced, "we will take control of your world, your corporation, your university and attempt to mold a world in which we and other people can live as human beings. Your power is directly threatened, since we will have to destroy that power before we take over." In conclusion, Rudd famously quoted the black arts poet LeRoi Jones: "Up against the wall, motherfucker, this is a stick-up."

The student takeover at Columbia combined all the elements of high political drama, moral theater, and sheer farce. Much to Rudd's chagrin, though SDS had initiated the week-long strike with its seizure of Hamilton Hall, black student activists who joined the protests hours later summarily expelled the white radicals and forced them to find other buildings to occupy. With city police officers encircling the campus and awaiting the order to raid Hamilton Hall, junior faculty members convened an ad hoc committee that issued a string of near-hysterical and often contradictory statements and then formed a human ring around Lowe Library in order to provide a buffer against a possible police attack.

Unimpressed but thoroughly amused, the left-wing *Village Voice* deemed the student takeover the "Groovy Revolution" and advised disapproving readers not to "underestimate the relationship between litter and liberty at Columbia. Until last Tuesday . . . the university was a clean dorm where students paid rent, kept the house rules, and took exams. Then the rebels arrived in an uneasy coalition of hip, black, and leftist militants. They wanted to make Columbia more like home, so they ransacked files, shoved furniture around, plastered walls with paint and placards."[4]

These excesses notwithstanding, some of the finer points of the SDS agenda were not without reason. The proposed university gym encroached on one of the few public parks available to Harlem residents. In a clumsy attempt to compensate local residents for the loss of open space, Columbia had proposed building a community gym on the bottom level of the larger structure with a separate subbasement entrance. Critics developed a predictable but fitting epithet for the offensive architectural design—"Gym Crow"—and argued, convincingly, that a predominately white, elite, private institution had no business appropriating public park space from an underprivileged urban community.

But critics appreciated how tenuous were the concrete grounds for the student takeover. Rudd later averred that at the time of the university takeover, he had no idea where the Morningside gym site actually was. The gym only provided a pretext for shutting down an institution that he and other student radicals viewed as the very embodiment of Cold War liberalism—a creed they rejected every bit as forcefully as Catholic backlash voters like Joe Kelly.

In an article written shortly after the student takeover, Daniel Bell drove home exactly this point. "The ethos of Columbia is liberalism," he explained. "There is complete academic freedom. . . . Most of the faculty is, politically, liberal. The men who give Columbia its reputation—Lionel Trilling, Meyer Schapiro, Ernest Nagel, Richard Hofstadter—have been in the forefront of liberal causes for more than thirty years. A number of Columbia's leading political scientists and law professors—Roger Hilsman, Zbigniew Brzezinski, Richard Gardner, Charles Frankel, William Cary, Wallace Sayre—have served in recent Democratic administrations." A whopping 70 percent of the university's faculty supported a withdrawal from Vietnam.[5]

Bell found that "in the last two years liberalism itself, particularly in the student movement, had come under severe attack." This was true at Columbia and across the nation. In this sense, students were not revolting so much against their alma mater as against the very foundation of liberal humanism that Columbia seemed to represent.

The Vietnam War and its resultant credibility gap was certainly one cause of the younger generation's loss of liberal faith. So was the civil rights movement: students coming of age in the early 1960s watched televised reports from Alabama and Mississippi and became increasingly skeptical of the grandiose promises they had been handed by their parents. The black struggle for equality not only challenged young people to question the discrepancy between American rhetoric and reality; it also drew well over 1,000 white students to the trenches of the Deep South between 1960 and 1964. In the fall of 1964, these students returned home from the Mississippi "Freedom Summer" project and sowed the seeds of activism that would define the "sixties generation."

Pronouncements such as, "Michigan State is the Mississippi of American universities"—an actual claim asserted by an activist in Lansing, circa 1965—resonated deeply with many students who felt equally betrayed by southern racism and collegiate life. Having grown up in a prosperous, middle-class culture that placed children at the center of domestic life, many members of the sixties generation came to feel both neglected and victimized by university administrators. They understood their plight as part of a larger pattern of American exploitation, the most egregious example of which was Jim Crow.

On one hand, undergraduates in the 1960s drifted, virtually anonymous, in a sea of bureaucracy. The postwar boom in higher education, fueled largely by the growth of government-funded scientific research, had bloated public and private institutions beyond recognition. Before 1940 no American university claimed a student population over 15,000; by 1970, more than fifty schools were at least that big, while eight institutions boasted enrollments of over 30,000. Berkeley's president, Clark Kerr, admitted that the new "multiversity" could be a "confusing place for the student." Freshmen accustomed to the doting atmosphere of home and high school quickly learned that their new environment was not constructed around their personal desires and opinions. In the wake of the 1968 Columbia takeover, David Truman, the university's vice president, remarked that "this is the most demanding generation for attention that I've ever seen in my life" and marveled at their "sense that they're just IBM cards, which is a general kind of thing." This was precisely the kind of observation that enraged enthusiasts of the New Left.[6] Many students agreed with the activist who complained, "They always seem to be wanting to make me into a number. I won't let them. I have a name and am important enough to be known by it. . . . I'll join any movement that comes along to help me."

Paradoxically, universities could sometimes be all *too* mindful of their students' names—as well as their whereabouts and extracurricular lives. Prevailing in loco parentis regulations gave administrators license to police the personal lives of their students—particularly coeds, whose comings and goings were subject to a crude double standard. At the University of Illinois, for example, only female undergraduates faced weeknight curfews of 10:30 P.M. and weekend curfews of 1:00 A.M. At the University of Massachusetts, coeds who broke curfew by five minutes lost privileges for the ensuing Friday night, ten minutes cost them Saturday night, and fifteen minutes warranted a hearing before the women's judiciary committee. At Barnard—Columbia University's all-women's affiliate—a man could visit a woman's dormitory room at set hours, but three of the couple's four legs had to be touching the floor at all times as a preventative against premarital sex.

By the mid-1960s, many collegians began to feel oppressed by this double-edged sword of benign neglect and in loco parentis. Events in the South galvanized a small but vocal core of activists who, in turn, inspired a somewhat larger number of their peers. "If there was one reason for increased student protest," recalled a journalist at the University of Utah, "it would probably be the civil rights movement. The movement . . . convinced many of them that non-violent demonstrations could be an effective device on the campus. It also served to make them more sensitive of their own civil rights."

Students who demonstrated on campuses in the latter half of the decade detected a great deal of continuity between their struggle and the struggle for black liberation. "The American university campus has become a ghetto," claimed one activist at the University of Florida. "Like all ghettos, it has its managers (the administrators), its Uncle Toms (the intimidated, status-berserk faculty), its raw natural resources processed for outside exploitation and consumption (the students)." A national survey conducted at the close of the 1964–65 school year revealed that students felt the most pressing issues facing them on campus concerned in loco parentis regulations. They named civil rights as the most important off-campus issue.

Some students also found common cause with victims of colonialism in the third world—particularly, as the decade wore on, in Vietnam. Again, civil rights leaders in the South blazed new intellectual paths in first making this association. "Not wanting to negotiate with the Vietcong is like the power structure in Mississippi not wanting to negotiate" with black political activists, argued one civil rights worker in 1966. Such cries became more common, especially among radical, white members of SDS and similar organizations.[7]

The student takeover at Columbia brought into sharp relief all of these ingredients of radical protest. It also highlighted another element of the New Left revolt: the university's SDS chapter was overwhelming Jewish in composition, as were the ranks of the nonaffiliated student protesters. The American Jewish Committee was so "frankly worried about the Jewish aspect of the Columbia trouble" that it commissioned a survey to ascertain whether Jews did, in fact, figure prominently in the upheaval. The AJC's worst fears were confirmed. "Prominent among the student rebels were Jewish students," explained a confidential, internal memorandum. "Frequently references to faculty supporters of the strike included Jewish names."[8] Subsequent national studies—more scientific than the AJC's informal poll of Columbia radicals—confirmed that Jews were disproportionately represented in the ranks of the New Left, more likely than non-Jews to participate in political protests, and more inclined to embrace radical political positions.[9]

Using a variety of criteria to identify adherents of New Left ideology, Stanley Rothman and S. Robert Lichter found that at Harvard, the University of Massachusetts at Amherst, the University of Michigan, and Boston University Jews comprised 53 percent of campus radicals, 63 percent of those who participated in seven or more protests, and 54 percent of those who led at least three protests. Generally, the more secular the Jewish student's upbringing, the more likely he or she was to embrace radical politics. Yet even Orthodox Jewish students were more radical and more likely to engage in political protests than secular Catholics and Protestants.

To some extent, these ideological differences were attributable to family background. Whereas over 50 percent of non-Jewish students surveyed identified their fathers as Republicans and only 15 percent as liberal Democrats, 40 percent of Jewish students claimed their fathers were liberal Democrats, 9 percent socialists or communists, and only 2 percent Republicans. Over two-thirds of Jewish radicals reported that their parents subscribed to at least one liberal (e.g., *New Republic*, *Dissent*) or left-wing (e.g., *Masses*, *Liberation*) periodical.[10]

Though their affinity for the New Left carried with it an implicit rejection of the mainstream liberal values that formed the heart of secular

Jewish culture, Jewish students were not rebelling against their parents as much as they were following to its logical conclusion the very instruction manual on which they had been raised. Taught that dissent and agitation were worthwhile and important endeavors, Jewish rebels like Mark Rudd were only heeding the best advice of their rabbis, parents, and teachers when they turned in full force against adult authority.[11]

Rudd was a perfect representative of Cold War–era Jewish culture: raised in a family that placed a high premium on dissent and intellectual choice—a family that sometimes valued the process of freethinking over the actual product of free thought—Rudd moved naturally into the ranks of SDS and claimed as his creed a rhetorical line that was decidedly in concert with his dissenting heritage. Far from viewing her son's protest activities as a form of rebellion against his family and upbringing, Mark's mother— a housewife from the northern New Jersey suburbs—spoke affectionately of "my revolutionary" and, with her husband, told reporters she was "100 percent behind" Mark even if she did not agree entirely with his current political stance. "I was a member of the depressed generation," Mark's father, a real estate agent and army veteran, explained, "and my greatest concern had always been making a living. Mark doesn't have to worry about that so much and we're glad he has time to spend on activities like politics."

Mark, a former Boy Scout who was raised in a conventionally middle-class suburb, made few excuses for his rejection of his parents' liberal politics. "People keep asking me why we take such strong stands," he explained, in a perfect reiteration of Jewish wisdom on the need to question and confront conventional social structures. "Well, liberals don't believe in the real world. They can rationalize anything. There will always be slums, they say, there will always be war. A lot of people never analyze that or challenge it. Those guys made me ask why war or slums have to exist. A radical doesn't accept that."

Other parents might have lamented their son's radical skepticism of their own values, but not the Rudds. In early May 1968, while Mark was busy reaping havoc at Columbia University, his proud parents found time to drive into Manhattan with a homemade meal of veal parmigiana (decidedly not kosher), which the family shared in a parked car on Amsterdam Avenue.[12]

The Rudd family was not unusual. During the height of the takeover crisis, several hundred parents of SDS activists—the most vocal of whom bore Jewish surnames—convened an ad hoc meeting to denounce the university administration. The parents endorsed their children's demand of total amnesty from disciplinary charges and condemned the university's threat to call in the New York City Police Department (NYPD) to restore order on campus. When Alan Temple, the vice chairman of the Columbia Board of Trustees, politely suggested that they might "guide" their children toward a peaceful surrender, the parents—according to their own meeting minutes—"replied that the 'generation gap' which Mr. Kirk has described 'is being swiftly bridged by the families of many of the strikers.'" Added Isabel Grossner, whose son, Morris, was a college junior: "We have learned a lot from our children the past week."

The problem, another parent maintained, was not the students' willful destruction of property or their use of physical coercion and violent threats to make a political point. Rather, it was "how to get the administration to take this seriously, because they have not—that is, to take the students seriously, because they have taken it seriously to send in the police, but to take the ideas and the concepts of change which the students are putting forth seriously. I think that is where the issue lies." When an enraged parent denounced leading Columbia academics like Lionel Trilling and Daniel Bell as "Cold war warriors" and expressed "outrage" that "our kids [might] be punished in any way for what they have done," his or her cry (the transcripts do not indicate the speaker's gender) was met with thunderous applause.[13]

A week into the campus takeover, the university finally loosed the NYPD on the student activists. Only the black activists occupying Hamilton Hall went quietly. White students pelted officers with food, trash cans, books, and any other office materials they could get their hands on. Fourteen police officers sustained injuries, including one who suffered a heart attack after student protesters repeatedly kicked him in the chest.

Even before the bust, police patience had worn thin. Diana Trilling reported that "revolutionary students spat at people they disliked, including senior faculty members. An old couple crossing the campus was shouted at: 'Go home and die, you old people, go home and die.' A law professor, my neighbor, walking with his wife near the campus gates, was gratuitously punched in the stomach by a passing student wearing the red armband of his militancy . . . a Barnard girl-demonstrator jumped up and down in front of the faculty line . . . shouting 'Shit, shit, shit, shit.'"

Radical Barnard students posed a special menace to the mostly Irish and Italian police, whose every instinct was to avoid tangling violently with members of the opposite sex. For days, young women bit and spat at the silent officers and besieged them with incendiary taunts like "Your sister sucks off your mother" and "Go fuck yourself, pig." A police sergeant spoke for many of his men when he wondered at the "language that [came] out of their mouths . . . you begin to wonder whether you're in a mental hospital. . . . Those kids go crazy when they see us. The uniform seems to trigger something in them. They become dirty, plain dirty. They use the worst language I've ever heard. They make insulting gestures to us. The girls make sexual overtures—when they're not swearing."

The police sergeant was onto something. His uniform represented authority and was therefore certain to enrage some of the young protesters who had been raised on a diet of skepticism and dissent. But none of this was much consolation to his beleaguered officers, who withstood days' worth of verbal and physical abuse without breaking rank. At 5 A.M. on the night of the bust, exhausted and worn down by the constant taunting and violence, many of the police officers snapped, chasing hundreds of protesters and innocent passers-by down Broadway, attacking them with clubs and kicking them to the ground.

In retrospect, Richard Hofstadter, a leading member of the Columbia history department, marveled that even some faculty members "were beginning to forget that force had been introduced on the campus by the seizure of the buildings by the students, and were thinking only of the force that might come if the police came." He might very well have said the same of the parents. Though they called for the "resignations of President Grayson Kirk, Dean [David] Truman, and those trustees who supported their action in calling the police onto campus" and decried the eventual police bust as a "holocaust," the parents said very little about the violence that their children directed against the police. In the after-hours of the initial raid, several student radicals brutally attacked patrolman Frank Gucciardi, leaving him with a permanent spinal injury.[14]

At a mass meeting held the following day, 200 parents gathered at nearby Riverside Church to condemn the Columbia administration and the police. "You get the feeling there's something sick about this university," said Leo Hurwitz, whose son, Thomas, was dragged out of Mathematics Hall and arrested during the bust. "The faculty and students don't seem to be important here. The administration—God help it—doesn't seem capable of running this place without brutality." Katherine Rosen, the mother of a college sophomore, agreed with the thrust of Hurwitz's statement. "I don't care about the politics of this campus," she declared. "But why did there have to be blood spilled here? When all this started, I had the feeling that the students were way out. Now I feel that the administration is way out." Isabel Grossner spoke for many of the parents when she called the police raid "an atrocity—completely unjustified. . . . The police created the riot here."[15]

At the time, it did not occur to many bystanders or participants that Jews played an unusually large role in the Columbia campus takeover. When asked years later about the roots of SDS radicalism, Robert Friedman, editor of the student newspaper in 1968, did not "think that Columbia College students were particularly leftist. I mean, there was a high concentration of kids like myself from suburbs and affluent backgrounds and Jewish upbringing, and so forth." When pressed on the point, Friedman did not attempt to explain this allegedly Jewish affinity for radical politics.[16]

The same question perplexed David Rothman, a university professor who noted in an interview just weeks after the takeover crisis that there had been a subtle split between non-Jewish and Jewish faculty members. "The people who worked with the Majority Coalition boys," he began, referring to a makeshift group of conservative students who opposed the SDS-led occupation of university buildings, "not in the sense of inciting them, but those who worked with the Majority Coalition boys—Seymour Harris, Warner Schilling, Orest Ranum—they're not Wasps, quite, but they may be close. On the other hand, if one looks at the [ad hoc faculty] steering committee, it's not exclusively by any means Jewish, but there's a disproportionate number of Jews on it, even in a place like Columbia."[17]

Lionel Trilling, one of the first Jews to hold a tenured position in the university's English department, was initially surprised that "students should lack confidence in the administration. I was simply feeling, out of my own undergraduate past, that if you got into trouble you saw the dean and the dean assigned you punishment if you deserved punishment and nobody ever thought to raise questions about it. The dean was the dean. He was the disciplinary officer of the university."

More to the point, Trilling was bemused to learn that students took an active interest in governing the academic community. "You see, I still can't understand why they give a God damn about how the university runs," he told an interviewer. "I didn't, why should they? You know, one went through, got one's degree, left, and had an affection for the place or resentment of the place. This sense of wanting to be part of it comes as a completely new thing to me. I still can't understand why anybody wants to be politically part of anything so dull as running the university."[18]

Living in the moment, and having grown up a product of New York Jewry, Trilling could not properly appreciate the extent to which young, Jewish students had been programmed to question and resist authority.

One SDS activist maintained that the dean of the college, David Truman, was "an intensely proud man, an *authoritarian* man, who will brook little contradiction. . . . So against this background, when Truman closed Low Library, took this very *authoritarian* step of saying, 'I am master,' in a symbolic way, 'I am master of my own house, and you are not really in any position of authority,' I think the students were terribly offended. This was kind of the catalyst that made many people put a lot of different things together that they had been unhappy about."[19]

Mark Rudd and the other Jewish members of SDS stand out as unusual: most young Jewish students did not become radical political activists, and the parents of those who did were not always as gleeful in supporting their children. Nevertheless, Rudd was the product of a distinctly middle-class, midcentury Jewish upbringing of a variety that inspired large numbers of Jewish youth to question, reject, and disavow the liberalism their parents viewed as central to American Jewish identity.

Not everyone was as enamored of the young, mostly Jewish protesters as their parents. Political guru David Garth, who served as a chief architect of John Lindsay's reelection campaign the following year, dismissed the radicals as the "Right on! kids from Great Neck" and added that he "probably would have shot one" of them had he been a police officer stationed at Columbia. Victor Gotbaum, an influential city labor leader, thought the students were "the biggest pains in the ass. . . . The truth is, they really didn't want to work with anybody."[20]

Among the sharpest critics of the Columbia takeover were the several dozen conservative students who formed the Majority Coalition. Chaired by Paul Vilardi, a twenty-two-year-old Columbia senior, the Majority Coalition gathered 2,000 signatures on a petition that decried the tactics employed by radical protesters without taking a formal stand on more substantive issues like the gymnasium or the university's participation in the Institute of Defense Analysis. Vilardi's faction demanded from the start that the administration summon the police to get "this place back in running order and that positive punishment be evoked against those that break the rules."

Though most faculty members wrote off the Majority Coalition as a consortium of "jocks," the group drew a disproportionate share of Catholic students, including Vilardi, Tony Cicione, and future New York governor George Pataki, and may have reflected a distinctly Catholic reaction to the specter of radical dissent and social disorder. Their complaint was with the radical *style*—not the radical substance—of the SDS takeover campaign. "Just looking at these dirty, bearded twerps with their sneers and their sloppy girlfriends is enough to make a guy vomit," remarked one of the conservatives. Another campus conservative summarized the chief difference between the Majority Coalition and sps: "We're Staten Island. They're Scarsdale." Almost half of Columbia undergraduates hailed from New York City and its suburbs; they surely understood that Scarsdale was overwhelmingly Jewish, while Staten Island was predominately Catholic.[21]

I f the disturbances that wracked Columbia University in 1968 tended on the whole to pit radical Jewish students against their more conservative Catholic peers, and if, nationwide, Jewish youth were statistically overrepresented in the ranks of the New Left, by no means were Catholic students or Catholic universities immune to the general revolt against authority that touched virtually every American institution in the late 1960s. Just months after the Columbia crisis, Fordham University endured two major waves of student protests that ultimately forced the school's administration to radically overhaul its governing rules and allow for an unprecedented degree of student participation in matters pertaining to discipline, curricula, and university finances.

At the start of the academic year in September 1969, the Ram, Fordham's student newspaper, predicted that several major issues—all of them left simmering from the year before—would boil over and create a general culture of unrest. First, considerable opposition to the ROTC program had been building up for some time. The prior spring, roughly around the time that Mark Rudd and his loose coalition of radicals shut down Columbia University, 200 students had protested outside the main administration building at Fordham, demanding an end to the military's presence on campus. At the same time, the Fordham student senate passed a nonbinding resolution calling on the administration to sever ties with the U.S. military. The results of a referendum staged two years earlier had revealed overwhelming student support for ROTC, but intervening events—particularly the Tet Offensive, the 1968 presidential campaign, and the steadily rising number of American soldiers killed—had turned a large portion of the Fordham campus against the Vietnam War. Second, students had been clamoring since the previous year for more representation at the university and departmental levels, a demand that dovetailed with a more specific third issue of contention—rising tuition costs. Taken together, the debate over these issues suggested that many Fordham students, no less then their counterparts at Columbia, believed they should enjoy more influence in governing their academic community.[22]

In September 1969 Fordham's students, faculty, and administrators nervously awaited the results of a new universitywide referendum on ROTC. Matters grew complicated when the Committee to Abolish ROTC, the main group opposing military recruitment and training on campus, announced its intention to boycott the vote. The committee's chairman dismissed the referendum as "a tool of the administration to use students against students" and charged that Rev. Michael Walsh, Fordham's president from 1969 to 1972, along with entrenched tenured faculty members, were attempting to manipulate student opinion to secure a ROTC victory. An op-ed columnist for the *Ram* agreed, concluding that the administration's official sponsorship of the referendum presented "opponents of ROTC with only one choice: to boycott it."[23]

Even as anti-ROTC forces held themselves at arm's length from the referendum process, preparations for the nationwide Moratorium Day protest against the Vietnam War electrified the Fordham campus. Just days before the 1969 mayoral election in New York, at least 3,000 students, a figure representing upwards of 75 percent of the undergraduate body, attended a rally at the campus gym, where they applauded a roster of antiwar speakers that included Paul Goodman, Herman Badillo, David Halberstam, Jacob Javits, Allard Lowenstein, and John Lindsay. The mayor may have been persona non grata among the city's Irish and Italian adults, but their children who attended Fordham gave Lindsay a "tumultuous applause," as a student journalist reported, when he told the assembled audience that "we have learned that the American people are brave enough, strong enough to change a mistaken course. And we have learned that at long last the time has come for this war to stop." Following the afternoon rally, 7,500 students from Fordham, Bronx Community College, and Hunter College's Bronx campus held a candlelight vigil at Fordham's Rose Hill campus.[24]

In the wake of the rally, Fordham's student newspaper issued a ringing endorsement of Lindsay's reelection bid, arguing that "as mayor of the largest city in the nation and the most important city in the world, Lindsay has been a powerful voice in the fight to reorder our nation's priorities away from Vietnam and back to the cities." In a sharp break with their parents—well over three-quarters of whom would soon vote, unsuccessfully, to boot the mayor out of Gracie Mansion—the editors concluded that "if John Lindsay has failed to live up to expectations during his first term in office, it is because he has refused to play the game of old time New York politics. If he fails to get the results of Chicago's Daley, it is because he believes in the power of the people, not the power of patronage. We would rather have John Lindsay try to make his view of government work than return to the surface calm of the Wagner days, while the roots of the city fester. Whether she likes it or not, New York needs Lindsay."[25]

In their opposition to the war and their support of Lindsay, Fordham students were breaking sharply with their elders. While some local residents of the predominately Catholic neighborhood surrounding the Rose Hill campus indicated quiet support for the Moratorium Day marchers, the prevailing attitude was one of disgust and anger. Cued by their parents, twelve-year-old schoolgirls skipped along the Moratorium Day parade route singing "Dirty pot smokers, dirty pot smokers," while adult onlookers chanted "Go to hell!" at the student protesters. Reporters for the *Ram* interviewed a number of neighborhood residents, most of whom seemed to agree with one man who said, "I don't believe in a protest against our form of government. I'm for America, they're for Ho Chi Min and all the rest." An Italian man told the student newspaper, "If I had my way, I'd turn the hose on them all," while another man asked rhetorically, "Why don't they go and fight like I did. They're terrible. Who are you reporting for, anyway, the 'Yellow Journal'?" A local Irish resident called out to a police officer, "They're a bunch of garbage benders!" while a more circumspect couple told reporters, "We're behind the government 100 percent. We are for peace but not necessarily for the march."[26]

By staking out liberal positions on the war and the mayoral election, Fordham students seemed to be itching for a more dramatic confrontation with adult authority. The same op-ed writer who suspected that the ROTC referendum was little more than a cynical ploy by the university administration to squelch dissent wondered why a straw poll was "suddenly the correct procedure for dealing" with contentious questions. "If a referendum is valid over this issue," he asked, "then why not university-wide referenda on other issues, such as tuition increases? Or open meetings of the Board of Trustees? Or the use of marijuana on campus (we would call that a reefer-rendum). Or Fr. Walsh as university president?"[27]

That Michael Walsh had joined seventy-six other college presidents in calling for an immediate pullout from Vietnam did little to ease suspicions among growing numbers of students that the war was just one of many topics that demanded greater parity in decision-making authority between the younger and older generations.[28] When the residents of a Fordham dorm at 610 East 191st Street protested the deteriorating physical condition of their building, their spokeswoman took pains to emphasize that her group was not only incensed by poor housing conditions, but also by the "whole attitude of the university." Another dorm resident agreed, telling the student newspaper that the problems stemming from 610 East 191st

Street were "just another example of the University's apathy toward housing and their whole attitude of not caring about the students."[29]

Amid this growing climate of suspicion and distrust, the pending ROTC debate threatened to erupt into an unmanageable crisis. Shortly after Moratorium Day, the student government commissioned a scientific poll that revealed that an overwhelming majority of Fordham undergraduates—68 percent in all—supported either downgrading the ROTC to an extracurricular activity or removing it from campus entirely. Of those surveyed, 59 percent also opposed the impending universitywide referendum, maintaining that the student senate's earlier, nonbinding vote to break ties with ROTC should have given the trustees ample evidence of student opinion about Fordham's relationship with the Department of Defense. Still firm in their determination to boycott the referendum, on 17 October members of the Committee to Abolish ROTC staged a formal picket outside the administration building. Mary Brennan, a spokeswoman for the committee, complained that Walsh had adopted a "condescending" attitude toward the student body and that he was "not being honest" in his stated opposition to the conflict in Southeast Asia. "He should carry his opposition to the war to its logical conclusion," she insisted, and announce the "abolition of ROTC on campus."[30]

Ultimately, the referendum failed to stave off the looming crisis. Only 24 percent of students participated in the vote—well short of the 40 percent threshold needed to make the poll binding on the student senate (though not on the university administration and trustees). Of those who turned in ballots, 53 percent—a slim majority—supported maintaining the university's relationship with ROTC, with 47 percent voting either to relegate the program to an extracurricular activity or eliminate it entirely. Even supporters of ROTC admitted that the widespread boycott of the referendum was probably an indication that an overwhelming majority of Fordham students wanted to change or sever the university's ties to the military.[31]

Events finally came to a head in mid-November, when seventy-five members of the Committee to Abolish ROTC marched into the administration building, forced dozens of university personnel—including President Walsh and Vice President Joseph Cammarosano—to vacate the premises, and occupied the presidential suite for several hours. Outside, 200 students cheered on the protestors and threw food to them through open windows until, late in the afternoon, New York City police arrived to break up the demonstration. Several students got into scrapes with university security personnel before being arrested, and in the days that followed, Walsh's office announced that the administration building had sustained $12,500 in damages (equivalent to roughly $66,000 in 2005 dollars).

In the immediate aftermath of the takeover, Fordham's campus emerged deeply divided. The faculty gave Walsh a unanimous vote of confidence for his decision to call in the police and press criminal charges against the arrested students, while roughly 350 students rallied to support the administration in its firm handling of the crisis. At the same time, 800 students signed a petition to protest the heavy-handed way in which the university was dealing with the arrested demonstrators, while upwards of 300 students attended a "Drop the Charges" rally at the campus center.[32]

If the student body was torn, with a sizeable number supporting the protesters and a compelling majority opposing ROTC's presence on campus, Fordham's alumni—most of whom hailed from New York and many of whom still lived there—were more united in their opposition to the demonstrators. In the weeks following the police raid, Walsh received scores of letters from Fordham graduates who demanded, as did one group of alumni from Long Island, that "the students who took part in the severe damaging of the administration building be expelled. We also want SDS removed from campus. We would also like to see litigation brought against the parents of these students if it can be legally done. Pending your decision we are withholding our contributions."[33] At an impromptu alumni meeting held at Fordham's Lincoln Center campus in Manhattan, once-faithful donors to the university railed against the student activists, characterizing them as "the lowest form of revolutionary scum" and calling on Walsh to "get them the hell off the campus."[34]

Many angry alumni invoked the time-honored vocabulary they grew up with, envisioning campus unrest as an example of general "lawlessness, disorder, physical and verbal abuse; and all of this under the guise of 'academic freedom,'" and criticizing the administration for being led "down the garden path of radical social experimentation and abdication to adolescent dissent." As one of Walsh's correspondent's explained, "In a society governed by law . . . one must live within the laws." Student protesters were not just breaking with the administration in Washington over the Vietnam War, or with the administration at Rose Hill over campus policies. They were challenging the very ethic of obedience to authority and allegiance to organic community that governed the city's insular Italian and Irish communities. "You Father Walsh and your liberal permissive attitude have caused the pall of shame and embarrassment to hang over many Catholic and indeed non-Catholic parents," wrote the sister of a Fordham alumnus and mother of five. "How can you tolerate vandalism and defiance of authority under the cloak of righteous dissent?"[35]

"When I went to Fordham," wrote one alumnus, "we were trained to be gentlemen. This called for a respect for authority among other thing." An Italian graduate of the college similarly argued that "we are now reaping what we have sowed by our policy of permissiveness and conciliation in the face of threats, abuse, obscene language, and violence." The letter writer expected this sort of capitulation to dissent and lawlessness at secular universities, which "have always raised and educated their students in an aura of permissiveness," but he found it "incredible . . . that such things are allowed in a Jesuit University. . . . [W]hen I went to Fordham there were certain rules and regulations which you had to abide by, and if you didn't, you were promptly punished. . . . I still find it hard to believe but I think that the Jesuits like all the other educators are succumbing to pressure from the liberals and Left wingers in the guise of freedom of speech and civil rights, and permitting the piece-meal destruction of our school, physically, morally, and spiritually."[36]

Not every guardian of authority and community hailed from the older generation. A graduate student at Fordham told Walsh that he viewed the school as "an oasis of order in a desert of chaos. Fordham is the last bastion of Classicism and as such she must furnish us with more than just intellectual leadership. I am glad that our university is using the Sword Temporal on the 'demonstrators,' but as a Jesuit Institution she has a further obligation. The Church's Sword Spiritual has grown rusty and blunted through the heinous outpourings of a clergy tottering on the brink of becoming the corporate voice of the Psychotic Malcontent." Another graduate student complained that he had chosen Fordham because "in addition to its academic offerings, it seemed to supply a vestige of order in a rapidly disintegrating university situation. . . . My shock at the rude and disgraceful actions of November 12, 1969 was very great. It was surpassed only by the subsequent shock I experienced upon learning that those involved in such violent actions actually expect amnesty. . . . Obviously, they have no concept of a society founded upon law."[37]

More representative of the youth generation, however, was recent alumnus John J. Kennedy, class of 1969, who urged leniency toward the protesters, reminding Walsh that

> the militant actions of the demonstrators was simply a response to the horrors of America's military adventures, especially Viet Nam. As an alumnus of Fordham, I would also like to register my objections to

ROTC. It trains men to be paid killers. How many Fordham trained officers were at Song My? How many Fordham officers are engaged in the wholesale destruction of Viet Nam? . . . Please, please, end this insane complicity on Fordham's part by abolishing ROTC completely. . . . The students involved in that demonstration were among the most prophetic in the Fordham community.

George Gilmore, one of the student protesters, went even further, quoting a long passage by the radical Catholic priest Daniel Berrigan and boldly insisting that "when compared to the rape of Vietnam and the ghetto, the destruction of Fordham University would indeed be mild!" Gilmore denounced the "irrelevant education we receive at Fordham" and ended his letter with "a question—some property has no right to exist, e.g., Hitler's concentration camps; does this University have a right to exist?"[38]

That some of the most devoted members of the city's Irish and Italian Catholic communities broke so sharply with adult authority—and with a worldview that counseled obedience to that same authority—to some degree signaled a victory of secular forces over ethnicity. The revolt against authority reached into every corner of American life by the late 1960s. Jewish youth may have been disproportionately inclined to participate in campus protests because they had been raised on an ethic of dissent and protest, but they were joined by millions of Catholic and Protestant youth who developed a similar, deep-seated suspicion of powerful institutions. Yet if the Irish and Italian Catholic subculture was cracking under the strain of secular social forces, internal developments within the community had also, ironically, helped sow the seeds of dissent that came to harvest at Fordham in 1969.

In cities around the country, working-class Catholics found themselves in the unfamiliar and uncomfortable position of opposing an increasingly liberal and activist core of clergy who demanded that lay Catholics embrace open housing and fair employment laws. It was easy enough for northern Catholics to apply church teachings on race to civil rights battles in the South. It was another matter, entirely, to invite African Americans into their communities, schools, and unions—to risk a devaluation of their property, an unraveling of tight-knit ethnic neighborhoods, and a loss of their already tenuous economic status. These questions, which often involved the very survival of working-class neighborhoods, opened up a chasm between the Catholic laity and clergy.

In Chicago, where priests and nuns waded into a racist mob in an effort to quell antiblack violence, they met with such taunts as "Hey, Father, are you sleeping with her?" and were occasionally knocked and stoned to the ground. "For the first time in the history of this city," the archdiocesan newspaper lamented, "a nun was attacked on the streets of Chicago in a public demonstration. And the attack came from a mob of howling Catholics." Catholic clerics quickly learned that "the sight of a Roman collar incited [the mob] to greater violence and nastier epithets." In Milwaukee, a group of activist priests led by Rev. James Groppi endorsed a school boycott and taught classes on black history at Freedom Schools to promote integration of the city's education system. Groppi's actions tore the community apart. Some parishioners supported Groppi, like a woman who wrote that "sixteen years of parochial school education taught me that Christ was always on the side of the underdog and gave not a second thought to civil disobedience or its consequences." Others complained that archdiocesan authorities should shut down Groppi's campaign and that it was "regrettable that Catholic clergy should encourage contempt for the law by urging children and young people to aid and abet this school boycott. During their formative years, children should be taught discipline in accord with the fourth commandment. Rebellion is a primary tenet of communism."[39]

Given the high stakes involved in these struggles between liberal clergy members and frightened, angry parishioners, the irony was probably lost on many backlash Catholics that, in violently protesting the actions of neighborhood priests and nuns, it was they who were breaking with authority. In Cicero, Illinois, a heavily Catholic, working-class suburb of Chicago that witnessed pitched battles over residential integration in the mid-1960s, angry white residents lashed out at John Cardinal Cody, the archbishop of Chicago, for his support of open housing laws. "They try and force integration on us and we'll rebel," John Pellegrini, a local man, announced. "Cody wasn't elected by us. He doesn't have the right to take away our rights. I suggest you refrain from contributing to your parish." An astute observer of racial and religious politics in Chicago noted that many whites "consider themselves good Catholics, yet utterly reject integration. And they are particularly bitter toward priests, bishops, and organizations who tell them they are in conflict with their religion. 'Since when?' they retort."[40]

Racial politics undermined Catholic authority more acutely in cities where large numbers of residents owned their own homes. This was not the case in New York, where renters predominated and where, consequently, residential politics played out in a more muted fashion. Nevertheless, the church's strident racial liberalism often inspired quiet dissent among the laity. In 1966 some 200 priests, nuns, and prominent lay Catholics bought an advertisement in the *New York Times* to support the police civilian review board; eighty-six priests in clerical garb also staged a televised press conference in Bedford-Stuyvesant to drum up support for the measure. Yet surveys showed that 83 percent of city Catholics voted against the creation of the review board in the ensuing public referendum.[41]

It remains unclear how much damage the divide between clergy and laity inflicted on Italian and Irish ethnic solidarity, but in subtle ways the revolt of so many adults against an ideal they once believed inviolate—that is, the sanctity of authority—undermined the worldview that had prevailed in urban Catholic communities for decades. Paradoxically, the rightward drift into dissent that many Irish and Italian Catholics followed actually gained force from liberal developments within the church. The Second Vatican Council (1962–65), known popularly as Vatican II, had ushered in sweeping changes that affected every aspect of the Catholic subculture. At its most basic level, Vatican II encouraged the use of the vernacular in celebrations of the Mass, effectively scrapping the old Latin rites that had kept church services uniform from country to country since the Council of Trent. Vatican II also moderated the century-old dogma of papal infallibility and broke down the cultural fire wall between laypersons and clergy.

It is difficult to imagine conflicts within the Catholic Church assuming as much force as they did in the mid-1960s without the liberalizing influence of Vatican II. Members of the congregation were now encouraged to participate actively, rather than passively, in religious services. After the late 1960s, Communion was administered in many Catholic parishes by lay "Eucharistic ministers" rather than solely by ordained priests. The relationship between pastors and their parishioners was essentially redefined as less hierarchical and more reciprocal and, as a result, lay people took a greater role in determining the content of religious services and in governing parish finances. Vatican II also gave bishops and priests the freedom to work with other faith-based groups to tackle nettlesome questions like poverty and racial strife. This new ecumenical policy signaled an important change in the church's relationship with non-Catholic institutions and helped ease American Catholic culture out of its separatist cast.[42]

Historians are still sorting out the grassroots-level impact of Vatican II on American Catholicism, but clearly the introduction of a less insular, more democratic ethos in church life created fault lines within the Catholic community. Many older Catholics were uncomfortable with changes in liturgy and worship. They missed the traditional Latin Mass and were unnerved by lay participation in religious services. In turn, Catholics who grew up in the late 1960s and 1970s were raised in a less austere and controlling church.[43] New York's Catholic subculture entered a period of great upheaval that, over time, challenged the ethnic separateness and distinction of New York's Irish and Italian communities.

The changes that Vatican II ushered in resonated almost immediately at the grassroots level. Upon the installation of Francis J. Mugavero as archbishop of Brooklyn in September 1968, the *Brooklyn Tablet*'s front page headline announced: "We Have a Bishop Standing in the Midst of His People as One Ready to Serve." Once a champion of ecclesiastical and political authority, the diocesan organ now celebrated the ideal of a democratic and participatory church culture. A year after Mugavero's elevation, the *Tablet* reported with favor that the new archbishop was unusually solicitous of parish priests (he even allowed them to form a pastors' association) and that he "scrupulously made himself available to any priest of the Diocese seeking to speak with him." Mugavero "revealed a radical commitment and untiring effort to establish a collegial spirit and the ecclesiastical structures which will lead to a practical broadening of decision making processes within the diocese." Just as the archbishop worked to democratize the church hierarchy, at the neighborhood level Catholic worshippers began forming parish councils in coordination with their pastors. By mid-1969, almost half of all parishes in the Archdiocese of New York, and probably a similar share in Brooklyn and Queens, had formed lay governing committees. The hierarchy urged pastors to defer to these bodies in all but extreme circumstances.[44]

The *Catholic News*, still the official organ of the Archdiocese of New York, began running weekly columns—some with clever and appealing titles like "Mass Confusion"—to walk parishioners through the maze of the sometimes confusing changes in liturgy and worship.[45] A columnist for the weekly newspaper noted that while there were "suggestions, exhortations, and perhaps implicit admonitions for pastors to grant greater opportunity for mutual communication and freedom of action of the laity on the parish level . . . as far as strict rights are concerned, I don't think anything new has evolved concerning the role of the laity in the Church."[46] While this assertion may have been true from a strictly doctrinal perspective, there was no denying that Vatican II had opened the floodgates to a more participatory church culture, and that on a day-to-day basis, the old lessons about corporal community and obedience to authority were being jettisoned in favor of a message that privileged both democratic participation in church institutions and the fundamental sanctity of the individual.

Concurrent with the rise of parish councils, throughout New York City clerical authorities began forming parish school boards to oversee finances, curricula, and disciplinary matters at church schools. As early as 1965 Monsignor O'Neil C. D'Amour, an official with the National Catholic Education Association, predicted that within five years, 90 percent of New York's Catholic schools would switch to such a model. The managing editor of the liberal Catholic journal *America* noted with guarded approval that Catholic parents "were being asked to come to the defense of the school structure as they have known it and to speak out in its behalf as citizens and as Catholics. To do so will require more than an act of will on the part of many parents." Before the introduction of lay school boards, he continued, Catholic schools had been run by "untrained, uncommunicative, most frequently incompetent administrators who qualify for their positions only because they have lived long enough to be pastors."[47]

However extreme this condemnation of pre–Vatican II Catholic schooling may have been, the change in Catholic classroom culture after 1965 was dramatic—at least if the rhetoric of leading education officials was any indication. "Rather than holding up submission and conformity as standards to meet," urged the president of Trinity College in Washington, D.C., at the National Catholic Education Association in 1965, "we have to encourage our students today to take stands that may be unpopular, may even expose them to ostracism. Debate, controversy, initiative—these must be the hallmark of educated people today." Such ideas stood in sharp contrast to the old dictums that once governed Catholic schools in Brooklyn, where, less than thirty years earlier, educators had warned that "inattention to the courtesies of life, crude *unconventionality* . . . far from being liberty, is the most cruel of servitudes—selfishness." Another speaker at the 1965 conference noted that "for years and years," lay Catholics had been taught "to pray and pay, and that is the extent of their responsibility." In this new climate of political and religious reform, parents needed to play a greater role in their children's education, and schools needed to foster a sense of individual curiosity and engagement on the part of their students.[48]

The new approach to Catholic education worked its way up to the highest levels. In September 1965, ninety administrators and professors at the College of Saint Vincent in New York City attended a teaching workshop, where they were encouraged to "teach in a way that is provocative, not didactic. Higher education must develop a high level of expectancy, with an attitude of willingness to experiment."[49]

Stirred by the same political and social forces that inspired students all around the country to demand a more relevant, participatory undergraduate experience—but also encouraged by the new ethic of innovation, democratic governance, and individualism in Catholic culture—a loose coalition of students and faculty at St. John's University staged a series of dramatic boycotts and demonstrations in late 1965. The professors—200 of whom walked out of a general faculty meeting in protest of administration policies (and many of whom were priests)—demanded better pay and benefits as well as more flexibility in classroom instruction, while students struck in favor of more academic freedom and an end to both censorship of student publications and "paternalism" by university administrators. Negotiations between the students, faculty, and administration grew so tense and complicated that, ultimately, John Meng, president of City University's Hunter College and a lay Catholic, was persuaded to take a six-month leave of absence from his job to serve as a special consultant and mediator at St. John's.[50]

Given the steady buildup of dissent within New York's Irish and Italian Catholic subculture, it is little wonder that students at Fordham University felt emboldened by 1969 to confront the highest vestiges of adult authority. Even before the disturbances at St. John's University several years earlier, a devout Catholic student from New York helped fire up the imagination of tens of thousands of collegians around the country and, to some degree, sparked the massive wave of campus disturbances that followed. In September 1964, returning from work as a Freedom Summer volunteer, Mario Savio, a twenty-one-year-old philosophy major at the University of California at Berkeley, announced, "Last summer I went to Mississippi to join the struggle there for civil rights. This fall I am engaged in another phase of the same struggle, this time in Berkeley. In Mississippi an autocratic and powerful minority rules, through organized violence, to suppress the vast majority. In California, the privileged minority manipulates the university bureaucracy to suppress the students' political expression." Savio proved a master at drawing powerful rhetorical connections between the plight of southern blacks and the daily tribulations faced by his fellow collegians. On the surface, Savio's experiences in Mississippi bore only superficial resemblance to events at Berkeley, where university administrators had banned on-campus political advocacy. But like activists on other campuses, he was able to make students feel personally affronted and affected by what they saw on television: the brutality of Jim Crow, the passivity and complacency of the federal government, and the seeming indifference of establishment figures who urged moderation and patience.[51]

Savio grew up in Italian neighborhoods in the East Village and in Queens, spoke both Italian and English fluently, and attended the first and second grades at a parish school before transferring to the public school system. His mother was a devout Catholic who instilled in her son a fierce love of the church and a hatred of religious and economic inequality—ideas that she identified as central to Catholic teachings. An altar boy who faithfully attended CCD classes and discussion groups each Friday night, even when he was in high school, Savio gravitated naturally to a group of young, progressive priests who had organized a monthly diocesan lecture series—the "Veritas Lectures"—that focused on social and political activism. A close friend recalled that Savio's "humanism was a direct outgrowth of his keen grasp of the Christian message of love. To Mario, scientists too easily accepted that there were no adequate proofs of divine presence, and they went about their lives as though there would always be a moral vacuum. What they filled it with often chilled his gentler soul. *Where was charity and humanity when efficiency became your god?* he demanded to know."

If the roots of his antiauthoritarianism and social conscience were in the church, Savio was ever mindful that his brand of radical politics was dissident in New York's Italian Catholic community. "Mario revered and cherished many truly Italian things," his friend remembered, "but he had not been comfortable growing up among other Italian Americans. . . . Except for the occasional Savio family, the type that is strong in union or humanistic traditions, the neighborhood where Mario and I grew up was reactionary and had very few real political convictions. Our Jewish friends and neighbors were more likely to hold the liberal views, and the children, our friends, were encouraged to ask questions of authority." In the years after his involvement with Freedom Summer and the Free Speech movement, Savio drifted away from his roots. He married twice, both times to Jewish women, and toward the end of his life considered converting to Buddhism.[52]

By the late 1960s, a key challenge facing Catholic institutions in New York and elsewhere was their ability to bend just enough to accommodate and keep faith with young people like Mario Savio without losing the allegiance of Irish and Italian adults for whom "older" virtues—like allegiance to authority and skepticism of radical politics—remained dogmatic. Few people better understood how difficult a balancing act was required of Catholic leaders than Fordham president Michael Walsh. Though final exams and Christmas vacation temporarily interrupted the campus tumult in late 1969, by the middle of the spring semester new issues spurred a large portion of the Fordham student population to return to the picket line.

The precipitating event was a decision by the English department to deny tenure to a thirty-two-year-old assistant professor named Ronald Friedman on the grounds that his publication record was too thin. Though there was something to the charge, Friedman was a gifted classroom teacher whose advocacy of liberal causes and easy rapport with students made him widely popular among Fordham's undergraduates. On the morning of 17 March, 400 students held a rally outside the administration building, where they turned over a petition in support of Friedman bearing 850 signatures. The assembled group then walked to the English department's offices, where student leaders confronted tenured faculty members. Friedman told a reporter for the *New York Times* that his particular case was "not the real issue. The real issue is student involvement. . . . My hope is that as a result of this the students will be involved in the issues of the university." Indeed, even as the embattled professor's supporters staged their sit-down at the English department, three busloads of students traveled to Fordham's Lincoln Center campus to confront a meeting of the board of trustees. Their demands included a repeal of the recent $200 tuition increase and representation on the board. By early April, the ad hoc student movement added to this list of demands a complete reorganization of university regulations, including the requirement that every academic department create a governing body equally composed of tenured faculty members, untenured faculty members, undergraduates, and graduate students.[53]

Matters came to a head in mid-April, when between 350 and 400 students occupied the administration building, vacating it only when a county sheriff arrived on campus bearing a court order that enjoined the students from continuing their protest. The demonstrators took pains to sweep, vacuum, and dust the offices they had seized and, upon leaving the building, called for a general boycott of classes. Within twenty-four hours, upwards of 75 percent of the student body was either participating in the strike or keeping clear of the campus in order to avoid being swept up in a possible police raid or protest. The editors of the *Ram* issued a stirring endorsement of the strike, affirming that "the students are together, and they are not about to stop until the administration and faculty accept them as full and equal partners in the educational experience."[54]

After several days, as it became clear that the students had effectively ground Fordham's institutional machinery to a halt, Walsh instructed all academic departments to begin discussions with students about the formation of joint faculty-undergraduate-graduate advisory boards and called for the creation of an interim, one-year university council composed of sixteen students, twenty-one faculty members, and ten administrators. The council was empowered to review administrative matters such as tenure and hiring decisions and to establish general academic policy. Within days, several academic departments adopted new governing bodies along the lines suggested by the student protesters, and in a referendum in early May, the student body approved the new arrangement by a 10-to-1 vote.[55]

With encouragement from the new university council, the administration also introduced a pilot program for a new "Open Curriculum"—an independent study elective "based on the idea that certain students receive the best education when they are able to pursue their own interests with close personal direction. . . . A truly liberal education thrives on personal interaction; so, the Open Curriculum is also a *learning community*. The students and faculty work on a number of problems together in required weekly seminar sessions." In a sharp break with traditional Catholic pedagogy, one of the program's faculty supporters boasted that the Open Curriculum was "in accord with Dewey's educational theory that if the student is left to pursue his own interest, he will be led eventually to all the elements of a liberal education."[56]

In the aftermath of the spring strike, the letters that flowed into Michael Walsh's office revealed the deep generational divide emerging within the Irish and Italian communities in and around New York City. Some parents, like an Italian American couple from the metropolitan area, were supportive of the student protesters:

> Our first reaction upon hearing that our daughter . . . was participating in a sit-in at the Administration Building was, "Get right out of there. We are paying for your education, and you are to concentrate on that alone." When it was carefully explained to us that education was the cause of their protest, and through the week, we observed their peaceful actions, we began to see the justice of their complaints. . . . Carole is our third college student, and we see the great contrast in their thinking and action, and can appreciate what you suffer in this crisis. However, because their reasons are truly reasonable for the most part, and their actions have so far been most retrospect, we hope that you will listen to them *now*.[57]

In general, however, the parents of Fordham students and the university's alumnae were incensed by the administration's capitulation to student demands and found fault with "the university's basic policies toward dissident students for the past few years." Wrote one such correspondent, "I don't like to mention it, but the president of Notre Dame has managed to keep things pretty level out at South Bend, because he showed strength at the beginning of this so-called students' revolt. Don't let them ruin Fordham. It's turned out a lot of useful citizens since 1841, let's continue to do so, not 'bums.' " Another alumnus, reacting to unconfirmed rumors that student demonstrators had burned an American flag during a rally, complained that "Fordham has always stood for God and Country and so should it stand now. Any student who can not live up to the simple rules and regulations of the school does not belong at Fordham."[58]

By 1970 social forces beyond the control of Italian and Irish New Yorkers, as well as unforeseen consequences of Vatican II, introduced cracks in the city's once-cohesive Catholic subculture. Like many of their Jewish counterparts, Irish and Italian youth demanded greater autonomy and a more equal partnership with their elders on and off college campuses. For many young Jews who had been taught from a young age to question authority, joining the ranks of the New Left was a logical step; certainly, many of their parents were willing to indulge the excesses of the antiwar movement. For many young Catholics, picketing an administration building or attending a Moratorium Day event represented a sharp break with a cherished ethnic worldview and often meant opening a breech between themselves and their parents.

The student uprisings of the late 1960s bore ominous implications for the liberal coalition. The house that Franklin Roosevelt built was bleeding Catholic adults on the right and a small but vocal minority of Jewish and Catholic youth on the left. But for white ethnic New York, the social upheavals of the late 1960s were a grave indication of what was still to come. By the early 1970s, in the face of new demographic realities, the old ethnic subcultures that once comprised the social, political, cultural, and even spatial map of New York City began to give way to new realities.

Conclusion

Roughly around the time that Rose Shapiro took to the synagogue circuit to denounce John Lindsay, and Joe Kelly took to the streets to defend God and country against the anarchic forces of urban liberalism, American scholars and public intellectuals began turning their attention to the question of ethnicity—particularly, white ethnicity—for the first time in several decades.[1] Wrote one such author,

> The religious and ethnic pluralism caused [by the migration of European immigrants between] 1820 and 1920 . . . is not the most important sort of diversity in American society, but because it is not the most important, it is not thereby unimportant. Quite the contrary, ethnic pluralism is part of the very fabric of American urban life (especially in the North Central and Northeast regions of the country). American social science has ignored this diversity for more than a quarter century and American policy makers ignored it in formulating the social policies of the 1960s.[2]

In the twenty years following World War II, the black struggle for civil rights had shifted attention away from pluralism among white Americans and instead focused public awareness on the political, social, and economic divide between whites and blacks. The late 1960s and 1970s saw renewed scholarly interest in the historic significance of ethnic pluralism throughout several centuries of American culture and politics.[3] Much of this new focus owed to the spirit of ethnic revivalism that seemed to be sweeping through the nation's Jewish, Italian, Irish, Polish, and other white communities. Books like Irving Howe's *World of Our Fathers* (1976) and William Shannon's *The American Irish* (1966), and films like *Fiddler on the Roof* (1971) and *The Godfather* (1972), celebrated the cultural richness and triumphs of the immigrant generation.[4]

This surge of ethnic pride and commemoration was in large part a popular reaction to more general political and social trends. Historian

Philip Gleason has written that the "revival of ethnicity" signaled a mounting rejection of the consensus view of American nationhood and history that prevailed in the 1940s and 1950s. "Against the impact of the Vietnam War and the racial crisis, [Gunnar] Myrdal's language about the American creed or [Horace] Kallen's about the American idea seemed inappropriate. . . . The revival of ethnicity was part of a deep crisis of confidence and self-respect among the American people." As they grew increasingly less certain that they shared a common ideology and culture, many Americans became more cognizant of their diverse, Old World roots. At the same time, the increased stridency and inward-looking disposition of certain minority communities (such as African Americans, Latinos, Asians, and American Indians) encouraged many white ethnics to also rediscover what was unique about their own pasts.[5]

Ironically, political observers began to consider anew the question of pluralism just as New York City's Catholic and Jewish communities started to experience sweeping changes that would undermine their cultural insularity and demographic strength. The dissipation of white ethnic culture that many observers thought had occurred immediately after World War II was in fact occurring more definitively in the 1970s.

Three phenomena contributed to a gradual decline and reordering of white ethnic New York after 1970. First, this period saw a precipitous decline in the city's Jewish population and the steady passing of the first generation, which had long anchored each community's sense of identity and distinctiveness. The influx of tens of thousands of Russian Jewish immigrants and the rapid-fire growth of the city's once-negligible Hasidic sects did not make up for net losses in the overall Jewish population, but it did introduce a new degree of ideological and religious pluralism in a community that had heretofore been overwhelmingly secular, liberal, and cosmopolitan. Second, the city itself changed. The mass arrival of new immigrants from Asia and Latin America helped diminish cultural distinctions between different white ethnic groups. Finally, Catholic culture, which had been remarkably uniform and insular throughout the early Cold War years, quickly fractured in the wake of sweeping changes—some of them handed down by Rome, others originating from the grassroots level. Together, these demographic and theological developments made the city's white ethnic communities less cohesive.

The 1970s saw Gotham's Jewish population drop off sharply. Over the course of the decade the community lost 38 percent of its total, or an aggregate of 700,000 people. Along with this population decline came a large-scale geographic reshuffling. By 1980 one-third of all Jews in metropolitan New York lived in the suburbs.[6] Within the city proper, old lines of demarcation vanished. Most Jewish neighborhoods in the Bronx quickly shrank or gave way to the growth of the black and Puerto Rican communities. In 1957 almost 500,000 Jews lived in the Bronx; they accounted for 35 percent of the borough's population. By the mid-1970s, only 95,000 remained, accounting for only 8 percent of Bronx residents. Around half of these Jews were over the age of fifty-five. Many continued to live in high-rise cooperatives ("co-ops"), relics of the 1920s and 1930s, when the garment unions erected thousands of housing units for the city's blue-collar workforce.

To the southeast, in Brooklyn, onetime Jewish enclaves like Williamsburg, Bensonhurst, and Flatbush saw quick racial turnover, though in some areas—notably, Borough Park and Crown Heights—a growing number of Orthodox families stayed behind, choosing to coexist, oftentimes in tension, with their new black and Latino neighbors. Brooklyn's Jewish population dipped from over 850,000 in the late 1950s to about 400,000 in 1980. To the west, in Manhattan, districts like the Upper West Side retained their historic, Jewish character, though steep rents generally kept the borough off limits to working-class and lower-middle-class urbanites. Jews accounted for 19 percent of Manhattan's population in 1980, roughly the same proportion as in the late 1950s, but the borough increasingly became a haven for young, unmarried Jews and wealthier members of the community.[7]

Replacing some of the Jews who left the city were a large portion of the roughly 100,000 Russian Jews who emigrated to the United States in the 1970s and 1980s. The sizable number who settled in New York had weathered decades of persecution in the Soviet Union, where the practice of Judaism or assertion of ethnic identity had been sharply proscribed. Consequently, they came to America with little formal knowledge of Jewish religion and culture and held themselves at a distance from religious and secular organizations that attempted to weave them into the preexisting fabric of Jewish life in New York. Because these Jews were forced to start anew in the United States, many also filled working-class jobs that the city's assimilated Jews had left behind.[8]

A second growth population in New York Jewry was in the various Hasidic sects. Until the 1940s most Orthodox Jews—a small portion of the city's overall Jewish population—were affluent and outwardly acculturated to American norms. They tended to be more observant than their Conservative and Reform coreligionists, kept strictly kosher homes, and preserved certain synagogue rituals that the other movements more freely discarded. But prewar Orthodoxy enjoyed a fluid relationship with the

Conservative movement and retained an easy comfort level with modern science, secular scholarship, and urban liberalism. This began to change after the war. Between 1947 and 1952 roughly 100,000 Jewish displaced persons came to the United States from Eastern Europe, many of whom settled in New York. Most of these new arrivals were Hungarian or Polish, and roughly half belonged to various Hasidic sects. In places like Williamsburg, Crown Heights, and the Lower East Side they replicated the insular, ultraobservant subcultures they had inhabited before the Holocaust. The Hasidic sects grew at a rapid pace, in large part because of their tendency to have large families. Their demographic explosion rejuvenated but also altered American Orthodoxy, moving it rightward both religiously and politically. By the 1980s, 13 percent of New York Jews were Orthodox, of whom many were ultra-Orthodox. Together with the Russians who arrived in the 1970s, the Hasidim introduced a new ideological and cultural pluralism within the city's Jewish population.[9]

For the Reform and Conservative Jews whose stories inform this book, events in the 1970s also posed a challenge to the liberal, cosmopolitan values that had guided Jewish life—at least externally—for a good portion of the twentieth century. In the aftermath of the 1973 Yom Kippur War, many Jews at the grassroots and organizational levels grew conscious of Israel's vulnerability to attack and began demanding that their community institutions devote less attention to national problems like poverty, race relations, and urban redevelopment and more attention to preserving Jewish civilization in Israel and at home. The emergence of new civil rights issues like affirmative action in colleges and universities also widened the gap between Jews, many of whom regarded education as a meritocratic stepping-stone to upward mobility, and African Americans, who tended to support measures aimed at achieving more diversity in admissions. New York Jews did not change their voting patterns or abandon liberalism; in fact, on election day they remain the second-most liberal racial, ethnic, or religious group, behind only African Americans. Instead, beginning in the 1970s they shifted their priorities.[10]

In the 1970s all three of New York's white ethnic constituencies experienced the passing of the immigrant generation. In 1950, 23 percent of all New Yorkers were foreign-born whites. But these immigrants comprised only 2 percent of city dwellers under the age of twenty and 60 percent of those aged sixty-five and over. By 1980 many of these white immigrants had died or moved away. At the start of World War II, the city was home to over 170,000 immigrants from Ireland; by 1980, the number had dwindled to 41,000.

During the same period, the city's foreign-born Italian population declined from 409,000 to 156,000. Although the city's foreign-born population numbered 1.7 million in 1980—accounting for about 24 percent of the total population—the majority of these residents hailed from countries that benefited from the Hart-Cellar Immigration Act (1965): the Dominican Republic, Jamaica, China, Guyana, Korea, and Haiti.[11] By the year 2000 roughly 3 million New Yorkers—just shy of half the city's population—were first-generation immigrants, and 60 percent of newborn babies had at least one immigrant parent. Critically, Europeans comprised just 19 percent of the city's foreign-born population.[12]

The passing of the immigrant generation, the aging of the second generation, and the mass influx of new immigrant groups from around the globe signaled a new era for the city's white ethnic populations. These older New Yorkers had played a leading role in determining the thrust and direction of the city's white ethnic subcultures in the postwar period. Now their children, the third generation, began to assume leadership of their communities and struggled to maintain leadership of a city where they no longer comprised a majority. By the mid-1970s, new political alignments emerged that drew white voters from across ethnic boundaries into common alliance.[13]

Finally, the challenges to Irish and Italian Catholic unity outlined in Chapter 8—particularly, the liberalization of Catholic religiosity and the increased entry of third-generation youth into universities and white-collar professions—shattered the insularity and solidarity of the city's once vibrant Catholic subculture.

The quarter century that preceded this period of decline and transition—the years roughly covering 1945 to 1970—had witnessed these groups at the pinnacle of their collective influence. Gotham's Jews, Italians, and Irish dominated the city's government during these years and together comprised at least half of the regional population. Their churches, synagogues, meeting halls, and newspapers provided a rich backdrop that underscored New York's historic diversity and pluralism. Though they peacefully and often amicably shared the subways, streets, stores, and (sometimes) schools, Irish, Italian, and Jewish New Yorkers retained a strong enough sense of group identity to carve out whole neighborhoods, institutions, and subcultures that were largely separate and distinct.

The postwar period gave rise to a rising, nationwide consciousness of the divide between black and white America, but the example of New York demonstrates that categories like white and black are only useful to a degree. Fewer and fewer New Yorkers after World War II could reasonably claim to be children of Ellis Island, but ethnic ties continued to exert great influence over first-, second-, and third-generation Americans.

Though a large influx of black and Latino migrants greatly altered New York's ethnographic landscape and elicited fears and anxieties from both Jews and Catholics, these white ethnic New Yorkers reacted differently to the challenges of a racially changing city. Gotham never played host to a unified white political culture, in no small part because the lessons of Catholicism and Judaism—and the fundamentals of Irish, Italian, and Jewish culture—differed significantly from each other.

Events in New York help explain why Franklin Roosevelt's storied New Deal coalition of blacks, Jews, and Catholics unraveled so easily between 1945 and 1970. Fault lines always ran through this political alliance, and they widened with every passing year. If racial polarization helped foment a white backlash against liberalism, in truth, the potential for backlash existed long before race politics injected itself into the center of the fray.

To be sure, between 1945 and 1970 race assumed primacy in American politics and culture. But in these same years, the survival of distinct ethnic worldviews among so-called white ethnics continued to produce a diversity of ideas about authority, dissent, popular governance, and culture. This diversity was evident in the city's homes, schools, and places of worship, at meetings of grassroots community groups, and in debates over censorship, communism, and social unrest.

Notes

Introduction

1. Ben Zion Bokser, untitled sermon, undated [ca. 1954], box 11, High Holiday Sermons Folder, BZB, RCSCJ.

2. Michael Pearson, *Dreaming of Columbus: A Boyhood in the Bronx* (Syracuse, 1999), 27–29.

3. Lawrence J. McCaffrey, *The Irish Catholic Diaspora in America* (Washington, D.C., 1997), chap. 7; Charles R. Morris, *American Catholic: The Saints and Sinners Who Built America's Most Powerful Church* (New York, 1997), chap. 10; Jerre Mangione

and Ben Morreale, *La Storia: Five Centuries of the Italian American Experience* (New York, 1993), pt. 8. See also Eli Lederhendler, *New York Jews and the Decline of Ethnicity, 1950–1970* (Syracuse, 2001); and Herbert Gans, *The Urban Villagers: Group and Class in the Life of Italian Americans* (New York, 1962), 32–36. Gans, a sociologist, emphasizes class rather than "ethnicity" as a primary behavioral and associational determinant.

4. Philip Roth, *American Pastoral* (New York, 1997), 73.

5. Eric Goldman, *The Crucial Decade: America, 1945–1955* (New York, 1956), 128. See also William Leuchtenburg, *A Troubled Feast: American Society since 1945*, rev. ed. (Boston, 1979), 70, 78; William Chafe, *The Unfinished Journey: America since World War II* (New York, 1986), 117–22, 141–44; and William O'Neill, *American High: The Years of Confidence, 1945–1960* (New York, 1986), 9–28. O'Neill and Chafe make almost no mention of ethnicity or religion, suggesting that the authors perceive neither as a significant element of identity and community in the 1950s and 1960s. Leuchtenburg contends that "long characterized as a polyglot society, the United States increasingly became a homogenous society. . . . [The nation] had moved a good distance from the world of Mulberry Bend and the East Side Ghetto" (70).

6. Will Herberg, *Protestant, Catholic, Jew: An Essay in American Religious Sociology* (Chicago, 1955), 22.

7. For a review of "consensus" history and its application to ethnic and religious history, see William Chafe, "America since 1945," in *The New American History*, ed. Eric Foner, 2nd ed. (Philadelphia, 1997), 164–68; Godfrey Hodgson, *America in Our Time* (New York, 1976), 67–98; John Morton Blum, *V Was for Victory: Politics and American Culture during World War II* (New York, 1976), 16–52; Edward S. Shapiro, *A Time for Healing: American Jewry since World War II* (Baltimore, 1992), chaps. 1 and 2; and Matthew Frye Jacobson, *Whiteness of a Different Color: European Immigrants and the Alchemy of Race* (New York, 1998), 91–138.

8. Michael Novak, *The Rise of the Unmeltable Ethnics: Politics and Culture in the Seventies* (New York, 1972); Jonathan Rieder, *Canarsie: The Jews and Italians of Brooklyn against Liberalism* (Cambridge, Mass., 1985); Andrew M. Greeley and Gregory Baum, eds., *Ethnicity* (New York, 1977); Andrew M. Greeley, *Ethnicity in the United States: A Preliminary Reconnaissance* (New York, 1974).

9. James P. Shenton and Kevin Kenny, "Ethnicity and Immigration," in Foner, *The New American History*, 366–67.

10. Nathan Glazer and Daniel Patrick Moynihan, *Beyond the Melting Pot: The Negroes, Puerto Ricans, Jews, Italians, and Irish of New York City* (New York, 1963), preface.

11. Jacobson, *Whiteness of a Different Color*, 91–136; Lizabeth Cohen, *Making a New Deal: Industrial Workers in Chicago, 1919–1939* (New York, 1990), 323–60; George Lipsitz, *The Possessive Investment in Whiteness: How White People Profit from Identity Politics* (Philadelphia, 1998), 1–46. See also Matthew Pratt Guterl, *The Color of Race in America, 1900–1940* (Cambridge, Mass., 2001); Thomas A. Guglielmo, *White on Arrival: Italians, Race, Color, and Power in Chicago, 1890–1945* (New York, 2003); Karen Brodkin, *How Jews Became White Folks and What That Says about Race in America* (New Brunswick, N.J., 1998); Dale T. Knobel,

Paddy and the Republic: Ethnicity and Nationality in the Antebellum Period (Middletown, Conn., 1986); and David Roediger, The Wages of Whiteness: Race and the Making of the American Working Class (London, 1999).

12. For a concise historiographical review of this new scholarship, see Gary Gerstle, "Race and the Myth of Liberal Consensus," Journal of American History 82, no. 2 (September 1995): 579–86. Important books include Thomas J. Sugrue, The Origins of the Urban Crisis: Race and Inequality in Postwar Detroit (Princeton, 1996); Arnold Hirsch, Making the Second Ghetto: Race and Housing in Chicago, 1940–1960 (New York, 1983); Stephen Grant Meyer, As Long as They Don't Move Next Door: Segregation and Racial Conflict in American Neighborhoods (New York, 2000); Matthew D. Lassiter, The Silent Majority: Suburban Politics in the Sunbelt South (Princeton, 2006); Kevin Kruse, White Flight: Atlanta and the Making of Modern Conservatism (Princeton, 2006); and Matthew J. Countryman, Up South: Civil Rights and Black Power in Philadelphia (Philadelphia, 2006).

13. The best example of this interpretation is Thomas Byrne Edsall with Mary D. Edsall, Chain Reaction: The Impact of Race, Rights, and Taxes on American Politics (New York, 1992). See also Clayborne Carson, "Black-Jewish Universalism in the Era of Identity Politics," in Struggles in the Promised Land: Towards a History of Black-Jewish Relations in the United States, ed. Jack Salzman and Cornel West (New York, 1997); and Jonathan Kaufman, Broken Alliance: The Turbulent Times between Blacks and Jews in America (New York, 1988). For an analysis that finds an earlier Jewish backlash against liberalism, see Michael E. Staub, Torn at the Roots: The Crisis of Jewish Liberalism in Postwar America (New York, 2002).

14. Another school of thought generally holds that race was only one of several concerns that drove white voters out of the liberal coalition. The emergence of new political agendas such as second-wave feminism, Black Power, antiwar activism, and gay rights caused many white liberals to reassess their politics. The Democratic Party's seeming embrace of such causes and constituencies— including but not limited to a redistributive civil rights agenda—inspired an electoral realignment that partly eviscerated the Roosevelt coalition. See Allen J. Matusow, The Unraveling of American Liberalism: A History of Liberalism in the 1960s (New York, 1984); Jonathan Rieder, "The Rise of the 'Silent Majority,' " in The Rise and Fall of the New Deal Order, 1930–1980, ed. Steve Fraser and Gary Gerstle (Princeton, 1989); Matthew Dallek, The Right Moment: Ronald Reagan's First Victory and the Decisive Turning Point in American Politics (New York, 2000); E. J. Dionne Jr., Why Americans Hate Politics (New York, 1991); and Kenneth D. Durr, Behind the Backlash: White Working-Class Politics in Baltimore, 1940–1980 (Chapel Hill, 2003).

15. Ronald H. Bayor, Neighbors in Conflict: The Irish, Germans, Jews, and Italians of New York City, 1929–1941 (Baltimore, 1978), 147; William Spinrad, "New Yorkers Cast Their Ballots" (Ph.D. diss., Columbia University, 1955), 14; "More in City Are Turning to the Right," NYT, 15 January 1974, 1; "Survey Confirms Politicians' Views of Attitudes of Ethnic Voters," ibid., 25 October 1970, 67.

16. John T. McGreevy, Parish Boundaries: The Catholic Encounter with Race in the Twentieth-Century Urban North (Chicago, 1996), 1–5.

17. Classic studies of nineteenth-century American political history hold that ethnicity and religion were key—though by no means singular or even primary—ingredients of voting behavior. See Lee Benson, *The Concept of Jacksonian Democracy: New York as a Test Case* (Princeton, 1961); Robert P. Swierenga, "Ethnoreligious Political Behavior in the Mid-Nineteenth Century: Voting, Values, Cultures," in *Religion and American Politics: From the Colonial Period to the 1980s*, ed. Mark A. Noll (New York, 1990); and William E. Gienapp, *The Origins of the Republican Party, 1852–1856* (New York, 1987). For a defense of using ethnicity and religion as categories of analysis in American political history, see Robert P. Formisano, "The Invention of the Ethnocultural Interpretation," *American Historical Review* 99, no. 2 (April 1994): 453–77.

18. A recent study that locates race as the primary determinant of city politics after the late 1960s is Jerald E. Podair, *The Strike That Changed New York: Blacks, Whites, and the Ocean Hill–Brownsville Crisis* (New Haven, 2001). Another recent study—one that is concerned with race but also attentive to the distinctiveness of Jewish political culture—is Wendell Pritchett, *Brownsville, Brooklyn: Blacks, Jews, and the Changing Face of the Ghetto* (Chicago, 2002).

19. Glazer and Moynihan, *Beyond the Melting Pot*, 7–9. Glazer and Moynihan note that in 1960, roughly 5 percent of the city's general population could be characterized as "old stock" or "WASP" (their terms), while 10 percent were of German (mostly Catholic) origin. They also count 240,000 foreign-born New Yorkers of various other nationalities. Adding in the black and Puerto Rican populations, the authors account for 93 percent of the city's general population.

Chapter One

1. Joshua Koreznick, interview, 23 March 1984, WWOHL; Emily Faust Koreznick, interview, 4 January 1983, WWOHL.

2. Brian McDonald, *My Father's Gun: One Family, Three Badges, One Hundred Years in the NYPD* (New York, 1999), 21–29.

3. Sociologists have long been aware of the tendency of Americans, particularly urbanites, to limit their associations to others of similar ethnic origin. See particularly Michael Parenti, "Ethnic Politics and the Persistence of Ethnic Identification," *American Political Science Review* 61, no. 3 (September, 1967): 717–26.

4. Jewish population counts are especially complicated by the U.S. Census Bureau's refusal to include religion as a category of analysis. It is also difficult to estimate the city's Irish and Italian populations. Figures for 1940, 1950, 1960, and 1970 are based on the number of respondents claiming to be of Irish or Italian "foreign stock" (foreign born, or of foreign-born parentage). Figures for 1980 are based on respondents' declaration of ethnic origin. Rising intermarriage rates between Irish and Italian New Yorkers complicate these estimates, as children of "mixed" parentage had to choose whether to count themselves as primarily Irish or Italian in origin. Figures for 1980 in Table 1 leave out 330,000 people claiming "Irish and other" origin. See Michael Hout

and Joshua R. Goldstein, "How 4.5 Million Irish Immigrants Became 40 Million Irish Americans: Demographic and Subjective Aspects of the Ethnic Composition of White Americans," *American Sociological Review* 59, no. 1 (February 1994): 64–82.

5. Nathan Glazer and Daniel Patrick Moynihan, *Beyond the Melting Pot: The Negroes, Puerto Ricans, Jews, Italians, and Irish of New York City* (New York, 1963), 7–9. Glazer and Moynihan further note that in 1960, roughly 5 percent of the city's general population could be characterized as "old stock" or "WASP" (their terms), while 10 percent were of German origin. They also count 240,000 foreign-born New Yorkers of various other nationalities. All totaled, the authors account for 93 percent of the city's general population. My estimate for 1970 assumes that the census undercounted the Irish and Italians by roughly 42 percent—the same undercount rate for 1960, if one accepts polling data as a more accurate gauge than census data.

6. Figures for metropolitan New York, 1930–57, in FJPNY, *Estimated Jewish Population of the New York Area, 1900–1975* (New York, 1959), 14, 22–30. Subsequent figures in Jacob Rader Marcus, *To Count a People: American Jewish Population Data, 1585–1984* (New York, 1990), 123, 139; FJPNY, "New York Jewish Population Study and Area Profile," 1981, General Collection, AJHS. The "greater metropolitan area" represents New York City and Suffolk, Nassau, and Westchester Counties in New York and Bergen, Passaic, and Essex Counties in New Jersey.

7. Ira Sheskin, "Jewish Metropolitan Homelands," *Journal of Cultural Geography* 13, no. 2 (Spring 1993): 99–132.

8. Ira Rosenwaike, *Population History of New York City* (New York, 1972), 167.

9. Deborah Dash Moore, *At Home in America: Second Generation New York Jews* (New York, 1981), 30–33. For a description of the New York City real estate boom in the early twentieth century, see Selma Berrol, "The Jewish West Side of New York City, 1920–1970," *Journal of Ethnic Studies* 14, no. 4 (Winter 1986): 21–45.

10. Among sociologists, the index of dissimilarity, or delta, is a popular mathematical estimation of demographic segregation. Running between 0.0 (no segregation) and 1.00 (total segregation), the delta quantifies the ethnic uniformity of a particular neighborhood or census tract. The problem with the dissimilarity index, however, and with any such mathematical device, is that its measurements are relative: inferring whether meaningful ethnic consolidation occurs at 0.35, 0.50, or 0.70 is purely subjective. Additionally, the delta does not account for further segregation or social selectivity within a spatial tract. With these caveats in mind, the delta is still a consistent and thus useful gauge of the persistence or decline of residential selectivity. See Otis Dudley Duncan and Beverly Duncan, "A Methodological Analysis of Segregation Indexes," *American Sociological Review* 20 (April 1955): 210–27; and Stanley Lieberson, *Ethnic Patterns in American Cities* (New York, 1963), app. A.

11. Moore, *At Home in America*, 31.

12. Tabulations based on FJPNY, *Estimated Jewish Population of the New York Area*, 25–42.

13. Anita Rogers, interview, 11 November 1986, WWOHL; Ruth Rogers, interview,

9 October 1986, WWOHL. Jews accounted for roughly 46 percent of the Rockaway area's population in 1957. FJPNY, *Estimated Jewish Population of the New York Area*, 312–13.

14. Jerry Della Femina and Charles Sopkin, *An Italian Grows in Brooklyn* (New York, 1978), 84–85.

15. Nathan Kantrowitz, "Ethnic and Racial Segregation in the New York Metropolis, 1960," *American Journal of Sociology* 74, no. 6 (May 1969): 690.

16. Richard D. Alba, John R. Logan, and Kyle Crowder, "White Ethnic Neighborhoods and Assimilation: The Greater New York Region, 1980–1990," *Social Forces* 75, no. 3 (March 1997): 893. The authors describe an "ethnic neighborhood" as a "set of contiguous [census] tracts, which must contain at least one tract where a group is represented as 40 percent or more of the residents and whose other tracts each have a level of ethnic concentration among residents of at least 35 percent" (893).

17. John T. McGreevy, *Parish Boundaries: The Catholic Experience with Race in the Twentieth-Century Urban North* (Chicago, 1996), 13.

18. Linda Dowling Almeida, "From Danny Boy to Bono: The Irish in New York City, 1945–1995" (Ph.D. diss., New York University, 1996), 228–29.

19. Marianna De Marco Torgovnick, *Crossing Ocean Parkway: Readings by an Italian American Daughter* (Chicago, 1994), 1–7.

20. Gloria Wills Landes, interview, 7 November 1983, WWOHL; FJPNY, *Estimated Jewish Population of the New York Area*, 250–51.

21. Henry L. Feingold, *A Time for Searching: Entering the Mainstream, 1920–1945* (Baltimore, 1992), 126–27; Works Progress Administration Federal Writer's Project, *The Italians of New York: A Survey* (New York, 1938), 64–67; David Reimers, "An End and a Beginning," in *The New York Irish*, ed. Ronald H. Bayor and Timothy J. Meagher (Baltimore, 1996), 419. See also Beth S. Wenger, *New York Jews and the Great Depression: Uncertain Promise* (New Haven, 1996), 10–32; Ronald H. Bayor, *Neighbors in Conflict: The Irish, Germans, Jews, and Italians of New York City, 1929–1941* (Baltimore, 1978), 8–29.

22. Sidney Goldstein, "Socioeconomic Differentials among Religious Groups in the United States," *American Journal of Sociology* 74, no. 6 (May 1969): 612–31, esp. 622.

23. Barry R. Chiswick, "The Postwar Economy of American Jews," *Studies in Contemporary Jewry* 8 (1992): 85–101.

24. Joshua B. Freeman, *Working-Class New York: Life and Labor since World War II* (New York, 2000), 3–22.

25. Lizabeth Cohen, *Making a New Deal: Industrial Workers in Chicago, 1919–1939* (New York, 1990).

26. Another counterargument to the Chicago-CIO model is Bruce Nelson, *Workers on the Waterfront: Seamen, Longshoremen, and Unionism in the 1930s* (Urbana, 1988).

27. Freeman, *Working-Class New York*, 45.

28. Nelson, *Workers on the Waterfront*, 43–45; Joshua B. Freeman, *In Transit: The Transport Workers Union in New York City, 1933–1966* (New York, 1989), 26–27;

Paul Ritterband, "Ethnic Power and the Public Schools: The New York City School Strike of 1968," *Sociology of Education* 47, no. 2 (Spring 1974): 251–58. For background on New York City's declining unskilled labor base, see Bayor, *Neighbors in Conflict*, 8–9.

29. Irving Howe, "New York in the Thirties: Some Fragments of Memory," *Dissent* 8, no. 3 (Summer 1961): 242.

30. Michael Pearson, *Dreaming of Columbus: A Boyhood in the Bronx* (Syracuse, 1999), 139.

31. Jay P. Dolan, *The Immigrant Church: New York's Irish and German Catholics, 1815–1965* (Notre Dame, 1983), 99–120; Charles R. Morris, *American Catholic: The Saints and Sinners Who Built America's Most Powerful Church* (New York, 1997), 3–5; Anthony E. Conte, *Catholic Education in New Jersey and the Nation: History, Statistics, and Outlook* (Trenton, 1970), 1–6.

32. NJWB, "Survey of the Cultural and Recreational Needs of the Jewish Population of New York City, Part Two: A Study of the Jewish Population of New York City," September 1946, 23, 48, box 20, AJHS.

33. All preceding estimates assume that children between the ages of five and fourteen in Manhattan, Brooklyn, the Bronx, and Queens reflected the city's overall religious composition: 51.5 percent Catholic (among whites). For the religious breakdown of New York City in 1952, see Neva Deardorff, "The Religio-Cultural Background of New York City's Population," *Milbank Memorial Fund Quarterly* 33, no. 2 (April 1955): 160. For 1945 enrollment figures, see Diocese of Brooklyn, *Brooklyn Educational Year Book: 1945* (Brooklyn, 1945), 26–31, copy housed in ADB. For successive enrollment figures, see *Official Catholic Directory: 1950* (New Providence, N.J., 1950); and *Official Catholic Directory: 1960* (New Providence, N.J., 1960). For the breakdown of school-age children, see FJPNY, *Estimated Jewish Population of the New York Area*, 112–19.

34. Diocese of Brooklyn, *Brooklyn Educational Year Book: 1945*, 26–31; *Official Catholic Directory: 1950*, 151–52; *Official Catholic Directory: 1960*, 188–90; BT, 10 June 1950, 4, 9; FJPNY, *Estimated Jewish Population of the New York Area*, 112–19; Lawrence J. McCaffrey, *The Irish Catholic Diaspora in America* (Washington, D.C., 1997), 176.

35. Andrew M. Greeley and Peter H. Rossi, *The Education of Catholic Americans* (Chicago, 1966), 37; Vincent Panella, *The Other Side: Growing Up Italian in America* (New York, 1979), 31.

36. David Blumberg, interview, 3 May 1984, WWOHL; Edna Rogers, interview, 29 October 1986, WWOHL.

37. Ruth Jacknow Markowitz, *My Daughter, the Teacher: Jewish Teachers in the New York City Schools* (New Brunswick, N.J., 1993), 2; Moore, *At Home in America*, 99–101.

38. On tracking, see Miriam Cohen, *Workshop to Office: Two Generations of Italian Women in New York City, 1900–1950* (Ithaca, 1992), 147–95.

39. Marcus Lee Hansen, "The Third Generation in America," *Commentary* 14 (November 1952): 492–500. Hansen's three-generation model of American immigration and ethnicity was challenged by such social scientists as Gerhard Lenski, whose study of religion and ethnicity in Detroit (1961) found that

church attendance among second-generation Catholics exceeded that of the first generation, while that of third-generation Catholics surpassed both. For a review of the scholarly debate, see Bernard Lazerwitz and Louis Rowitz, "The Three-Generation Hypothesis," *American Journal of Sociology* 69, no. 5 (March 1964): 529–38, esp. 529–31.

40. Greeley and Rossi, *The Education of Catholic Americans*, 39. Irish Catholics reported the following rates of parochial school attendance: "all Catholic" education, 41 percent for first/second generations and 27 percent for third/fourth generations; "some Catholic" education, 39 percent for first/second generations and 49 percent for third/fourth generations; and "no Catholic" education, 20 percent for first/second generations and 27 percent for third/fourth generations. The drop in the percentage of respondents claiming a complete K–12 Catholic education may be attributable to the rise in high school attendance and completion over the generations. Diocesan high schools generally captured a lower proportion of the Catholic population than parish elementary schools.

41. Nicholas John Russo, "Three Generations of Italians in New York City: Their Religious Acculturation," *International Migration Review* 3, no. 2 (Spring 1969): 3–16. On Italian American religiosity, see Leonard Covello, *The Social Background of the Italo-American School Child: A Study of the Southern Italian Family Mores and Their Effect on the School Situation in Italy and America* (Totowa, N.J., 1972), 103–25; Robert Anthony Orsi, *The Madonna of 115th Street: Faith and Community in Italian Harlem, 1880–1950* (New Haven, 1985); and Mary Elizabeth Brown, *Churches, Communities, and Children: Italian Immigrants in the Archdiocese of New York, 1880-1945* (New York, 1995).

42. Data on family and individual services and Catholic Youth Organization membership: Catholic Charities of the Archdiocese of New York, *Report for 1963* (New York, 1963), 16, 39. Data on Catholic Youth Organization: Diocese of Brooklyn, *50th Anniversary, Catholic Charities, Diocese of Brooklyn* (New York, 1949), 35–40. For estimated attendance at parish dances, see Catholic Charities of the Archdiocese of New York, *Report for 1960* (New York, 1960), 38. Data on the Knights of Columbus: "Knights of Columbus Increase," *NYT*, 30 May 1954. Hospital data: *Official Catholic Directory: 1955* (New Providence, N.J., 1955).

43. Pete Hamill, *A Drinking Life* (New York, 1994), 9; Society of the Friendly Sons of Saint Patrick in the City of New York, *Yearbook: 1966* (New York, 1966), 5–6.

44. Doris Kearns Goodwin, *Wait Till Next Year: A Memoir* (New York, 1997), 84–88.

45. George Kelly, *Inside My Father's House* (New York, 1989), 3–4.

46. *JEC Bulletin*, January 1954. Full collection housed in the New York Public Library—Dorot Jewish Division.

47. Marshall Sklare, ed., *America's Jews* (New York, 1971), 120–21; Jack Elinson, Paul W. Haberman, and Cyrelle Gell, *Ethnic and Educational Data on Adults in New York City, 1963–1964* (New York, 1967). Three surveys conducted in 1959 revealed that 19 percent of all New York City Jews never attended synagogue, while 50 percent attended only a few times each year—primarily on the High

Holidays. Corresponding national figures for Jews not residing in New York City were 12 percent and 50 percent. See Bernard Lazerwitz, "Jews In and Out of New York City," *Jewish Journal of Sociology* 3, no. 2 (December 1961): 254–60.

48. *JEC Bulletin*, January 1954.

49. Ibid., April 1945, November 1948; *American Jewish Yearbook* (Philadelphia, 1948), 155.

50. In 1980 the FJPNY found that 13 percent of New York City Jews identified themselves as Orthodox. While no such figures are available for the early postwar years, it is likely that a smaller portion of the Jewish community counted itself as Orthodox in the 1940s, 1950s, and 1960s. After losing numbers to the Conservative movement in the 1920s and 1930s, American Orthodoxy gained its real strength in the 1940s and 1950s, when Hassidic and other stringently Orthodox émigrés from the Soviet Union and Poland made their way to New York. Their demographic explosion, and the consequent rightward shift in Orthodox Judaism since the 1970s, has rejuvenated but also altered American Orthodoxy. See FJPNY, "New York Jewish Population Study and Area Profile," New York, 1981, General Collection, AJHS. For background on postwar Orthodox Judaism, see Jeffrey S. Gurrock, "The Orthodox Synagogue," in *The American Synagogue: A Sanctuary Transformed*, ed. Jack Wertheimer (Hanover, N.H., 1987), 64–68.

51. Simon Rifkind, interview, 10 December 1983; Robert Rifkind, interview, 14 September 1983; Richard Rifkind, interview, 21 October 1983; all in WWOHL.

52. Ben Zion Bokser, "Kol Nidre Sermon," September 1952, box 11, High Holiday Sermons Folder, BZB, RCSCJ.

53. Ibid.; Paula E. Hyman, "The Introduction of the Bat Mitzvah in Conservative Judaism in Postwar America," in *YIVO Annual* 19 (New York, 1990), 133–46.

54. *JEC Bulletin*, May 1945, 2. The *Catholic Directory's* annual head counts of Catholics in the Archdiocese of New York and the Diocese of Brooklyn show an almost even split between girls and boys in elementary and high schools.

55. NJWB, "Survey of the Leisure Time Needs of Jewish Population in Stuyvesant Town Area," November 1950, box 15, AJHS. Forty-nine percent of the neighborhood's Jews—and fully 63 percent of its Jewish males—had graduated from college; 41 percent of employed men were professionals; and there were "no semi-skilled or unskilled workers."

56. Mandell L. Berman, "Memorandum to Committee on Federation Planning for Jewish Education," 2 June 1966, box 384, Council of Jewish Federations and Welfare Funds, G.A.-1966-Jewish Education-Miscellaneous and All Matters-January–June Folder, AJHS.

57. AAJE, "Test on Fundamentals of Hebrew—I, for Grades 3–6, Elementary Hebrew Schools, 1956," box 10, Tests-Samples Folder, AJHS; Daniel Biederman, interview, 25 May 1983, WWOHL; Jane Blumberg, interview, 8 December 1983, WWOHL.

58. AAJE, "Amounts Budgeted for All Jewish Local Needs through Federation or/and Chest Allocations and Amounts Allocated for Jewish Education (55 Communities), 1947–1957: Cities Having Jewish Population over 100,000,"

box 20, Budgets-Financing Education Folder, AJHS; Jack Wertheimer, *A People Divided: Judaism in Contemporary America* (Hanover, N.H., 1993), 5–6.

59. NJWB, "Survey of the Cultural and Recreational Needs of the Jewish Population of New York City, Part One: Summary and Recommendations for New York City," September 1946, box 20, AJHS.

60. FJPNY, *Let Us Build a City of Life* (New York, 1961); BT, 10 June 1950; AAJE, "Reported Cost of Operating Weekday Afternoon and Sunday Schools," ca. 1958–59, box 20, Budgets-Financing Education Folder, AJHS; NYT, 3 February 1946, 1 February 1946, 21 February 1946, and 15 February 1946; Glazer and Moynihan, *Beyond the Melting Pot*, 280. See also Wenger, *New York Jews and the Great Depression*, 136–65, esp. 164.

61. Sklare, *America's Jews*, 120–21; Lazerwitz, "Jews In and Out of New York City"; Wertheimer, *A People Divided*, chap. 1 (quote from p. 14).

62. In a survey conducted in 1980, the FJPNY estimated that 89 percent of Jews in New York City, Westchester County, and Long Island held Passover seders. This chapter assumes that this percentage is no higher than those that a comparable study in the 1950s or 1960s would have revealed. See FJPNY, "New York Jewish Population Study and Area Profile," 1981, General Collection, AJHS. On religious school attendance see *JEC Bulletin*, January 1954.

Chapter Two

1. Woody Allen, "Annie Hall," in *Four Films of Woody Allen* (New York, 1982), 20.

2. YIVO Institute for Jewish Research, *Image before My Eyes* (1980), film directed by Josh Waletzky.

3. Joseph Telushkin, *Jewish Literacy: The Most Important Things to Know about the Jewish Religion, Its People, and Its History* (New York, 1991), 40.

4. Friedman's biblical references include three important episodes in the Torah. Sodom and Gomorrah were two ancient cities famous for their alleged depravity. In Genesis 19:24–25, God destroys both cities despite the entreaties of the patriarch Abraham, who pleads that even if only one righteous man could be found amid the rabble, God must spare the cities. In Numbers 16, Korach and his coalition of Israelites from the tribes of Levi and Ruben attempt a populist-style overthrow of Moses; God punishes them with death. Friedman refers to Moses' plea that the innocent be spared, and in fact Korach's sons are not killed, as they are not among the conspirators. In the biblical book bearing his name, Job faces a string of divine trials: the loss of his wealth, the death of his ten children, and painful physical afflictions. Job does not renounce God but demands repeatedly that God justify these tribulations.

5. Rabbi Theodore Friedman (Congregation Beth-El, South Orange, N.J.), "Question or Answer?" (sermon delivered at High Holiday Sermon Seminar, September 1961), box 6, folder 32, Samuel Penner Papers, RCSCJ.

6. Rabbi Leon Jick (Free Synagogue of Westchester, N.Y.), "To Ease the Burden of Our Brothers Rosh Hashanah Morning" (sermon delivered at the High Holiday Sermon Seminar, Park Avenue Synagogue, New York City, 8 Sept. 1965), box 6, folder 32, Samuel Penner Papers, RCSCJ.

7. George Lieberman, "The Excommunication of Spinoza: An Ageless Controversy and Its Lessons for Today" (sermon, ca. 1955), box 2, folder 5, George Lieberman Papers, AJA.

8. Ben Zion Bokser, untitled sermon, undated (ca. 1953), box 11, High Holiday Sermons Folder, BZB, RCSCJ. In his sermon, Bokser refers to the cessation of hostilities in Korea, which suggests that he delivered it at High Holiday services in the fall of 1953, roughly two months after the armistice of 27 July 1953.

9. Samuel Penner, "Rosh Hashanah Sermon Ideas," ca. 1944, box 6, folder 6, Samuel Penner Papers, RCSCJ.

10. Joseph P. Sternstein (Temple Ansche Chesed, New York, N.Y.), "Sons or Slaves—Which?" (sermon delivered at High Holiday Sermon Seminar, 8 Sept. 1965), box 6, folder 32, Samuel Penner Papers, RCSCJ.

11. Benjamin Z. Kreitman, "The Escape to Life: The Jewish View of Activism: A Sermon on the Sidrach Toledot," *Brooklyn Jewish Center Review* 43 (September 1964), copy housed in RCSCJ. The story of Jacob's struggle with the angel appears in Genesis 32:28–29.

12. For a brief description of religious and social arrangements in the traditional Ashkenazic community, see Jacob Katz, *Out of the Ghetto: The Social Background of Jewish Emancipation, 1770–1870* (New York, 1973), chap. 2. On Hassidism, see Bernard D. Weinryb, *The Jews of Poland: A Social and Economic History of the Jewish Community in Poland from 1100 to 1800* (Philadelphia, 1972), 206–303.

13. For background on the gradual erosion of traditional Jewish political authority, see Eli Lederhendler, *The Road to Modern Jewish Politics: Political Tradition and Political Reconstruction in the Jewish Community of Tsarist Russia* (New York, 1989); Michael Stanislawski, *Czar Nicholas I and the Jews: The Transformation of Jewish Society in Russia, 1825–1855* (Philadelphia, 1983); and John Doyle Klier, *Russia Gathers Her Jews: The Origins of the "Jewish Question" in Russia, 1772–1825* (DeKalb, Ill., 1986), 3–8, 179–80.

14. For a review of the Jewish community's factious social and political reaction to pogroms and czarist oppression, see Alexander Orbach, "The Development of the Russian Jewish Community, 1881–1903," in *Pogroms: Anti-Jewish Violence in Modern Russian History*, ed. John Doyle Klier and Shlomo Lambroza (New York, 1992), 137–63. Useful essays include Jonathan Frankel, "The Crisis of 1881–1882 as a Turning Point in Modern Jewish History," and Michael Stanislawski, "The Transformation of Traditional Authority in Russian Jewry: The First Stage," both in *The Legacy of Jewish Immigration: 1881 and Its Impact*, ed. David Berger (New York, 1983), 9–30. On the rapid urbanization and proletarianization of Russian Jewry, see Ezra Mendelsohn, *Class Struggle in the Pale* (Cambridge, 1970).

15. On the development of a distinctly democratic form of American Christianity in the colonial period and the early Republic, see Gordon S. Wood, *The Radicalism of the American Revolution* (New York, 1991), 111–12, 144–45; and Nathan Hatch, *The Democratization of American Christianity* (New Haven, 1989).

16. Leon A. Jick, *The Americanization of the Synagogue, 1820–1870* (Hanover, N.H., 1976), esp. chaps. 4, 6, and 7; Hasia Diner, *A Time for Gathering: The Second*

Migration, 1820–1880 (Baltimore, 1992), chap. 5; Jick, "The Reform Synagogue," in *The American Synagogue: A Sanctuary Transformed* ed. Jack Wertheimer (Hanover, N.H., 1987), 85–110.

17. Michael A. Meyer, *Response to Modernity: A History of the Reform Movement in Judaism* (Detroit, 1988), chap. 6. See also Jack Wertheimer, *A People Divided: Judaism in Contemporary America* (Hanover, N.H., 1993), 43–46; and Wade Clark Roof and William McKinney, *American Mainline Religion: Its Changing Shape and Future* (New Brunswick, N.J., 1987).

18. Congregation B'nai Jeshurun, Annual Report, 14 Jan. 1951, box 36, folder 3, Congregation B'nai Jeshurun Papers, RCSCJ.

19. Irving Howe, "New York in the Thirties: Some Fragments of Memory," *Dissent* 8, no. 3 (Summer 1961): 242–43.

20. Aileen Robbins, interview, 17 March 1983, WWOHL.

21. Emily Faust Koreznick, interview, 4 January 1983, WWOHL.

22. Lisa Goodkind Hathaway, interview, 27 December 1983, WWOHL.

23. Ruth Messinger, interview, 25 February 1982, WWOHL; AJCongress, National Women's Division, Scarsdale–White Plains–Harrison Chapter, *Bulletin*, October 1954, box 131, AJCongress Papers, AJHS.

24. Marcy Oppenheimer, interview, 31 May 1983; Jean Bennet, interview, 19 September 1983; Hannah Hofheimer, interview, 24 August 1983; all in WWOHL.

25. Beth S. Wenger, *New York Jews and the Great Depression: Uncertain Promise* (New Haven, 1996), 63–64; Henry L. Feingold, *A Time for Searching: Entering the Mainstream, 1920–1945* (Baltimore, 1992), 14–15. Scholars disagree sharply about the roots of American Jewish educational achievement. For background on this debate, see Selma C. Berrol, "Education and Economic Mobility: The Jewish Experience in New York City, 1880–1920," *American Jewish Historical Quarterly* 65, no. 3 (Fall 1976): 269–70; Feingold, *A Time for Searching*, 139–40; and Susan A. Glenn, *Daughters of the Shtetl: Life and Labor in the Immigrant Generation* (Ithaca, 1990), chap. 1, esp. 8–16.

26. Jack Elinson, Paul W. Haberman, and Cyrelle Gell, *Ethnic and Educational Data on Adults in New York City, 1963–1964* (New York, 1967), 14; George Lieberman, "Confirmation Speech, Shuvuos, June 12, 1959," box 2, folder 1, George Lieberman Papers, AJA.

27. Charles S. Liebman, *The Ambivalent American Jew: Politics, Religion, and Family in American Jewish Life* (Philadelphia, 1973), 163–64.

28. Bernard C. Rosen, "Race, Ethnicity, and the Achievement Syndrome," *American Sociological Review* 24, no. 1 (February 1959): 47–60; Theodore Bienstok, "Antiauthoritarian Attitudes in the Eastern European Shtetl Community," *American Journal of Sociology* 57, no. 2 (September 1951): 150–58; George Psathas, "Ethnicity, Social Class, and Adolescent Independence from Parental Control," *American Sociological Review* 22, no. 4 (August 1957): 415–23.

29. Bienstok, "Antiauthoritarian Attitudes," 156.

30. Psathas, "Ethnicity, Social Class, and Adolescent Independence." The results were based on the teenagers' perceptions of their family lives. Parental impressions and opinions were not included in the survey.

31. For comparative income levels and occupations, see Chapter 1.

32. Deborah Dash Moore, *At Home in America: Second Generation New York Jews* (New York, 1981), 11; Jenna Weissman Joselit, *The Wonder of America: Reinventing Jewish Culture, 1880–1950* (New York, 1994), 5–6.

33. For background on the child-centered orientation of middle-class domestic culture, see Elaine Tyler May, *Homeward Bound: American Families in the Cold War Era* (New York, 1988), chap. 6; Paula Fass, *The Damned and the Beautiful: American Youth in the 1920s* (New York, 1977), chap. 2; Dominick Cavallo, *A Fiction of the Past: The Sixties in American History* (New York, 1999), chap. 3; and Alan Petigny, "The Permissive Turn" (unpublished paper, courtesy of Alan Petigny).

34. Robert H. Landis, interview, 28 November 1983, WWOHL.

35. Richard Rifkind, interview, 21 October 1983, WWOHL.

36. Ruth Rogers, interview, 9 October 1986; Arthur Rodgers, interview, 10 November 1986; both in WWOHL.

37. Carole Rifkind, interview, 18 October 1983; Nancy Rifkind, interview, 23 November 1983; both in WWOHL.

38. Hannah Hofheimer, interview, 14 August 1983; Jean Bennet, interview, 19 September 1983; both in WWOHL.

39. Arthur Rogers, interview, 10 November 1986, WWOHL.

40. Simon Rifkind, interview, 10 December 1983; Richard Rifkind, interview, 21 October 1983; both in WWOHL.

41. "Ways of Building Relationships with Children," Camp Ramah training material, 1963, box 2, folder 1, Jerome Abrams Papers, RCSCJ.

42. Diane Ravitch, *The Troubled Crusade: American Education, 1945–1980* (New York, 1983), chap. 2.

43. BJCC, "Statement on Religious and Spiritual Needs of Boys and Girls between the Ages of 12–18 for the Little White House Conference on Children and Youth in Brooklyn," draft, ca. 1950, box 11, folder 1, AJA; *JEC Bulletin*, January 1951, copy housed in New York Public Library—Dorot Jewish Division.

44. New York City Board of Education, *Curriculum Design of the New York City Schools* (New York, 1956). Copy housed at New York City Public Library. Italics added.

45. For background on Jewish school enrollment, see Chapter 1.

46. David H. Panitz, "Rabbi's Column," *B'nai Jeshurun Topics*, vol. 23, no. 14 (6 April 1951), B'nai Jeshurun Papers, RCSCJ.

47. Lieberman, "Confirmation Speech, Shuvuos, June 12, 1959."

48. The students are quoted in Morris M. Goldberg, "Let Us Pray," *Shaare Zedek Newsletter*, vol. 5, no. 13 (22 January 1954), box 2, folder 1, Shaare Zedek Papers, RCSCJ. Goldberg's column supported the students.

49. The episode is all the more striking given the prevalence of in loco parentis laws governing American universities through the mid-1960s. See Terry H. Anderson, *The Movement and the Sixties: Protest in America from Greensboro to Wounded Knee* (New York, 1995), intro., chap. 2.

50. Joseph Stein, *Fiddler on the Roof* (New York, 1965), 72–75, 121–26.

51. George Lieberman, "Fiddler on the Roof" (sermon, 19 February 1965), box 3, folder 1, George Lieberman Papers, AJA.

52. The original Broadway production of *Fiddler on the Roof* (1964) portrays Tevye's departure for America as a joyous and optimistic occasion. Norman Jewison's film adaptation of the musical (1971) restores some of Aleichem's original negativity about America; the closing scene casts Tevye's departure as exilic rather than buoyant. Nevertheless, even in the film's final sequence, the Fiddler follows Tevye and his family to America rather than go with the matchmaker Yente, who is bound for Palestine. This is a significant departure from Aleichem's story line.

53. Seth L. Wolitz, "The Americanization of Tevye, or Boarding the Jewish 'Mayflower,'" *American Quarterly* 40, no. 4 (December 1988): 514–16, quote on 527. Aleichem's original stories also reflect his deep concern over the infusion of capitalistic relationships and ethics into Jewish culture. Wolitz notes that Aleichem's Tevye would never have sung "If I Were a Rich Man," a song that acknowledges simultaneously the virtue of material comfort and nonmaterial values.

54. An example of Aleichem's original ambivalence about free choice—but *Fiddler*'s embrace of it—is Tevye's relationship with his third daughter, Khava. Tevye declares Khava dead to the family after she marries a gentile. In Aleichem's original version (1914), Khava leaves her Russian husband and begs readmission to the family. The scene offers no resolution; the narrator says simply, "What should Tevye have done? Should he have embraced her? . . . What would you have done?" In *Fiddler*, Khava and her husband stay together but announce their solidarity with the shtetl's Jews, who have been banished by the Russian authorities. Reflecting the second generation's ambivalence about intermarriage and assimilation, the play's producers do not effect a complete reconciliation. But Tevye speaks to Khava and her husband—"May God be with you"—and therefore reaches an accommodation between tradition and familial love.

Chapter Three

1. Bernard Klein, "Idealism—An Ingredient of Life," reprinted in *Thoughts of the Week*, 20 December 1957, box 7, folder 15, Samuel Penner Papers, RCSCJ. *Thoughts of the Week* was published by Yeshiva Torah Vodaath and Mestiva (Brooklyn).

2. Rev. Brother Aloysius Edward (brother of the Christian Schools, teacher in St. Augustine Diocesan High School, Brooklyn), "The Catholic Concept of American Citizenship" (paper read at the teachers' conference, Diocese of Brooklyn, 5 June 1948), reprinted in Diocese of Brooklyn, *Brooklyn Educational Year Book: 1948* (Brooklyn, 1948), 58–62, copy housed in ADB.

3. "Address of the Most Reverend Bishop" (presented at St. James Pro-Cathedral, 9 September 1934), reprinted in Diocese of Brooklyn, *Brooklyn Educational Year Book: 1934* (Brooklyn, 1934), copy housed in ADB; "Vital Provisions for Efficient Schools" (paper presented and read by Rev. Sister Sperata, teacher at St. Savior High School, at the teacher's conference, Diocese of Brooklyn, 9 January 1938), reprinted in Diocese of Brooklyn, *Brooklyn Educational Year Book: 1938* (Brooklyn, 1938), copy housed in ADB.

4. "Sermon of the Very Reverend Edward J. Walsh" (presented at St. James Pro-Cathedral, 13 September 1936), reprinted in Diocese of Brooklyn, *Brooklyn Educational Year Book: 1936* (Brooklyn, 1936), copy housed in ADB.

5. "Sermon of the Reverend Joseph A. Murphy, Ph.D." (pastor, St. Bonaventure's Church, Alban Manor, Long Island, N.Y.), reprinted in Diocese of Brooklyn, *Brooklyn Educational Year Book: 1937* (Brooklyn, 1937), copy housed in ADB.

6. Diocese of Brooklyn, *Revised Handbook of Regulations: Elementary and High Schools* (Brooklyn, 1946), 100.

7. Rev. Mother Mary Williams (principal, St. Francis de Sales School, Patchogue, Long Island, N.Y.), "What Makes a Catholic Teacher?" (paper prepared and read at the teachers' conference, Diocese of Brooklyn, 12 January 1946), reprinted in Diocese of Brooklyn, *Brooklyn Educational Year Book: 1946* (Brooklyn, 1946), 50–52, copy housed in ADB; Rev. Brother Germain (Holy Cross Brothers, teacher in St. Thomas Aquinas School, Flatlands, Brooklyn), "Mathematics in Our Schools" (paper prepared and read at the teachers' conference, Diocese of Brooklyn, 10 Jan. 1948), reprinted in Diocese of Brooklyn, *Brooklyn Educational Year Book: 1948* (Brooklyn, 1948), 46–47, copy housed in ADB.

8. Diocese of Brooklyn, *Syllabus for the Catholic Elementary Schools, Effective September 1937* (Brooklyn, 1937), 12–18, copy housed in ADB.

9. Catholic School Board (Archdiocese of New York), *Course of Study Prescribed for the Elementary Schools* (New York, 1938), 5–8; Diocese of Brooklyn, *Syllabus for the Catholic Elementary Schools*, 64, 268; New York City Board of Education, *Curriculum Design of the New York City Schools* (New York, 1956), 10. Copy housed at New York City Public Library.

10. For a comprehensive study of academic subject matter covered in Brooklyn's Catholic schools through the early 1930s, see Rev. William P. A. Maguire, S.M., M.A., "Catholic Secondary Education in the Diocese of Brooklyn" (Ph.D. diss., Catholic University of America, 1932).

11. Allan Luke, "The Secular Word: Catholic Reconstruction of Dick and Jane," in *The Politics of the Textbook*, ed. Michael W. Apple and Linda K. Christian-Smith (New York, 1991), 178.

12. "The Service of Morality, Public Order, and Religion" (paper prepared and read by a sister of St. Dominic, Brooklyn Community, at the teacher's conference, Diocese of Brooklyn, 11 November 1933), reprinted in Diocese of Brooklyn, *Brooklyn Educational Year Book: 1934* (Brooklyn, 1934), 42, copy housed in ADB.

13. Theresa R. Aulincio (St. Catherine of Alexandria School), "Fitting Students for Modern Life" (paper prepared and read at the teachers' conference, Diocese of Brooklyn, 4 April 1936), reprinted in Diocese of Brooklyn, *Brooklyn Educational Year Book: 1936* (Brooklyn, 1936), 63–66, copy housed in ADB.

14. Rev. Sister Mary Madeline (Grey Nun of the Sacred Heart, Blessed Sacrament School, Jackson Heights, Queens), "What Makes an American Teacher?" (paper read at the Teachers' College Conference, 6 April 1946), reprinted in Diocese of Brooklyn, *Brooklyn Educational Year Book: 1946* (Brooklyn, 1946), 55–60, copy housed in ADB.

15. Diocese of Brooklyn, *Syllabus for the Catholic Elementary Schools*, 284

16. Catholic School Board (Archdiocese of New York), *Course of Study*, 8; Diocese of Brooklyn, *Revised Handbook of Regulation*, 18.

17. Catholic School Board (Archdiocese of New York), *Course of Study*, 249–55; Diocese of Brooklyn, *Revised Handbook of Regulation*, 64, 284–86.

18. Michael Pearson, *Dreaming of Columbus: A Boyhood in the Bronx* (Syracuse, 1999), 135.

19. Diocese of Brooklyn, *Revised Handbook of Regulations*, 17–18, 139.

20. Dennis Smith, *A Song for Mary: An Irish-American Memory* (New York, 1999), 3–5.

21. Pearson, *Dreaming of Columbus*, 91.

22. Pete Hamill, *A Drinking Life* (New York, 1994), 104; John R. Powers, *Do Black Patent Leather Shoes Really Reflect Up?* (New York, 1975), excerpts reprinted in *Saints and Sinners: The American Catholic Experience through Stories, Memoirs, Essays, and Commentary*, ed. Greg Tobin (New York, 1999).

23. Doris Kearns Goodwin, *Wait Till Next Year: A Memoir* (New York, 1997), 90–91.

24. Diane Ravitch, *The Troubled Crusade: American Education, 1945–1980* (New York, 1983), 43–80; Diane Ravitch, *The Great School Wars: New York City, 1805–1973* (New York, 1974), 236–38. For background on Catholic opposition to progressive education theories, see Timothy Walch, *Parish School: American Catholic Parochial Education from Colonial Times to the Present* (New York, 1996), 118–33.

25. "Results of Intellectual Disintegration Cited," BT, 14 July 1951.

26. "Godless Courts Scored in Sermon," ibid., 9 October 1948.

27. "Hits Secularism in U.S. Schools," ibid., 16 October 1948.

28. Joshua B. Freeman, *Working-Class New York: Life and Labor since World War II* (New York, 2000), 79–80; John Cooney, *The American Pope: The Life and Times of Francis Cardinal Spellman* (New York 1984), 187–95.

29. See Chapter 2 for a synopsis of the events at Yeshiva University.

30. Charles R. Morris, *American Catholic: The Saints and Sinners Who Built America's Most Powerful Church* (New York, 1997), 41.

31. Emmet Larkin, "The Devotional Revolution in Ireland, 1850–1875," *American Historical Review* 77, no. 3 (June 1972): 625–52; Morris, *American Catholic*, 40–47; Jay P. Dolan, *The Immigrant Church: New York's Irish and German Catholics, 1815–1865* (New York, 1975), esp. 159–69.

32. For background, see Garry Wills, *Papal Sin: Structures of Deceit* (New York, 2000), chap. 1.

33. This review of American Catholicism relies heavily on Jay P. Dolan, *In Search of an American Catholicism: A History of Religion and Culture in Tension* (New York, 2002), chaps. 1–2. See also Patrick W. Carey, *People, Priests, and Prelates: Ecclesiastical Democracy and the Tensions of Trusteeism* (Notre Dame, Indiana, 1987); and Dale Light, *Rome and the New Republic: Conflict and Community in Philadelphia Catholicism between the Revolution and the Civil War* (Notre Dame, 1996).

34. Dolan, *In Search of an American Catholicism*, 32–33; Joseph P. Chinnici, "American Catholics and Religious Pluralism, 1775–1820," *Journal of Ecumenical Studies* 16 (Fall 1979): 733–36.

35. Joseph H. Fitcher, S.J., "Conceptualizations of the Urban Parish," *Social Forces* 31, no. 2 (October 1952): 43–47. Other dioceses, like Chicago and Boston, organized their parishes along even more authoritarian lines. Under the legal principle of corporation sole, the bishop owned exclusive title to all church and parish properties throughout the diocese.

36. "The Top of My Mind," *Catholic News*, 2 April 1949; "Request for Church Vote on Melish 'Activity' Defended by Vestrymen as 'Legally Sound,'" *NYT*, 6 April 1948.

37. John T. McGreevy, *Catholicism and American Freedom: A History* (New York, 2003), 28–29.

38. See Chapter 1 for a review of the Catholic school system in New York City, which captured anywhere between one-half and two-thirds of the Catholic school-age population in any given year by the mid-twentieth century.

39. On anti-Catholic and anti-Irish nativism, see Dale T. Knobel, *Paddy and the Republic: Ethnicity and Nationality in the Antebellum Period* (Middletown, Conn., 1986); and John Higham, *Strangers in the Land: Patterns of American Nativism, 1860–1925* (New York, 1963). Dolan's *In Search of an American Catholicism* makes the strong case that the popular rejection of Enlightenment Catholicism, acquiescence to ecclesiastical authority, and the embrace of devotional Catholicism was in large part an act of retrenchment. See Dolan, *In Search of an American Catholicism*, chap. 2.

40. McGreevy, *Catholicism and American Freedom*, 37.

41. Ibid., 105, 139.

42. For background on the acculturation of Italian Americans to the Irish American Church, see Nicholas John Russo, "Three Generations of Italians in New York City: Their Religious Acculturation," *International Migration Review* 3, no. 2 (Spring 1969): 3–16. For a concurring opinion, see Donald Tricario, *The Italians of Greenwich Village: The Social Structure and Transformation of an Ethnic Community* (New York, 1984), 46–55. Good descriptions of Italian Catholic religiosity include Leonard Covello, *The Social Background of the Italo-American School Child: A Study of the Southern Italian Family Mores and Their Effect on the School Situation in Italy and America* (Totowa, N.J., 1972), 103–25; Robert Anthony Orsi, *The Madonna of 115th Street: Faith and Community in Italian Harlem, 1880–1950* (New Haven, 1985); Mary Elizabeth Brown, *Churches, Communities, and Children: Italian Immigrants in the Archdiocese of New York, 1880–1945* (New York, 1995); and Salvatore Primeggia, "The Social Context of Religious Devotion: How Saint Worship Expresses Popular Religiosity," in *The Saints in the Lives of Italian Americans: An Interdisciplinary Investigation*, ed. Joseph A. Varacalli et al. (New York, 1999), 60–90. A study that finds strong political and theological connections between the American and Italian churches is Peter R. D'Agostino, *Rome in America: Transnational Catholic Ideology from the Risorgimento to Fascism* (Chapel Hill, 2004).

43. See Chapter 1. See also Russo, "Three Generations of Italians in New York City," 15.

44. See Kerby A. Miller, *Emigrants and Exiles: Ireland and the Irish Exodus to North America* (New York, 1985), 102–30.

45. McGreevy, *Catholicism and American Freedom*, 96.

46. In particular, see Covello, *The Social Background of the Italo-American School Child*; Orsi, *The Madonna of 115th Street*; and Virginia Yans-McLaughlin, *Family and Community: Italian Immigrants in Buffalo, 1880–1930* (New York, 1980).

47. McGreevy, *Catholicism and American Freedom*, 180–82.

48. See Paula Fass, *The Damned and the Beautiful: American Youth in the 1920s* (New York, 1977), chap. 2; Dominick Cavallo, *A Fiction of the Past: The Sixties in American History* (New York, 1999), chap. 3; and Alan Petigny, "The Permissive Turn" (unpublished paper, courtesy of Alan Petigny).

49. Herbert J. Gans, *The Urban Villagers: Group and Class in the Life of Italian-Americans* (New York, 1962), 54–73.

50. George Psathas, "Ethnicity, Social Class, and Adolescent Independence from Parental Control," *American Sociological Review* 22, no. 4 (August 1957): 415–23.

51. Bernard C. Rosen, "Race, Ethnicity, and the Achievement Syndrome," *American Sociological Review* 24, no. 1 (February 1959): 47–60.

52. See Chapter 1. See also U.S. Bureau of the Census, *United States Census of Population, 1960*, "Nativity and Parentage," Table 11 (Washington, D.C., 1961).

53. Michael James Eula, "Between Contandino and Urban Villager: Italian Americans of New Jersey and New York, 1880–1980: A Comparative Exploration of the Limits of Bourgeois Hegemony" (Ph.D. diss., University of California–Irvine, 1987), chaps. 4 and 5; Covello, *The Social Background of the Italo-American School Child*, 229–37.

54. Vincent Panella, *The Other Side: Growing Up Italian in America* (New York, 1979), 14, 30.

55. Jonathan Rieder, *Canarsie: The Jews and Italians of Brooklyn against Liberalism* (New York, 1985), 34.

56. A summary of the report is provided in Nathan Glazer and Daniel P. Moynihan, *Beyond the Melting Pot: The Negroes, Puerto Ricans, Jews, Italians, and Irish of New York City* (New York, 1963), 338, n. 44.

57. George Kelly, *Inside My Father's House* (New York, 1989), 10.

58. Smith, *A Song for Mary*, 8–9.

59. New York City Police Department, "Remarks of Commissioner Stephen P. Kennedy at the Clerical Conference of Catholic Students, Mission Crusade, Catholic University, Washington, D.C., on Friday, November 7th, 1958 at 8:00 P.M." (press release), BJCC, box 11, folder 3, AJA.

60. "Address of Dean William Hughes Mulligan," 2 May 1967, reprinted in Society of the Friendly Sons of Saint Patrick in the City of New York, *Yearbook: 1967* (New York, 1967), 67–72, copy housed at the New York Public Library.

61. "Address of Commissioner Bowie Kent Kuhn," 5 May 1969, in Society of the Friendly Sons of Saint Patrick in the City of New York, *Yearbook: 1969* (New York, 1969), 65–67, copy housed at the New York Public Library.

62. Daniel Callahan, "Contraception and Abortion: American Catholic Responses," *Annals of the American Academy of Political and Social Science* 387 (January 1970): 114.

63. For background on the Legion of Decency, see James M. Skinner, *The Cross and the Cinema: The Legion of Decency and the National Catholic Office for Motion Pictures, 1933–1970* (New York, 1993).

64. Stephen J. Whitfield, *The Culture of the Cold War* (Baltimore, 1996), 96–99.

65. "Spellman Censors *Moon Is Blue* Film," NYT, 25 June 1953; "Priest Lauds Protest on Film," ibid., 21 October 1953; "Elizabeth Protests Bar Film," ibid., 29 October 1953.

66. "Eisenhower Urged to Curb McCarthy," NYT, 25 June 1953.

67. BJCC, "Memorandum to Presidents and Rabbis, from Community Relations Committee of the Brooklyn Jewish Community Council, re: *Oliver Twist*," undated, box 6, folder 8, AJA.

68. "By the Way," *Catholic News*, 2 October 1948; "Johnson Answers Rabbis on Protest," NYT, 10 September 1948.

69. "K. of C. Is Warned of Soviet Threat," BT, 19 August 1950.

70. Israel Goldstein (Congregation B'nai Jeshurun, New York, N.Y.), "True to Our-selves" (a Kol Nidre sermon), reprinted in *B'nai Jeshurun Topics*, vol. 25, no. 2 (October 1952), box 36, folder 38, B'nai Jeshurun Papers, RCSCJ. Italics added.

Chapter Four

1. Ellen J. Broidy, "Enforcing the ABCs of Loyalty: Gender, Subversion, and the Politics of Education in the New York City Public Schools, 1948–1954" (Ph.D. diss., University of California–Irvine, 1997), 128–43.

2. For a brief synopsis of the two Quinn controversies (1943, 1949–50), see Joshua B. Freeman, *Working-Class New York: Life and Labor since World War II* (New York, 2000), 72–74.

3. Quotes drawn from photographs of protesters taken at the time. BJCC, box 11, folder 7, AJA.

4. BT, 31 October 1953; "Urges People Not to Be Led Like Lambs to Bigotry," ibid., 15 April 1950.

5. BJCC, meeting minutes, 18 January 1950, box 9, folder 1, AJA; Metropolitan Presidents Advisory Committee Meeting, minutes, 28 December 1949, box 80, Metropolitan Advisory Committee Folder, AJCongress, AJHS.

6. See protest photographs, n. 3.

7. Richard Hofstadter, "The Pseudo-Intellectual Revolt—1954," in *The Paranoid Style in American Politics and Other Essays* (Cambridge, Mass., 1963), 54. Concur-ring studies include Seymour Martin Lipset, "Democracy and Working-Class Authoritarianism," *American Sociological Review* 24, no. 4 (August 1959): 482–501; and Robert Sokol, "Power Orientation and McCarthyism," *American Journal of Sociology* 73, no. 4 (January 1968): 443–52.

8. See Donald Crosby, *God, Church, and Flag: Senator Joseph R. McCarthy and the Catholic Church, 1950–1957* (Raleigh, N.C., 1978), esp. chap. 11; and Richard Gid Powers, *Not without Honor: The History of American Anticommunism* (New York, 1996). Powers argues that anticommunism was a broad-based move-ment whose fringe elements have earned too much attention. By implication, Catholics were merely one constituent group in the anticommunist con-

sensus. For a more equivocal opinion—that "messianic ardor among [Catholic] parishioners and prelates . . . was found mainly on the Right," though most Catholics continued to vote for Democrats and support the New Deal welfare state in the 1950s—see Michael Kazin, *The Populist Persuasion: An American History* (New York, 1995), 174. For an opposing view, see Stephen J. Whitfield, *The Culture of the Cold War* (Baltimore, 1996), 91–99; and Michael Paul Rogin, *The Intellectuals and McCarthy: The Radical Specter* (Cambridge, Mass., 1967), 238–39, 256.

9. See Stuart Svonkin, *Jews against Prejudice: American Jews and the Fight for Civil Liberties* (New York, 1997), 116; Edward Shapiro, *A Time for Healing: American Jewry since World War II* (Baltimore, 1992), 34–36. An early study of Joseph McCarthy's appeal concluded that the Wisconsin senator was not an anti-Semite, though his movement earned the support of some avowed Jew-baiters. See Richard H. Rovere, *Senator Joe McCarthy* (New York, 1959), 141.

10. The most adamant expression of this interpretation is Peter Novick, *The Holocaust in American Life* (New York, 1999), esp. 103–23. More measured examples of the same interpretation include Arthur Hertzberg, *The Jews in America: Four Centuries of an Uneasy Encounter; A History* (New York, 1989), 301–03; Jack Wertheimer, *A People Divided: Judaism in Contemporary America* (Hanover, N.H., 1993), 28–29; and Howard M. Sachar, *A History of the Jews in America* (New York, 1992), 839.

11. "Sursum Corda," *Catholic News*, 27 November 1948.

12. William Leuchtenburg, *Franklin D. Roosevelt and the New Deal, 1932–1940* (New York, 1963), 321. Leuchtenburg notes that by 1944, "Irish Americans, who had backed [Roosevelt] more strongly than any other ethnic group in 1932, had grown more prosperous and tended to take on some of the conservatism of anti–New Dealers. They also thought Roosevelt's foreign policy too Anglophile. Some Italian-Americans . . . turned against him in 1940 because they resented the contemptuous implications of the Charlottesville speech [against Italian fascism]. Democratic workers could enter Italian sections of the Bronx only under police protection."

13. Deborah Dash Moore, *At Home in America: Second Generation New York Jews* (New York, 1981), chap. 8; David M. Esposito and Jackie R. Esposito, "LaGuardia and the Nazis, 1933–1938," *American Jewish History* 78, no. 1 (September 1988): 38–53; Ronald H. Bayor, *Neighbors in Conflict: The Irish, Germans, Jews, and Italians of New York City, 1929–1941* (Baltimore, 1978), 143.

14. Roughly 85 percent of O'Dwyer's Italian and Irish Catholic supporters voted the Democratic line for mayor.

15. All preceding election figures drawn from William Spinrad, "New Yorkers Cast Their Ballots" (Ph.D. diss., Columbia University, 1955); Chris McNickle, *To Be Mayor of New York: Ethnic Politics in the City* (New York, 1993), 332–33; and Hugh A. Bone, "Political Parties in New York City," *American Political Science Review* 40, no. 2 (April 1946): 272–82. Spinrad and McNickle arrived at the preceding figures by overlaying census tracts on election districts; the figures are the best available estimates.

16. McNickle, *To Be Mayor of New York*, 332–33.

17. Saul Brenner, "Patterns of Jewish-Catholic Voting and the 1960 Presidential Vote," *Jewish Social Studies* 26, no. 3 (1964): 169–78. Jews comprised 49.3 percent of Borough Park's population in 1940 and 55.6 percent in 1957. In Bay Ridge, Jews comprised only 1 percent or less of the population. Since the African American population remained negligible in both neighborhoods, it is likely that the balance of voters in Borough Park, and the vast majority in Bay Ridge, were Irish and Italian Catholics. See FJPNY, *Estimated Jewish Population of the New York Area, 1900–1975* (New York, 1959), 232–33. For poll data, see Alan Fisher, "Continuity and Erosion of Jewish Liberalism," *American Jewish Historical Quarterly* 65, no. 2 (1976): 332–33, 341.

18. "President Scores New High in State," *NYT*, 7 November 1956.

19. AIPO 133, 23 Sept. 1938; NORC 230, November 1944; NORC S-089, November 1944; AIPO 454, 24 March 1950; AIPO 527, 23 March 1954; AIPO 647, 10 May 1955; AIPO 577, 15 January 1957. All in Alfred Hero, *American Religious Groups View Foreign Policy: Trends in Rank and File Opinion, 1937–1969* (Durham, N.C., 1973), app.

20. See Fisher, "Continuity and Erosion of Jewish Liberalism," 322–62; J. J. Goldberg, *Jewish Power: Inside the American Jewish Establishment* (New York, 1996), chaps. 1, 2; and Marc Dollinger, *Quest for Inclusion: Jews and Liberalism in Modern America* (Princeton, 2000), 3.

21. Lawrence H. Fuchs, *The Political Behavior of American Jews* (Glencoe, Ill., 1956), 177–84.

22. See Ben Halpern, "The Roots of American Jewish Liberalism," *American Jewish Historical Quarterly* 65, no. 2 (1976): 190–214; William Spinrad, "Explaining American-Jewish Liberalism: Another Attempt," *Contemporary Judaism* 11, no. 1 (1990): 107–19.

23. For a synthesis of the traditional Judaism and socialism/radicalism theses, see Gerald Sorin, *The Prophetic Minority: American Jewish Radicals, 1880–1920* (New York, 1985). Other authors combine several of the aforementioned theories in assessing the causes of Jewish liberalism. See Jonathan Rieder, *Canarsie: The Jews and Italians of Brooklyn against Liberalism* (New York, 1985), 43–54; Clayborne Carson, "Black-Jewish Universalism in the Era of Identity Politics," in *Struggles in the Promised Land: Toward a History of Black-Jewish Relations in the United States*, ed. Jack Salzman and Cornel West (New York, 1997), 192.

24. Arthur Liebman, "The Ties That Bind: The Jewish Support for the Left in the United States," *American Jewish Historical Quarterly* 65, no. 2 (1976): 285–321. For a vivid account of the immigrant-socialist milieu, see Irving Howe, *World of Our Fathers: The Journey of the Eastern European Jews to America and the Life They Found and Made* (New York, 1976), 287–324. For Yiddish daily circulation figures, see Henry L. Feingold, *A Time for Searching: Entering the Mainstream, 1920–1945* (Baltimore, 1992), 69–70. Quote from Irving Howe, "New York in the Thirties: Some Fragments of Memory," *Dissent* 8, no. 3 (Summer 1961): 243. See also Tony Michels, *A Fire in Their Hearts: Yiddish Socialists in New York* (Cambridge, Mass., 2005).

25. Moore, *At Home in America*, chap. 8; Edward Fogel, interview, 29 January 1983, WWOHL.

26. See Moore, *At Home in America*, 222–24.

27. The Torah (translated literally as "instruction," "teaching," or "law") is the Hebrew term for the five books of Moses (Genesis, Exodus, Leviticus, Numbers, and Deuteronomy). The Prophets include Joshua, Judges, Samuel, Kings, Isaiah, Jeremiah, Ezekiel, and the Twelve Prophets. The Reform movement placed particular emphasis on the Prophets as a foundation for social justice and social action. Bokser's sermon is evidence of a similar tendency, by the postwar years, among Conservative rabbis. See Bruce M. Metzger and Michael D. Coogan, eds., *The Oxford Companion to the Bible* (New York, 1993), 79; Michael Meyer, *Response to Modernity: A History of the Reform Movement in Judaism* (Detroit, 1988), 273–75, 287–89, 301-2; and Shapiro, *A Time for Healing*, 190–94.

28. Ben Zion Bokser, untitled Rosh Hashanah sermon, undated, box 11, High Holiday Sermons Folder, BZB, RCSCJ. The bulk of the dated materials in his sermon folder suggest that Bokser wrote this document in the 1940s and 1950s. Italics added.

29. Ruth Messinger, interview, 25 February 1982, WWOHL.

30. Israel Mowshowitz (Hillcrest Jewish Center, Flushing, N.Y.), "Breaking the Shackles" (sermon delivered at the High Holiday Sermon Seminar, Jewish Theological Seminary, 1961), box 6, folder 32, Samuel Penner Papers, RCSCJ.

31. Here the term "Israel" represents the ancient Israelites as a group but also Jewry in the broader sense; religious texts often use "Israel" to denote the Jewish people either in a specific place and time or throughout the ages.

32. *Congregation Shaari Israel Bulletin*, April 1963, box 4, folder 1, Congregation Shaari Israel (Brooklyn) Papers, RCSCJ.

33. Rabbi Jacob Pressman (Forest Hills Jewish Center, Queens, N.Y.), "There Were Four Sons," *Forest Hills Home News for the Men and Women in the Armed Forces*, vol. 1. no. 4 (March 1945), box 15, Forest Hills Correspondence 1944/1945 Folder, BZB, RCSCJ.

34. William L. Rubin (senior vice commander, Manhattan Post No. 1), "Passover and Human Freedom," *Manhattan Post No. 1–JWV Bulletin*, Passover Edition, April 1946, box 3, Printed Materials of Local J.W.V. Posts Folder, AJHS. See "Passover and Human Freedom" in same edition.

35. Rabbi Morris Goldberg, "Let My People Go," *Shaare Zedek Newsletter*, vol. 4, no. 23 (27 March 1953); reprinted in ibid., vol. 5, no. 25 (16 April 1954). Both housed in box 2, folder 1, Shaare Zedek Papers, RCSCJ. Other Jewish religious leaders also drew a parallel between Lincoln and Moses. In February 1945 Rabbi Pressman of the Forest Hills Jewish Center delivered a sermon titled "Let My People Go" on the occasion of Lincoln's birthday. See *The Message* (Forest Hills Jewish Center), vol. 11, no. 20 (8 February 1945), box 15, Forest Hills Correspondence Folder, BZB, RCSCJ.

36. Rabbi Israel Levinthal (Brooklyn Jewish Center), "Passover and the Freedom Ideal," *Brooklyn Jewish Center Review*, April 1954, RCSCJ.

37. Samuel Penner, "On Freedom" (Passover sermon), undated (ca. late 1940s), box 6, folder 5, Samuel Penner Papers, RCSCJ.

38. Cheryl Lynn Greenberg, *"Or Does It Explode?" Black Harlem in the Great Depression* (New York, 1991), chap. 1; Hasia Diner, *In the Almost Promised Land: American Jews and Blacks, 1915–1935* (Westport, Conn., 1977), 79–81.

39. *JEC Bulletin*, May 1949, April 1948.

40. Ibid., November 1950.

41. AJCongress, National Women's Division, Scarsdale–White Plains–Harrison Chapter, *Bulletin*, October 1954, box 131, AJCongress Papers, AJHS.

42. Alfred Warner, "Passion for Peace: A Striving for Peace Has Been a Jewish Inheritance," *Brooklyn Jewish Center Review*, November 1946, BJCC, box 34, RCSCJ. The ideas in Warner's article were broadly representative. Another example is Congregation Shaari Israel (Manhattan), which ran a similar essay in its bulletin one year earlier arguing that "it is not enough to win the war, we must also win the peace. . . . As members of the human race and as citizens of the various countries of the world, we too hope for the day when we 'shall dwell safely, every man under his vine and under his fig tree.' We therefore look with favor upon the accomplishments at such conferences as were held recently at San Francisco and Potsdam." See *Congregation Shaari Israel Bulletin*, September 1945, box 3, folder 9, Congregation Shaari Israel (Brooklyn) Papers, RCSCJ.

43. Meeting notices drawn from *Brooklyn Jewish Center Review*, November 1948, November 1949, November 1950, and November 1951. Information on Catholic anticommunism drawn from BT, 8 May 1948 (for support of banning the Communist Party); 27 May 1950 (for "guilt by association" editorial); 15 May and 15 June 1948 (for attacks on Henry Wallace); 18 February 1950 (for exposé on socialized medicine); and 19 August 1950 (for Spellman's speech to the Knights of Columbus). For background on the controversy surrounding Eleanor Roosevelt, see Diane Ravitch, *The Troubled Crusade: American Education, 1945–1980* (New York, 1983), chap. 1, esp. 35–40.

44. AJCongress, Scarsdale–White Plains–Harrison Chapter, *Bulletin*, March 1954, box 131, Untitled Folder, AJCongress Papers, AJHS.

45. Murray Friedman, *What Went Wrong: The Creation and Collapse of the Black-Jewish Alliance* (New York, 1995), 136–50; Lee O'Brien, *American Jewish Organizations and Israel* (Washington, D.C., 1986), 63–103.

46. The CLSA was the Committee for Legal and Social Action of the AJCongress.

47. David Schine was an aide and close personal confidant to Roy Cohn, McCarthy's chief subcommittee counsel. Many observers credit Schine's army induction—over Cohn's strong objections—to McCarthy's fateful decision to investigate alleged communist influences in the U.S. Army.

48. A dramatic moment in the "Army-McCarthy hearings" came when Joseph Welch, a Boston attorney who served as counsel to the army, exposed one of Cohn's exhibits as a doctored photograph.

49. AJCongress, Brooklyn Chapter, National Women's Division, "Your Show by Shmoes of 1954," box 134, National Women's Division Brooklyn Reports

"Your Show by Shmoes" Folder, AJCongress Papers, AJHS. McCarthy's stock line was "point of order," a parliamentary device he employed liberally, even when procedurally inappropriate.

50. The "Frankfurt School" was actually the popular designation of the Institute of Social Research (ISR), which was founded in 1923 in Frankfurt, Germany. Many of the ISR's predominantly Jewish membership fled Germany in 1933 and relocated, first in Geneva and then in New York, where the ISR was relaunched as an affiliate of Columbia University. See Svonkin, *Jews against Prejudice*, 33.

51. Svonkin, *Jews against Prejudice*, 32–40. See chap. 2 for full citation of Levinthal's remarks.

52. Prominent examples of popular social science scholarship in the 1940s and 1950s include Gunnar Myrdal, *An American Dilemma*, 2 vols. (New York, 1944); William H. Whyte, *The Organization Man* (New York, 1956); John Kenneth Galbraith, *The Affluent Society* (Boston, 1958); and David Riesman and Nathan Glazer, eds., *The Lonely Crowd: A Study of the Changing American Character* (New Haven, 1950).

53. Louis Levitsky, "What's on My Mind," *Oheb Shalom Review*, 1 February 1950, box 2, folder 9, Louis Levitsky Papers, RCSCJ. Along similar lines, officials of the AJCongress reminded members in 1948 that "the fight against anti-Semitism is not separate and distinct from the fight against lynching, the poll tax and defamation and discrimination in employment, education and housing." See AJCongress, South Shore Women's Division, *American Jewish Congress*, Summer Edition 1948, box 131, South Shore Correspondence 48–49 Folder, AJCongress Papers, AJHS.

54. "Sursum Corda," *Catholic News*, 26 February 1949.

55. AJCongress, West Side Chapter, "Hanukkah Living: A Candle Lighting Dramatization," 15 December 1955, box 131, National Women's Division West Side Chapter Folder, AJCongress Papers, AJHS.

56. "Invitation: Brooklyn Conference on Germany, Democracy or Nazism, Sponsored by the Jewish Community Council," box 134, National Women's Division Brooklyn Folder, AJCongress Papers, AJHS.

57. Israel Goldstein, "Can Germany Be Forgiven?," Rosh Hashanah sermon, reprinted in *B'nai Jeshurun Topics*, vol. 24, no. 2 (12 October 1951), box 36, folder 38, B'nai Jeshurun Papers, RCSCJ; " 'No Innocents in Germany,' Nazis Admit," *Brooklyn Jewish Center Review*, February 1945, box 34, Brooklyn Jewish Center Papers, RCSCJ.

58. NYT, 3 February 1946, 1 February 1946, 21 February 1946, 15 February 1946; Shapiro, *A Time for Healing*, 63. See also Chapter 1.

59. *JEC Bulletin*, February 1946; ibid., June–July 1948.

Chapter Five

1. Stuart Svonkin, *Jews against Prejudice: American Jews and the Fight for Civil Liberties* (New York, 1997), 135–44; and David King Dunaway, *How Can I Keep from Singing: Pete Seeger* (New York, 1981), 13–23.

2. "Robeson, Officials Differ on Disorder," NYT, 6 September 1949; "Budding Fascism Seen by Wallace," ibid., 3 September 1949.

3. AJCongress, Brooklyn Division and Brooklyn Women's Division, "A Petition for the Protection of Full Civil Liberties," box 134, NWD Brooklyn Reports Folder, AJCongress Papers, AJHS; AJCongress, "Can it happen here?," box 134, NWD Brooklyn Reports Folder, AJCongress Papers, AJHS; BJYC, "Minutes of the Meeting of the Executive Committee," 20 October 1949, box 4, folder 2, AJA.

4. "Dewey Aide Urged for Robeson Row," NYT, 31 August 1949. The term "wool-hatters" referred to a white supremacist group in Georgia.

5. "Gossip, Threats Divide Peekskill as Aftermath of Robeson Fight," ibid., 10 September 1949.

6. "The Peekskill Affair," BT, 24 June 1950; untitled column, ibid., 29 July 1950.

7. "By the Way," Catholic News, 3 September 1949; "By the Way," ibid., 11 March 1949.

8. "The Victory of Easter," ibid., 16 April 1949.

9. Dale T. Knobel, Paddy and the Republic: Ethnicity and Nationality in Antebellum America (Middletown, Conn., 1986).

10. Charles R. Morris, American Catholic: The Saints and Sinners Who Built America's Most Powerful Church (New York, 1997), 150–51; see also Alan Brinkley, Voices of Protest: Huey Long, Father Coughlin, and the Great Depression (New York, 1982), 86–89.

11. "Sursum Corda," Catholic News, 1 January 1949.

12. David O'Brien, American Catholics and Social Reform: The New Deal Years (New York, 1968), esp. 97–119; Richard Camp, The Papal Ideology of Social Reform: A Study in Historical Development, 1878–1967 (New York, 1969); Lawrence B. DeSaulniers, The Response in American Catholic Periodicals to the Crises of the Great Depression (New York, 1984); and "Warns Against Crushing Taxes," BT, 22 April 1950.

13. Robert Frank, "Prelude to the Cold War: American Catholics and Communism," Journal of Church and State 34, no. 1 (Winter 1992): 39–56; Wilson Miscamble, "Catholics and American Foreign Policy: From McKinley to McCarthy," Diplomatic History 4, no. 3 (Summer 1980): 223–40; J. David Valaik, "Catholics, Neutrality, and the Spanish Embargo, 1937–1939," Journal of American History 54, no. 1 (June 1967): 73–85; Leo Kanawanda, Franklin D. Roosevelt's Diplomacy and American Catholics, Italians, and Jews (New York, 1982); and John Stack, International Conflict in an American City: Boston's Irish, Italians, and Jews, 1935–1944 (Westbury, Conn., 1979), 58–72. AIPO 147, 2 February 1939; NORC T-46, DU-1, 21 May 1946.

14. BT, 17 April 1948; "Food for Thought," Irish Echo, 6 January 1951.

15. Kerby A. Miller, Emigrants and Exiles: Ireland and the Irish Exodus to North America (New York, 1985), 3–8, 102–30.

16. See Knobel, Paddy and the Republic.

17. John T. McGreevy, Catholicism and American Freedom: A History (New York, 2003), 95.

18. Paul Blanshard, "The Catholic Church and Democracy, Part 1," *Nation*, 29 May 1948, 601–5; Blanshard, "The Catholic Church and Democracy, Part 2," *Nation*, 5 June 1948, 630–31.

19. Nathan Glazer and Daniel Patrick Moynihan, *Beyond the Melting Pot: The Negroes, Puerto Ricans, Jews, Italians, and Irish of New York City* (New York, 1963), 271.

20. "Food for Thought," *Irish Echo*, 23 December 1950; "Food for Thought," ibid., 11 September 1954.

21. Jonathan Rieder, "The Rise of the Silent Majority," in *The Rise and Fall of the New Deal Order, 1930–1980*, ed. Steve Fraser and Gary Gerstle (Princeton, 1989), 245. Lubell is quoted in Rieder's article.

22. Stephen J. Whitfield, *The Culture of the Cold War* (Baltimore, 1991), 94–96.

23. BT, 18 September 1948, 25 September 1948, 2 October 1948, 9 October 1948, and 6 November 1948.

24. "Pope John Acclaims Sodalities," NYT, 21 August 1959, 11; "Hibernians Laud the Catholic News as 'Powerful Weapon' against Reds," *Catholic News*, 5 February 1949.

25. For a general history of the events at Fatima, see William T. Walsh, *Our Lady of Fatima* (New York, 1947).

26. Ibid, 229; Thomas A. Kselman and Steven Avella, "Marian Piety and the Cold War in the United States," *Catholic Historical Review* 72, no. 3 (July 1986): 403–24; *Life*, 29 August 1950.

27. John T. McGreevy, "Bronx Miracle," *American Quarterly* 52, no. 3 (Fall 2000): 405–43.

28. "Statue of Virgin Is Enthroned Here," NYT, 12 January 1948, 22; "City-Wide Prayers for Cardinal Set," ibid., 31 January 1949, 16; "20,000 Celebrate World Sodality Day at Fordham," ibid., 3 May 1945, 11.

29. "50,000 Worshippers at Marian Ritual," ibid., 11 October 1954, 10.

30. See Robert A. Orsi, *Thank You, St. Jude: Women's Devotion to the Patron Saint of Hopeless Causes* (New Haven, 1996).

31. "Priest Recounts Fatima Prophecy," NYT, 14 October 1957, 24.

32. "Display of Loyal Youth Surpasses Borough Record," BT, 7 May 1949.

33. "Weekly Instruction: Employers and the Employed," ibid., 25 June 1949. Gary Gerstle has found that French Canadian workers in Woonsocket, Rhode Island, proved receptive to the quasicorporatist vision of their left-wing union organizers, but the leadership's increased agitation for "industrial democracy" at the shop floor level eventually alienated devout Catholics, whose understanding of proper industrial relations accorded certain rights and prerogatives to the plant owners. See Gerstle, *Working-Class Americanism: The Politics of Labor in a Textile City, 1914–1960* (New York, 1989), chaps. 9 and 10.

34. "Labor Day Theme Is Social Justice" and "Asks Religious Labor Day Rites," BT, 1 September 1951.

35. "Cardinal Calls Workers' Withdrawal from Red-Tinged Union Heartening," *Catholic News*, 12 March 1949.

36. Joshua B. Freeman, *Working-Class New York: Life and Labor since World War II* (New York, 2000), 90–94

37. Ibid., 93–94. See also Martha Biondi, *To Stand and Fight: The Struggle for Civil Rights in Postwar New York City* (Cambridge, Mass., 2003).

38. John T. McGreevy, *Parish Boundaries: The Catholic Encounter with Race in the Twentieth-Century Urban North* (Chicago, 1996), 69, 133.

39. Much of this discussion is elucidated in the following pages.

40. "Practical Tolerance," BT, 31 July 1948. For background on Wallace's dangerous campaign forays in the South, see Alonzo L. Hamby, *Beyond the New Deal*, 206, 260–62.

41. BT, 5 June 1948; Numan V. Bartley, *The New South, 1945–1980: The Story of the South's Modernization* (Baton Rouge, 1995), chap. 2.

42. AIPO 557, 6 December 1955; SRC 417, September–November 1956; Pete Hamill, *A Drinking Life* (New York, 1994), 11.

43. "Jim Crowism Rules in the Six Counties," *Irish Echo*, 12 December 1949.

44. "Negro and White Children at Same Camp to Test Theory No Bias Exists in Youths," NYT, 18 July 1947; "A Summer Appeal," *Irish Echo*, 22 May 1957; "CYO Fight on Ban against Negroes in ABC Defeated," BT, 24 April 1948.

45. "Father Carow Honored by Interracial Group," BT, 8 May 1948; "Tennis Officials Face Discrimination Question," ibid., 24 July 1950; "The ABC About-Face," ibid., 20 May 1950.

46. "President's Victory," ibid., 6 November 1948.

47. "Martin Dies Sees Work Vindicated," ibid., 17 June 1950; "Positive Note," ibid., 6 May 1950.

48. "Positive Note," ibid., 6 May 1950; Bartley, *The New South*, 52, 62–63.

49. Alden Brown, *The Tablet: The First Seventy-Five Years* (New York, 1983), 52–65; Diocese of Brooklyn, *Revised Handbook of Regulations: Elementary and High Schools* (Brooklyn, 1946), 14, 37–38, ADB. Brown also explains that by the late 1940s, the *Tablet*'s "focus of attention now was anti-communism, with little qualification. The *Tablet*'s earlier criticism of American capitalism virtually disappeared" (44). Jerry Della Femina and Charles Sopkin, *An Italian Grows in Brooklyn* (New York, 1978), 150.

50. Hamill, *A Drinking Life*, 125.

51. George Combs (chairman, Speakers Bureau, William O'Dwyer Mayoral Campaign), interview, 2 November 1949, OHP-CU.

52. "Group Backs McCarthy," NYT, 24 July 1950, 23.

53. Whitfield, *The Culture of the Cold War*, 96–97; Linda Dowling Almeida, "From Danny Boy to Bono: The Irish in New York City, 1945–1995" (Ph.D. diss., New York University, 1996), 309–11; "Vote of Confidence in Sen. McCarthy," BT, 29 July 1950.

54. "God Must Be Angry," *Irish Echo*, 11 May 1957.

55. "McCarthy Services Attended by 2,800," NYT, 12 May 1957, 86.

56. BT, 15 May and 15 June 1948.

57. One bicoastal study of the predominantly Catholic longshoremen in San Francisco and New York attributes differences between "the radical-led union on the West Coast [and] its conservative union counterpart in the Port of New York" to several factors, including "patterns of occupational recruitment,

industry structure, organizing strategies, generational experiences, and labor force stability." This chapter raises the possibility that New York City's unique political landscape compelled many Catholic workers to embrace a more conservative outlook. See Howard Alex Kimeldorf, "Reds or Rackets: Sources of Radical and Conservative Union Leadership on the Waterfront" (Ph.D. diss., University of California–Los Angeles, 1985).

58. George Hermann Derry, *How the Reds Get That Way: Some Big Words to Discuss*, (New Haven, 1948), 5.

59. "C.W.V. Convention Lauds McCarthy," BT, 13 May 1950; "Act Now on Reds, Women Advised," ibid., 20 May 1950; "Archbishop Scores Anti-Bias Measure," NYT, 3 March 1947.

60. Freeman, *Working-Class New York*, chaps. 3, 7–9.

61. Joshua B. Freeman, *In Transit: The Transport Workers Union in New York City, 1933–1966* (New York, 1989), 26–27.

62. Joshua B. Freeman, "Catholics, Communists, and Republicans: Irish Workers and the Organization of the Transport Workers Union," in *Working-Class America: Essays on Labor, Community, and American Society*, ed. Michael H. Fritsch and Daniel J. Walkowitz (Chicago, 1983), 256–76.

63. Vito Marcantonio, interview, 3 November 1949, OHP-CU.

64. Gerald Meyer, *Vito Marcantonio: Radical Politician, 1902–1954* (New York, 1989), 53–86, 122.

65. "City's Catholics Split on Election: Lean to Kennedy," NYT, 20 September 1960, 1.

Chapter Six

1. James J. Graham, "Backlash in Brooklyn: Why the Review Board Failed," *Commonweal*, 9 December 1966, 287–91; "Symbol of Backlash," *Nation*, 7 November 1966, 46–49.

2. Tamar Jacoby, *Someone Else's House: America's Unfinished Struggle for Integration* (New York, 1998), 61.

3. For background on the Reagan-Brown contest, see Matthew Dallek, *The Right Moment: Ronald Reagan's First Victory and the Decisive Turning Point in American Politics* (New York, 2000), chaps. 8–10; "Symbol of Backlash," 46–49.

4. The aforementioned articles are examples of this interpretation.

5. Garry Wills, *Nixon Agonistes: The Crisis of the Self-Made Man* (Boston, 1970), 51–52.

6. Jonathan Rieder, *Canarsie: The Jews and Italians of Brooklyn against Liberalism* (New York, 1985); Thomas Byrne Edsall and Mary D. Edsall, *Chain Reaction: The Impact of Race, Rights, and Taxes on American Politics* (New York, 1992), chaps. 3, 4; Jonathan Kaufman, *Broken Alliance: The Turbulent Times between Blacks and Jews in America* (New York, 1988), chaps. 4, 5; J. Anthony Lukas, *Common Ground: A Turbulent Decade in the Lives of Three American Families* (New York, 1986); and Robert Formisano, *Boston against Busing: Race, Class, and Ethnicity in the 1960s and 1970s* (Chapel Hill, 1991).

7. Arnold R. Hirsch, *Making the Second Ghetto: Race and Housing in Chicago, 1940–1960* (New York, 1983); Thomas Sugrue, *The Origins of the Urban Crisis: Race,*

Industrial Decline, and Housing in Detroit, 1940–1960 (Princeton, 1996); Thomas Sugrue, "Crabgrass-Roots Politics: Race, Rights, and the Reaction against Liberalism in the Urban North, 1940–1964," Journal of American History 82, no. 2 (September 1995): 551–78; and George Lipsitz, The Possessive Investment in Whiteness: How White People Profit from Identity Politics (Philadelphia, 1998), chaps. 1–2.

8. Gary Gerstle, "Race and the Myth of Liberal Consensus," Journal of American History 82, no. 2 (September 1995): 584. See also Ira Katznelson, When Affirmative Action Was White: An Untold History of Racial Inequality in Twentieth-Century America (New York, 2005).

9. Louis Harris and Associates, Inc., "A Survey of Voter Attitude toward New York City and Its Government," May 1959, 24–34, in private possession of the author.

10. Louis Harris and Associates, Inc., "A Study of the Election for Mayor of New York with a Special Focus on the Democratic Primary," 4 August 1961, in private possession of the author. Five percent of Jews volunteered a "pro-integration" opinion, while 6 percent (and 5 percent of Italians) complained of "too many Puerto Ricans." Twenty-one percent of African Americans voiced "pro-integration" sentiment, while 3 percent complained of "too many Puerto Ricans."

11. For background on the American public's general disinterest in civil rights between 1955 and 1960, see James T. Patterson, Brown v. Board of Education: A Civil Rights Milestone and Its Troubled Legacy (New York, 2001), 118–20.

12. Jerald Podair, The Strike That Changed New York: Blacks, Whites, and the Ocean-Hill Brownsville Crisis (New York, 2002), 15.

13. Martha Biondi, To Stand and Fight: The Struggle for Civil Rights in Postwar New York City (Cambridge, Mass., 2003), 80–84.

14. Oliver Quayle and Company, "A Survey of the Special Election for State Assembly in New York's 8th A.D.," October 1963, box 10, Edward N. Costikyan Papers, BLRM.

15. Louis Harris and Bert E. Swanson, Black-Jewish Relations in New York City (New York, 1970), 67–69. These figures cut across all age groups and educational cohorts, though not without some variation. Seventy-one percent of Jews with high school or eighth grade diplomas believed that the civil rights revolution was proceeding "too fast," an opinion shared by 46 percent of Jews with college diplomas. Only 17 percent of the latter group felt that civil rights gains were moving "too slow." Among older Jews (fifty-plus), 71 percent felt race relations were changing "too fast," an opinion shared by 47 percent of younger Jews (age twenty-one to thirty-four). But only 16 percent of younger Jews believed that change was occurring "too slow."

16. Sugrue, The Origins of the Urban Crisis, 140–41; Numan V. Bartley, The New South, 1945–1980: The Story of the South's Modernization (Baton Rouge, 1995), chaps. 1, 2; and Joshua B. Freeman, Working-Class New York: Life and Labor since World War II (New York, 2000), 147–48.

17. Freeman, Working-Class New York, 149.

18. Arnold Markoe, "Brooklyn Navy Yard," in *The Encyclopedia of New York City*, ed. Kenneth T. Jackson (New Haven, 1995), 159–60; Freeman, *Working-Class New York*, 165.

19. Ira Rosenwaike, *Population History of New York City* (New York, 1972), 133. For background on the "great migration" of southern blacks to the urban North —a demographic shift influenced in great part by the mechanization of southern agriculture, as well as the pull of northern freedom—see Nicholas Lemann, *The Promised Land: The Great Black Migration and How It Changed America* (New York, 1992), 1–58.

20. Craig Steven Wilder, *A Covenant with Color: Race and Social Power in Brooklyn* (New York, 2000), 169, 173; Freeman, *Working-Class New York*, 180–81; Nathan Glazer and Daniel Patrick Moynihan, *Beyond the Melting Pot: The Negroes, Puerto Ricans, Jews, Italians, and Irish of New York City* (New York, 1963), 30–31.

21. Kenneth T. Jackson, *Crabgrass Frontier: The Suburbanization of the United States* (New York, 1985), 203–18; James T. Patterson, *Grand Expectations: The United States, 1945–1974* (New York, 1996), 71–72.

22. Wilder, *A Covenant with Color*, chap. 9, quote on 191. For background on the HOLC's redlining policies, see Jackson, *Crabgrass Frontier*, chap. 11.

23. Biondi, *To Stand and Fight*, 114.

24. Sylvie Murray, "Suburban Citizens: Domesticity and Community Politics in Queens, New York, 1945–1960" (Ph.D. diss., Yale University, 1994), 16–17, 60.

25. For background on the expansion of Brooklyn's black ghetto—an area anchored by Bedford-Stuyvesant and encompassing the greater part of north-central Brooklyn—see Harold X. Connolly, *A Ghetto Grows in Brooklyn* (New York, 1977), 136–39. For white population figures, see Rosenwaike, *Population History of New York City*, 133.

26. Alex Campbell, "Is New York Possible? Lindsay's Poor, Rich City," *New Republic*, 16 November 1968, 13–16. By 1968 three times as many New Yorkers were on welfare as were employed by the city; the cost to the city to support these welfare recipients—above and beyond what the state and federal governments provided—exceeded the total operating costs of New York's public school system.

27. Jim Sleeper, *The Closest of Strangers: Liberalism and the Politics of Race in New York* (New York, 1990), chap. 5; Biondi, *To Stand and Fight*, 114.

28. New York City Commission on Jewish Affairs, "Blockbusting in New York: A Background Report," box 1, Negro-Jewish Relations 1961–1963 Folder, AJHS.

29. Glazer and Moynihan, *Beyond the Melting Pot*, 50–51, 61.

30. "Polls Show Whites Resent Civil Rights Drive," *NYT*, 21 September 1964, 1.

31. Harris and Swanson, *Black-Jewish Relations in New York City*, 76–79.

32. Rieder, *Canarsie*, 62–63.

33. Biondi, *To Stand and Fight*, 124–36, 226–41.

34. "By the Numbers," *Newsweek*, 18 April 1966; "The City: Crime Underground," *Time*, 19 February 1965.

35. "Death in the City," *Time*, 24 April 1964.

36. David W. Abbott, Louis H. Gold, and Edward T. Rogowsky, *Police, Politics, and Race: The New York City Referendum on Civilian Review* (New York, 1969), 22; Harris and Swanson, *Black-Jewish Relations in New York City*, 98–99.

37. Harris and Swanson, *Black-Jewish Relations in New York City*, 98–99.

38. Charles R. Morris, *The Cost of Good Intentions: New York City and the Liberal Experiment, 1960–1975* (New York, 1980), 67–74, quote on 67.

39. Frances Fox-Piven and Richard Cloward, *Regulating the Poor: The Functions of Public Welfare* (New York, 1971), 321–38; Morris, *The Cost of Good Intentions*, 67–74; Larry R. Jackson and William A. Johnson, *Protest by the Poor: The Welfare Rights Movement in New York City* (New York, 1973), 75–207.

40. Louis Harris and Associates, Inc., "A Survey of Voter Attitude," 5, 11.

41. Louis Harris and Associates, Inc., "A Study of the Election for Mayor," 24; "Better Definition of Issues" (memorandum from [John] Kraft to G.D.), 9 August 1965, box 10, Edward N. Costikyan Papers, BLRM.

42. Morris, *The Cost of Good Intentions*, 29–30. For background on Catholic resentment of the double-tax burden, see Diane Ravitch, *The Troubled Crusade: American Education, 1945–1980* (New York, 1983), 27–41.

43. For background on the school desegregation controversy in New York City, see Adina Back, "Up South in New York: The 1950s School Desegregation Struggles" (Ph.D. diss., New York University, 1997), esp. chaps. 1, 2, 6. Back's study is well researched and detailed, though thoroughly ideological in its assumptions and conclusions. The author sees systematic racism at the heart of every controversy over school districting and tends to overstate her argument.

44. Vincent J. Cannato, *The Ungovernable City: John Lindsay and His Struggle to Save New York* (New York, 2001), 269–72, 447.

45. Nathan Kantrowitz, "Ethnic and Racial Segregation in the New York Metropolis, 1960," *American Journal of Sociology* 74, no. 6 (May 1969): 690.

46. For background on the close relationship between city Jews and the public school system, see David Rogers, *110 Livingston Street Revisited: Politics and Bureaucracy in the New York City School System* (New York, 1968), 79–83; and Ruth Jacknow Markowitz, *My Daughter, the Teacher: Jewish Teachers in the New York City Schools* (New Brunswick, N.J., 1993).

47. "Academic Sickness in New York," *Time*, 24 March 1967, 35.

48. The following summary of the Ocean Hill–Brownsville controversy relies primarily on Diane Ravitch, *The Great School Wars: New York City, 1805–1973* (New York, 1974), 292–378. Ravitch's account is fair and extremely well documented, although she is highly critical of the community activists. For a more biased account favoring proponents of local control, see Mario Fantini, Marilyn Gittell, and Richard Magnate, *Community Control and the Urban School* (New York, 1970). An equally biased account favoring the teachers' union is Philip Taft, *United They Teach: The Story of the UFT* (Los Angeles, 1974). See also Kaufman, *Broken Alliance*, chap. 4. Kaufman provides useful and colorful anecdotes, but his account tends to soft-pedal the anti-Semitic component of the controversy and downplay the local community board's defiance of court orders, due process, and binding agreements.

49. Cannato, *The Ungovernable City*, 275–76.

50. Ibid., 307.

51. Ibid., 282–85, 297, 318–19, 326.

52. Robert G. Weisbord and Arthur Stein, *Bittersweet Encounter: The Afro-American and the American Jew* (Westport, Conn., 1970), 102–7; and Lucy S. Dawidowicz, "American Public Opinion," in *American Jewish Yearbook* (Philadelphia, 1968), 228.

53. Ronald Radosh, *Divided They Fell: The Demise of the Democratic Party, 1964–1996* (New York, 1996), 27–49; James Ridgeway, "Freak-Out in Chicago," *New Republic*, 16 September 1967, 9–12; Peter Steinfels, "Alice in Newleftland," *Commonweal*, 29 September 1967, 608–10; *Newsweek*, 18 September 1967, 40; Richard Blumenthal, "New Politics at Chicago," *Nation*, 25 September 1967, 273–76; Walter Goodman, "When Black Power Runs the New Left," *New York Times Magazine*, 24 September 1967, 28, 124–27; "Letter from the Palmer House," *New Yorker*, 23 September 1967, 56–88.

54. Cannato, *The Ungovernable City*, 288, 306.

55. Harris and Swanson, *Black-Jewish Relations in New York City*, 110–11.

56. Podair, *The Strike That Changed New York*, 37.

57. Cannato, *The Ungovernable City*, 343.

58. Podair, *The Strike That Changed New York*, 44.

59. Sleeper, *The Closest of Strangers*, 99; Cannato, *The Ungovernable City*, 343.

60. Wendell Pritchett, *Brownsville, Brooklyn: Blacks, Jews, and the Changing Face of the Ghetto* (Chicago, 2002), chap. 5.

61. See Ronald H. Bayor, *Neighbors in Conflict: The Irish, Germans, Jews, and Italians of New York City, 1929–1941* (Baltimore, 1978); and John Stack, *International Conflict in an American City: Boston's Irish, Italians, and Jews, 1935–1944* (Westbury, Conn., 1979).

62. Miriam Cohen, *Workshop to Office: Two Generations of Italian Women in New York City, 1900–1950* (Ithaca, 1992), 147–95.

63. Ibid., 95. Harris and Swanson defined "backlash" districts as areas where an overwhelming majority of voters opposed the 1966 police review board. Since 87.5 percent and 86.6 percent of Irish and Italian Catholics, respectively, opposed the review board, it is likely that Harris's non-Jewish, white backlash voters were overwhelmingly Catholic. For the review board vote, see Abbott, Gold, and Rogowsky, *Police, Politics, and Race*, 15.

64. Sleeper, *The Closest of Strangers*, 72.

65. Freeman, *Working-Class New York*, xiii, 34–35.

66. Glazer and Moynihan, *Beyond the Melting Pot*, 1; Sugrue, *The Origins of the Urban Crisis*, 13. Sugrue notes that "in some cities, most notably New York, Los Angeles and Chicago, the presence of other minority groups . . . complicated racial politics in ways that diverge from the experience of Detroit, which had a small Mexican-American population, a tiny Asian enclave, and hardly any Puerto Ricans, Dominicans or Cubans" (13).

Chapter Seven

1. Louis Harris and Associates, Inc., "A Study of Where Mayor Robert F. Wagner Stands in the 1961 Race for Mayor of New York and What New Yorkers Think of His Incumbent Administration," 29 March 1961, in private possession of the author. Harris's memorandum suggests that John F. Kennedy lost New York's Irish vote in 1960; no other matters of public record exist to substantiate this remarkable claim. Italics added.

2. Louis Harris and Associates, Inc., "A Study of the Election for Mayor of New York," 4 August 1961, 5, in private possession of the author.

3. Oliver Quayle and Company, "A Survey of Public Opinion in the First Assembly District, South, New York City, July 1963," box 10, Edward N. Costikyan Papers, BLRM. Sixty-three percent of De Sapio supporters and 65 percent of Koch supporters volunteered a position in favor of more housing opportunities and rent control. On crime, 44 percent of De Sapio voters and only 27 percent of Koch voters volunteered support for more police action. Among De Sapio voters, 45 percent volunteered an antitax sentiment, compared with only 20 percent of Koch supporters. But 80 percent of Koch voters offered a position in favor of more school funding and better educational standards, compared with only 14 percent of De Sapio supporters, many of whom probably enrolled their children in parochial schools. Forty-nine percent of Koch's supporters volunteered a position in favor of better race relations, compared with 7 percent of De Sapio voters.

4. Vincent J. Cannato, The Ungovernable City: John Lindsay and His Struggle to Save New York (New York, 2001), 37–39.

5. Ibid., 53–55.

6. O'Brien-Sherwood Associates, Inc., "New York City Voter Opinion and Attitude Study," 20–25 September 1965, box 10, Edward N. Costikyan Papers, BLRM; "Highlights of Findings—Political Study No. 2" (memorandum from William J. O'Brien to Independent Citizens Committee for the Election of Beame, O'Connor, and Procaccino), box 10, Edward N. Costikyan Papers, BLRM; Cannato, The Ungovernable City, 59.

7. Commonweal, 19 November 1965, 202; "How Voter Swings Elected Lindsay," NYT, 4 November 1965.

8. Chris McNickle, To Be Mayor of New York: Ethnic Politics in the City (New York, 1993), 208.

9. E. J. Dionne Jr., Why Americans Hate Politics (New York, 1991), 79; Jonathan Rieder, Canarsie: The Jews and Italians of Brooklyn against Liberalism (Cambridge, Mass., 1985), 128; Jim Sleeper, The Closest of Strangers: Liberalism and the Politics of Race in New York (New York, 1990), 62–63; Jerald Podair, The Strike That Changed New York: Blacks, Whites, and the Ocean-Hill Brownsville Crisis (New York, 2002), 144.

10. "Five Democratic Mayoral Candidates in Primary," NYT, 17 June 1969; "Liberal Democrats Begin Move toward Lindsay Endorsement," ibid., 20 June 1969.

11. Tamar Jacoby, Someone Else's House: America's Unfinished Struggle for Integration (New York, 1998), 220–26.

12. "Procaccino Offers Job Program to Cut Relief Rolls by 200,000," NYT, 29 October 1969; "Five Democratic Mayoral Candidates in Primary," ibid., 17 June 1969; "Procaccino Lays Deals to Lindsay: Calls Mayor Candidate of 'Limousine Liberals,'" ibid., 18 August 1969; Jacoby, *Someone Else's House*, 220–26.

13. "Procaccino Says He's Progressive," NYT, 19 June 1969; "Procaccino Accuses Lindsay of Deceit," ibid.; "Procaccino Sees Himself as More of a LaGuardia Than a Yorty," ibid., 2 June 1969; "Procaccino Warns Lindsay on Charges of Racist Campaign," ibid., 17 September 1969; "Procaccino: Candidate on the Go," ibid., 6 June 1969, 29.

14. "John Marchi: Republican-Conservative for Mayor," BT, 4 September 1969; "Marchi Says Issue Is Law and Order: Assails Lindsay for Linking Him to 'Reactionaries,'" NYT, 9 June 1969.

15. Charles R. Morris, *The Cost of Good Intentions: New York City and the Liberal Experiment, 1960–1975* (New York, 1980), 57–82.

16. Cannato, *The Ungovernable City*, 138–39, 162–63, 222.

17. "Lord of the Flies," *Newsweek*, 19 February 1968; A. H. Raskin, "Why New York Is 'Strike City,'" *New York Times Magazine*, 22 December 1968, 7.

18. Cannato, *The Ungovernable City*, 39.

19. Ibid., 391–93.

20. "Jews Debating Black Anti-Semitism," NYT, 26 January 1969; "Jewish Voters Wooed," ibid., 15 September 1969; "Poor and Rich, Not Middle Class: The Key to Lindsay's Re-Election," ibid., 6 November 1969; "How the Lindsay Strategy Developed," ibid.

21. "School for Hate?," *Newsweek*, 25 November 1968; memorandum from Robert A. Morse to Robert Sweet (deputy mayor), 14 November 1968, box 56, folder 102, John V. Lindsay Papers, NYCMA.

22. Confidential memorandum from Jay Kriegal to Barbara Chertock, 11 November 1968, box 56, folder 102, John V. Lindsay Papers, NYCMA; Rowland Evans and Robert Novak, "Lindsay's Vote Power," *New York Post*, 2 March 1969.

23. Cannato, *The Ungovernable City*, 368–71, 397.

24. For a review of Lindsay's strategy, see McNickle, *To Be Mayor of New York*. McNickle based his account on personal interviews with most of Lindsay's key advisors, including pollster Louis Harris and media consultant David Garth.

25. Cannato, *The Ungovernable City*, 424.

26. "Ex-Convict Hiring Backed by Lindsay; Procaccino Scored," NYT, 22 October 1969, 1.

27. "Lindsay Presses the 'High Risk' Issue of Vietnam," NYT, 19 October 1969; "Bells Toll and Crosses Are Planted around U.S. as Students Say 'Enough!' to War," ibid., 16 October 1969, 19; Cannato, *The Ungovernable City*, 423.

28. Cannato, *The Ungovernable City*, 404, 430–431.

29. Andrew Hacker, *The New Yorkers: A Profile of an American Metropolis* (New York, 1975), 59.

30. Morris Shapiro's involvement with the Scottsboro defense is well-documented. See James Goodman, *Stories of Scottsboro* (New York, 1994), esp. 342–

47; and Dan T. Carter, *Scottsboro: A Tragedy of the American South* (Baton Rouge, 1969), 361–90.

31. Rose Shapiro, interview, 9 November 1981, WWOHL; Emily Faust Koreznick, interview, 4 January 1983, WWOHL.

32. "New York: The Hard Hats," *Newsweek*, 25 May 1970.

33. Richard Rogin, "Joe Kelly Has Reached His Boiling Point: Why the Construction Workers Holler, 'U.S.A., All the Way!,'" *New York Times Magazine*, 28 June 1970, 12.

34. Richard Reeves, "Mayoralty: All the Earmarks of a Very Rough Campaign," *NYT*, 7 September 1969, E4.

35. These stereotypes were actually on the mark. See Gerald Gamm, *Urban Exodus: Why the Jews Left Boston and Why the Catholics Stayed* (Cambridge, Mass., 1999); and John T. McGreevy, *Parish Boundaries: The Catholic Encounter with Race in the Twentieth Century Urban North* (Chicago, 1996), 102–3.

36. I. Sherman, "Low-Income Project in Forest Hills Will Destroy Community" (letter to the editor), undated, *Jewish Press*, clipping in box 27, folder 1, BZB, RCSCJ; "Jewish Council Blasts City on Low-Income Housing Site," *Long Island Press*, 18 September 1971.

37. Letter from Sidney Cohn to Ben Zion Bokser, 6 December 1971, box 26, folder 6, BZB, RCSCJ.

38. Mario Cuomo, *Forest Hills Diary: The Crisis of Low-Income Housing* (New York, 1974; repr. 1983), 49, 57.

39. Letter to Ben Zion Bokser from a Resident [anonymous], 25 October 1971, box 26, folder 1, BZB, RCSCJ.

40. Joshua B. Freeman, *Working-Class New York: Life and Labor since World War II* (New York, 2000), 30; Michael A. Stegman, *The Dynamics of Rental Housing in New York City* (Piscataway, N.J., 1982), 64. Freeman writes: "The fact that the New York working class did not own real property had important political implications. It meant . . . that homeowners associations were not a major political force among the working class" (30).

41. Sylvie Murray, "Suburban Citizens: Domesticity and Community Politics in Queens, New York, 1945–1960" (Ph.D. diss., Yale University, 1994), intro.

42. Letter to Ben Zion Bokser from Harry Helpern, 26 May 1972, box 27, folder 7, BZB, RCSCJ; letter to Ben Zion Bokser from Rabbi Joseph Sternstein, 18 May 1972, box 27, folder 7, BZB, RCSCJ.

43. "Neighborhoods: Baychester Racially Tense beneath Calm Veneer," *NYT*, 15 September 1969, 43.

44. Rieder, *Canarsie*, 24, 83.

45. "Backlash Vote Falls Short of Wallace's Hopes Here," *NYT*, 6 November 1968.

46. "Nixon's Landslide Is Traced to Democratic Defections," ibid., 9 November 1972; "Study Analyzes Ethnic Vote in '72," ibid., 19 August 1973, 40.

47. "More in City Are Turning to the Right," ibid., 15 January 1974, 1; "Survey Confirms Politicians' Views of Attitudes of Ethnic Voters," ibid., 25 October 1970, 67. These numbers were only so instructive, as 31 percent and 29 percent of black and Puerto Rican New Yorkers, respectively, also claimed the

conservative label, despite their overwhelming support of the Democratic Party.

48. For a compelling empirical study that finds little erosion on the national level of Jewish liberalism in the 1970s, see Alan Fisher, "Realignment of the Jewish Vote?," *Political Science Quarterly* 94, no. 1 (Spring 1979): 97–116.

49. Allen J. Matusow, *The Unraveling of America: A History of Liberalism in the 1960s* (New York, 1984), 343–44.

Chapter Eight

1. Prominent among books that focus on generational conflict (including conflict within the black civil rights movement) are Terry H. Anderson, *The Movement and the Sixties: Protest in America from Greensboro to Wounded Knee* (New York, 1995); Harvard Sitkoff, *The Struggle for Black Equality, 1954–1992* (New York, 1981; rev. ed., 1993); Dominick Cavallo, *A Fiction of the Past: The Sixties in American History* (New York, 1999); Allen Matusow, *The Unraveling of America: A History of Liberalism in the 1960s* (New York, 1984); Maurice Isserman and Michael Kazin, *America Divided: The Civil War of the 1960s* (New York, 2003); and Clayborne Carson, *In Struggle: SNCC and the Black Awakening of the 1960s* (Cambridge, Mass., 1981).

2. Sara Evans, *Personal Politics: The Roots of Women's Liberation in the Civil Rights Movement and the New Left* (New York, 1979); Kenneth J. Heineman, *Put Your Bodies upon the Wheels: Student Revolt in the 1960s* (Chicago, 2001); and Rusty L. Monhollon, *This is America? The Sixties in Lawrence, Kansas* (New York, 2002).

3. This account relies heavily on Daniel Bell, "Columbia and the New Left," *Public Interest* 13 (Fall 1968): 61–101.

4. Vincent J. Cannato, *The Ungovernable City: John Lindsay and His Struggle to Save New York* (New York, 2001), 249.

5. Bell, "Columbia and the New Left," 87–88.

6. David Truman, interview, 4 October 1968, OHP-CU.

7. Joshua Zeitz, "Back to the Barricades," *American Heritage* 52, no. 7 (2001): 70–72, 74–75.

8. Cannato, *The Ungovernable City*, 246.

9. There is wide agreement among scholars that Jewish students played a disproportionate role in the New Left, but less agreement about the sources of Jewish radicalism. Among those sources on the New Left that do not account in detail for the preponderance of Jewish students are Anderson, *The Movement and the Sixties*; Peter Collier and David Horowitz, *Destructive Generation: Second Thoughts about the Sixties* (New York, 1989); John Patrick Diggins, *The Rise and Fall of the American Left* (New York, 1992); and Todd Gitlin, *The Sixties: Years of Hope, Days of Rage* (New York, 1987). Sources that acknowledged more directly the Jewish role in the New Left without thoroughly explaining it include Nathan Glazer, "The Jewish Role in Student Activism," *Fortune*, January 1969; Nathan Glazer, "Jewish Interests and the New Left," *Midstream* 17, no. 1 (January/February 1971): 32–37; Dorothy Rabinowitz, "Are Jewish Students Different?," *Change* 3, no. 4 (Summer 1971): 47–50.

10. Stanley Rothman and S. Robert Lichter, *Roots of Radicalism: Jews, Christians, and the New Left*, rev. ed. (New York, 1996), 213–21.

11. For a counter opinion rooted in sociopsychological theory—that Jewish radicals were rebelling against their parents—see Rothman and Lichter, *Roots of Radicalism*. Prominent among other studies that emphasize psychological ingredients of Jewish and non-Jewish radicalism is Kenneth Keniston, *Young Radicals: Notes on Committed Youth* (New York, 1968).

12. "Leader of S.D.S. Unit: From a Jersey Suburb to the Picket Lines," NYT, 19 May 1968, 1.

13. "Columbia Concerned Parents" (transcript), 6 May 1968, Columbia University Crisis Project, OHP-CU.

14. Richard Hofstadter, interview, 15 May 1968, Columbia University Crisis Project, OHP-CU; Cannato, *The Ungovernable City*, 257.

15. "Parents in Clash on Campus Riot," NYT, 3 May 1968, 53.

16. Robert Friedman, interview, 4 October 1983 and 9 December 1983, Columbia University Crisis Project, OHP-CU.

17. David Rothman, interview, 15 May 1968, Columbia University Crisis Project, OHP-CU.

18. Lionel Trilling, interview, 23 May 1968, Columbia University Crisis Project, OHP-CU.

19. Jeffrey Kaplow, interview, 13 May 1968, Columbia University Crisis Project, OHP-CU.

20. Cannato, *The Ungovernable City*, 261.

21. Paul Vilardi, interview, 17 May 1968, Columbia University Crisis Project, OHP-CU. Cannato, *The Ungovernable City*, 246; "Brooklyn vs. Columbia," NYT, 24 May 1968, 33.

22. "Four Basic Issues Spark Unrest at Fordham," *Ram*, 9 September 1969.

23. Bill Arnone, "The Referendum as a Tool," ibid., 25 September 1969.

24. "Local Doves Speak in Gym," "Convocation Draws 3000," and "7,500 Crowd Parade Field," ibid., 17 October 1969.

25. "The Mayor for Mayor," ibid.

26. "Middle Americans, Bronx Style, Vocalize Their Moratorium Views," ibid.

27. Arnone, "The Referendum as a Tool," ibid., 26 September 1969.

28. "Walsh Joins College Leaders Asking Vietnam Pullout," ibid., 15 October 1969.

29. "Girls to Protest '610' Dorm Condition," ibid., 19 September 1969.

30. "ROTC Change Favored," ibid., 24 October 1969; "Anti-ROTC Group Plans Protest Rally, March Today," ibid., 17 October 1969.

31. " 'No Change' Wins in ROTC Vote," ibid., 31 October 1969.

32. "ROTC Opponents Take Administration Building," ibid., 13 November 1969; "Students for Campus Peace Demonstrate," ibid., 18 November 1969; "Rally Urges End to Criminal Charges," ibid., 21 November 1969; "Open Hearing on Seizure Set," ibid., 25 November 1969; "Faculty Endorses Walsh Actions," ibid.; "6 Held in Fordham R.O.T.C. Protest Could Get Terms up to 8 Years," NYT, 14 November 1969.

33. E. G. F. Corrigan '51, Anthony Di Perna '52, and Dr. John Nidds '52 to Michael P. Walsh, telegram, 14 December 1969, box 2, RLDF, MPW.

34. James D. Harper (Haven Avenue, New York, 10032) '68 to Walsh, 11 December 1969, box 2, RLDF, MPW.

35. Austin Kilcullen '43 to Walsh, 1 December 1969, box 2, RLDF, MPW; Brian T. Jordan B.S. '61, M.A. '62 to Walsh, 28 November 1969, box 2, RLDF, MPW; Howard Seitz to Walsh, 24 November 1969, box 2, RLDF, MPW; Mrs. Thomas Mahon to Walsh, 25 November 1969, box 2, RLDF, MPW.

36. Eugene G. Galvin to Walsh, 19 November 1969, box 2, RLDF, MPW; Joseph A. Izzillo to Walsh, 17 November 1969, box 2, RLDF, MPW.

37. Robert H. Fischer to Walsh, 19 November 1969, box 2, RLDF, MPW; Daniel M. Muchinsky to Walsh, 12 December 1969, box 2, RLDF, MPW.

38. John J. Kennedy (Fordham College, Class of 1968) to Walsh, 3 January 1970, box 2, RLDF, MPW; George T. Gilmore '72 to Walsh, 18 November 1969, box 2, RLDF, MPW.

39. John T. McGreevy, *Parish Boundaries: The Catholic Encounter with Race in the Twentieth Century Urban North* (Chicago, 1996), 189–90, 197–200.

40. McGreevy, *Parish Boundaries*, 190–91.

41. Ibid., 182.

42. For background on Vatican II and its impact on Catholic life in the United States, see Charles R. Morris, *American Catholic: The Saints and Sinners Who Built America's Most Powerful Church* (New York, 1997).

43. Benedict M. Ashley, "The Loss of Theological Unity: Pluralism, Thomism, and Catholic Morality," in *Being Right: Conservative Catholics in America*, ed. Mary Jo Weaver and R. Scott Appleby (Bloomington, Ind., 1995), 63–87.

44. "We Have a Bishop Standing in the Midst of His People as One Ready to Serve," BT, 12 September 1968; "Bishop Mugavero's First Year: Toward Institutional Renewal," ibid., 4 September 1969; "Bay Ridge Parish, after Long Planning, Ready to Pick Council Members," ibid., 6 November 1969; NYT, 31 May 1969, 12:2.

45. "The New Look of the Mass," *Catholic News*, 25 February 1965; "When to Genuflect," ibid., 8 March 1965; "Mass Confusion," ibid., 8 April 1965.

46. "The Church and the Laity," ibid., 25 February 1965.

47. "Sees Increase in Parish School Boards," ibid., 29 April 1965.

48. Diocese of Brooklyn, *Syllabus for the Catholic Elementary Schools, Effective September 1937* (Brooklyn, 1937), 284, ADB; "Stress Freedom, Not Obedience," *Catholic News*, 22 April 1965.

49. " 'Self-Starting' Students is Theme of Workshop," *Catholic News*, 16 September 1965.

50. "Broad Self-Study at St. John's," ibid., 15 April 1965.

51. Zeitz, "Back to the Barricades," 70–72, 74–75.

52. Arthur Gatti, "Mario Savio's Religious Influences and Origins," *Radical History Review* 71 (Spring 1998): 122–32.

53. "Friedland Protest Slated for Today," *Ram*, 17 March 1969; "Students Stand Trial, Sit-in, Picket This Week," ibid., 17 March 1960; "400 Protesters Crowd

English Department," ibid., 20 March 1970; "Students Occupy Fordham Building to Back Teacher," NYT, 13 April 1970; "Orderly Students Protest at Fordham," ibid., 14 April 1970; "Coalition Lists Demands," Ram, 24 March 1970.

54. "Strike," Ram, 15 April 1970.

55. "Protesters Debate Walsh Offer," ibid., 14 April 1970; "400 Students End 2-day Building Occupation," ibid., 15 April 1970; "Protesters Leave Fordham Building," NYT, 15 April 1970; "Boycott Snarls Fordham Classes," ibid., 16 April 1970; "Strike Continues," Ram, 16 April 1970; "Students Demand Academic Governing Role," ibid., 17 April 1970; "Walsh to Face Students Today," ibid., 21 April 1970; "Strike Ends at Fordham," NYT, 22 April 1970; "Walsh Cancels Tomorrow's Rose Hill Classes," Ram, 22 April 1970; "Fordham Students Vote," NYT, 2 May 1970.

56. Memorandum from Raymond A. Schroth, S.J. (coordinator), "The Open Curriculum, History/Introduction," March 1971, box 2, Curriculum Folder, MPW; press release, 20 December 1970–1971?, box 2, Curriculum Folder, MPW.

57. Mr. and Mrs. Peter Scagnetti to Michael P. Walsh, 18 April 1970, box 2, Demonstration April 13–16, 1970 Folder, MPW.

58. Michael J. Mangan '64 to Walsh, 10 May 1970, box 2, Demonstration April 13–16, 1970 Folder, MPW; Joseph C. O'Neill '51 to Walsh, 18 May 1970, box 2, Demonstration April 13–16, 1970 Folder, MPW; William E. Neilson to Walsh, 27 May 1970, box 2, Demonstration April 13–16, 1970 Folder, MPW.

Conclusion

1. Examples include Joseph Ryan, ed., White Ethnics: Their Life in Working-Class America (Englewood Cliffs, 1971); Richard Krickus, Pursuing the American Dream: White Ethnics and the New Populism (Garden City, N.Y., 1976); Andrew M. Greeley, "Political Attitudes among American White Ethnics," Public Opinion Quarterly 36, no. 2 (Summer 1972): 213–20; and Michael Novak, The Rise of the Unmeltable Ethnics: Politics and Culture in the Seventies (New York, 1972).

2. Andrew M. Greeley, Why Can't They Be More Like Us? America's White Ethnic Groups (New York, 1971), 13.

3. A particularly influential article that synthesized the "ethno-religious" factor in American politics from the early Republic through the 1970s is Robert Kelley, "Ideology and Political Culture from Jefferson to Nixon," American Historical Review 82, no. 3 (June 1977): 531–62. See also Stephen A. Garrett, "Eastern European Ethnic Groups and American Foreign Policy," Political Science Quarterly 93, no. 2 (Summer 1978): 301–23.

4. William V. Shannon, The American Irish (New York, 1966); Irving Howe, World of Our Fathers (New York, 1976).

5. Philip Gleason, "American Identity and Americanization," in Harvard Encyclopedia of American Ethnic Groups, ed. Stephan Thernstrom (Cambridge, Mass., 1980), 31–58; Godfrey Hodgson, America in Our Time (New York, 1976), 409; and Scott L. Malcomson, One Drop of Blood: The American Misadventure with Race (New York, 2000), 386–87.

6. See Chapter 1, Table 1.

7. FJPNY, "New York Jewish Population Study and Area Profile," New York, 1981, General Collection, AJHS; FJPNY, *Estimated Jewish Population of the New York Area, 1900–1975* (New York, 1959), 22–23.

8. Edward Shapiro, *A Time For Healing: American Jewry since World War II* (Baltimore, 1992), 126.

9. Howard M. Sachar, *A History of the Jews in America* (New York, 1992), 692–700. In 1980 the FJPNY found that 13 percent of New York City Jews identified themselves as Orthodox. No such figures are available for the early postwar years, although it is likely that a smaller portion of the Jewish community counted itself as Orthodox in the 1940s, 1950s, and 1960s. See FJPNY, "New York Jewish Population Study and Area Profile." For background on postwar Orthodox Judaism, see Jeffrey S. Gurrock, "The Orthodox Synagogue," in *The American Synagogue: A Sanctuary Transformed*, ed. Jack Wertheimer (Hanover, N.H., 1987), 64–68.

10. Joshua Michael Zeitz, " 'If I Am Not for Myself': The American Jewish Establishment in the Aftermath of the Six-Day War," *American Jewish History* 88, no. 2 (June 2000): 253–86.

11. Carole Groneman and David M. Reimers, "Immigration," in *The Encyclopedia of New York City*, ed. Kenneth T. Jackson (New Haven, 1995), 184–85.

12. "Record Immigration Changing New York's Neighborhoods," NYT, 24 January 2005.

13. Jerald E. Podair, *The Strike That Changed New York: Blacks, Whites, and the Ocean Hill–Brownsville Crisis* (New Haven, 2001).

Index

Brennan, Mary, 210
Breslin, Jimmy, 166
Brooklyn Board of Rabbis, 111
Brooklyn College, 51
Brooklyn Jewish Center: liberalism of, 105–6
Brooklyn Jewish Community Council (BJCC), 56–57
Brooklyn Jewish Youth Committee (BJYC), 115, 135–36
Brooklyn Naval Yard, 148
Brooklyn Tablet, 70, 131, 136, 216; and May Quinn controversy, 90; political conservatism of, 106; and Peekskill riots, 115–16; and Spain, 119–20; and Cold War, 122; anticommunism of, 126, 134; and race, 129, 131–32; and 1969 mayoral campaign, 179
Brotherhood of Painters, Decorators, and Paperhangers, 23
Brown, Edmund, 142
Brownsville and East New York Jewish Community Council, 125
Brzezinski, Zbigniew, 198
Buckley, William F., Jr., 174–75, 181, 189
Bundy, McGeorge, 166

Cahan, Abraham, 98
Cammarosano, Joseph, 210
Campbell, Les, 164, 183
Campbell, Margaret, 164
Campion, Raymond, 131
Carberry, Jim, 175
Carey, Matthew, 74
Carroll, John (layman), 73
Carroll, John (bishop of Baltimore), 73
Carson, Sonny, 164
Cary, William, 198
Catholic Charities of New York, 30–31
Catholic Church: as agent of ethnicity, 18, 23–32; parish and diocesan schools of, 23–32; and birth con-

trol, 85–86. See also Catholics; Diocese of Brooklyn
Catholic News, 75, 110, 216; on Harry Truman, 91; on Peekskill riots, 116; on labor strikes, 118
Catholics: voting patterns of, 6, 93–97, 133–34, 172–76; New York population of, 9; occupational patterns of, 19–23; and self-employment, 21–22; and anti-Catholicism, 77; and student unrest, 84–85; and censorship of films, 84–87; and birth control, 85–86; Francis Spellman against communism, 87–88; and communism, 90–93, 125–26; political identification of, 97, 194; and Peekskill riots, 115–16; roots of Catholic anticommunism, 117–25, 131–32; and Spanish Civil War, 119; and American Labor Party, 126–29; and Liberal Party, 126–29; and Popular Front, 127–29, 131; and race, 128–32; support of Joseph McCarthy, 134–35; and anti-Semitism, 136–37; left-wing Catholics, 138–40; and John F. Kennedy, 140; and 1968 presidential election, 194; and Fordham student protests, 207–22; and African Americans, 213–15
—history and culture of: 2, 6–7; views on authority and dissent, 1–2, 61, 65–72, 84–88, 213–18; parish culture, 18, 31–32; religious practices of, 29–30; church attendance, 32; infrastructure of churches, 37; rise of modern church in Ireland and United States, 72–73; Enlightenment Catholicism in early America, 73–74; Thomistic revival, 73–78; ultramontanism, 73–78; Tridentine Catholicism, 74–78; redemptive suffering and Catholic culture, 75–76; morality and sin, 110; Cath-

ulation of, 9, 12–15, 226–27; residential patterns of, 11–12, 15–18, 233 (n. 10); occupational patterns of, 19–23; and self-employment, 21–22; and education, 23–32, 51; parochial school attendance of, 26, 235 (n. 33), 236 (n. 40); attitude toward authority and dissent, 61–62, 84–85; rise of modern church in Ireland and United States, 72–73; and deemphasis of individual agency, 78–79; and Gaelic, 79; child-rearing practices of, 83–84; and censorship of films, 85–86; and exilic culture, 120; and anti-Irish prejudice, 120–22; and anticommunism, 121–22; and American Labor Party, 126–29; and Liberal Party, 126–29; support of Joseph McCarthy, 135; left-wing Irish Catholics, 138–39; and civil rights, 147, 154, 156; and taxes, 159; and African Americans, 168; voting patterns of, 172–76; and Police Department, 180; as portion of the electorate, 182; and 1969 mayoral election, 186–87

Irish Counties Association, 135

Irish Echo, 18; anticommunism of, 120–22; opposition to Jim Crow, 130; support of Joseph McCarthy, 135

Israel: Jewish fund-raising for, 37

Italian Americans: voting patterns of, 6, 93–97, 172–76; New York City population of, 9, 12–15, 227; residential patterns of, 15–18, 233 (n. 10); and Italian language, 17; ethnic solidarity of, 19; occupational patterns of, 19–23; and self-employment, 21–22; education of, 23–32, 51; parochial school attendance of, 26, 28, 235 (n. 33); in public schools, 27; religiosity of, 28–29; child-rearing practices of, 52–53, 81–83; attitude toward

authority and dissent, 61–62, 83–84; deemphasis of personal agency, 79–80; working-class profile of, 81–82; and American Labor Party, 126–29; and Liberal Party, 126–29; political patterns of, 133–34, 159; support of Vito Marcantonio, 139–40; and civil rights, 147, 154, 156; and taxes, 159; and African Americans, 168; as portion of the electorate, 182; and 1969 mayoral election, 186–87

Janowitz, Morris, 109

Javits, Jacob, 199, 208

Jewish Education Committee of New York, 37, 57, 104–5

Jewish Labor Committee, 111

Jewish People's Fraternal Order (JPFO), 98, 135–36

Jewish War Veterans (JWV), 90; on prejudice, 102–3, 111; on Peekskill riots, 115

Jews: voting patterns of, 6, 93–97, 172–76; New York City population of, 9, 12–15; residential patterns of, 11–12, 15–18, 233 (n. 10); ethnic solidarity of, 19; occupational patterns of, 19–23; and self-employment, 20–21; as white-collar workers, 22; educational achievement of, 22, 50–52; Jewish women as public schoolteachers, 26–27; and public schools, 26–27, 57; sectarian philanthropy of, 37; fund-raising for Israel by, 37, 112; described as intellectuals, 39–41; described as argumentative, 39–41; and anticommunism, 42–44, 88, 90–93, 109, 135–36; child-centered parenting of, 49–50, 52–58, 59–60, 81–82; middle-class identity of, 53; Israel Goldstein on communism, 88; political identification of, 97–100; on prejudice,